MAKING POOR NATIONS RICH

THE INDEPENDENT INSTITUTE is a non-profit,
non-partisan, scholarly research and educational organization
that sponsors comprehensive studies of the political economy
of critical social and economic issues.

The politicization of decision-making in society has too
often confined public debate to the narrow reconsideration
of existing policies. Given the prevailing influence of partisan interests, little social innovation
has occurred. In order to understand the nature of and possible solutions to major public issues,
the Independent Institute adheres to the highest standards of independent inquiry, regardless
of political or social biases and conventions. The resulting studies are widely distributed as
books and other publications, and are publicly debated in numerous conference and media
programs. Through this uncommon depth and clarity, the Independent Institute expands
the frontiers of our knowledge, redefines the debate over public issues, and fosters new and
effective directions for government reform.

THE INDEPENDENT INSTITUTE
100 Swan Way, Oakland, California 94621-1428, U.S.A.
Telephone: 510-632-1366 • Facsimile: 510-568-6040
Email: info@independent.org • Website: www.independent.org

MAKING

POOR

NATIONS

RICH

Entrepreneurship

and the Process

of Economic

Development

Edited by Benjamin Powell

STANFORD ECONOMICS AND FINANCE
An imprint of Stanford University Press
Stanford, California
Published in association with The Independent Institute

Stanford University Press
Stanford, California

Printed in the United States of America on acid-free, archival-quality paper

Library of Congress Cataloging-in-Publication Data

Making poor nations rich : entrepreneurship and the process of economic development / edited by Benjamin Powell.
    p. cm.
  Includes bibliographical references and index.
  ISBN 978-0-8047-5731-7 (cloth : alk. paper)—ISBN 978-0-8047-5732-4
  (pbk. : alk. paper)
  1. Entrepreneurship.   2. Economic development.   I. Powell, Benjamin, 1978–
HB615.M343 2008
338.4—dc22

                                                          2007030460

Typeset by Newgen in 10/13.5 Sabon

Contents

Illustrations

Tables

Figures

Map

Foreword

I am delighted to write a foreword to this splendid collection of articles on a very important subject, the role of entrepreneurship in the process of economic development. One of the important conclusions of *The Political Economy of Poverty, Equity and Growth—A Comparative Study*, in which Hal Myint and I directed the study of the economic history of twenty-one developing countries until the late 1980s, was the importance of entrepreneurship and what may be called a classical liberal policy framework in explaining the differing economic performances of developing countries in the post–World War II period. The case studies in this volume, particularly of developed countries not included in the Lal–Myint (1996) study—namely, Romania, Sweden, China, India, Ireland, New Zealand, and Botswana—add strength to its conclusions besides providing incisive accounts of the processes of economic repression and reform (however limited) in these countries.

Particularly noteworthy are the case studies of Sweden and New Zealand. The former, which has become the poster boy of the New Dirigiste backlash against the classical liberal policy package embodied in the so-called Washington consensus (see Lal 2006), represents a country that has succeeded in creating a "capitalism with a human face." The latter is an example of a country that has supposedly adopted the classical liberal package without any marked effect on its growth rate. The authors of the careful case studies of these two countries show that Sweden's overexpansion of its welfare state has led to a sclerotic economic performance compared with its earlier performance. On the other hand, it is the failure of New Zealand to fully implement the classical liberal package that has led to its relatively poor economic turnaround. The same can be seen to be true of Latin America in the excellent Chapter 7 surveying its economic performance.

It might, however, be useful to put these essays into a broader theoretical and historical perspective in this foreword, even if that means rather vaingloriously blowing my own trumpet! Over the last decade, I have been trying to put some content into the black box of "institutions" that, it is increasingly agreed, provides the basic reasons for the differing wealths of nations. Particularly in my Ohlin lectures (Lal 1998, 2006), I have argued that institutions are the means to constrain the self-seeking instincts that we are endowed with as part of our basic human nature. They reduce the transactions costs involved in the efficiency of exchange and those associated with policing opportunistic behavior by economic agents. These two types of transactions costs are in turn related to a distinction I make between the "material" and the "cosmological" beliefs of a culture—which is the informal aspect of institutions that constrains human behavior. "Material" beliefs relate to ways of making a living and can change quite quickly as the material environment changes—see Chapters 10 and 11 on China and India, respectively, in this volume. "Cosmological" beliefs concern, in Plato's words, "how one should live." They provide the moral anchor of different civilizations and are slow to change. They are determined by the ecological conditions in which different civilizations arose as well as the language group to which the cultures belong. They are transmitted through child-rearing practices using the moral emotions of shame and guilt to perpetuate them through the generations. I also argued that it is the material beliefs that are relevant for economic performance.

The material beliefs of all the agrarian Eurasian civilizations were inimical to the risk-taking and novelty-seeking merchants and entrepreneurs who, with their capitalist institutions such as markets, banking, bills of exchange, and business firms, go back to ancient Mesopotamia (see Baechler 1975). Tolerated as a necessary evil to extract and transfer the food needed by the men of the sword and the book in the towns, they were subject to constant predation by the state. It was due to the eleventh-century papal legal and administrative revolution of Pope Gregory VII that western Europe alone of all the agrarian Eurasian civilizations broke from these dysfunctional material beliefs. The legal papal revolution created a church-state that protected property rights across western Christendom (see Berman 1984). This led to the Great Divergence, with the slow rise of the West from the twelfth century onward until it overtook the other hitherto richer Eurasian civilizations by the eighteenth century (Maddison 2001). This legal and administrative infrastructure for a market economy, which makes the risk-taking and novelty-seeking activities of entrepreneurs secure, can and has been transferred (however imperfectly) to many non-Western countries, first as part of globalization in the nineteenth century under the aegis of the British empire and today, after the interwar breakdown of this liberal international economic order, under U.S. hegemony (Lal 2004, 2006).

This globalization of capitalism has, however, been resisted by two groups—the cultural nationalists of the Third World and various dirigistes in all three worlds. The origins of this hatred of capitalism and its main agents—entrepreneurs—arise because the change in material beliefs associated with the eleventh-century legal papal revolution was preceded and precipitated by an earlier papal family revolution in the sixth century by Pope Gregory the Great. This changed the West's cosmological beliefs by promoting individualism, the independence of the young, and love marriages (see Goody 1983), as contrasted to the communalist values and arranged marriages that remain common to this day in the rest of Eurasia. This change in the West's cosmological beliefs can be characterized as Westernization, whereas the later change in its material beliefs associated with the eleventh-century legal papal revolution can be characterized as modernization. Although temporally conjoined in the trajectory of the West for economic prosperity and the promotion and protection of the entrepreneur on which it is based, it is only the material beliefs associated with modernization that the rest need to adopt. They can modernize without Westernizing (i.e., accepting the cosmological beliefs of the West), as shown by Japan in its Meiji revolution and more recently by the increasing (although still incomplete) acceptance of the market by the two ancient Eurasian civilizations of China and India (see Lal 1998, 2000a).

The dirigisme that began in the late nineteenth century in Europe with the creation of welfare states and became rampant in the post–World

War II Third World was based on the attractions of various varieties of socialism as a route that offered modernity without sacrificing traditional communalist cosmological beliefs. The socialist panaceas combined the rationalism of the Enlightenment with the critique of the Romantic revolt as represented in the writings of the young Marx and the Fabian socialism of the Webbs and William Morris in the United Kingdom. They offered a route whereby countries could modernize without losing their souls. With the death of the countries of "really existing socialism," the harder socialist panaceas based on the plan were seen to be dead ends, but a softer version based on the desire to have "capitalism with a human face" still survives (see Lal 2006). Chapter 9 on Sweden in this volume is thus salutary in showing that this, too, is a dead end for sustaining long-term economic growth.

The cycles of repression and reform representing changes in material beliefs documented in the case studies in this volume also underline two other major themes of the earlier Lal–Myint (1996) comparative study. The first is the role of crises arising from past dirigisme in initiating reform (see Lal 1987). The chapters on China and India exemplify the process, whilst the excellent survey in Chapter 6 on sub-Saharan Africa's decades-long crisis of growth shows why even an enduring long-term crisis might not lead to reform in natural resource–rich economies. Here my model of the predatory state (first outlined in Lal 1984 and incorporated in Lal 1988–2005), combined with the different paths to development in a model incorporating land along with the traditional factors of production—labor and capital—charted by Krueger (1977) and Leamer (1987), provides a theoretical framework for explaining the political economy of countries for whom natural resources become a "precious bane." It was used by Lal–Myint (1996) to provide an explanatory framework for the changing economic policies adopted by twenty-five developing countries until the late 1980s. The Chapter 6 survey on Africa and the rather sad Chapter 14 on the deteriorating performance of the hitherto star African performer Botswana in this volume show how the continent's natural resource abundance is still proving a precious bane, not least because of the predatory behavior of its postindependence nationalist elites (also see Lal 2004 on these problems of creating and maintaining the minimal "order" required for economic prosperity).

Finally, although not explicitly dealt with in this volume, there is

the question of whether a particular type of polity is conducive for economic development. The current political panacea is the promotion of democracy in the Third World. However, the Lal–Myint volume found no
relationship between the type of polity and economic performance. In con-
tradistinction to the technocratic economic explanation for dictatorship
and democracy recently provided by Acemoglou and Robinson (2005),
which I find unpersuasive, I have argued (Lal 1998, 2000b) that political
habits are part of a civilization's cosmological beliefs, determined in large
part by the exigencies of the geography in the region where the civilization is born. Thus I do not see China giving up its ancient bureaucratic
authoritarian political habits nor India eschewing its democratic ones.

The tragedy of Africa is that its traditional polities, based on the
legitimacy of tribal chiefs, were destroyed by the colonial impact. The
artificial states bequeathed to nationalist successors cut through ancient
configurations and amalgamated historically opposing tribes within their
borders. So, apart from intertribal conflict within their borders to garner
the rents from their natural resources, they have also been threatened
by claimants from "across the border." The shining exception (as documented in Chapter 14 in this volume) is Botswana. It was fortunate that,
largely because of its backwardness and seeming lack of natural resources,
the British allowed it to preserve its precolonial internal autonomy and
tribal chiefs. They delivered unparalleled economic growth after independence. But, as the chapter shows, the rent seeking associated with natural
resources, after diamonds were discovered in the country, seems to be
emerging in even this African success story.

Latin America is also a region plagued by the curse of natural resources. Given its Christian heritage, its egalitarian cosmological beliefs
are in dissonance with its ecology, which generates large inequalities of
income and wealth. The neo-Thomist beliefs it inherited from Spain and
Portugal involve a form of fundamentalist universalism not found in its
Protestant neighbor to the north. It also accounts, in my view, for the con-
tinent-wide shifts and fashions in economic policy over the last two hundred years. These swings in fashion are rather like religious conversions,
while the dissonance between an unequal social reality and egalitarian
cosmological beliefs has led to cycles of democratic populism followed by
authoritarian repression as the distributional consequences of the populist phase are found unacceptable by the upper classes. Chile seems the

only one to have broken the cycle, while in the others—particularly in the Andean countries and Venezuela—we seem to have swung back to democratic populism, however unjustly its proponents criticize the previous decade of half-hearted liberal reforms, as Chapter 7 on Latin America in the volume ably demonstrates.

I hope this puts the essays in this book into a broader perspective. These excellent essays demonstrate how departures from classical liberalism and the ensuing atavistic suppression of the entrepreneurial instinct continue to hamper continuing economic progress in the world.

Deepak Lal
James S. Coleman Professor of
International Development Studies
University of California, Los Angeles

References

Acemoglu, D., and J. A. Robinson. 2005. *The Economic Origins of Democracy and Dictatorship*. Cambridge: Cambridge University Press.

Baechler, J. 1975. *The Origins of Capitalism*. Oxford, UK: Blackwell.

Berman, H. 1983. *Law and Revolution*. Cambridge, MA: Harvard University Press.

Goody, J. 1983. *The Development of the Family and Marriage in Europe*. Cambridge: Cambridge University Press.

Krueger, A. O. 1977. *Growth, Distortions and Patterns of Trade among Many Countries*. Princeton Studies in International Finance no. 40. Princeton, NJ: Princeton University.

Lal, Deepak. (1984). "The Political Economy of the Predatory State." Discussion Paper DRD 105. Washington, DC: Development Research Department, World Bank.

———. 1987. "The Political Economy of Economic Liberalization." *World Bank Economic Review* 1 (2): 273–299.

———. 1988–2005. *The Hindu Equilibrium*, vols. 1 and 2, rev. and abr. ed. Oxford, UK: Clarendon Press.

———. 1998. *Unintended Consequences—The Impact of Factor Endowments, Culture and Politics on Long-Run Economic Performance*. Cambridge, MA: MIT Press.

———. 2000a. "Does Modernization Require Westernization?" *The Independent Review* 5 (1): 5–24.

————. 2000b. "Political Habits and the Political Economy of Economic Repression and Reform." *Cuadernos de Economia* 37 (112): 415–443.

————. 2004. *In Praise of Empires—Globalization and Order.* New York: Palgrave-Macmillan.

————. 2006. *Reviving the Invisible Hand—The Case for Classical Liberalism in the Twenty-First Century.* Princeton, NJ: Princeton University Press.

Lal, Deepak, and Hal Myint. 1996. *The Political Economy of Poverty, Equity and Growth—A Comparative Study.* Oxford, UK: Clarendon Press.

Leamer, E. 1987. "Patterns of Development in the Three-Factor n-Good General Equilibrium Model." *Journal of Political Economy* 95 (5): 961–999.

Maddison, A. 2001. *The World Economy—A Millennial Perspective.* Paris: OECD.

Contributors

Benjamin Powell is an assistant professor of economics at Suffolk University, an economist with the Beacon Hill Institute, and a research fellow at the Independent Institute. He received his PhD from George Mason University. Much of his research has focused on economic development. He is the author of more than two dozen scholarly articles and policy studies.

George B. N. Ayittey, a native of Ghana, is a distinguished economist at American University and president of the Free Africa Foundation, both in Washington, DC. He received his PhD from the University of Manitoba, Winnipeg. He is the author of several books on Africa, including *Africa Unchained*, *Africa in Chaos*, *Africa Betrayed*, and *Indigenous African Institutions*.

William J. Baumol is a professor of economics at New York University, senior research economist and professor emeritus at Princeton University, and the Harold Price professor of entrepreneurship and academic director at the Berkley Center for Entrepreneurial Studies. He received his PhD from the University of London. He is the author of more than thirty-five books and more than five hundred articles published in professional journals and newspapers.

Scott A. Beaulier is an assistant professor of economics at Beloit College and a fellow at the Center on Entrepreneurial Innovation at the Independent Institute. He received his PhD from George Mason University. He has conducted field research in Botswana and authored numerous articles on Botswana's economic development.

Peter J. Boettke is the BB&T professor for the study of capitalism at George Mason University and the research director of the Global Prosperity Initiative at the Mercatus Center. He received his PhD from George Mason University. He is the author of several books on the history, collapse, and transition from socialism in the former Soviet Union.

Christopher J. Coyne is an assistant professor of economics at West Virginia University. He received his PhD from George Mason University. He has conducted field research in Romania.

James A. Dorn is a professor of economics at Towson University and vice president for academic affairs at the Cato Institute. He received his PhD from the University of Virginia. Professor Dorn has edited or co-edited several books on China, most recently *China's Future: Constructive Partner or Emerging Threat?*

Randall G. Holcombe is DeVoe Moore professor of economics at Florida State University and senior fellow at the Madison Institute. He received his PhD from Virginia Polytechnic Institute. He is the author of ten books and more than one hundred articles published in academic and professional journals.

Dan Johansson is a research fellow at the Ratio Institute. He received his PhD from the Royal Institute of Technology. His research deals with the role of entrepreneurs, the effects of institutions on entrepreneurship, and firm formation and growth.

Robert A. Lawson is professor of economics and George H. Moor chair at Capital University. His PhD is from Florida State University. He is the co-author of *The Economic Freedom of the World Annual Report*.

Peter T. Leeson is a BB&T professor for the study of capitalism with the Mercatus Center at George Mason University, where he also earned his PhD. He has conducted field research in Romania.

Mancur Olson Jr. was distinguished university professor of economics and principal investigator of the Center for Institutional Reform and the Informal Sector (IRIS) at the University of Maryland. He received his doctorate from Harvard. He was the author of seminal works in economics and political science, including *The Logic of Collective Action* and *The Rise and Decline of Nations*.

Renuka Sane is a consultant for the Centre for Monitoring Indian Economy. He holds a master's degree in economics from the University of Mumbai and has previously served as a research associate at the Invest India Economic Foundation.

Frederic Sautet is a senior research fellow at the Mercatus Center at George Mason University. He has a PhD in economics from the Université de Paris Dauphine and has served as a senior analyst at the New Zealand Treasury and as a senior economist at the New Zealand Commerce Commission.

Parth J. Shah is president of the Centre for Civil Society, New Delhi. He received his PhD from Auburn University. He has edited several books dealing with India, including *Profiles in Courage: Dissent on Indian Socialism*.

Alvaro Vargas Llosa is the director of the Center on Global Prosperity at the Independent Institute. He received his BSE in international history from the London School of Economics. He is the author of *Liberty for Latin America* and numerous other books on Latin America.

Acknowledgments

Thanks are due to everyone who helped produce this volume. In particular, I thank David Theroux, president of the Independent Institute; Alex Tabarrok, research director; and members of the Independent Institute staff for their assistance and support throughout the entire process. The manuscript benefited from revisions suggested by J. Robert Subrick, Russell Sobel, and an anonymous reviewer from Stanford University Press. I also thank my editors at Stanford University Press, Geoffrey Burn, Jared Smith, and their staff for their good work. Independent Institute interns David Skarbek, Matt Ryan, Andrew Neumann, and Nicholas Curott all provided valuable research, administrative, and manuscript preparation assistance. Finally I would like to acknowledge the University of Chicago Press, the American Economics Association, the Ludwig Von Mises Institute, and the Cato Institute for permission to reprint articles.

MAKING POOR NATIONS RICH

1   Introduction

BENJAMIN POWELL

Why do some nations become rich while others remain poor? This has been a central question in economics since at least the time of Adam Smith. China, India, and Botswana are booming and in the process lifting hundreds of millions of people out of wretched poverty, while most of sub-Saharan Africa not only fails to get rich but is instead actually getting poorer.

Traditional mainstream economic growth theory doesn't help us much to answer this question—through most of the twentieth century it focused on models that assumed growth is a simple function of labor, capital, and technology. The new growth theory, of which this book is part, looks more to institutions and policy. How well does a nation protect its entrepreneurs? In what countries do you get rich by inventing a new product, and in what countries do you get rich by wresting control of government from your rivals?

Entrepreneurs drive the market toward efficient outcomes by exploiting profit opportunities and causing the market process to tend toward equilibrium (Kirzner 1973). Entrepreneurs also play a central role in the market's process of creative destruction, whereby new innovations constantly replace old technologies and send the market on a path toward a new equilibrium (Schumpeter 1934). The interaction of these two roles of the entrepreneur drives the process of economic development.

Entrepreneurs exist in almost all cultures and historical contexts. Why, then, doesn't the process of economic development occur in all countries equally? Human decision making responds to perceived costs and benefits, and not all societies have an environment that rewards productive entrepreneurship. Look at the case of imperial China. A brilliant young man would devote all of his energies to studying law in preparation for the exams that gave entrance into the upper echelons of the ruling bureaucracy. That same young man today may study electrical engineering with the dream of one day opening his own firm because now Chinese businessmen can earn greater prestige and profits than they could in the past. In which society should we expect greater economic growth?

In recent years the economics profession and policy world have begun to pay more attention to the institutional environment necessary for economic growth. Geography and other explanations for success have begun to be pushed aside as institutions have become increasingly recognized as the main driver of economic success (Rodrik, Subramanian, and Trebbi 2004). Some in the profession have moved toward detailed analytical narratives to explain individual cases in economic development. There has also been a virtual explosion in research measuring economic freedom and using it to explain economic performance. In Washington, DC, people in policy circles now generally, though incompletely, acknowledge the need for private property rights and the rule of law for economic development.

Making Poor Nations Rich seeks to push the current debate further in the direction of an appreciation for the critical role that entrepreneurs and the institutional environment of private property rights and economic freedom play in economic development. The book begins by collecting the key essays that explain how entrepreneurs create economic growth and why some particular institutional environments encourage more productive entrepreneurship than do others. Part 1 ends with a chapter explaining the overall empirical findings on the importance of economic freedom for prosperity. With the theoretic underpinning and overall empirical results in place, the final two parts of the book provide detailed case studies of individual countries and regions by examining the institutional environment that entrepreneurs operate in and the effect this environment has on economic prosperity. Part 2 focuses on countries and regions that have failed to develop because of barriers to productive entrepreneurship. Part 3 contains case studies of countries that have developed by reforming their institutional environment to better protect private property rights and grant greater levels of economic freedom.

This book is similar to Rodrik's edited volume *In Search of Prosperity*. Both books employ an analytical narrative approach using case studies. Both find that institutions are important for development. This book differs from Rodrik's by emphasizing the primary importance of entrepreneurship and what specific type of institutional environment is necessary for encouraging the productive entrepreneurship that promotes growth. This is most evident in our three country studies, Botswana, China, and India, which overlap with Rodrik's volume. In each case, the authors in this book illustrate more forcefully the primacy of reforms that promoted property rights and enhanced economic freedom in creating growth in these countries.

This book begins by examining alternative explanations for the vast differences in wealth around the world. In Chapter 2 Mancur Olson begins with the standard economic assumption that any economic gains that can be had are exploited. He pushes the argument to its logical conclusion that "what is, is efficient." However, when one looks around the world and sees the dramatically differing standards of living between countries it seems unlikely that the most efficient policies are in place everywhere. Olson identifies two possible explanations for the differing economic performance of countries. The first is that national borders may mark areas of differing resource endowments. Poor countries are poor because they lack land and natural resources, physical and human capital, or access to the latest technology. If differences in these endowments explain the differing performances, then poor countries are, in fact, doing as well as they can given their endowment. The second possible explanation is that national boundaries mark the borders of public policies and different institutional environments. Some of these policies and institutions are better than others. In those that are better, more profit opportunities are seized, whereas those with poor institutions leave potential gains from trade unexploited—big bills are left on the sidewalk.

Olson first deals with the possibility of each of the differing resource endowments as the explanation for differing economic performance. He finds that differing access to knowledge is not an adequate explanation. In Korea royalties and other payments for disembodied technology were minuscule—less than one-thousandth of GDP. If knowledge can be had so cheaply it is not likely to be holding countries back from developing. The standard assumption that knowledge is equally available to all countries is well founded.

Olson finds that overpopulation and diminishing returns to labor do not cause differences in performance. If they did, we should find countries with net out-migration converging in incomes with countries with in-migration. We do not. Furthermore, population density does not explain differing performance. Many of the most densely settled countries in the world have high per capita incomes.

What about differences in capital? With diminishing returns to capital we should see capital flow from capital-rich countries to capital-poor countries. As Olson puts it, "Capital should be struggling at least as hard to get into the third world as labor is struggling to migrate into the high-wage countries" (p. 38). Instead, we see the lion's share of capital in a few wealthy nations, and we see capital continue to flow to these countries. Labor and capital often migrate in the same direction, but if all countries had the most efficient policies they should move in opposite directions due to diminishing returns. Olson drives home the point that something else, namely institutions, is driving the flow of capital, so a country's capital stock cannot be taken as exogenous in explaining economic performance. Other research, such as Hall and Jones (1999), has followed up on this point by creating measures of institutional quality and finding that institutions do, as Olson predicts, play a major role in the accumulation of capital and achievement of growth.

Next he looks at human capital and divides it into two parts: "marketable human capital" and "public good human capital." Marketable human capital reflects the skills, propensities, or cultural traits that affect the quantity and quality of productive inputs that an individual can sell in the market. Public good human capital is knowledge about what types of public policies are good. Migration allows us examine each of these separately and see which is more important for explaining differing economic performances between countries. When people migrate, they take both forms of human capital with them. However, only the marketable human capital impacts performance in the new country. Because even large migrations do not dramatically alter the public policy outcomes in the new country, we can isolate the effects of each type of human capital.

What do we find? New immigrants earn about 55 percent of the income of an American of the same age, sex, and years of schooling, whereas many come from countries whose incomes per capita are only one-tenth or one-fifth as large as America's. Cut a different way, we can look at two immigrant groups in America—one from a rich country and one from a poor country—and see what the gap between their incomes is. Germany is much richer than Haiti. If this difference existed because Germans are better educated or smarter than Haitians, then we would expect German immigrants in the United States to also be much richer than Haitian immigrants. But Haitians and Germans in the United States have much closer income levels than do Haitians and Germans in their home countries. It's not the people that differ; it's the institutions.

Olson's overall finding is that "the large differences in per capita income across countries cannot be explained by differences in access to the world's stock of productive knowledge or to its capital markets, by differences in the quality of marketable human capital or personal culture." The only plausible explanation left is that differing performances are caused by differences in the quality of countries' institutions and policies. There are big bills left on the sidewalk. If a country improves its institutions, it can pick up these bills.

In Chapter 3, "Entrepreneurship and Economic Growth," Randall Holcombe describes the process that creates profit opportunities that lead to economic growth. He provides the theoretic underpinning of a central theme in this book: the importance of entrepreneurs for economic growth. Instead of viewing growth merely as a function of inputs, Holcombe argues that "Smithian growth," in which the division of labor is limited by the extent of the market, is a better description of real-world development. As markets grow, this growth leads to continual innovation and specialization in the division of labor. Growth is essentially unlimited. What is the mechanism that causes more innovation to occur? Holcombe introduces the Kirznerian (1973) entrepreneur for this purpose.

The Kirznerian entrepreneur seizes profit opportunities that had previously gone unnoticed. Although Kirzner used the entrepreneur to explain how the market process attains a particular equilibrium, Holcombe connects the entrepreneur to economic growth. The profit opportunities that the entrepreneur seizes must come from somewhere. As Olson pointed out, profit opportunities do not last very long before they are grasped in a market economy. Most profit opportunities that are acted on must be new. Where do they come from? Holcombe argues that the profit opportunities that entrepreneurs seize come mainly from the actions of other entrepreneurs. Individual acts of entrepreneurship create new profit opportunities for other entrepreneurs to act on.

Holcombe argues that entrepreneurial opportunities emerge from the actions of other entrepreneurs for at least three reasons. One reason is that even in a general equilibrium setting, any change made by one entrepreneur necessarily alters the economic environment and will require additional adjustments by other entrepreneurs to attain a new equilibrium. A second source of opportunities comes from the fact that entrepreneurial activity generates wealth and increases the extent of the market. The third source of opportunities comes through the creation of market niches that did not previously exist. New entrepreneurs enter and expand a market niche after it is created. All of these entrepreneurial opportunities come into being because of prior acts of entrepreneurship. As Holcombe puts it in one example, "Bill Gates could not have made his fortune had not Steve Jobs seen the opportunity to build and sell personal computers, and Steve Jobs could not have built a personal computer had not Gordon Moore invented the microprocessor" (p. 61).

What are the implications of Holcombe's model of entrepreneurial growth? Maybe most important, the implication is that growth is not limited. As long as entrepreneurs make innovations, there will be new opportunities for others. Another implication is that just forcing education, investment, or research and development into a production function will not necessarily improve growth. Instead, these things occur in response to entrepreneurial opportunities. The more opportunities there are, the greater incentive there is to search for them by engaging in these activities. How can we explain differing economic performances of countries? The differences must lie in the entrepreneurial opportunities that are available and hence the new ones that will be created. Holcombe links Kirzner's entrepreneur with Friedrich Hayek's (1945) emphasis on the particular knowledge of time and place. Because opportunities arise in this context, people must be free to act on them and seize the profits when they see them. So a decentralized free economy will likely lead to more entrepreneurial opportunities. After they are seized entrepreneurship builds on itself and acts as an endogenous engine of economic growth. Holcombe does not elaborate very much on the institutional structure that is necessary for entrepreneurial development. For that we turn to Chapters 4 and 5.

Chapter 4 builds on Holcombe's and Olson's insights by examining how the cultural and policy environment impacts the allocation of entrepreneurial activity. William Baumol begins with Schumpeter's five types of entrepreneurial acts—introducing a new good; introducing a new method of production; opening a new market; discovering a new source of supply of raw material or intermediate good; and carrying out the new organization of an industry—and then adds rent seeking as a sixth type of entrepreneurial activity. The rent seeking may take the form of lobbying regulators or legislators for favors, suing in the courts to harm competitors, or conducting military activity. Baumol observes that, unlike the other forms of entrepreneurship, rent-seeking activity is not socially beneficial. He argues that differing economic performances of countries can be explained in part not by the total supply of entrepreneurial activity but rather by the allocation of entrepreneurial efforts among these activities. He further argues that the allocation of entrepreneurship is influenced by the institutions in society. Countries with cultures and economic policies that reward unproductive entrepreneurship will channel more of their entrepreneurial effort to those activities, and consequently the economies will perform poorly. He neatly summarizes his main argument in three propositions.

1. The rules of the game that determine the relative payoffs to different entrepreneurial activities do change dramatically from one time and place to another.
2. Entrepreneurial behavior changes direction from one economy to another in a manner that corresponds to the variations in the rules of the game.
3. The allocation of entrepreneurship between productive and unproductive activities, though by no means the only pertinent influence, can have a profound effect on the innovativeness of the economy and the degree of dissemination of its technological discoveries.

Baumol illustrates the importance of these propositions by briefly surveying a variety of historic episodes. He shows that in ancient Rome

persons of honorable status could accumulate wealth through land holding, usury, and political payments but not through industry or commerce.
Though productive entrepreneurship was rewarded with financial gains,
those gains were partially offset by the loss of prestige. Baumol argues
that this situation made the Romans divert more entrepreneurial effort to
unproductive political entrepreneurship. The result was that although the
Romans had a great deal of technical knowledge, such as many forms of
machine gearing still used today and the steam engine, this knowledge
was not translated into commercial gain and instead often amounted to
"elaborate toys." A similar claim is made for medieval China. Prestige
and wealth came with attaining a high rank in the bureaucracy, whereas
high social standing was denied to people engaged in commerce. Instead
of efforts being focused on serving consumers, efforts were focused on
scoring well on the exams that were used to allocate bureaucratic positions. The result, much like the Romans, was a squandered chance at an
industrial revolution.

As was done for Rome and China, many periods of history in
Europe from the Middle Ages through the Industrial Revolution are examined to see how the changing rules of the game and cultural norms impacted the allocation of entrepreneurial activity. The historical episodes
considered lend support to Baumol's three main propositions.

The chapter's main contribution—that entrepreneurs respond to
incentives and that rules of the game that reward unproductive entrepreneurship will harm economic performance—seems intuitive and obvious.
Yet this contribution has strong policy implications. Countries performing
poorly may have cultural attitudes that punish some forms of productive
entrepreneurship, but they also likely have poor economic institutions
that bias entrepreneurial innovation toward unproductive activities. To
improve economic performance all they need to do is change the rules
of the game that govern economic activity. As Chapter 5 will show, the
rules of the game that promote productive entrepreneurship are rules that
protect private property and promote economic freedom.

Chapter 5, "Economic Freedom and Property Rights: The Institutional Environment of Productive Entrepreneurship," provides the
bridge between our more theoretical chapters and the case studies that
follow. The central message of Chapters 2 through 4 is that a country's
institutional environment is an important determinant of its economic

performance. This chapter, by Robert Lawson, describes the environment necessary for economic growth—economic freedom and property rights—and then systematically examines the evidence and literature to support his claim.

Although we understand intuitively what economic freedom entails—namely, private ownership, personal choice, voluntary exchange, and free entry into markets—it is not easily objectively quantifiable. The *Economic Freedom of the World* report, published annually by the Fraser Institute (and co-authored by Lawson), is the most widely used scholarly index that attempts to measure economic freedom. In this chapter the index and the scholarly literature based on it are used to show that economic freedom is correlated with prosperity.

Some of the chapter's main findings are that higher levels of economic freedom are associated with

- Higher levels of per capita income
- Higher rates of economic growth
- Higher levels of entrepreneurial activity
- Higher rates of domestic investment
- Larger amounts of foreign investment attracted
- Longer life expectancies
- Better access to safe water

One finding in particular fits very well with Olson's message from Chapter 2. Not only do levels of economic freedom matter, but also changes in freedom matter. Countries that improve in economic freedom, regardless of their initial position, tend to grow faster than other countries. This fact is consistent with Olson's description of how big bills that are left on the sidewalk are quickly picked up. Countries initially well inside their production possibilities frontier enact policies that move them closer to the frontier. In the process, a number of profit opportunities that were previously just sitting ungrasped on the sidewalk because of institutional barriers now become available, and economic growth increases while they are acted on. Although this chapter reviews the overall empirical relationship, it also identifies some of the countries that have improved the most in recent years. A number of them—Botswana, China, India, Ireland, and New Zealand—are the subjects of later chapters in this book.

The overall message of this chapter is quite clear. "After over a decade of research, the empirical evidence is overwhelmingly clear: Societies that organize themselves with private property, rule of law, and free markets outperform, on almost every measurable margin, societies that are less economically free" (p. 131).

It is with this message in mind that we turn to the case studies presented in this book. In each case study a particular country or region of the world is examined in detail. Looking at each on an individual basis allows us to examine the precise policy changes that have occurred in each area and how they have impacted economic performance. We first look at countries and regions where a poor institutional environment has prevented entrepreneurs from promoting sustained economic growth. Then we turn to success stories about countries that have improved their institutions and economic performance.

1. Failures in Entrepreneurial Development

Africa has been the biggest failure in the quest for economic development during the last fifty years. Africa is mired in poverty, famine, disease, and illiteracy. Not only are most African countries extremely poor, but also they're getting poorer. Since 1975 sub-Saharan Africa has averaged a 1 percent annual decrease in per capita GDP. In Chapter 6 George Ayittey explains the causes of Africa's problems and how development efforts could be more successful.

Under colonial rule African institutions contained elements of capitalism, but they were far from perfect. They often focused on resource extraction rather than development. After gaining independence many African countries rebelled against all things colonial—including capitalism. Africa's problems stem from embracing socialist ideologies after independence. Ayittey argues that the failure of socialist policies led to African governments transforming into what he terms "vampire states." The vampire state exists only to enrich the rulers. The general population has little or no say in state activities, finding themselves impoverished as the rulers suck the wealth from the economy. Ayittey argues that these states follow a general pattern of evolution to their own collapse. As people begin to exit and move into the informal economy, governments resort to inflation to raise revenue. As the situation of the population deteriorates, the people eventually rise up and rebel. Then the struggle for political power eventually plunges the country into civil war.

The West has played a role in prolonging Africa's poverty through aid sent to leaders of these vampire states and through programs that have displaced indigenous institutions.

Ayittey argues that Africa needs investment in order to develop but that to get investment Africa needs an enabling economic environment. This environment includes property rights, incentives, rule of law, and freedom. How can Africa get it? We must first stop the aid/reform dance with African leaders who continually game Western donors. Instead, we must fundamentally change our view of Africa. We must distinguish between modern Africa and traditional Africa. Much of the African population works in the traditional and informal sectors. These are the sectors that had sustained Africa for centuries and that have been neglected or squashed by the modern African states that have developed in the postcolonial period. Ayittey argues that the modern sector is nonreformable. What is to be done with it? Instead of sending African governments more aid, "The rogue African state should be left to the fate it deserves—implosion and state collapse" (p. 173). Instead, development assistance should be channeled to the informal sectors where the majority of Africans live. He argues that we need to have a "bottom-up" approach to development rather than a "top-down" approach. Instead of looking to African elites, we should look to the free enterprise spirit of the general population and help them foster the institutions necessary to create the right environment for attracting investment and growth.

Much of Latin America has also experienced disappointing levels of economic growth. Much like Africa, natural resources abound, yet development lacks. It is a region characterized by state power, political instability, corruption, and poverty for the masses. In Chapter 7 Alvaro Vargas Llosa explains the region's colonial history, twentieth-century policies, and more recent attempts at reform. Overall, he summarizes the region's history as a mix of corporatism, state mercantilism, privilege, wealth transfer, and political law and argues that these have caused the region's poverty.

Although Latin American peasants had little access to landed property and trade during the colonial period, they have not fared much better since. Vargas Llosa argues that land reform after independence did not lead to full private property rights but that instead the new states became the real owners in most cases. The dominant postindependence institutional environment could be better classified as economic nationalism than as property rights and economic freedom. Leaders believed that their countries were at a structural disadvantage because rich nations "monopolized" capital and technology and Latin American exports would not earn enough foreign exchange to pay for the capital needed to improve living standards. He argues that leaders implemented barriers to imports, subsidies, legal discrimination, and even nationalization of certain industries to "correct" for their structural disadvantage. The result was continually lagging economic performance. Overall, economic nationalism was just a new way of doing what was done before in Latin America: draining resources from ordinary people to sustain those living off government privilege.

The 1980s and 1990s promised to be a period of reform in Latin America. With the exception of Chile, Vargas Llosa maintains that there was only the mirage of reform. As state assets were sold off, the revenue was used to make unsustainable increases in government spending in many countries. Although some effort was made to reform monetary and fiscal policies, reforms were often offset with new interventions into the economy. As he puts it, "reform meant replacing inflation with new taxes, high tariffs with regional trading blocs, government monopolies with private monopolies, price controls with regulatory bodies" (p. 202). In one particularly crucial area, the judiciary, Vargas Llosa maintains that there was negligible reform. He argues that the judiciary in Latin America is just a corrupt arm of the government, not a limit on political power or a safeguard of individual rights.

Latin America experienced essentially no economic growth between 1989 and 2004 because of the various institutional impediments to development. Vargas Llosa concludes his chapter with a discussion of a few of the areas where reforms could help reverse Latin America's five hundred years of state oppression and begin to promote the growth that will lift ordinary people out of poverty.

With the fall of the Berlin Wall in 1989 and the collapse of the Soviet Union in 1991, hopes were high that the former Communist bloc would embrace markets and converge to western Europe's standard of living. Some eastern European countries have been relatively successful at reforming their economies. Others have not. In Chapter 8 Peter Boettke,

Christopher Coyne, and Peter Leeson explain Romania's relatively unsuccessful transition to a market economy by examining the incentives facing entrepreneurs. Consistent with Baumol's (1990) theory, they show that unproductive entrepreneurship is better rewarded than productive entrepreneurship in Romania.

The chapter identifies Romania's excessive and continually changing regulatory environment as a main cause of unproductive entrepreneurship. In a World Bank survey 86 percent of respondents claimed that "constant changes in the laws and regulations are a main obstacle to doing business." The constant changes stem in part from "emergency ordinances" that are immediately active executive decrees. In some years these decrees account for more than 50 percent of all new laws. A constantly fluctuating legal and regulatory environment makes it hard for entrepreneurs to do long-term business planning in the aboveground market. The widespread corruption in government courts also raises the costs of operating in the aboveground market, as do the bribes that must be paid to regulators. Overall, Transparency International found Romania was the third most corrupt country in Europe. The extensive system of bribes and the changing regulatory framework lower the benefits of participating in aboveground productive activities and simultaneously divert entrepreneurs to unproductive activities by making it more profitable to try to become one of the system's administrators. The chapter argues that due to other factors such as financing availability, a poorly functioning land market, and distance from the political center, the entrepreneurial environment is even worse in rural areas of the country.

For Romania to develop it will need to promote an environment of more productive entrepreneurship. Enacting judicial and regulatory reforms, as well as aligning de jure and de facto property rights, is one of the most urgently needed changes. Whether the failure of past policies or membership in the European Union will be enough to induce the needed reforms is yet to be determined.

Sweden is the final case of failed economic development policy that we examine. It may at first seem strange to consider Sweden a case of development failure because it has a relatively high per capita income and is often used as an example of a successful interventionist state. However, in Chapter 9 Dan Johansson shows that most of Sweden's growth occurred before it implemented a comprehensive welfare state and that since the rise of the welfare state rates of entrepreneurial creation and economic growth have fallen.

From 1870 to 1970 Sweden was one of the fastest-growing countries in the world. In 1970 it was the fourth-richest country in the Organisation for Economic Co-operation and Development (OECD), but three decades later it had fallen below the median country to fourteenth. This fall coincides with the creation of the Swedish welfare state. Swedish tax revenues as a percent of GDP were lower than those of both the United States and Britain until the end of the 1950s. By 1970 they had increased to 40 percent of GDP and to 50 percent by 1976. This high level of taxation has remained to the present.

Johansson argues that regulations and the financing of the Swedish welfare state put up barriers to entrepreneurship that inhibited economic growth. He finds that many industries are off-limits to entrepreneurs because they are reserved for the government. Very high real tax rates have often made entrepreneurial action unprofitable even when ventures would have been nominally profitable. The tax system is also biased against young, small, independent, and less-capital-intensive firms. Yet these are the types of firms that promote much new growth. Wealth is also taxed, and by 1990 Sweden's wealth per capita stood at about $13,000 or roughly 17 percent of the U.S. level. New firm formation has been limited because wealth per capita is important to enable start-ups. Plus, private markets play only a limited role in directing wealth flows because the bulk of Swedish savings is tied up in compulsory pension savings. Labor market rigidities also stifle the willingness of new firms to hire employees.

All of this taxation and regulation has limited new job creation. The total population has increased by about two million since 1950, but only 155,000 new jobs have been created in the private sector, while 770,000 have been created in the public sector. Not surprisingly, Johansson finds that entrepreneurial activity is lower in Sweden than in other countries. In a survey of thirty-four countries Sweden had the sixth-lowest share of its population engaged in entrepreneurial activity.

Overall, Johansson's chapter demonstrates that Sweden is not an example of high growth and a pervasive welfare state. He finds that Sweden grew before it had its welfare state and that because of interventions that harm small and fast-growing firms Swedish economic growth has slowed.

2. Reform and Success in Entrepreneurial Development

The final part of this book examines the experiences of countries that have made major economic reforms that have enabled them to develop. Some countries, such as Ireland and New Zealand, were already moderately developed when they were able to improve their institutional environment. Others, such as China, India, and Botswana, were very poor prior to reform. These examples give us a very diverse set of countries from different regions of the world, with different cultures and access to resources. The one common element in all of the countries is that they achieved higher rates of economic growth by making pro-property rights and pro-market reforms.

China provides a perfect example of how improvements in institutional quality, no matter how poor the initial institutional environment, can improve economic performance. China is still far from a full-fledged market economy. Its 2002 economic freedom ranking was still only ninetieth out of 123 countries ranked. However, its improvement during the last twenty-five years is dramatic. Its freedom score has improved 66 percent from its 1980 level. The nonstate sector produces two-thirds of industrial output today, up from one-third when reforms began in 1978. China is a perfect illustration of how institutional barriers keep a country from reaching its production possibilities frontier. The reforms in China still have a long way to go, but the initial changes in the entrepreneurial environment created profit opportunities for productive entrepreneurship to exploit, and this development has led to the growth China has achieved.

In Chapter 10 James Dorn describes the pre- and postreform institutional environment in China, the resulting economic performance, and what areas are still in greatest need of reform. Dorn shows that much of the reform has taken place spontaneously at the local level and then has often been sanctioned after the fact by the national government. Reforms in the ownership of small enterprises and agriculture started this way. A major area of reform has been in freeing trade with foreigners and allowing foreign investment into the country. Of particular importance have been special enterprise zones where more freedom is granted. Dorn shows that the regions of China with the highest degree of "marketization" are the areas where most of the economic growth has occurred. With the opening of trade, thirty-five thousand Chinese firms had the right to engage in foreign trade by 2001. In 1978 only twelve state-owned enterprises had this privilege. Since the start of reforms it is estimated that 400 million people had been lifted out of poverty in China by 2001.

Although many reforms have been made, China still has much untapped potential. Large state-owned enterprises still exist, and private entrepreneurs are still discriminated against. Interest rates are regulated, and the bulk of investment funds are allocated to state-owned enterprises through state-owned banks. Private entrepreneurs often have to turn to foreign investors or informal capital markets to raise funds. Meanwhile nonperforming loans pile up in the state-run banks. The challenge for China is to more fully embrace the market mechanism and to spread the economic freedom that has been achieved out from the coastal zones to the rest of the country.

India, much like China, remains heavily interventionist but has made significant reforms since its financial crisis in 1991. From 1991 to 2002 India improved its economic freedom index score by nearly 33 percent. During the period of reform India was finally able to exceed its "hindu" rate of economic growth. In Chapter 11 Parth Shah and Renuka Sane document India's reforms and what remains to be done.

They find that one of India's biggest areas of reform has been in its freedom to trade with foreigners. Tariffs have been dramatically lowered, the number of goods that there are other restrictions on has fallen, and foreign direct investment and capital flows have been liberalized. Individual industries, including telecommunications and airlines, have seen the introduction of competition. India's stock markets have become increasingly competitive with the introduction of a new exchange. Two key industries—information technology and back-office processing/call centers—have emerged and remain relatively unregulated. These sectors benefited greatly from the improvements in the international trade environment.

Unfortunately India's reforms still have a long way to go. While new industries that are engaged in internationally traded services and are free from India's industrial licensing have emerged, much of the domestic economy remains heavily regulated. Starting a business still takes a long time to get approval and entails significant costs. Many small-scale enterprises remain subject to licensing that restricts the number of legal vendors and forces many to work in the black market. A host of agricultural restrictions remain. Shah and Sane argue that although the poor have seen some improvements during India's period of reform, the main industries that most of them work in have been the areas of least reform. Although India has made many improvements, and its growth has accelerated, they say that a more comprehensive change in the mind-set of Indians that more fully embraces markets will be necessary to get meaningful across-the-board reform.

Compared with China and India, Ireland has enjoyed a relatively high standard of living during the past fifty years. It had neither the poverty nor the quantity of socialist policies that both China and India had. In fact, the rule of law, to a greater or lesser extent, was always present, and Ireland had an economy relatively open to international trade since the late 1960s. Despite this fact, by European standards, Ireland was underdeveloped. A 1988 survey article in the *Economist* about Ireland was even titled "The Poorest of the Rich." For decades Ireland experienced out-migration while continually lagging behind Britain's and Europe's standards of living. Then, beginning in the late 1980s, Ireland's growth began improving, and suddenly by the late 1990s Ireland was growing at nearly a 10 percent annual rate and had caught and surpassed Britain's and Europe's standards of living.

In Chapter 12 Benjamin Powell documents the series of economic reforms that allowed Ireland to achieve its dramatic growth. Although some aspects of economic freedom had been present in Ireland for years, other crucial aspects were missing. Monetary and fiscal restraint in particular had been lacking in Ireland. Ireland had engaged in extensive increases in government spending during the 1970s to try to stimulate aggregate demand in response to the oil shocks. The spending increases failed to stimulate the economy but did create fiscal imbalance. By the mid-1980s the government debt-to-GDP ratio was well over 100 percent. To deal with the crisis, dramatic cuts in government spending were made. Government spending as a percent of GDP fell from 55 percent in 1985 to 40 percent by 1990. As the role of government in the economy was slashed, growth began to pick up, and Ireland improved its precarious fiscal position. The initial cuts were followed up with decreases in personal and corporate tax rates throughout the 1990s. These reforms, coupled with Ireland's free trade regime and access to the European market, fueled investment in its economy and helped achieve dramatic rates of economic growth in the 1990s.

Although some have claimed that Ireland's growth was driven by EU structural funds, this chapter shows that these funds have diminished in importance as Ireland began to grow and offers a host of theoretical reasons for why these funds cannot explain Ireland's growth. The overall explanation of Ireland's dramatic growth comes from the large increase in economic freedom it experienced from 1985 through 2000. The improvement in the institutional environment attracted the foreign direct investment and productive entrepreneurship that fueled Ireland's growth.

New Zealand is another case of a relatively developed yet underachieving country where crisis led to reform. In Chapter 13 Frederic Sautet describes the effects of New Zealand's economic reforms that began in the early 1980s. New Zealand had fallen from being one of the five richest countries in the world in the early twentieth century to being about the twentieth richest by the early 1980s. During the 1970s until the beginning of the reform period New Zealand had high levels of taxation and government spending, high inflation, inflexible labor markets, many barriers to trade, and a host of other interventions that hampered economic performance. In response to a currency crisis in 1984 New Zealand began reforming its policies.

Sautet argues that four main areas of reform were responsible for New Zealand's turnaround. The first area was tax reform. Marginal income tax rates were cut in half as the tax base was broadened so that entrepreneurial business decisions were guided more by market forces and less by tax considerations. The Employment Contract Act of 1991 was of critical importance in the area of labor reform. The act made the labor market more fluid by giving employees and employers the choice to negotiate either individual employment contracts or collective ones. With union power diminished, unemployment fell from 11 percent to 4 percent by 2004. Labor is an important factor of production, and in an entrepreneurial environment of economic growth it is crucial that it be possible to easily reshuffle labor to reflect changing economic realities. A third major area of reform was in trade liberalization. Because New Zealand is a small economy it is essential that it be integrated into a larger world market. New Zealand went from having one of the least open economies in the OECD during the 1970s to having a much more open economy during reform. Complete free trade with Australia was adopted, while tariffs against other countries were gradually reduced. Finally, monetary reforms were important. Inflation had been high, and with the adoption of the 1989 Reserve Bank Act, many of the bank's conflicting goals were eliminated, and it was mandated to target inflation rates of 1–3 percent (originally 0–2 percent). Since 1991 inflation has averaged 2.1 percent. The overall impact of reforms in New Zealand resulted in its economic freedom score improving from 5.9 in 1985 to 8.2 in 2002.

Despite the widespread reforms and improvements in performance, New Zealand hasn't experienced as dramatic a turnaround as some other reforming nations have. Sautet argues that the reason is that the reforms have not gone far enough. Although the efficiency of taxation has improved, the overall size of government has remained large. Marginal tax rates have been lowered, but average taxes remain high. The high levels of government spending continue to misdirect entrepreneurship toward unproductive activities. Despite the opening of New Zealand's economy, barriers put in place by other nations limit New Zealand's access to markets. If it could join the free trade agreement with Australia and the United States, then it would have better access to a larger market, much like Ireland has with the EU. Finally, regulations and interventions remain in labor and industry. Some aspects of the Employment Contract Act have been repealed, and the government remains a player in industry by owning commercial enterprises such as Kiwibank, Air New Zealand, and the railway system. Sautet concludes that further reform in all of these areas could promote an environment of more productive entrepreneurship that would lead to even better performance than New Zealand has achieved thus far in the reform process.

Botswana rounds out our cases of productive reformers. In Chapter 14 Scott Beaulier explains how Botswana transformed itself from one of the poorest nations in the world in the early 1960s to an upper-middle-income nation today. Botswana was a land-locked British protectorate with few natural resources, an arid climate, little infrastructure, and widespread poverty. Upon gaining independence in the 1960s it embarked on a series of reforms that reduced the government presence in the economy and promoted economic freedom. Botswana, unlike other African governments, kept much of the British common law. Meanwhile, government spending as a percent of GDP fell from 23 percent in the mid-1960s to 15 percent by the early 1970s, and an overall environment of openness, toleration, and respect for the rule of law promoted economic development. The result was an increase in incomes from $372 per capita in 1965 to $1,032 a decade later.

Since 1975 Botswana has remained more free than most of its African neighbors and has continued to increase its standard of living. During the period of 1966 through 1996 Botswana was the fastest-growing nation in the world, averaging 7.7 percent for the period. However, Beaulier points out that Botswana's institutional environment has deteriorated since the mid-1970s and that it could face problems going forward.

Beaulier argues that the formation of interest groups and the discovery of diamonds are the two main factors contributing to Botswana's institutional deterioration. He argues that the formation of interest groups has fueled demands for increased government spending, particularly in education and defense. Since diamonds were discovered in the early 1970s they have grown increasingly important in Botswana's economy and have given the government a source of revenue to finance interest-group spending demands. Government spending has grown from 15 percent of GDP in the early 1970s to nearly 33 percent of GDP today. Meanwhile, overall marginal tax rates have remained low because the government continually renegotiates with Debswana, the major diamond-mining corporation, to get more revenue. It is now estimated that anywhere from 35 to 50 percent of government revenue comes from the diamond industry. Although most of the economy has not had to bear the burden of increased government spending, there are some indications that diamond reserves are shrinking, and if Botswana does not reduce spending in the future other industries might have to face higher taxes.

Overall, Botswana is an extreme success story. It started out with little prospect of development in a region of the world where few countries succeed. Yet it was able to dramatically improve living standards by adopting pro-market policies.

3. Conclusion

Foreign aid and state planning have failed to promote economic growth in impoverished regions of the world. As case studies in this book make clear, countries that are poor suffer from too much government intervention, not too little. Countries that have developed rapidly have done so by improving the institutional environment in which entrepreneurs operate. They better respected private property rights and granted greater levels of economic freedom.

This lesson is crucial for the poorer countries of the world, where increased economic growth can literally be a matter of life and death. It is also important for "developed" countries. No country has a perfect institutional environment. Even Hong Kong, which consistently ranks first in the economic freedom indexes, has interventions that distort housing markets. The United States and western European nations all have numerous interventions that distort entrepreneurial incentives, preventing the economies from reaching their potential. Whether in Africa or the United States, institutional reforms that promote economic freedom will lead to achieving higher standards of living.

A crucial question is how to get beneficial reforms. This book answers that question only tangentially. In New Zealand, Ireland, and India, financial crises disrupted existing political equilibria and allowed reforms to be made without major ideological shifts. However, there is evidence of backsliding in both New Zealand and Ireland, and India's reforms still have a long way to go. Crisis alone is not enough to guarantee reform. Africa has no shortage of crises, but few nations have seized the opportunity to make pro-freedom reforms. In Botswana's case, a British legacy, a committed leader, and a lack of interest groups were enough to set the country on the right path. In China, experimentation at the local level that succeeds is later endorsed by the central party in a kind of bottom-up process of reform. Britain, which is not covered in this book, did experience more of an ideological shift during its period of reform. Although it is not a central theme in this book, the findings are consistent with those of Glaser and colleagues (2004) in finding that democratic political reforms are not a prerequisite for beneficial policy changes that induce growth. Dictatorships such as China and democracies such as Ireland are both capable of reform. There is likely not one unique path to achieving beneficial social change. However, this remains an area of crucial importance for future research. We know the right institutional environment for economic growth. The question remains as to how to get it adopted. One thing is for certain: a step that is crucial for getting the right institutional environment in place is to convince more people of exactly what the right institutional environment is. That is the purpose of this book.

The overall message of this book is simple, yet it is vitally important for the millions who reside in underdeveloped regions of the world. Economic freedom and private property rights are essential for promoting the productive entrepreneurship that leads to economic growth. In countries where this institutional environment is lacking, sustained economic development remains elusive. When countries make pro-market reforms that enhance their institutional environment, growth improves—sometimes dramatically. This message had been lacking in most of the theoretical academic literature and international policy organizations for much of the past sixty years. Fortunately, this situation is changing, and the importance of property rights and economic freedom is now recognized more frequently in both circles. Hopefully, by carefully studying individual cases of success and failure, this book can help to further promote the importance of this institutional environment.

References

Economist. 1988. "Survey Republic of Ireland," January 16, 1988, 3–26.

Glaeser, Edward, Rafael La Porta, Florencio Lopez-de-Silanes, and Andrei Shleifer. 2004. "Do Institutions Cause Growth?" *Journal of Economic Growth* 9:271–303.

Gwartney, James, and Robert Lawson. 2005. *Economic Freedom of the World*. Vancouver, Canada: Fraser Institute.

Hall, Robert, and Charles Jones. 1999. "Why Do Some Countries Produce So Much More Output Per Worker Than Others?" *The Quarterly Journal of Economics* 114 (1): 83–116.

Hayek, F. 1945. "The Use of Knowledge in Society." *American Economic Review* 35 (4): 519–530.

Kirzner, Israel. 1973. *Competition and Entrepreneurship*. Chicago: University of Chicago Press.

Rodrik, Dani, ed. 2003. *In Search of Prosperity*. Princeton, NJ: Princeton University Press.

Rodrik, Dani, Arvind Subramanian, and Francesco Trebbi. 2004. "Institutions Rule: The Primacy of Institutions over Geography and Integration in Economic Development." *Journal of Economic Growth* 9:131–165.

Schumpeter, Joseph. 1934. *The Theory of Economic Development*. Cambridge, MA: Harvard University Press.

I *Institutions and Entrepreneurship*

2 Big Bills Left on the Sidewalk: Why Some Nations Are Rich, and Others Poor

MANCUR OLSON JR.

There is one metaphor that not only illuminates the idea behind many complex and seemingly disparate articles, but also helps to explain why many nations have remained poor while others have become rich. This metaphor grows out of debates about the "efficient markets hypothesis" that all pertinent publicly available information is taken into account in existing stock market prices, so that an investor can do as well by investing in randomly chosen stocks as by drawing on expert judgment. It is embodied in the familiar old joke about the assistant professor who, when walking with a full professor, reaches down for the $100 bill he sees on the sidewalk. But he is held back by his senior colleague, who points out that if the $100 bill were real, it would have been picked up already. This story epitomizes many articles showing that the optimization of the participants in the market typically eliminates opportunities for supranormal returns: big bills aren't often dropped on the sidewalk, and if they are, they are picked up very quickly.

Many developments in economics in the last quarter century rest on the idea that any gains that can be obtained are in fact picked up. Though primitive early versions of Keynesian macroeconomics promised huge gains from activist fiscal and monetary policies, macroeconomics in the last quarter century has more often than not argued that rational individual behavior eliminates the problems that activist policies were supposed to solve. If a disequilibrium wage is creating involuntary unemployment, that would mean that workers had time to sell that was worth less to them than to prospective employers, so a mutually advantageous employment contract eliminates the involuntary unemployment. The market ensures that involuntarily unemployed labor is not left pacing the sidewalks.

Similarly, profit-maximizing firms have an incentive to enter exceptionally profitable industries, which reduces the social losses from monopoly power. Accordingly, a body of empirical research finds that the losses from monopoly in U.S. industry are slight: Harberger triangles are small. In the same spirit, many economists find that the social losses from protectionism and other inefficient government policies are only a minuscule percentage of the GDP.

The literature growing out of the Coase theorem similarly suggests that even when there are externalities, bargaining among those involved can generate socially efficient outcomes. As long as transactions costs are not too high, voluntary bargaining internalizes externalities, so there is a Pareto-efficient outcome whatever the initial distribution of legal rights among the parties. Again, this is the idea that bargainers leave no money on the table.

Some of the more recent literature on Coaseian bargains emphasizes that transactions costs use up real resources and that the value of these resources must be taken into account in defining the Pareto frontier. It follows that, if the bargaining costs of internalizing an externality exceed the resulting gains, things should be left alone. The fact that rational parties won't leave any money on the table automatically insures that laissez faire generates Pareto efficiency.

More recently, Gary Becker (1983, 1985) has emphasized that government programs with deadweight losses must be at a political disadvantage. Some economists have gone on to treat governments as institutions that reduce transactions costs, and they have applied the Coase theorem to politics. They argue, in essence, that rational actors in the polity have an incentive to bargain politically until all mutual gains have been realized, so that democratic government, though it affects the distribution of income, normally produces socially efficient results (Stigler 1971, 1992; Wittman 1989, 1995; Thompson and Faith 1981; Breton 1993). This is true even when the policy chosen runs counter to the prescriptions of economists: if some alternative political bargain would have left the rational parties in the polity better off, they would have chosen it! Thus, the elemental idea that mutually advantageous bargaining will obtain all gains that are worth obtaining—that there are no bills left on the sidewalk—leads to the conclusion that, whether we observe laissez faire or rampant interventionism, we are already in the most efficient of all possible worlds.[1]

The idea that the economies we observe are socially efficient, at least to an approximation, is not only espoused by economists who follow their logic as far as it will go, but is also a staple assumption behind much of the best-known empirical work. In the familiar aggregate-production-function or growth-accounting empirical studies, it is assumed that economies are on the frontiers of their aggregate production functions.

Profit-maximizing firms use capital and other factors of production up to the point where the value of the marginal product equals the price of the input, and it is assumed that the marginal private product of each factor equals its marginal social product. The econometrician can then calculate how much of the increase in social output is attributable to the accumulation of capital and other factors of production and treat any increases in output beyond this—"the residual"—as due to the advance of knowledge. This procedure assumes that output is as great as it can be, given the available resources and the level of technological knowledge.

If the ideas evoked here are largely true, then the rational parties in the economy and the polity ensure that the economy cannot be that far from its potential, and the policy advice of economists cannot be especially valuable. Of course, even if economic advice increased the GDP by just 1 percent, that would pay our salaries several times over. Still, the implication of the foregoing ideas and empirical assumptions is that economics cannot save the world, but at best can only improve it a little. In the language of Keynes's comparison of professions, we are no more important for the future of society than dentists.

1. The Boundaries of Wealth and Poverty

How can we find empirical evidence to test the idea that the rationality of individuals makes societies achieve their productive potential? This question seems empirically intractable. Yet there is one type of place where evidence abounds: the borders of countries. National borders delineate areas of different economic policies and institutions, and so—to the extent that variations in performance across countries cannot be explained by the differences in their endowments—they tell us something about the extent to which societies have attained their potentials.

Income levels differ dramatically across countries. According to the best available measures, per capita incomes in the richest countries are more than twenty times as high as in the poorest. Whatever the causes of high incomes may be, they are certainly present in some countries and absent in others. Though rich and poor countries do not usually share common borders, sometimes there are great differences in per capita income on opposite sides of a meandering river, like the Rio Grande, or where opposing armies happened to come to a stalemate, as between North and South Korea, or where arbitrary lines were drawn to divide a country, as not long ago in Germany.

At the highest level of aggregation, there are only two possible types of explanations of the great differences in per capita income across countries that can be taken seriously.

The first possibility is that, as the aggregate-production-function methodology and the foregoing theories suggest, national borders mark differences in the scarcity of productive resources per capita: the poor countries are poor because they are short of resources. They might be short of land and natural resources, or of human capital, or of equipment that embodies the latest technology, or of other types of resources. On this theory, the Coase theorem holds as much in poor societies as in rich ones: the rationality of individuals brings each society reasonably close to its potential, different as these potentials are. There are no big bills on the footpaths of the poor societies, either.

The second possibility is that national boundaries mark the borders of public policies and institutions that are not only different, but in some cases better and in other cases worse.[2] Those countries with the best policies and institutions achieve most of their potential, while other countries achieve only a tiny fraction of their potential income. The individuals and firms in these societies may display rationality, and often great ingenuity and perseverance, in eking out a living in extraordinarily difficult conditions, but this individual achievement does not generate anything remotely resembling a socially efficient outcome. There are hundreds of billions or even trillions of dollars that could be—but are not—earned each year from the natural and human resources of these countries. On this theory, the poorer countries do not have a structure of incentives that brings forth the productive cooperation that would pick up the big bills, and the reason they don't have it is that such structures do not emerge automatically as a consequence of individual rationality. The structure of incentives depends not only on what economic policies are chosen in each period, but also on the long-run or institutional arrangements: on the legal systems that enforce contracts and protect property rights and on political structures, constitutional provisions, and the extent of special-interest lobbies and cartels.

How important are each of the two foregoing possibilities in explaining economic performance? This question is extraordinarily important. The answer must not only help us judge the theories under discussion, but also tell us about the main sources of economic growth and development.

I will attempt to assess the two possibilities by aggregating the productive factors in the same way as in a conventional aggregate-production-function or growth-accounting study and then consider each of the aggregate factors in turn. That is, I consider separately the relative abundance or scarcity of "capital," of "land" (with land standing for all natural resources) and of "labor" (with labor including not only human capital in the form of skills and education, but also culture). I will also consider the level of technology separately, and I find some considerations and evidence that support the familiar assumption from growth-accounting studies and Solow-type growth theory that the same level of technological knowledge is given exogenously to all countries.[2] With this conventional taxonomy and the assumption that societies are on frontiers of their aggregate neoclassical production functions, we can derive important findings with a few simple deductions from familiar facts.

The next section shows that there is strong support for the familiar assumption that the world's stock of knowledge is available at little or no cost to all the countries of the world. I next examine the degree to which the marginal productivity of labor changes with large migrations and evidence on population densities, and I show that diminishing returns to land and other natural resources cannot explain much of the huge international differences in income. After that, I borrow some calculations from Robert Lucas on the implications of the huge differences across countries in capital intensity—and relate them to facts on the direction and magnitude of capital flows—to show that it is quite impossible that the countries of the world are anywhere near the frontiers of aggregate neoclassical production functions. I then examine some strangely neglected natural experiments with migrants from poor to rich countries to estimate the size of the differences in endowments of human capital between the poor and rich countries, and I demonstrate that they are able to account for only a small part of the international differences in the marginal product of labor.

Since neither differences in endowments of any of the three classical aggregate factors of production nor differential access to technology explains much of the great variation in per capita incomes, we are left with the second of the two (admittedly highly aggregated) possibilities set out above: that much the most important explanation of the differences in income across countries is the difference in their economic policies and institutions. There will not be room here to set out many of the other types of evidence supporting this conclusion, nor to offer any detailed analysis of what particular institutions and policies best promote economic growth. Nonetheless, by referring to other studies—and by returning to something that the theories with which we began overlook—we shall obtain some sense of why variations in institutions and policies are surely the main determinants of international differences in per capita incomes. We shall also obtain a faint glimpse of the broadest features of the institutions and policies that nations need to achieve the highest possible income levels.

2. The Access to Productive Knowledge

Is the world's technological knowledge generally accessible at little or no cost to all countries? To the extent that productive knowledge takes the form of unpatentable laws of nature and advances in basic science, it is a nonexcludable public good available to everyone without charge. Nonpurchasers can, however, be denied access to many discoveries (in countries where intellectual property rights are enforced) through patents or copyrights, or because the discoveries are embodied in machines or other marketable products. Perhaps most advances in basic science can be of use to a poor country only after they have been combined with or embodied in some product or process that must be purchased from firms in the rich countries. We must, therefore, ask whether most of the gains from using modern productive knowledge in a poor country are mainly captured by firms in the countries that discovered or developed this knowledge.

Since those Third World countries that have been growing exceptionally rapidly must surely have been adopting modern technologies from the First World, I tried (with the help of Brendan Kennelly) to find out how much foreign technologies had cost some such countries. As it happens, there is a study with some striking data for South Korea for the years from 1973 to 1979 (Koo 1982). In Korea during these years, royalties and all other payments for disembodied technology were minuscule—often less than one-thousandth of GDP. Even if we treat all profits on foreign direct investment as solely a payment for knowledge and add them to royalties, the total is still less than 1.5 percent of the *increase* in Korea's GDP over the period. Thus the foreign owners of productive knowledge obtained less than a fiftieth of the gains from Korea's rapid economic growth.[3]

The South Korean case certainly supports the long-familiar assumption that the world's productive knowledge is, for the most part, available to poor countries, and even at a relatively modest cost.[4] It would be very difficult to explain much of the differences in per capita incomes across countries in terms of differential access to the available stock of productive knowledge.[5]

3. Overpopulation and Diminishing Returns to Labor

Countries with access to the same global stock of knowledge may nonetheless have different endowments, which in turn might explain most of the differences in per capita income across countries. Accordingly, many people have supposed that the poverty in the poor countries is due largely to overpopulation, that is, to a low ratio of land and other natural resources to population. Is this true?

There is some evidence that provides a surprisingly persuasive answer to this question. I came upon it when I learned through Bhagwati (1984) of Hamilton and Whalley's (1984) estimates about how much world income would change if more workers were shifted from low-income to high-income countries. The key is to examine how much

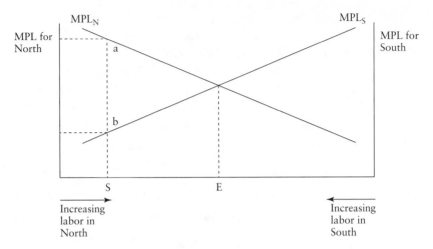

FIGURE **2.1** Population distribution and relative wages

migration from poorer to richer countries *changes* relative wages and the marginal productivities of labor.

For simplicity, suppose that the world is divided into only two regions, North and South, and stick with the conventional assumption that both are on the frontiers of their aggregate production functions. As we move left to right from the origin of Figure 2.1, we have an ever-larger workforce in the North until, at the extreme right end of this axis, all of the world's labor force is there. Conversely, as we move right to left from the right-hand axis, we have an ever larger workforce in the South. The marginal product of labor or wage in the rich North is measured on the vertical axis at the left of Figure 2.1. The curve MPL_N gives the marginal product or wage of labor in the North, and, of course, because of diminishing returns, it slopes downward as we move to the right. The larger the labor force in the South, the lower the marginal product of labor in the South, so MPL_S, measured on the right-hand vertical axis, slopes down as we move to the left. Each point on the horizontal axis will specify a distribution of the world's population between the North and the South. A point like S represents the status quo. At S, there is relatively little labor and population in relation to resources in the North, and so the northern marginal product and wage are high. The marginal product and wage in the overpopulated South will be low, and the marginal product of labor in the North exceeds that in the South by a substantial multiple.

This model tells us that when workers migrate from the low-wage South to the high-wage North, world income goes up by the difference between the wage the migrant worker receives in the rich country and what that worker earned in the poor country, or by amount *ab*. Clearly, the world as a whole is not on the frontier of its aggregate production, even if all of the countries in it are: some big bills have not been picked up on the routes that lead from poor to rich countries.[6] Of course, the argument that has just been made is extremely simple, and international migration involves many other considerations. We can best come to understand these considerations—as well as other matters—by staying with this simple factor-proportions story a while longer.

4. The Surprising Results of Large Migrations

This elementary model reminds us that, if it is diminishing returns to land and other natural resources that mainly explain international differences in per capita incomes, then large migrations from poorer to richer societies will, if other things (like the stocks of capital) remain equal, necessarily reduce income differentials.

Such migration obviously raises the resource-to-population ratio in the country of emigration and reduces it in the country of immigration, and if carried far enough will continue until wages are equalized, as at point *E* in Figure 2.1.

Now consider Ireland, the country that has experienced much the highest proportion of outmigration in Europe, if not the world. In the census of 1821, Ireland had 5.4 million people, and Great Britain a population of 14.2 million.[7]

Though the Irish have experienced the same rates of natural population increase that have characterized other European peoples since 1821, in 1986, Ireland had only 3.5 million people. By this time, the population of Great Britain had reached 55.1 million. In 1821, the population density of Ireland was greater than that of Great Britain; by 1986, it was only about a fifth as great.[8]

If the lack of "land" or overpopulation is decisive, Ireland ought to have enjoyed an exceptionally rapid growth of per capita income, at least in comparison with Great Britain, and the outmigration should eventually have ceased. Not so. Remarkably, the Irish level of per capita income is still only about five-eighths of the British level and less than half of the level in the United States, and the outmigration from Ireland is still continuing. As we shall see later, such large disparities in per capita income cannot normally be explained by differences in human capital. It is clear that in the United States, Britain, and many other countries, immigrants from Ireland tend to earn as much as other peoples, and any differences in human capital could not explain the *increase* in wage that migrants receive when they go to a more productive country. Thus we can be sure that it is not the ratio of land to labor that has mainly determined per capita income in Ireland.

Now let us look at the huge European immigration to the United States between the closing of the U.S. frontier in about 1890 and the imposition of U.S. immigration restrictions in the early 1920s. If diminishing returns to labor were a substantial part of the story of economic growth, this vast migration should have caused a gradual reduction of the per capita income differential between the United States and Europe. In fact, the United States had a bigger lead in per capita income over several European countries in 1910 and 1920 than it had in the nineteenth century. Although many European countries did *not* narrow the gap in per capita incomes with the United States in the nineteenth century when they experienced a large outmigration to the United States, many of these same countries did nearly close that gap in the years after 1945, when they had relatively little emigration to the United States, and when their own incomes ought to have been lowered by a significant inflow of migrants and guest workers. Similarly, from the end of World War II until the construction of the Berlin Wall, there was a considerable flow of population from East to West Germany, but this flow did not equalize income levels.

Consider also the irrepressible flow of documented and undocumented migration from Latin America to the United States. If diminishing returns to land and other natural resources were the main explanation of the difference in per capita incomes between Mexico and the United States, these differences should have diminished markedly at the times when this migration was greatest. They have not.

Several detailed empirical studies of relatively large immigration to isolated labor markets point to the same conclusion as the great migrations we have just considered. Card's (1990) study of the Mariel boatlift's effect on the wages of natives of Miami, Hunt's (1992) examination of the repatriation of Algerian French workers to southern France, and

Carrington and De Lima's (1996) account of the repatriates from Angola and Mozambique after Portugal lost its colonies all suggest that the substantial immigration did not depress the wages of natives.[9]

Perhaps in some cases the curves in Figure 2.1 would cross when there was little population left in a poor country. Or maybe they would not cross at all: even that last person who turned the lights out as he left would obtain a higher wage after migrating.

5. Surprising Evidence on Density of Population

Let us now shift focus from changes in land/labor ratios due to migration to the cross-sectional evidence at given points in time on ratios of land to labor. Ideally, one should have a good index of the natural resource endowments of each country.

Such an index should be adjusted to take account of changes in international prices, so that the value of a nation's resources index would change when the prices of the resources with which it was relatively well endowed went up or down. For lack of such an index, we must here simply examine density of population. Fortunately, the number of countries on which we have data on population and area is so large that population density alone tells us something.

Many of the most densely settled countries have high per capita incomes, and many poor countries are sparsely settled. Argentina, a country that fell from having one of the highest per capita incomes to Third World status, has only 11 persons per square kilometer; Brazil, 16; Kenya, 25; and Zaire, 13. India, like most societies with a lot of irrigated agriculture, is more densely settled, with 233 people per square kilometer. But high-income West Germany, with 246 people per square kilometer, is more densely settled than India. Belgium and Japan have half again more population density than India, with 322 and 325 people per square kilometer, and Holland has still more density with 357. The population of Singapore is 4,185 per square kilometer; that of Hong Kong, over 5,000 persons per square kilometer (United Nations 1986). These two densely settled little fragments of land also have per capita incomes ten times as high as the poorest countries (and as of this writing they continue, like many other densely settled countries, to absorb migrants, at least when the migrants can sneak through the controls).

The foregoing cases could be exceptions, so we need to take all countries for which data are available into account and summarily describe the overall relationship between population density and per capita income. If we remember that the purpose is description and are careful to avoid drawing causal inferences, we can describe the available data with a univariate regression in which the natural log of real per capita income is the left-hand variable, and the natural log of population per square kilometer is the "explanatory" variable. Obviously, the per capita income of a country depends on many things, and any statistical test that does not take account of all important determinants is misspecified, and thus must be used only for descriptive and heuristic purposes. It is nonetheless interesting—and for most people surprising—to find that there is a *positive* and even a statistically significant relationship between these two variables: the *greater* the number of people per square kilometer the *higher* per capita income.[10]

The law of diminishing returns is indisputably true: it would be absurd to suppose that a larger endowment of land makes a country poorer. This consideration by itself would, of course, call for a negative sign on population density. Thus, it is interesting to ask what might account for the "wrong" sign and to think of what statistical tests should ultimately be done. Clearly, there is a simultaneous two-way relationship between population density and per capita income: the level of per capita income affects population growth just as population, through diminishing returns to labor, affects per capita income.

The argument offered here suggests that perhaps countries with better economic policies and institutions come to have higher per capita incomes than countries with inferior policies and institutions, and that these higher incomes bring about a higher population growth through more immigration and lower death rates. In this way, the effect of better institutions and policies in raising per capita income swamps the tendency of diminishing returns to labor to reduce it. This hypothesis also may explain why many empirical studies have not been able to show a negative association between the rate of population growth and increases in per capita income.

One reason why the ratio of natural resources to population does not account for variations in per capita income is that most economic activity can now readily be separated from deposits of raw materials and arable land. Over time, transportation technologies have certainly improved, and products that have a high value in relation to their weight, such as most services and manufactured goods like computers and airplanes, may have become more important. The Silicon Valley is not important for the manufacture of computers because of deposits of silicon, and London and Zurich are not great banking centers because of fertile land. Even casual observation suggests that most modern manufacturing and service exports are not closely tied to natural resources. Western Europe does not now have a high ratio of natural resources to population, but it is very important in the export of manufactures and services. Japan has relatively little natural resources per capita, but it is a great exporter of manufactures. Certainly the striking successes in manufactures of Hong Kong and Singapore cannot be explained by their natural resources.

6. Diminishing Returns to Capital

We have seen that large migrations of labor do not change the marginal productivities of labor the way that they would if societies were at the frontiers of aggregate neoclassical production functions and that there is even evidence that labor is on average more highly paid where it is combined with less land. We shall now see that the allocation of capital across countries—and the patterns of investment and migration of capital across countries of high and low capital intensities—contradict the assumption that countries are on the frontiers of aggregate neoclassical production functions in an even more striking way.

This is immediately evident if we return to Figure 2.1 and relabel its coordinates and curves. If we replace the total world labor supply given along the horizontal axis of Figure 2.1 with the total world stock of capital and assume that the quantity of labor as well as natural resources in the North and South do not change, we can use Figure 2.1 to analyze diminishing returns to capital in the same way we used it to consider diminishing returns to labor.

As everyone knows, the countries with high per capita incomes have incomparably higher capital intensities of production than do those with low incomes. The countries of the Third World use relatively little capital, and those of the First World are capital rich: most of the world's stock of capital is "crowded" into North America, western Europe and Japan.

If the countries of the world were on the frontiers of neoclassical production functions, the marginal product of capital would therefore be many times higher in the low-income than in the high-income countries. Robert Lucas (1990) has calculated, albeit in a somewhat different framework,[11] the marginal product of capital that should be expected in the United States and in India. Lucas estimated that if an Indian worker and an American worker supplied the same quantity and quality of labor, the marginal product of capital in India should be fifty-eight *times* as great as in the United States. Even when Lucas assumed that it took *five* Indian workers to supply as much labor as one U.S. worker, the predicted return to capital in India would still be a multiple of the return in the United States.

With portfolio managers and multinational corporations searching for more profitable investments for their capital, such gigantic differences in return should generate huge migrations of capital from the high-income to the low-income countries. Capital should be struggling at least as hard to get into the Third World as labor is struggling to migrate into the high-wage countries. Indeed, since rational owners of capital allocate their investment funds across countries so that the risk-adjusted return at the margin is the same across countries, capital should be equally plentiful in all countries. (As we know from the Heckscher–Ohlin–Stolper–Samuelson discovery, if all countries operate on the same aggregate production functions, free trade alone is sometimes enough to equalize factor price ratios and thus factor intensities even in the absence of capital flows.)

Obviously, the dramatically uneven distribution of capital around the world contradicts the familiar assumption that all countries are on the frontiers of aggregate neoclassical production functions. A country could not be Pareto efficient and thus could not be on the frontier of its aggregate production unless it had equated the marginal product of capital in the country to the world price of capital.[12] If it were not meeting this law-of-one-price condition, it would be passing up the gains that could come from borrowing capital abroad at the world rate of interest, investing it at home to obtain the higher marginal product of capital and pocketing the difference—it would be leaving large bills on the sidewalk. Accordingly, the strikingly unequal allocation of the world's stock of capital across nations proves that the poor countries cannot be anywhere near the frontiers of their aggregate production functions.

Sometimes the shortcomings of the economic policies and institutions of the low-income countries keep capital in these countries from earning rates of return appropriate to its scarcity, as we may infer from Harberger's (1978) findings and other evidence. Sometimes the shortcomings of the economic policies and institutions of poor countries make foreign investors and foreign firms unwelcome, or provoke the flight of locally owned capital, or make lending to these countries exceedingly risky. Whether the institutional and policy shortcomings of a country keep capital from having the productivity appropriate to its scarcity or discourage the investments and lending that would equalize the marginal product of capital across countries, they keep it from achieving its potential.

On top of all this, it is not rare for capital and labor to move in *the same direction*: both capital and labor are sometimes trying to move out of some countries and into some of the same countries. Of course, in a world where countries are on the frontiers of their aggregate production functions, capital and labor move in opposite directions.[13]

Given the extraordinarily uneven allocation of capital across the countries of the world and the strong relationship between capital mobility and the economic policies and institutions of countries, the stock of capital cannot be taken to be exogenous in any reasonable theory of economic development.

7. Distinguishing Private Good and Public Good Human Capital

The adjustment of the amount of human capital per worker in Lucas's (1990) foregoing calculation for India and the United States raises a general issue: Can the great differences in per capita income be mainly explained by differences in the third aggregate factor, labor, that is, by differences in the *human* capital per capita, broadly understood as including the cultural or other traits of different peoples as well as their skills? The average level of human capital in the form of occupational skills or education in a society can obviously influence the level of its per capita income.

Many people also argue that the high incomes in the rich countries are due in part to cultural or racial traits that make the individuals in these countries adept at responding to economic opportunities: they have the "Protestant ethic" or other cultural or national traits that are supposed to make them hard workers, frugal savers, and imaginative entrepreneurs. Poor countries are alleged to be poor because they lack these traits.[14] The cultural traits that perpetuate poverty are, it is argued, the results of centuries of social accumulation and cannot be changed quickly.

Unfortunately, the argument that culture is important for economic development, though plausible, is also vague: the word "*culture,*" even though it is widely used in diverse disciplines, has not been defined precisely or in a way that permits comparison with other variables in an aggregate production function. We can obtain conceptions of culture that are adequate for the present purpose by breaking culture down into two distinct types of human capital.

Some types of human capital are obviously marketable: if a person has more skill, or a propensity to work harder, or a predilection to save more, or a more entrepreneurial personality, this will normally increase that individual's money income. Let us call these skills, propensities, or cultural traits that affect the quality or the quantity of productive inputs that an individual can sell in the marketplace "marketable human capital" or, synonymously, "personal culture." Max Weber's analysis of what he called the Protestant ethic was about marketable human capital or personal culture.

The second type of culture or human capital is evident when we think of knowledge that individuals may have about how they should vote: about what public policies will be successful. If enough voters acquire more knowledge about what the real consequences of different public policies will be, public policies will improve and thereby increase real incomes in the society. But this better knowledge of public policy is usually not marketable: in a society with *given* economic policies and institutions, the acquisition of such knowledge would not in general have any effect on an individual's wage or income. Knowledge about what public policy should be is a public good rather than a private or marketable good. Thus this second kind of human capital is "public good human capital" or "civic culture." Whereas marketable human capital or personal culture increases an individual's market income under given institutions and public policies, public good human capital or civic culture is not normally marketable and only affects incomes by influencing public policies and institutions.

With the aid of the distinction between marketable and public good human capital, we can gain important truths from some natural experiments.

8. Migration as an Experiment

As it happens, migration from poor to rich countries provides researchers with a marvelous (and so far strangely neglected) natural experiment. Typically, the number of individuals who immigrate to a country in any generation is too small to bring about any significant change in the electorate or public policies of the host country. But the migrant who arrives as an adult comes with the marketable human capital or personal culture of the country of origin; the Latin American who swims the Rio Grande is not thereby instantly baptized with the Protestant ethic. Though the migrant may in time acquire the culture of the host country, the whole idea behind the theories that emphasize the cultural or other characteristics of peoples is that it takes time to erase generations of socialization: if the cultural or other traits of a people could be changed overnight, they could not be significant barriers to development. Newly arrived immigrants therefore have approximately the same marketable human capital or personal culture they had before they migrated, but the institutions and public policies that determine the opportunities that they confront are those of the host country. In the case of the migration to the United States, at least, the data about newly arrived migrants from poor countries are sufficient to permit some immediate conclusions.

Christopher Clague (1991), drawing on the work of Borjas (1987), has found that individuals who had just arrived in the United States from poor countries, in spite of the difficulties they must have had in adjusting to a new environment with a different language and conditions, earned about 55 percent as much as native Americans of the same age, sex, and years of schooling.[15] New immigrants from countries where per capita incomes are only a tenth or a fifth as large as in the United States have a wage more than half as large as comparable American workers.[16] Profit-maximizing firms would not have hired these migrants if they did not have a marginal product at least as large as their wage. The migrant's labor is, of course, combined with more capital in the rich than in the poor country, but it is not an accident that the owners of capital chose to invest it where they did: as the foregoing argument showed, the capital-labor ratio in a country is mainly determined by its institutions and policies.

Migrants might be more productive than their compatriots who did not migrate, so it might be supposed that the foregoing observations on immigrants are driven by selection bias. In fact, no tendency for the more productive people in poor countries to be more likely to emigrate could explain the huge increases in wages and marginal products of the *migrants themselves*. The migrant earns and produces much more in the rich country than in the poor country, so no tendency for migrants to be more productive than those who did not migrate could explain the *increase* in the migrant's marginal product when he or she moves from the poor to the rich country.[17] In any event, developing countries often have much more unequal income distributions than developed nations, and the incentive to migrate from these countries is greatest in the least successful half of their income distributions. In fact, migrants to the United States are often drawn from the lower portion of the income distribution of underdeveloped countries (Borjas 1990).

It is also instructive to examine the differences in productivity of migrants from poor countries with migrants from rich countries and then to see how much of the difference in per capita incomes in the countries of origin is likely to be due to the differences in the marketable human capital or personal culture of their respective peoples. Compare, for example, migrants to the United States from Haiti, one of the world's least successful economies, with migrants from West Germany, one of the most successful. According to the 1980 U.S. Census, self-employed immigrants from Haiti earned $18,900 per year, while those from West Germany earned $27,300; salaried immigrants from Haiti earned $10,900, those from West Germany, $21,900. Since the average Haitian immigrants earned only two-thirds or half as much as their West German counterparts in the same American environment, we may suspect that the Haitians had, on average, less marketable human capital than the West Germans.

So now let us perform the thought experiment of asking how much West Germans would have produced if they had the same institutions and economic policies as Haiti, or conversely how much Haitians would have produced had they had the same institutions and economic policies as West Germany. If we infer from the experience of migrants to the United

States that West Germans have twice as much marketable capital as the Haitians, we can then suppose that Haiti with its present institutions and economic policies, but with West German levels of marketable human capital, would have about twice the per capita income that it has. But the actual level of Haitian per capita income is only about a tenth of the West German level, so Haiti would still, under our thought experiment, have less than one-fifth of the West German per capita income. Of course, if one imagines Haitian levels of marketable human capital operating with West German institutions and economic policies, one comes up with about half of the West German per capita income, which is again many times larger than Haiti's actual per capita income.

Obviously, one of the reasons for the great disparity implied by these thought experiments is the different amounts of tangible capital per worker in the two countries. Before taking this as given exogenously, however, the reader should consider investing his or her own money in each of these two countries. It is also possible that different selection biases for immigrants from different countries help account for the results of the foregoing thought experiments. Yet roughly the same results hold when one undertakes similar comparisons for migrants from Switzerland and Egypt, Japan and Guatemala, Norway and the Philippines, Sweden and Greece, the Netherlands and Panama, and so on.[18] If, in comparing the incomes of migrants to the United States from poor and rich countries, one supposes that selection bias leads to an underestimate of the differences in marketable human capital between the poor and rich countries, and then makes a larger estimate of this effect than anyone is likely to think plausible, one still ends up with the result that the rich countries have vastly larger leads over poor countries in per capita incomes than can possibly be explained by differences in the marketable human capital of their populations. Such differences in personal culture can explain only a small part of the huge differences in per capita income between the rich and the poor countries.

History has performed some other experiments that lead to the same conclusion. During most of the postwar period, China, Germany, and Korea have been divided by the accidents of history, so that different parts of nations with about the same culture and group traits have had different institutions and economic policies. The economic performances of Hong Kong and Taiwan, of West Germany, and of South Korea have been incomparably better than the performances of mainland China, East Germany, and North Korea. Such great differences in economic performance in areas of very similar cultural characteristics could surely not be explained by differences in the marketable human capital of the populations at issue.

It is important to remember that the foregoing experiments involving migration do not tell us anything about popular attitudes or prejudices in different countries regarding what public policy should be. That is, they do not tell us anything about the public good human capital or civic cultures of different peoples. As we know, the migrants from poor to rich countries are normally tiny minorities in the countries to which they migrate, so they do not usually change the public policies or institutions of the host countries. The natural experiments that we have just considered do not tell us what would happen if the civic cultures of the poor countries were to come to dominate the rich countries. For example, if traditional Latin American or Middle Eastern beliefs about how societies should be organized came to dominate North America or western Europe, institutions and economic policies—and then presumably also economic performance—would change.

9. The Overwhelming Importance of Institutions and Economic Policies

If what has been said so far is correct, then the large differences in per capita income across countries cannot be explained by differences in access to the world's stock of productive knowledge or to its capital markets, by differences in the ratio of population to land or natural resources, or by differences in the quality of marketable human capital or personal culture. Albeit at a high level of aggregation, this eliminates each of the factors of production as possible explanations of most of the international differences in per capita income. The only remaining plausible explanation is that the great differences in the wealth of nations are mainly due to differences in the quality of their institutions and economic policies.

The evidence from the national borders that delineate different institutions and economic policies not only contradicts the view that societies produce as much as their resource endowments permit, but also directly suggests that a country's institutions and economic policies are decisive for its economic performance. The very fact that the differences in per capita incomes across countries—the units with the different policies and institutions—are so large in relation to the differences in incomes across regions of the same country supports my argument. So does the fact that national borders sometimes sharply divide areas of quite different per capita incomes.

10. Old Growth Theory, New Growth Theory, and the Facts

The argument offered here also fits the relationships between levels of per capita income and rates of growth better than does either the old growth theory or the new. As has often been pointed out, the absence of any general tendency for the poor countries with their opportunities for catch-up growth to grow faster than the rich countries argues against the old growth theory. The new or endogenous growth models feature externalities that increase with investment or with stocks of human or tangible capital and can readily explain why countries with high per capita incomes can grow as fast or faster than low-income countries.

But neither the old nor the new growth theories predict the relationship that is actually observed: *the fastest-growing countries are never the countries with the highest per capita incomes but always a subset of the lower-income countries.* At the same time that low-income countries as a whole fail to grow any faster than high-income countries, a subset of the lower-income countries grows far faster than *any* high-income country does. The argument offered here suggests that poor countries on average have poorer economic policies and institutions than rich countries, and, therefore, in spite of their opportunity for rapid catch-up growth, they need not grow faster on average than the rich countries.

But any poorer countries that adopt relatively good economic policies and institutions enjoy rapid catch-up growth: since they are far short of their potential, their per capita incomes can increase not only because of the technological and other advances that simultaneously bring growth to the richest countries, but also by narrowing the huge gap between their actual and potential income (Barro 1991). Countries with the highest per capita incomes do not have the same opportunity.

Thus the argument here leads us to expect what is actually observed: no necessary connection between low per capita incomes and more rapid rates of growth, but much the highest rates of growth in a subset of low-income countries—the ones that adopt better economic policies and institutions. During the 1970s, for example, South Korea grew seven times as fast as the United States. During the 1970s, the four countries that (apart from the oil-exporting countries) had the fastest rates of growth of per capita income grew on average 6.9 percentage points faster per year than the United States—more than five times as fast. In the 1980s, the four fastest growers grew 5.3 percentage points faster per year than the United States—four times as fast. They outgrew the highest-income countries as a class by similarly large multiples. All four of the fastest-growing countries in each decade were low-income countries.

In general, the endogenous growth models do not have anything in their structures that predicts that the most rapid growth will occur in a subset of low-income countries, and the old growth theory is contradicted by the absence of general convergence.

Note also that, as the gap in per capita incomes between the relatively poor and relatively rich countries has increased over time, poor countries have also fallen further behind their potential. Therefore, the argument offered here predicts that the maximum rate of growth that is possible for a poor country—and the rate at which it can gain on the highest per capita income countries—is increasing over time. This is also what has been observed. In the 1870s, the four continental European countries with the fastest growth of per capita incomes grew only 0.3 of 1 percent per annum faster than the United Kingdom. The top four such countries in the 1880s also had the same 0.3 percent gain over the United Kingdom. As we have seen, the top four countries in the 1970s grew 6.9 percentage points faster than the United States, and the top four in the 1980s, 5.3 percentage points faster. Thus the lead of the top four in the 1970s was twenty-three times as great as the lead of the top four in the 1870s, and the lead of the top four in the 1980s was more than seventeen times as great as the top four a century before.[19] Thus neither the old nor the new growth theory leads us to expect either the observed overall relationship between the levels and rates of growth of per capita incomes or the way this relationship has changed as the absolute gap in per capita incomes has increased over time. The present theory, by contrast, suggests that there should be patterns like those we observe.

11. Picking Up the Big Bills

The best thing a society can do to increase its prosperity is to wise up. This means, in turn, that it is very important indeed that economists, inside government and out, get things right. When we are wrong, we do a lot of harm. When we are right—and have the clarity needed to prevail against the special interests and the quacks—we make an extraordinary contribution to the amelioration of poverty and the progress of humanity. The sums lost because the poor countries obtain only a fraction of—and because even the richest countries do not reach—their economic potentials are measured in the trillions of dollars.

None of the familiar ideologies is sufficient to provide the needed wisdom. The familiar assumption that the quality of a nation's economic institutions and policies is given by the smallness, or the largeness, of its public sector—or by the size of its transfers to low-income people—does not fit the facts very well (Levine and Renelt 1992; Rubinson 1977; Olson 1986).

But the hypothesis that economic performance is determined mostly by the structure of incentives—and that it is mainly national borders that mark the boundaries of different structures of incentives—has far more evidence in its favor. This lecture has set out only one of the types of this evidence; there is also direct evidence of the linkage between better economic policies and institutions and better economic performance. Though it is not feasible to set out this direct evidence here, it is available in other writings (Clague, Reefer, Knack, and Olson 1995; Olson 1982, 1987a, 1987b, 1990).

We can perhaps obtain a glimpse of another kind of logic and evidence in support of the argument here—and a hint about what kinds of institutions and economic policies generate better economic performance—by returning to the theories with which we began. These theories suggested that the rationality of the participants in an economy or the parties to a bargain implied that there would be no money left on the table. We know from the surprisingly good performance of migrants from poor countries in rich countries, as well as from other evidence, that there is a great deal of rationality, mother wit, and energy among the masses of the poor countries: individuals in these societies can pick up the bills on the sidewalk about as quickly as we can.

The problem is that the really big sums cannot be picked up through uncoordinated individual actions. They can only be obtained through the efficient cooperation of many millions of specialized workers and other inputs: in other words, they can only be attained if a vast array of gains from specialization and trade are realized. Though the low-income societies obtain most of the gains from self-enforcing trades, they do not realize many of the largest gains from specialization and trade. They do not have the institutions that enforce contracts impartially, and so they lose most of the gains from those transactions (like those in the capital market) that require impartial third-party enforcement. They do not have institutions that make property rights secure over the long run, so they lose most of the gains from capital-intensive production. Production and trade in these societies is further handicapped by misguided economic policies and by private and public predation. The intricate social cooperation that emerges when there is a sophisticated array of markets requires far better institutions and economic policies than most countries have. The effective correction of market failures is even more difficult.

The spontaneous individual optimization that drives the theories with which I began is important, but it is not enough by itself. If spontaneous Coase-style bargains, whether through laissez faire or political bargaining and government, eliminated socially wasteful predation and obtained the institutions that are needed for a thriving market economy, then there would not be so many grossly inefficient and poverty-stricken societies. The argument presented here shows that the bargains needed to create efficient societies are not, in fact, made. Though that is another story, I can show that in many cases such bargains are even logically inconsistent with rational individual behavior.[20] Some important trends in economic thinking, useful as they are, should not blind us to a sad and all-too-general reality: as the literature on collective action demonstrates (Olson 1965; Hardin 1982; Sandler 1992; and many others), individual rationality is very far indeed from being sufficient for social rationality.

Notes

This article originally appeared in the *Journal of Economic Perspectives* (vol. 10, no. 2) in the spring of 1996. The author is grateful to the U.S. Agency for International Development for supporting this research and many related inquiries through the IRIS Center at the University of Maryland. He is indebted to Alan Auerbach, Christopher Clague, David Landes, Wallace Oates, Robert Solow, Timothy Taylor, and especially to Alan Krueger for helpful criticisms, and to Nikolay Gueorguiev, Jac Heckelman, Young Park, and Robert Vigil for research assistance.

1. A fuller statement of this argument, with additional citations to the literature on "efficient redistribution," appears in my draft paper on "Transactions Costs and the Coase Theorem: Is This Most Efficient of All Possible Worlds?" which is available on request.

2. The different assumptions of endogenous growth theory are explored later.

3. My calculation leaves out that portion of the cost of new equipment that is an implicit charge for the new ideas embodied in it. We must also remember that by no means all of Korea's growth was due to knowledge discovered abroad.

4. It is sometimes said that developing countries do not yet have the highly educated people needed to use modern technologies, and so the world's stock of knowledge is not in fact accessible to them. This argument overlooks the fact that the rewards to those with the missing skills, when other things are equal, would then be higher in the poor societies than in societies in which these skills were relatively plentiful. If difficulties of language and ignorance of the host country's markets can be overcome, individuals with the missing skills would then have an incentive to move (sometimes as employees of multinational firms) to those low-income countries in which they were most needed.

5. We shall see, when we later consider a heretofore neglected aspect of the relationship between levels and rates of growth of per capita incomes, that the new or endogenous growth-theory objection to this assumption need not concern us here.

6. In other words, there has not been a Coase-style bargain between rich and poor regions. Given that income increases by, say, tenfold when labor moves from the poor to the rich countries, there would be a continuing incentive for the poor to migrate to the rich countries even if the rich countries took, for example, half of this increase and kept it for their citizens. The transactions costs of such a deal would surely be minute in relation to the gains.

7. At the time I wrote this, I had not read Joel Mokyr's (1983) analysis of nineteenth-century Ireland. For a richer analysis of nineteenth-century Ireland, see his *Why Ireland Starved*. After detailed quantitative studies, he concludes that "there is no evidence that pre-famine Ireland was overpopulated in any useful sense of the word" (p. 64).

8. Northern Ireland is excluded from both Great Britain and Ireland. See Mitchell (1962), Mitchell and Jones (1971), Ireland Central Statistics Office (1986), and Great Britain Central Statistical Office (1988).

9. I am grateful to Alan Krueger for bringing these studies to my attention.

10. Specifically, the regression results are PER CAPITA GDP = 6.986 + 0.1746(POPULATION DENSITY). The $R^2 = 0.05$, and the t-statistic is 2.7.

11. Lucas's calculations are set in the context of Solow's theory of long-run growth. To bring the contradiction between the assumption that societies are on the frontiers of aggregate neoclassical production functions and what is actually observed, most starkly and simply, I have focused on a single point in time and used the framework Solow put forth for empirical estimation. It would add little insight to the present argument to look at the growth paths of different countries.

12. Since each Third World economy is small in relation to the world economy, it is reasonable to assume that no one of them could change the world price of capital, so that the marginal cost of capital to the country is equal to its price.

13. In a neoclassical world with only capital and labor, they would necessarily move in opposite directions, but when there is a disequilibrium with respect to land or other natural resources, both capital and labor could both move to correct this disequilibrium.

14. In his Ely lecture, Landes (1990) made an argument along these lines.

15. Clague takes the intercept of Borjas's regression about how the migrants' wages increase with time in the United States as the wage on arrival.

16. Apparently, somewhat similar patterns can be found when there is migration from areas of low income to other high-income countries. The increases in the wages that migrants from low-wage countries like Turkey, or from the German Democratic Republic, have received in West Germany are well known and in accord with the argument I am making. As Krueger and Pischke (1995) show, after German unification, East German workers who work in West Germany earn more than those who work in East Germany. By my reading of their numbers, the increase from this migration is less than it was before German unification. If Germany is succeeding in its efforts to create the same institutional and policy environment in East as in West Germany, the gains from east to west migration in Germany should diminish over time. But the structures of incentives in East and West Germany are not yet by any means identical.

17. To account for this result in terms of selection bias, one would have to argue that those workers who remained in the poor countries would not have a similar increase in marginal product had they migrated.

18. I am thankful to Robert Vigil for help in studying the incomes of migrants from other countries to the United States.

19. Germany was the fastest-growing European country in the 1870s, but its borders changed with the Franco-Prussian war, and so the "1870s" growth rate used for Germany is that from 1872 to 1882. Angus Maddison's estimates were used for the nineteenth century; World Bank data for the twentieth. The

top four qualifying growth countries in each decade were the following: for the 1980s, Korea, China, Botswana, and Thailand; for the 1970s, Botswana, Malta, Singapore, and Korea; for the 1880s, Germany, Finland, Austria, and Denmark; for the 1870s, Germany, Belgium, the Netherlands, and Austria. Those countries that still had open frontiers in the nineteenth century, or in some cases even until World War I, or that were major oil-exporting countries at the times of the oil shocks are not apt countries for the comparisons at issue now. It would be going much too far to extend the argument here about the limited importance of land and natural resources to growth to countries that are in major disequilibrium because of open frontiers or huge changes in their terms of trade. That is why I excluded the oil-exporting countries and compared the fastest-growing continental European countries with Britain in order to analyze the speed of catch-up after the industrial revolution.

I am thankful to Nikolay Gueorguiev for gathering and analyzing the data on this issue.

20. The logic at issue is set out in a preliminary way in the aforementioned Olson (1995) working paper, "Transactions Costs and the Coase Theorem."

References

Barro, Robert J. 1991. "Economic Growth in a Cross Section of Countries." *Quarterly Journal of Economics* 106 (2): 407–443.

Becker, Gary. 1983. "A Theory of Competition among Pressure Groups for Political Influence." *Quarterly Journal of Economics* 98:371–400.

———. 1985. "Public Policies, Pressure Groups, and Dead Weight Costs." *Journal of Public Economics* 28 (3): 329–347.

Bhagwati, Jagdish. 1984. "Incentives and Disincentives: International Migration." *Weltswirtscha.-liches Archiv* 120:678–701.

Borjas, George. 1987. "Self-Selection and the Earnings of Immigrants." *American Economic Review* 77:531–553.

———. 1990. *Friends or Strangers: The Impact of Immigrants on the U.S. Economy.* New York: Basic Books.

Breton, A. 1993. "Toward a Presumption of Efficiency in Politics." *Public Choice* 77 (1): 53–65.

Card, David. 1990. "The Impact of the Mariel Boatlift on the Miami Labor Market." *Industrial and Labor Relations Review* 43 (2): 245–257.

Carrington, William J., and Pedro J. F. De Lima. 1996. "The Impact of 1970s Repatriates from Africa on the Portuguese Labor Market." *Industrial and Labor Relations Review* 49 (2): 330–347.

Clague, Christopher. 1991. "Relative Efficiency Self-Containment and Comparative Costs of Less Developed Countries." *Economic Development and Cultural Change* 39 (3): 507–530.

Clague, Christopher, P. Keefer, S. Knack, and Mancur Olson. 1995. "Contract-Intensive Money: Contract Enforcement, Property Rights, and Economic Performance." IRIS Working Paper no. 151, University of Maryland.

Great Britain Central Statistical Office. 1988. *Annual Abstract of Statistics.* London: H.M.S.O.

Hamilton, Bob, and John Whalley. 1984. "Efficiency and Distributional Implications of Global Restrictions on Labour Mobility: Calculations and Policy Implications." *Journal of Development Economics* 14 (January/February): 61–75.

Harberger, Arnold. 1978. "Perspectives on Capital and Technology in Less Developed Countries." In *Contemporary Economic Analysis*, ed. M. Artis and A. Nobay, 12–72. London: Croom Helm.

Hardin, Russell. 1982. *Collective Action.* Baltimore: Johns Hopkins University Press.

Hunt, Jennifer. 1992. "The Impact of the 1962 Repatriates from Algeria on the French Labor Market." *Industrial and Labor Relations Review* 45 (3): 556–572.

Ireland Central Statistics Office. 1986. *Statistical Abstract.* Dublin, Ireland: Stationery Office.

Koo, Bohn-Young. 1982. "New Forms of Foreign Direct Investment in Korea." Korean Development Institute Working Paper no. 82-02.

Krueger, Alan B., and Jorn-Steffen Pischke. 1995. "A Comparative Analysis of East and West German Labor Markets." In *Differences and Changes in Wage Structures*, ed. Richard Freeman and Lawrence Katz, 405–445. Chicago: University of Chicago Press.

Landes, David. 1990. "Why Are We So Rich and They So Poor?" *American Economic Review* 80:1–13.

Levine, Ross, and David Renelt. 1992. "A Sensitivity Analysis of Cross-Country Growth Regressions." *American Economic Review* 82:942–963.

Lucas, Robert. 1990. "Why Doesn't Capital Flow from Rich to Poor Countries?" *American Economic Review* 80:92–96.

Mitchell, Brian R. 1962. *Abstract of British Historical Statistics.* Cambridge: Cambridge University Press.

Mitchell, Brian R., and H. G. Jones. 1971. *Second Abstract of British Historical Statistics.* Cambridge: Cambridge University Press.

Mokyr, Joel. 1983. *Why Ireland Starved: A Quantitative and Analytical History of the Irish Economy 1800–1850.* London and Boston: Allen & Unwin.

Olson, Mancur. 1965. *The Logic of Collective Action.* Cambridge, MA: Harvard University Press.

———. 1982. *The Rise and Decline of Nations.* New Haven, CT: Yale University Press.

———. 1986. "Supply-Side Economics, Industrial Policy, and Rational Ignorance." In *The Politics of Industrial Policy,* ed. Claude E. Barfield and William A. Schambra, 245–269. Washington, DC: American Enterprise Institute for Public Policy Research.

———. 1987a. "Diseconomies of Scale and Development." *The Cato Journal* 7 (1): 77–97.

———. 1987b. "Economic Nationalism and Economic Progress: The Harry Johnson Memorial Lecture." *The World Economy* 10 (3): 241–264.

———. 1990. "The IRIS Idea." IRIS, University of Maryland.

———. 1995. "Transactions Costs and the Coase Theorem: Is This Most Efficient of All Possible Worlds?" Working paper.

Rubion, Richard. 1977. "Dependency, Government Revenue, and Economic Growth, 1955–1970." *Studies in Comparative Institutional Development* 12 (2): 3–28.

Sandier, Todd. 1992. *Collective Action.* Ann Arbor: University of Michigan Press.

Stigler, George J. 1977. "The Theory of Economic Regulation." *Bell Journal of Economics and Management Science* 2:3–21.

———. 1992. "Law or Economics?" *The Journal of Law and Economics* 353:455–468.

Thompson, Earl, and Roger Faith. 1981. "A Pure Theory of Strategic Behavior and Social Institutions." *American Economic Review* 71 (3):366–380.

United Nations. 1986. *Demographic Yearbook.* New York: United Nations.

Wittman, Donald. 1989. "Why Democracies Produce Efficient Results." *Journal of Political Economy* 97 (6): 1395–1424.

———. 1995. *The Myth of Democratic Failure: Why Political Institutions Are Efficient.* Chicago: University of Chicago Press.

3   Entrepreneurship and Economic Growth

RANDALL G. HOLCOMBE

What causes economic growth? At the risk of some oversimplification, the answers economists have given to this question can be divided into two broad camps, one following the ideas of Adam Smith (1776) and the other following the ideas of David Ricardo (1821). Smith, whose overriding goal was to understand the wealth-creation process, began his treatise with the lesson that the[1] division of labor is limited by the extent of the market. As markets grew,[2] entrepreneurship would lead to innovation, which would lead to an increasing division of labor and increased productivity. Ricardo, in contrast, envisioned economic output as being a function of the inputs of land, labor, and capital. Investment could produce more capital, but because of diminishing marginal factor productivity and the existence of fixed factors such as land, population growth would always dominate economic growth, keeping most of the population at a subsistence level of income. The ideas of Ricardo and his friend and contemporary Malthus (1798) created the view of economics as the dismal science, which contrasts sharply with Smith's view of entrepreneurship and innovation that would lead to ever-increasing wealth.

This characterization of Smithian and Ricardian growth is an oversimplification in the sense that both authors had a deeper understanding of the growth process than the above characterization reveals. In one sense, it is unfair to Smith and Ricardo because it does not take account of the richness of their views and insights. In another sense, however, it is an eminently fair characterization. After all of their analysis of the process of economic growth, Smith ultimately concluded that the potential for economic growth was virtually unlimited, whereas Ricardo viewed the potential for economic growth as limited by the availability of economic resources (and in particular, land). If it is possible to contrast the ideas of various economists at all, it is certainly fair to characterize them according to their ultimate conclusions.

With hindsight, Smith's vision of economic growth was more accurate than Ricardo's, but the economics profession has followed Ricardo more closely than Smith in developing a theory of economic growth. Part of the reason is that the comparative static nature of economic modeling has made the production function approach of Ricardo amenable to economic modeling, whereas the innovation that leads to an increased division of labor is more difficult to model precisely. As economics has become more scientific over the twentieth century, economists have been more ready to attack problems that fit into a general equilibrium model of the economy than those that are more difficult to parameterize.[1] In the Ricardian production function approach, investment is the key to economic growth, whereas in the Smithian view, innovation leading to increases in the division of labor is the key. The Smithian answer seems right, but Smith did not explain the process by which that innovation occurs. Kirzner (1973) provides an important insight in this regard, by describing entrepreneurship as the process of acting upon a previously unnoticed profit opportunity. Thus, Kirzner's entrepreneurship can provide an engine to drive Smithian economic growth.

As Kirzner sees it, entrepreneurial insights are profit opportunities that had previously gone unnoticed. Entrepreneurs act upon these insights and the economy becomes more productive because it is able to produce more consumer satisfaction at a lower cost. The connection between entrepreneurship and economic growth is that these previously unnoticed profit opportunities must come from somewhere, and the most common source of profit opportunities is the insights of other entrepreneurs. Entrepreneurial ideas arise when an entrepreneur sees that the ideas developed by earlier entrepreneurs can be combined to produce a new process or output. Entrepreneurial opportunities tend to appear within the context of a specific time and place, so following Hayek (1945), a decentralized economy that allows individuals to act on their entrepreneurial insights, and rewards them for doing so, produces an environment where additional entrepreneurial insights are likely to be produced. Looked at in this way, entrepreneurship is the foundation for economic growth. Entrepreneurial insights lay the foundation for additional entrepreneurial insights, which drive the growth process.[2]

Before discussing the details of economic growth, it is worth drawing a distinction between the process of economic growth and the environment within which growth takes place. After the collapse of the centrally planned economies in Europe beginning in 1989, it is apparent that a market environment is more conducive to economic growth than is a centrally planned environment, and empirical analysis confirms this observation.[3]

This issue of the role that markets play in the process of growth is relevant to the public-policy question of what institutions foster economic growth, but is peripheral to the more theoretical issues considered here. The question considered in this article is how, within a market setting, economic growth occurs. The answer, in a sentence, is that acts of entrepreneurship create an environment within which innovations build on themselves, leading to continually increasing productivity.

1. Smithian Versus Ricardian Growth

Perhaps the simplest way to differentiate Smithian from Ricardian growth within the setting of contemporary economics is to use the Solow (1956) growth model as a framework. If output in year t is denoted Y_t and capital and labor are represented as K_t and L_t, Solow envisioned output as a function of capital, labor, and time,

$$Y_t = F[K_t, L_t, t],$$

with time entering the production function, because over time technology can advance, making a given amount of capital and labor more productive. This simple mathematical formulation allows considerable development by making simple assumptions about the production function.[4] The model can be used to derive the "golden rule" growth path, which implies that there is an optimal amount of investment, and can be used as a foundation for showing "convergence," which is the idea that economies with lower per capita incomes should grow faster than those with higher per capita incomes, so that over time incomes will converge. In fact, convergence has not occurred, casting some doubt on the basic framework of the Solow model, and creating its own strand of literature on convergence.[5]

Within the Solow model it has been relatively easy to formulate mathematical relationships among Y, K, and L, but modeling the effect oft has been more problematic, so it has often been treated as exogenous over time. Often, L is also treated as exogenous, and if one is considering per capita income, it is easy to divide by L, leaving only K and the exogenous t as explanatory factors.[6] The implication is straightforward. By investing, K can be increased, which will increase Y. This provides the foundation for the Ricardian view of economic growth.

The Ricardian model of growth has been taken seriously by both economists and policy makers. As Kreuger (1993) notes, it was at the foundation of world economic development policy for three decades after World War II, and application of the Ricardian model points out the advantages of central planning over market allocation, because planners are in a better position both to increase a nation's saving and investment rate, and to direct investment toward those sectors that can be most productive. Yet, despite the advice of economic growth theorists, undeveloped economies remain undeveloped even though they have undertaken substantial investment initiatives. Furthermore, the data make clear that only a small part of economic growth can be explained by increases in investment. The answer must lie somewhere else.

The problem with the Solow framework is that the most reasonable alternatives for the causes of growth are K or t, and the effects of capital are easy to analyze, so they have been analyzed extensively, whereas the effects of time are nebulous and hard to analyze, so they have tended to remain exogenous. In fact, it is unlikely that time, by itself, causes growth, but rather something else that changes over time. That something else has been called technological change and, as the other alternative in the Solow framework, has itself come under close scrutiny. There is, for example, a substantial literature on research and development, under the thought that R&D can increase productivity over time.

Other avenues might be taken within the basic Ricardian framework. Jones and Manuelli (1990) find that under different constraints, a Ricardian model need not imply convergence, suggesting that this framework might be able to be rehabilitated to conform more closely with reality. Taking a different tack, Lucas (1988) suggests that the key may be *L*, not *K*, and that in particular human capital can play the major role in development. Toward the end of his paper, Lucas discusses the idea of the external effects of human capital, and suggests that a higher population density may result in a finer division of labor and that the human capital of one person may make others more productive. Thus, Lucas begins moving the Ricardian framework toward a Smithian view of economic growth.

The Smithian view of growth focuses less on the quantities of factors of production and more on the processes that are used to combine them into aggregate output. Young (1928) viewed economic growth as occurring because of increasing returns, and explicitly recognized the Smithian foundations of his analysis, but increasing returns does not sit well in the neoclassical framework, as Kaldor (1972) argued. In frequently cited articles, Paul Romer has steered the literature in a neoclassical direction. Romer (1986) shows that growth can be modeled with a factor having increasing returns, and that in such a model growth rates need not converge over the long run, which fits the facts better than the simple Solow framework. Romer (1990) focuses attention on human capital, and argues that additional investment in research could promote more economic growth. Like earlier developments from the Solow model, however, this line of reasoning focuses on the inputs into the production process rather than the process itself.

2. The Production Process

The most basic facts of economic growth weigh against focusing on the inputs into the production process, and point toward an examination of the process itself. Within the neoclassical framework, changes in the production function have had a bigger impact on economic growth than changes in the inputs into the production function. The quantity and quality of both human and physical capital are important, beyond a doubt, but they are a product of an economy and not factors given exogenously to it. Both existed in abundance in ancient China, and even today the pyramids of Egypt (physical capital) and the knowledge of Leonardo da Vinci (human capital) inspire awe, yet economic growth, as it is understood today, is a recent phenomenon. Blanchard and Fischer (1989, 1–2) note, "real GNP is about 37 times larger than it was in 1874, 7 times larger than in 1919, and 3 times larger than in 1950. Extrapolating backwards leads to the well-known conclusion that economic growth at these rates cannot have been taking place for more than a few centuries." Land, labor, and capital long predate the transformation to economic growth. It is the process by which they are combined that has created sustained economic growth.

Rather than viewing production in a Ricardian production function setting, Bohm-Bawerk (1959) depicted a structure of production that would become more roundabout as more indirect methods of production were used. Bohm-Bawerk's ideas about heterogeneous capital and more roundabout methods of production have remained an integral part of Austrian capital theory (Hayek 1941), and have, among other things, been applied to explain business cycles (Hayek 1933, 1935) and even to illuminate the process of economic growth (Kirzner 1986). This literature, which focuses on incentives for altering the production process, also has implications for the ways in which entrepreneurs discover new production processes. Within the Solow framework, the new production processes fall within t in the production function, and the effect of t is generally viewed as working through technological change. That still leaves the question of what produces technological change.

3. Entrepreneurship and Technological Change

Within a neoclassical framework, where things are produced by combining inputs in a production function, the most straightforward way to get technological change is to produce it. Research and development can be undertaken by combining land, labor, and capital, to produce technological change. The successes attributable to investment in research and development are indisputable, but research-and-development expenditures cannot be the whole story, because once the research is done, the results need to be applied to make production less costly, or even more mysteriously, to produce goods and services that have never been produced before. This is the role of entrepreneurship.

Kirzner (1973) depicts entrepreneurs as people who are alert enough to spot previously unseen profit opportunities and then act on them. As Kirzner describes it, <u>entrepreneurship involves noticing something that nobody has noticed before</u>. <u>However, some people are in a better position to notice certain profit opportunities than others</u>. Those with training in mechanical engineering are more likely to spot potential profit opportunities in the design of internal combustion engines than those with training in law, for example, and somebody who never goes to the beach will not be in a position to notice the opportunity to open an ice-cream shop or T-shirt shop there. People who travel a lot might notice opportunities because of the amenities they find in one place that might not be available in another. There is, for example, an opportunity for the person who notices that a profit might be made in Indianapolis by offering a service similar to one already available and profitable in Cincinnati. Thus, there is more of a relationship between Hayek's (1945) view of the use of knowledge in society and Kirzner's vision of entrepreneurship than at first is apparent.

Entrepreneurial alertness is itself unrelated to knowledge, and is costless in the sense that it does not use up resources. However, one's past activities do influence one's ability to recognize an opportunity when one presents itself, as the examples in the previous paragraph suggest. All individuals have knowledge specific to their own activities—knowledge of time and place that others do not share. This specific knowledge of time and place gives some people the chance to notice profit opportunities that others could not possibly see. How does it happen that one can see a profit opportunity that nobody before has noticed? In part, it has to do with the differences in knowledge that different individuals possess. For example, it was not a coincidence that the microprocessor was invented by an electrical engineer and not a poet. Of course, knowledge does not create entrepreneurial insight, but it does create the opportunity to notice things that could not be noticed without that knowledge, which creates a direct connection between Hayekian knowledge and Kirznerian entrepreneurship. Economic theory biases economists against thinking that it is possible to come upon previously unexploited profit opportunities, because in neoclassical competitive equilibrium, all profit opportunities have been competed away.[7]

In fact, most profit opportunities get noticed by entrepreneurs because they are new. This is true whether the entrepreneurial successes are spectacular or more mundane. Consider some great American fortunes.

Andrew Carnegie was able to build the foundations of U.S. Steel by capitalizing on the newly developed Bessemer process. John D. Rockefeller's Standard Oil Company developed because he was able to control the distribution network, which at the time relied on the recently constructed railroad infrastructure. Henry Ford's assembly lines were feasible only when there was enough of a mass market for automobiles. The fortunes of Bill Gates rose along with the fledgling personal computer industry. None of these individuals invented the technology that made them wealthy, but they had the insight to take advantage of an entrepreneurial opportunity. Note, however, that in each case the opportunity was newly developed, and the entrepreneurial opportunity did not go unnoticed for long. Entrepreneurial opportunities are not just lying around waiting for someone to notice them. Rather, they appear and then entrepreneurs rapidly move to take advantage of them.

Where do entrepreneurial opportunities come from? Many of them come from the actions of other entrepreneurs. Henry Ford could not have succeeded in mass-producing automobiles until there was a substantial market, including infrastructure such as roads, gasoline stations, and repair facilities. Bill Gates could not have made his fortune had not Steve Jobs seen the opportunity to build and sell personal computers, and Steve Jobs could not have built a personal computer had not Gordon Moore invented the microprocessor. When entrepreneurs take advantage of profit opportunities, they create new entrepreneurial opportunities that others can act upon. Entrepreneurship creates an environment that makes more entrepreneurship possible.

4. Increasing Returns and Knowledge Externalities

The Smithian view of economic growth is based on the concept of increasing returns, and twentieth-century contributors to the Smithian idea, like Young (1928) and Kaldor (1972), have explicitly acknowledged that they were building on Adam Smith's insights. Yet increasing returns is a problematic concept in an economic framework because it implies that average cost continually declines. Kaldor (1972) notes the problems for general equilibrium models when firms are characterized by increasing returns, but another possibility is that the production functions of firms do not exhibit increasing returns, but firms generate positive externalities that lower the costs of production for other firms in close proximity. Individual firms do not exhibit increasing returns, but the entire economy does. This is easy to visualize as a Smithian idea. The division of labor is limited by the extent of the market, so additional firms in an area enlarge the market and allow all firms to be more productive by becoming increasingly specialized. Increased specialization is but one way in which firms can become more innovative, so a more general way to envision this idea is that the knowledge created by firms benefits other firms in close proximity, so that when one firm innovates, others find themselves in a better position to innovate also.

Romer (1986, 1990) depicts the process as a knowledge spillover. Knowledge, embodied in human capital, is the factor with increasing returns, meaning that investments in human capital make future investments in human capital more productive. Because human capital must be combined with other factors of production, there will be a tendency for productivity increases to be geographically concentrated, which results in some areas manifesting more economic growth than others.[8] This raises two questions, only one of which will be dealt with here. The first is, What conditions cause economic growth to be concentrated in some areas but not in others? A plausible answer, but outside the scope of the present article, is that market institutions make the difference.[9] The second question is, By what process does the productive activity of some result in a positive externality that increases the productivity of others? This is the question that Kirzner's model of entrepreneurship answers. Kirzner clearly distinguishes between knowledge and entrepreneurship.

But as closely as the element of knowledge is tied to the possibility of winning pure profits, the elusive notion of entrepreneurship is, as we have seen, not encapsulated in the mere possession of greater knowledge of market opportunities. The aspect of knowledge which is crucially relevant to entrepreneurship is not so much the substantive knowledge of market data as *alertness, the "knowledge" of where to find market data* (1963, 67, emphasis in original).

Entrepreneurship, in Kirzner's vision, clearly excludes research and development activities, and the accumulation of human capital. These activities can augment factors of production, but by themselves do not provide the insights that lead to new goods and services, or new processes for producing existing goods and services. If this seems like an overly fine

distinction, consider the policy implications. Centrally planned economies tried unsuccessfully for decades to produce growth through investment in research and education, but were missing the institutions that
enabled entrepreneurship.

5. The Process of Entrepreneurship

One might imagine an entrepreneur spotting a profit opportunity
in the same way that a pedestrian spots a $20 bill on the sidewalk. Many
people might walk by the bill, not noticing it, until one alert individual
spots it and reaps the $20 reward. This analogy fits Kirzner's model of
entrepreneurship in some respects, but falls short in others. One problem with the analogy is that it is rare to find money on the sidewalk, so
there is little incentive to look for it. In contrast, it is not uncommon, for
example, to find scavengers with metal detectors on a beach looking for
lost watches, rings, and other valuables. If more money were lying on
sidewalks, people would become more alert to the opportunity of finding
it. The idea that people will be more alert for profit opportunities when
they are more likely to exist helps illuminate the reason why more profit
opportunities are seized in growing economies. Economic growth creates
profit opportunities.

When economies are organized around traditional lines, people's
economic roles are given and there is little possibility for capitalizing on
innovation. The ancient Chinese economy had more capital than other
economies at the time, had a well-developed legal system, had well-defined
property rights, and had advanced the state of knowledge further than
any other place in the world. Yet the traditional nature of the economy
meant that individuals found their employment dictated by historical factors outside their control, and more significantly, found little change in
the status quo over the course of their lifetimes.[10] When the status quo
changes relatively little, one is not likely to spot an entrepreneurial opportunity today that was not apparent yesterday. Even a substantial opportunity will tend to blend in with the status quo, and because it is familiar,
will tend to go unnoticed. This is one reason why economies organized
along traditional lines tend not to grow, even when they have substantial
endowments of basic factors of production, when they are technologically
advanced, and when their population has substantial human capital.

This observation holds not only for traditional economies, but for market economies too, if they are unchanging. Consider the neoclassical concept of general equilibrium in which all firms are pricing at minimum average costs and there are no economic profits to be had. By definition, entrepreneurs have no profit opportunities to find; they have all been exploited already. Starting from this situation of general equilibrium, one can see that if an innovation occurs that disturbs the equilibrium, it opens profit opportunities in other areas of the economy. If a new good is introduced, consumers will shift their purchases toward that good, creating profits for some and losses for others. Those who sell complementary goods have a profit opportunity, and once a new good is produced, it may produce the opportunity for others to introduce new complementary goods for which there would not have been a market before. New production processes can be developed for the new goods, and the innovative opportunities go on.

This example points toward two shortcomings of analyzing economic growth in a general equilibrium framework. First, the models are not well suited for depicting the process of introducing new goods into the economy. In the neoclassical framework, growth occurs by producing more of the old goods. Second, because they are equilibrium models, they do not depict the profit opportunities that entice innovation. Thus, innovation tends to be depicted as research-and-development activity that is produced by applying inputs in a production function, rather than as an entrepreneurial discovery process. If one imagines the activities of those who run the black boxes that are firms in such models, they must be imagined as managers, whose job it is to combine pre-specified inputs into pre-specified outputs in a Pareto-efficient manner, rather than being entrepreneurs who innovate by undertaking production in a previously untried manner, producing goods that have not previously been produced, aiming at markets that do not yet exist.

There is some merit to considering research and development as a component of innovation and entrepreneurship, in the same way that one considers the purchase of a metal detector as a method for finding objects on the beach.[11] If there are not very many entrepreneurial opportunities, it does not pay to look for them, but when entrepreneurial opportunities abound, it makes sense to invest in the search for entrepreneurial profits. But focusing on research and development as the main component of innovation and technological advance misses the point. In most cases, a metal detector will not help people find lost objects, so one rarely sees people with metal detectors searching for lost objects in shopping centers, apartment buildings, or schools. On the beach, however, lost objects are more likely to be hidden from view in the sand, and because beachgoers do lose objects with some regularity, using a metal detector on a beach may turn up valuable objects. Similarly, research-and-development activity takes place in those areas where entrepreneurial profits seem promising. Research and development expenditures are not the cause of entrepreneurial opportunities, they are the result of entrepreneurial opportunities. More research and development occurs in the electronics industry than in the garment industry because there are more potential entrepreneurial insights to be found in electronics than in garment manufacture.

Thus, while it is reasonable to consider research and development to be a factor pushing technological change, research and development is not the cause of growth, it is a response to growth opportunities. The question is, What creates such opportunities? The answer is: entrepreneurship. In a static setting, where there is little change, there will be relatively little in the way of entrepreneurial opportunities. Those that might be lying in wait must be relatively obscure to have remained unnoticed, and the static environment precludes the creation of new opportunities. Furthermore, with few opportunities, there is little incentive to devote any resources toward seeking them out. In an environment of economic change, new opportunities will continually be presenting themselves. When entrepreneurs take advantage of some opportunities, the economic environment changes, creating with it additional opportunities. Thus, entrepreneurship leads to more entrepreneurship.

Several factors lead entrepreneurial insights to build on one another. First, the changes that result from entrepreneurship alter the economic environment, creating new profit opportunities. This is easy to see even within a comparative static general equilibrium setting. If the equilibrium is upset, the equilibrium condition that eliminates profit opportunities is removed, and profit opportunities arise to lead the adjustment to a new general equilibrium. Second, entrepreneurial activity generates wealth, and thereby increases the extent of the market, to use Adam Smith's phrase. The increase in income alone will generate new market opportunities, but an increase in the volume of goods also produces the opportunity for greater specialization. Third, entrepreneurial insights create new market niches that go along with innovation. This third factor, the creation of market niches, is the key link between entrepreneurship and economic growth.

Consider, for example, one innovative insight in the rapidly developing computer industry. Somebody had the idea that if a computer mouse communicated with the computer via an infrared connection, the mouse could be used without a cord. It is a small development, to be sure, but it is a good example of an entrepreneurial insight and the capitalization of a previously unnoticed profit opportunity. The profit opportunity arose solely because of a previously nonexistent market niche, and once that market niche appeared, it did not take very long for an entrepreneur to seize on the idea. Notice that this entrepreneurial insight did not arise for either of the first two reasons listed in the previous paragraph. It did not arise because of a profit opportunity created by a temporary disequilibrium in the market. Before personal computers used mice (which also is an example of an entrepreneurial insight), there would have been no possibility for the insight, regardless of how far the market was out of equilibrium. It did not arise because of the second reason either, which is a bigger market. The division of labor has nothing to do with the insight that a mouse could communicate with a computer through infrared technology (although it might have something to do with what type of firm produces the technology). An increase in wealth could not create the demand for infrared mice without the innovation of the mouse as a computer input device. This entrepreneurial insight capitalized on a new opportunity, which was created by other entrepreneurial insights.

One can go through a chain of events, seeing that the entrepreneurial insight that led to infrared mice could not have been made without the insight that a mouse could be used as a computer peripheral, and the insight that a mouse could be used to control a computer could not have been made without the insight that there was a market for personal computers. As is well known, the major computer manufacturers of the 1970s completely overlooked this market, leaving it to entrepreneurial start-ups. And the insight that there is a market for personal computers could not have been made without the development of the microprocessor, a result of yet another entrepreneurial insight. The computer industry provides a good example of the way that entrepreneurial insights lead to additional entrepreneurial insights. The economy does not simply offer a fixed set of entrepreneurial opportunities which then can be harvested.

Rather, new entrepreneurial opportunities continually arise as the result of past entrepreneurial activity.

This does not imply that one cannot invest in looking for entrepreneurial opportunities. Research and development, and the production of human capital, can be systematic ways of producing additional opportunities, and of finding those that already exist. That specific knowledge of time and place that Hayek emphasized can play a role in revealing entrepreneurial opportunities. However, if one focuses exclusively on investment in human capital and technological advance, the mechanism by which innovation occurs is left out of the picture entirely. Such investments can produce a more fertile environment within which to search for entrepreneurial opportunities, but it is the entrepreneurial act of seizing those opportunities that produces the engine for economic growth, and that lays the foundation for more entrepreneurial discoveries.[12]

To see that this is true, one need only look at the centrally planned economies of the twentieth century. Those economies placed a big premium on the development of both human and physical capital, and on the production of advances in technology. Their collapse at the end of the twentieth century shows that it is not the advancement of human capital, physical capital, and technology by itself that leads to economic growth, but rather the environment within which these advances take place. Hayek (1945) emphasized the specific knowledge of time and place possessed by every individual in the economy, and when the economy allows every individual to take advantage of this knowledge and become entrepreneurial, economic growth is the result. Centrally planned economies failed because central planning precludes entrepreneurship, which is necessarily decentralized in nature.

The market system produces this setting, and entrepreneurship within the market setting that makes the process work. Innovations produce profit opportunities which are then seized by entrepreneurs, and those entrepreneurial activities create more profit opportunities.

6. Implications for Kirzner's Model of Entrepreneurship

The linking of entrepreneurship with the environment of economic growth helps to illuminate the process by which entrepreneurial opportunities arise, and the process by which they are observed and acted upon. While, in a sense, profit opportunities lie unseen until entrepreneurs observe them and capitalize on them, profit opportunities are not like a fixed stock of resources waiting to be claimed. Rather, they arise in the course of economic activity and in many cases are seized shortly after they appear. Most entrepreneurial opportunities are created as a result of past entrepreneurship. Seeing entrepreneurship within the context of economic growth helps clarify the origin of entrepreneurial ideas, and the way in which entrepreneurs are able to spot them and act on them.

A view that opportunities for entrepreneurial insights are produced exogenously and lie in wait for entrepreneurs to notice them is fundamentally misleading. Furthermore, it would be misleading to think that at any moment in time there is an abundance of entrepreneurial opportunities that are unnoticed, waiting to be discovered. Entrepreneurial opportunities constantly arise in a growing economy, and when they do they are, except in rare circumstances, rapidly acted upon. Entrepreneurial insights are produced in the process of economic advancement. More rapid advancement brings more entrepreneurial opportunities, and more entrepreneurial opportunities produce greater incentives for potential entrepreneurs to become more alert to them. Entrepreneurship generates more entrepreneurship. In contrast, a stagnant economy blunts the incentives for entrepreneurial activity, and can remain stagnant because of the lack of entrepreneurial opportunities.[13]

If one wanted to focus solely on the activities of entrepreneurs, then entrepreneurial opportunities might be viewed as exogenous creations that entrepreneurs act upon. However, when one extends Kirzner's model of entrepreneurship to examine its results, it is a straightforward conclusion that entrepreneurial activities create more entrepreneurial opportunities. This has the advantage of endogenizing the creation of entrepreneurial opportunities, so that Kirzner's model then explains the origin of entrepreneurial opportunities as well as the competitive process that results from their existence. When one sees that entrepreneurial insights build upon one another, the creation of entrepreneurial insights is endogenized and the Kirznerian model of entrepreneurship becomes more complete.

Kirzner (1973, 72–75) distinguishes his view of entrepreneurship, which he envisions as equilibrating, with Schumpeter's (1934), which he depicts as disequilibrating. "Schumpeter's entrepreneur acts to *disturb* an existing equilibrium situation. . . . The entrepreneur is pictured as *initiat-*

ing change and generating new opportunities" (pp. 72–73, emphasis in original). Kirzner then quotes Schumpeter as concluding that entrepreneurship is at odds with equilibrating activity. Kirzner, in contrast, argues that the entrepreneur "*brings into mutual adjustment* those discordant elements which resulted from prior market ignorance" (p. 73, emphasis in original). Kirzner takes issue with Schumpeter because his discussion of entrepreneurship is "likely to generate the utterly mistaken view that the state of equilibrium can establish itself without any social device to deploy and marshal the scattered pieces of information which are the only source of such a state" (pp. 73–74).

When Kirznerian entrepreneurship is considered within the framework of economic growth, however, there may be more common ground between Kirzner's and Schumpeter's views on entrepreneurship than Kirzner implies in the above passages. Kirzner's entrepreneurs explicitly begin their activity within a disequilibrium situation.

It is necessary to postulate that out of the mistakes which led market participants to choose less-than-optimal courses of action yesterday, there can be expected to develop systematic changes in expectations concerning ends and means that can generate corresponding alterations in plans (1973, 71).

In such a situation, entrepreneurial insights would bring individuals closer and closer to their optimal courses of action, eventually causing entrepreneurial opportunities to vanish. However, new opportunities could arise from Schumpeterian entrepreneurship, which would create a disequilibrium situation with new profit opportunities for Kirznerian entrepreneurs to act upon.

In fact, there is no difference between the actions of Kirznerian and Schumpeterian entrepreneurs. Both are seizing unexploited profit opportunities, and in both cases the market environment will be different for all market participants in the future. One must note, however, that in any developing economy, the equilibrium toward which the economy tends changes from day to day, and when the Kirznerian model is expanded to recognize this, the tendency toward equilibrium in a static sense is less important than the exploitation of new profit opportunities, which implies greater gains from trade and economic growth. The difference that Kirzner emphasizes between his and Schumpeter's views largely arises because of the different objectives of the two writers. Schumpeter was discussing directly the role of entrepreneurship in economic growth, while Kirzner was interested in showing how entrepreneurship is an essential but underrecognized element in the allocation of economic resources.[14]

Schumpeter's discussion of entrepreneurship flows from his vision of economic growth as a spontaneous, revolutionary, and discontinuous process,[15] implying that the motive forces of growth are exogenous to his model of growth, if not to the economic process itself. From an initial equilibrium, entrepreneurial activity disturbs that equilibrium, leading Schumpeter to the idea that entrepreneurial activity is disequilibrating. Kirzner begins from a disequilibrium condition to show how entrepreneurial activity helps equilibrate an economy. Neither view is complete, because in Schumpeter's model some force must equilibrate an economy before entrepreneurial activity can disequilibrate it, and that force is Kirznerian entrepreneurship. Likewise, in Kirzner's model, if entrepreneurial activity continually works to equilibrate an economy, some force must push it away from equilibrium to allow the equilibrating process to operate, and that force is Schumpeterian entrepreneurship. Both forces have the same origin, however, which is entrepreneurs acting on previously unrecognized profit opportunities.

Kirzner is justly concerned that Schumpeter ignores the equilibrating role of entrepreneurship, but at the same time Schumpeter does correctly note that entrepreneurial activity is essential for growth. But Kirzner's theory of entrepreneurship gives no indication of the origin of entrepreneurial opportunities, and when Kirznerian entrepreneurship is depicted as an integral part of the process of economic growth, entrepreneurial opportunities can be seen as originating from past entrepreneurial activity, making Kirzner's theory of entrepreneurship more self-contained and complete.

7. Implications for Growth Theory

While growth theory has become far more formalized in the last half of the twentieth century, the fundamental ideas behind the engine of economic growth can be traced back to Adam Smith. As noted in the earlier review of the literature, current theorists are focusing on the role of human capital, knowledge externalities, and increasing returns. These insights certainly are not wrong, but at the same time they do not go very

far toward illuminating the process by which knowledge externalities produce growth, or by which increasing returns can be manifested in the production process. The recognition of entrepreneurship's role in the market
process fills this gap. Knowledge externalities occur when the entrepreneurial insights of some produce entrepreneurial opportunities for others. Increasing returns occur because the more entrepreneurial activity an
economy exhibits, the more new entrepreneurial opportunities it creates.

When one recognizes that entrepreneurship gives rise to knowledge
externalities and increasing returns, it then becomes apparent that growth
theory should focus less on the Ricardian production function approach
where inputs are combined in a black box to produce outputs, and more
on the process by which production processes are determined. The engine
of economic growth is not better inputs, but rather an environment in
which entrepreneurial opportunities can be capitalized upon. As Kreuger
(1993) notes, for decades after World War II, the production-function approach dominated economic thinking, and economic policy advisors, applying state-of-the-art growth theory, advised nations to industrialize, to
save and invest, and to develop their human capital. The result has been
that many Third World nations have inefficient industries that require constant subsidies to keep them running, further draining their economies.
They have tried educating their citizens, but because of lack of opportunities, many of their better minds have emigrated to other countries. The
biggest beneficiaries of the whole process may have been the high-priced
consultants who recommended these inefficient growth strategies.

When entrepreneurship is seen as the engine of growth, the
emphasis shifts toward the creation of an environment within which
opportunities for entrepreneurial activity are created, and successful entrepreneurship is rewarded. Human and physical capital remain inputs
into the production process, to be sure, but by themselves they do not
create economic growth.[16] Rather, an institutional environment that encourages entrepreneurship attracts human and physical capital, which is
why investment and growth are correlated. When the key role of entrepreneurship is taken into account, it is apparent that emphasis should
be placed on market institutions rather than production function inputs.
The importance of market institutions has now been generally recognized
in practice, but has not been integrated into the mainstream theory of
economic growth.

Contemporary growth theory, built on complex mathematical models, must make simplifying assumptions to keep the models tractable. In the process of simplifying models to make them more manageable, it is easy to assume away the institutional details that provide the foundation for economic growth. The temptation to assume away these institutional details is increased because often institutional details are hard to measure. One can come up with plausible measures for capital and labor, but it is more difficult to measure the degree to which property rights are protected in an economy, or the degree to which government regulations hamper economic activity or push it underground.[17] By recognizing entrepreneurship as the foundation for economic growth, the emphasis then must be turned toward those features of the economy that foster entrepreneurial activity. Surely research-and-development activity and investment in physical and human capital provide inputs that make growth possible, but by focusing on these inputs, contemporary mainstream growth models look past the process by which growth occurs. Research and development and investment do not cause economic growth, they take place in response to growth opportunities, and those opportunities are created by entrepreneurship.

Recent work that focuses on human capital as the engine of economic growth is just as misleading as the growth theory of decades ago that focused on physical capital investment as providing a "golden rule" for economic growth. Human capital is correlated with economic growth because a growing economy provides a greater return to human capital. The direction of causation is from an environment conducive to growth of human capital, not the other way around. This becomes apparent when entrepreneurship is viewed as the engine of economic growth. The existence of institutions conducive to entrepreneurship creates the profit opportunities which increase the return to education and lead to an increase in human capital. Human capital is important because it is a component of the production process, but entrepreneurship, not capital of any kind, is the underlying cause of growth.[18]

8. Conclusion

The incorporation of entrepreneurship into the framework of economic growth contributes both to growth theory and to Kirzner's theory of entrepreneurship. Each framework helps enlighten the other. The growth framework furthers Kirzner's model of entrepreneurship by helping to illustrate where entrepreneurial opportunities originate, why more opportunities arise in some sectors of the economy than others, and what factors can provide incentives for entrepreneurs to more intensively search for new entrepreneurial insights. Entrepreneurial opportunities are not just exogenously delivered to an economy; in large part they are produced by entrepreneurial activities in the recent past. This expansion of Kirzner's framework explains the origins of entrepreneurial opportunities as well as the process of entrepreneurship.

Incorporating entrepreneurship into the framework of economic growth adds to growth theory by showing the nature of increasing returns to scale, knowledge externalities, and the role of human capital. These processes appear as a black box in mainstream growth theory, but when they are depicted as a part of the entrepreneurial process, it becomes apparent that the engine of economic growth is entrepreneurship, not technological advance or investment in human capital per se. This focus on entrepreneurship pushes growth theory in a direction that emphasizes the institutional setting within which growth occurs, and away from a neoclassical growth theory that focuses on inputs into the production process. The incorporation of entrepreneurship into the framework of economic growth not only fills in the institutional details to help make the growth process more understandable, but also points toward more promising economic policy recommendations for fostering economic growth.

In the latter half of the twentieth century a production function approach to economic growth has led both growth theory and growth policy to conclude that increases in output could best be produced by increasing the inputs into the production process. Policies were aimed at increasing both the quantity and quality of inputs through investment, incorporation of modern technology, and education. In many less-developed economies, the results have been disappointing. In contrast, this Austrian framework for viewing economic growth shows that the key element in economic growth is the production of entrepreneurial opportunities. When such opportunities are available, individuals have the incentive to invest in human and physical capital without government intervention. Mainstream growth theory has seen the problems with the mechanistic application of the production function approach to economic growth, but has responded by incorporating increasing returns and knowledge externalities into formal models in a way that obscures the way in which these factors might actually manifest themselves in the real world. The answer is the type of entrepreneurship that Kirzner described, and the straight-forward prescription for economic growth is to create an institutional environment that encourages markets and rewards productive activity.

Notes

This article originally appeared in the *Quarterly Journal of Austrian Economics* (vol. 1, no. 2) in 1998. The author gratefully acknowledges helpful comments from Peter Boettke, Tyler Cowen, Roger Garrison, two anonymous reviewers at the *Quarterly Journal of Austrian Economics*, and offers special thanks to Israel Kirzner for his comments and advice. The article's shortcomings remain the responsibility of the author.

1. As one observer has said, "When the only tool you have is a hammer, everything looks like a nail." The economics profession's approach to economic growth reminds one of the old joke about the man who is standing under a streetlight looking for his keys when another man offers to help him. "Where did you drop them," the helper asks. "Across the street," the man answers. "Then why are you looking here?" "The light is better." This article heads where the light is not so good, but where the answer is more likely to be found.

2. Schumpeter (1934, 154), discussing a framework in which all profit is competed away in a competitive equilibrium, and in which profit is the return to entrepreneurship, observed, "Without development there is no profit, without profit no development." While this sentiment captures the way in which entrepreneurship leads to growth, Kirzner notes some differences between his approach and Schumpeter's, which are discussed below.

3. See, for examples, Gwartney, Lawson, and Block (1996), Scully (1988, 1992), and Knack (1996). See also Olson's (1996) insightful discussion of institutions and economic growth.

4. Barro and Sala-i-Martin (1995) give a good exposition of the ways that the Solow model has been developed, and the implications that have arisen from the model. Barro and Sala-i-Martin use the production function given here to depict the Solow model, although another specification would have been $Y_t = \theta_t[K_t, L_t]$. This seems to suggest a constant rate of change over time for θ, however, which is clearly at odds with the evidence.

5. Quah (1996) presents empirical evidence showing that national incomes are becoming bi-modal, with some nations converging at high levels of income while others stagnate at low levels. Quah suggests, based on the evidence, that under the right conditions nations can converge as the Solow model suggests, but that low-income nations do not exhibit the right conditions.

6. Of course, in the general functional form above, dividing by L may not eliminate it from the right side of the equation, but it would eliminate population growth per se as a factor in income growth.

7. An economist joke, repeated in Olson (1996), illustrates the point. Two economists, an assistant professor and a full professor, are walking down the street. Assistant professor: "Hey, there's a $20 bill on the sidewalk." Professor: "Couldn't be. If there was, somebody would have picked it up." (In order to retain an air of seriousness, this article has relegated all of its jokes to footnotes.)

8. See Krugman (1991) and Audretsch and Feldman (1996) for models in which increasing returns occur in geographically concentrated areas.

9. Gwartney, Lawson, and Block (1996), Olson (1996), Scully (1988, 1992), and Knack (1996) are some examples of studies that come to this conclusion. Scully uses a measure of economic and political freedom, while Gwartney, Lawson, and Block deliberately confine their analysis to economic freedoms. Barro (1996) and Perotti (1996) present some evidence that economic freedoms are what count, and that democratic political institutions may even have a negative effect on economic growth.

10. Heilbroner (1962) divides economic systems into traditional, command, and market economies, and that is the distinction used here when discussing economies based on tradition.

11. Note, however, that Kirzner (1973, 40) would make the distinction between the entrepreneurial insight that a metal detector might be used to discover previously undiscovered profit opportunities, which requires no resources, and the investment in the metal detector, which is the employment of capital in the production process.

12. Weitzman (1996) outlines a theory of growth along these lines.

13. Young (1993) develops a model along these lines. Mokyr (1990) classifies technological advances as "macroinventions" and "microinventions." The idea is that major inventions like the steam engine and the microprocessor create entrepreneurial opportunities for microinventions that further drive economic growth.

14. Kirzner (1979, chapter 7) argues that there are important differences between his and Schumpeter's ideas, and takes Schumpeter to task for not discussing the equilibrating role of entrepreneurship. Elsewhere, however, Kirzner (1985, chapter 4) develops the idea of entrepreneurship in a manner that encompasses the spirit of Schumpeter's ideas, and in private correspondence Kirzner has told me that he believes Schumpeter's ideas on entrepreneurship are important, and that they can be reconciled with his ideas.

15. Schumpeter (1934, 63) discusses the revolutionary nature of economic growth, and later (1934, 65) describes the motive forces as "spontaneous and discontinuous."

16. In an interesting bit of speculation, Weitzman (1996) argues that the former Soviet Union took neoclassical growth theory as the foundation for economic policy, and when their continual efforts at increasing output by increasing inputs into their production functions failed, the Soviet economy and government collapsed. The prediction of collapse goes back to Mises (1922), but the underlying faulty model to which Weitzman refers was not developed until decades later. It is interesting to conjecture that the Soviet Union may have collapsed because its leaders took neoclassical growth theory too seriously.

17. DeSoto (1989) presents a fascinating study of the way in which government restrictions have pushed a substantial fraction of Peru's economic activity into what he calls the informal sector of the economy, and the way in which this impedes economic development.

18. Academic economists may have an incentive to overstate the importance of human capital because they receive their incomes from the production of education. If academics can convince the population at large of the importance of education, their incomes will rise. Thus, as Holcombe (1997) notes, one must be inherently suspicious of academics who argue the importance of education.

References

Audretsch, David B., and Maryann P. Feldman. 1996. "R&D Spillovers and the Geography of Innovation and Production." *American Economic Review* 86 (3): 630–640.

Barro, Robert J. 1996. "Democracy and Growth." *Journal of Economic Growth* 1 (1): 1–27.

Barro, Robert J., and Xavier Sala-i-Martin. 1995. *Economic Growth*. New York: McGraw-Hill.

Blanchard, Oliver Jean, and Stanley Fischer. 1989. *Lectures on Macroeconomics*. Cambridge, MA: MIT Press.

Bohm-Bawerk, Eugen von. 1884/1959. *Capital and Interest*. 3 vols. Spring Mills, PA: Libertarian Press.

de Soto, Hernando. 1989. *The Other Path: The Invisible Revolution in the Third World*. New York: Harper and Row.

Gwartney, James, Robert Lawson, and Walter Block. 1996. *Economic Freedom of the World. 1975–1995*. Vancouver, Canada: Fraser Institute.

Hayek, Friedrich A. 1933/1966. *Monetary Theory and the Trade Cycle*. New York: Augustus M. Kelley.

———. 1935. *Prices and Production*, 2nd ed. New York: Augustus M. Kelley.

———. 1941. *The Pure Theory of Capital*. Chicago: University of Chicago Press.

———. 1945. "The Use of Knowledge in Society." *American Economic Review*
35 (51): 9–30.

Heilbroner, Robert L. 1962. *The Making of Economic Society*. Englewood
Cliffs, NJ: Prentice Hall.

Holcombe, Randall G. 1997. "A Theory of the Theory of Public Goods." *Review of Austrian Economics* 10 (1): 1–22.

Jones, Larry E., and Rodolfo Manuelli. 1990. "A Convex Model of Equilibrium
Growth: Theory and Policy Implications." *Journal of Political Economy* 98
(5), pt. 1: 1008–1038.

Kaldor, Nicholas. 1972. "The Irrelevance of Equilibrium Economics." *Economic Journal* 82 (1): 237–255.

Kirzner, Israel M. 1973. *Competition and Entrepreneurship*. Chicago: University of Chicago Press.

———. 1979. *Perception, Opportunity, and Profit: Studies in the Theory of Entrepreneurship*. Chicago: University of Chicago Press.

———. 1985. *Discovery and the Capitalist Process*. Chicago: University of Chicago Press.

———. 1986. "Roundaboutness, Opportunity, and Austrian Economics." In
The Unfinished Agenda, ed. Martin J. Anderson, 93–103. London: Institute
of Economic Affairs.

Knack, Steve. 1996. "Institutions and the Convergence Hypothesis: The Cross-
National Evidence." *Public Choice* 87 (3/4): 207–228.

Kreuger, Anne O. 1993. *Political Economy of Policy Reform in Developing
Countries*. Cambridge, MA: MIT Press.

Krugman, Paul. 1991. "Increasing Returns and Economic Geography." *Journal
of Political Economy* 99 (3): 483–499.

Lucas, Robert E., Jr. 1988. "On the Mechanics of Economic Development."
Journal of Monetary Economics 22 (1): 3–42.

Malthus, Thomas Robert. 1798/1914. *An Essay on Population*. New York:
E. P. Dutton.

Mises, Ludwig von. 1922/1951. *Socialism*. New Haven, CT: Yale University
Press.

Mokyr, Joel. 1990. *The Lever of Riches*. Oxford, UK: Oxford University Press.

Olson, Mancur, Jr. 1996. "Big Bills Left on the Sidewalk: Why Some Nations
Are Rich, Others Poor." *Journal of Economic Perspectives* 10 (2): 3–24.

Perotti, Roberto. 1996. "Growth, Income Distribution, and Democracy: What
the Data Say." *Journal of Economic Growth* 1 (2): 149–187.

Quah, Danny T. 1996. "Convergence Empirics across Economies with (Some)
Capital Mobility." *Journal of Economic Growth* 1 (1) (March): 95–124.

Ricardo, David. 1821/1912. *The Principles of Political Economy*, 3rd ed. London: J. M. Dent.

Romer, Paul M. 1986. "Increasing Returns and Long-Run Growth." *Journal of Political Economy* 94 (5): 1002–1037.

———. 1990. "Endogenous Technological Change." *Journal of Political Economy* 98 (5) pt. 2: S71–S102.

Schumpeter, Joseph A. 1934. *The Theory of Economic Development*. Cambridge, MA: Harvard University Press.

Scully, Gerald W. 1988. "The Institutional Framework and Economic Development." *Journal of Political Economy* 96 (3): 652–662.

———. 1992. *Constitutional Environments and Economic Growth*. Princeton, NJ: Princeton University Press.

Smith, Adam. 1776/1937. *An Inquiry into the Nature and Causes of the Wealth of Nations*. New York: Modern Library.

Solow, Robert M. 1956. "A Contribution to the Theory of Economic Growth." *Quarterly Journal of Economics* 70 (1): 65–94.

Weitzman, Martin L. 1996. "Hybridizing Growth Theory." *American Economic Review* 86 (2): 207–212.

Young, Allyn. 1928. "Increasing Returns and Economic Progress." *Economic Journal* 38:527–542.

Young, Alwyn. 1993. "Invention and Bounded Learning by Doing." *Journal of Political Economy* 101 (3): 443–472.

4   Entrepreneurship: Productive, Unproductive, and Destructive

WILLIAM J. BAUMOL

The basic hypothesis is that, while the total supply of entrepreneurs varies among societies, the productive contribution of the society's entrepreneurial activities varies much more because of their allocation between productive activities such as innovation and largely unproductive activities such as rent seeking or organized crime. This allocation is heavily influenced by the relative payoffs society offers to such activities. This implies that policy can influence the allocation of entrepreneurship more effectively than it can influence its supply. Historical evidence from ancient Rome, early China, and the Middle Ages and Renaissance in Europe is used to investigate the hypotheses.

It is often assumed that an economy of private enterprise has an automatic bias towards innovation, but this is not so. It has a bias only towards profit (Hobsbawm 1969, 40).

When conjectures are offered to explain historic slowdowns or great leaps in economic growth, there is the group of usual suspects that is regularly rounded up—prominent among them, the entrepreneur. Where growth has slowed, it is implied that a decline in entrepreneurship was partly to blame (perhaps because the culture's "need for achievement" has atrophied). At another time and place, it is said, the flowering of entrepreneurship accounts for unprecedented expansion.

This paper proposes a rather different set of hypotheses, holding that entrepreneurs are always with us and always play *some* substantial role. But there are a variety of roles among which the entrepreneur's efforts can be reallocated, and some of those roles do not follow the constructive and innovative script that is conventionally attributed to that person. Indeed, at times the entrepreneur may even lead a parasitical existence that is actually damaging to the economy. How the entrepreneur acts at a given time and place depends heavily on the rules of the game—the reward structure in the economy—that happen to prevail. Thus the central hypothesis here is that it is the set of rules and not the supply of entrepreneurs *or the nature of their objectives* that undergoes significant changes from one period to another and helps to dictate the ultimate effect on the economy via the *allocation* of entrepreneurial resources. Changes in the rules and other attendant circumstances can, of course, modify the composition of the class of entrepreneurs and can also alter its size. Without denying this or claiming that it has no significance, in this paper I shall seek to focus attention on the allocation of the changing class of entrepreneurs rather than its magnitude and makeup. (For an excellent analysis of the basic hypothesis, independently derived, see Murphy, Shleifer, and Vishny [1990].)

The basic proposition, if sustained by the evidence, has an important implication for growth policy. The notion that our productivity problems reside in "the spirit of entrepreneurship" that waxes and wanes for unexplained reasons is a counsel of despair, for it gives no guidance on how to reawaken that spirit once it has lagged. If that is the task assigned to policymakers, they are destitute: they have no means of knowing how to carry it out. But if what is required is the adjustment of rules of the game to induce a more felicitous allocation of entrepreneurial resources, then the policymaker's task is less formidable, and it is certainly not hopeless. The prevailing rules that affect the allocation of entrepreneurial activity can be observed, described, and, with luck, modified and improved, as will be illustrated here. Here, extensive historical illustrations will be cited to impart plausibility to the contentions that have just been described. Then a short discussion of some current issues involving the allocation of entrepreneurship between productive and unproductive activities will be offered. Finally, I shall consider very briefly the means that can be used to change the rules of the game, and to do so in a manner that stimulates the productive contribution of the entrepreneur.

1. On the Historical Character of the Evidence

Given the inescapable problems for empirical as well as theoretical study of entrepreneurship, what sort of evidence can one hope to provide? Since the rules of the game usually change very slowly, a case study approach to investigation of my hypotheses drives me unavoidably to examples spanning considerable periods of history and encompassing widely different cultures and geographic locations. Here I shall proceed on the basis of historical illustrations encompassing all the main economic periods and places (ancient Rome, medieval China, Dark Age Europe, the later Middle Ages, etc.) that the economic historians almost universally single out for the light they shed on the process of innovation and its diffusion. These will be used to show that the relative rewards to different types of entrepreneurial activity have in fact varied dramatically from one time and place to another and that this seems to have had profound effects on patterns of entrepreneurial behavior. Finally, evidence will be offered *suggesting* that such reallocations can have a considerable influence on the prosperity and growth of an economy, though other variables undoubtedly also play substantial roles.

None of this can, of course, be considered conclusive. Yet, it is surely a standard tenet of scientific method that tentative confirmation of a hypothesis is provided by observation of phenomena that the hypothesis helps to explain and that could not easily be accounted for if that hypothesis were invalid. It is on this sort of reasoning that I hope to rest my case. Historians have long been puzzled, for example, by the failure of the society of ancient Rome to disseminate and put into widespread practical use some of the sophisticated technological developments that we know to have been in its possession, while in the "High Middle Ages," a period in which progress and change were hardly popular notions, inventions that languished in Rome seem to have spread like wildfire. It will be argued that the hypothesis about the allocability of entrepreneurial effort between productive and unproductive activity helps considerably to account for this phenomenon, though it certainly will not be claimed that this is all there was to the matter.

Before I get to the substance of the discussion, it is important to emphasize that nothing that follows in this article makes any pretense of constituting a contribution to economic history. Certainly it is not intended here to try to explain any particular historical event. Moreover, the analysis relies entirely on secondary sources, and all the historical developments described are well known to historians, as the citations will indicate. Whatever the contribution that may be offered by the following pages, then, it is confined to enhanced understanding and extension of the (nonmathematical) theory of entrepreneurship in general, and not to an improved analysis of the historical events that are cited.

2. The Schumpeterian Model Extended: Allocation of Entrepreneurship Evidence

The analysis of this paper rests on what seems to be the one theoretical model that effectively encompasses the role of the entrepreneur and that really "works," in the sense that it constitutes the basis for a number of substantive inferences.[1] This is, of course, the well-known Schumpeterian analysis, whose main shortcoming, for our purposes, is the paucity of insights on policy that emerge from it. It will be suggested here that only a minor extension of that model to encompass the *allocation* of entrepreneurship is required to enhance its power substantially in this direction.

Schumpeter tells us that innovations (he calls them "the carrying out of new combinations") take various forms besides mere improvements in technology:

> This concept covers the following five cases: (1) the introduction of a new good—that is one with which consumers are not yet familiar—or of a new quality of a good. (2) The introduction of a new method of production, that is one not yet tested by experience in the branch of manufacture concerned, which need by no means be founded upon a discovery scientifically new, and can also exist in a new way of handling a commodity commercially. (3) The opening of a new market, that is a market into which the particular branch of manufacture of the country in question has not previously entered, whether or not this market has existed before. (4) The conquest of a new source of supply of raw materials or half-manufactured goods, again irrespective of whether this source already exists or whether it has first to be created. (5) The carrying out of the new organization of any industry, like the creation of a

monopoly position (for example through trustification) or the breaking up of a monopoly position. (1912/1934, 66)

The obvious fact that entrepreneurs undertake such a variety of tasks all at once suggests that theory can usefully undertake to consider what determines the *allocation* of entrepreneurial inputs among those tasks. Just as the literature traditionally studies the allocation of other inputs, for example, capital resources, among the various industries that compete for them, it seems natural to ask what influences the flow of entrepreneurial talent among the various activities in Schumpeter's list.

Presumably the reason no such line of inquiry was pursued by Schumpeter or his successors is that any analysis of the allocation of entrepreneurial resources among the five items in the preceding list (with the exception of the last—the creation or destruction of a monopoly) does not promise to yield any profound conclusions. There is no obvious reason to make much of a shift of entrepreneurial activity away from, say, improvement in the production process and toward the introduction of new products. The general implications, if any, for the public welfare, for productivity growth, and for other related matters are hardly obvious.

To derive more substantive results from an analysis of the allocation of entrepreneurial resources, it is necessary to expand Schumpeter's list, whose main deficiency seems to be that it does not go far enough. For example, it does not explicitly encompass innovative acts of technology transfer that take advantage of opportunities to introduce already-available technology (usually with some modification to adapt it to local conditions) to geographic locales whose suitability for the purpose had previously gone unrecognized or at least unused.

Most important for the discussion here, Schumpeter's list of entrepreneurial activities can usefully be expanded to include such items as innovations in rent-seeking procedures, for example, discovery of a previously unused legal gambit that is effective in diverting rents to those who are first in exploiting it. It may seem strange at first blush to propose inclusion of activities of such questionable value to society (I shall call them acts of "unproductive entrepreneurship") in the list of Schumpeterian innovations (though the creation of a monopoly, which Schumpeter does include as an innovation, is surely as questionable), but, as will soon be seen, this is a crucial step for the analysis that follows. If entrepreneurs are defined, simply, to be persons who are ingenious and creative in finding ways that add to their own wealth, power, and prestige, then it is to be expected that not all of them will be overly concerned with whether an activity that achieves these goals adds much or little to the social product or, for that matter, even whether it is an actual impediment to production (this notion goes back, at least, to Veblen [1904]). Suppose that it turns out, in addition, that at any time and place the magnitude of the benefit the economy derives from its entrepreneurial talents depends *substantially*, among other variables, on the allocation of this resource between productive and unproductive entrepreneurial activities of the sorts just described. Then the reasons for including acts of the latter type in the list of entrepreneurial activities become clear.

Here no exhaustive analysis of the process of allocation of entrepreneurial activity among the set of available options will be attempted. Rather, it will be argued only that at least *one* of the prime determinants of entrepreneurial behavior at any particular time and place is the prevailing rules of the game that govern the payoff of one entrepreneurial activity relative to another. If the rules are such as to impede the earning of much wealth via activity A, or are such as to impose social disgrace on those who engage in it, then, other things being equal, entrepreneurs' efforts will tend to be channeled to other activities, call them B. But if B contributes less to production or welfare than A, the consequences for society may be considerable.[2]

As a last preliminary note, it should be emphasized that the set of active entrepreneurs may be subject to change. Thus if the rules of the game begin to favor B over A, it may not be just the same individuals who switch their activities from entrepreneurship of type A to that of type B. Rather, some persons with talents suited for A may simply drop out of the picture, and individuals with abilities adapted to B may for the first time become entrepreneurs. Thus the allocation of entrepreneurs among activities is perhaps best described in the way Joan Robinson (following Shove's suggestion) analyzed the allocation of heterogeneous land resources (1933, chapter 8): as the solution of a jigsaw puzzle in which the pieces are each fitted into the places selected for them by the concatenation of pertinent circumstances.

3. Entrepreneurship, Productive and Unproductive: The Rules Do Change Evidence

Let us now turn to the central hypothesis of this paper: that the exercise of entrepreneurship can sometimes be unproductive or even destructive, and that whether it takes one of these directions or one that is more benign depends heavily on the structure of payoffs in the economy—the rules of the game. The rather dramatic illustrations provided by world history seem to confirm quite emphatically the following proposition.

PROPOSITION 1. *The rules of the game that determine the relative payoffs to different entrepreneurial activities do change dramatically from one time and place to another.*

These examples also suggest strongly (but hardly "prove") the following proposition.

PROPOSITION 2. *Entrepreneurial behavior changes direction from one economy to another in a manner that corresponds to the variations in the rules of the game.*

A. Ancient Rome Evidence

The avenues open to those Romans who sought power, prestige, and wealth are instructive. First, it may be noted that they had no reservations about the desirability of wealth or about its pursuit (e.g., Finley 1985, 53–57). *As long as it did not involve participation in industry or commerce*, there was nothing degrading about the wealth acquisition process. Persons of honorable status had three primary and acceptable sources of income: landholding (not infrequently as absentee landlords), "usury," and what may be described as "political payments":

> The opportunity for "political moneymaking" can hardly be over-
> estimated. Money poured in from booty, indemnities, provincial taxes,
> loans and miscellaneous extractions in quantities without precedent in
> Graeco-Roman history, and at an accelerating rate. The public treasury
> benefited, but probably more remained in private hands, among the
> nobles in the first instance; then, in appropriately decreasing proportions,
> among the *equites*, the soldiers and even the plebs of the city of Rome. . . .

> Nevertheless, the whole phenomenon is misunderstood when it is classi-
> fied under the headings of "corruption" and "malpractice," as historians
> still persist in doing. Cicero was an honest governor of Cilicia in 51 and
> 50 B.C., so that at the end of his term he had earned only the legitimate
> profits of office. They amounted to 2,200,000 sesterces, more than treble
> the figure of 600,000 he himself once mentioned (*Stoic Paradoxes* 49)
> to illustrate an annual income that could permit a life of luxury. We are
> faced with something structural in the society. (Finley 1985, 55)

Who, then, operated commerce and industry? According to Veyne (1961),
it was an occupation heavily undertaken by freedmen, former slaves
who, incidentally, bore a social stigma for life. Indeed, according to this
writer, slavery may have represented the one avenue for advancement
for someone from the lower classes. A clever (and handsome) member
of the lower orders might deliberately arrange to be sold into slavery to
a wealthy and powerful master.[3] Then, with luck, skill, and drive, he
would grow close to his owner, perhaps managing his financial affairs
(and sometimes engaging in some homosexual activity with him). The
master then gained cachet, after a suitable period, by granting freedom
to the slave, setting him up with a fortune of his own. The freedmen,
apparently not atypically, invested their financial stakes in commerce,
hoping to multiply them sufficiently to enable them to retire in style to the
countryside, thereafter investing primarily in land and loans in imitation
of the upper classes.

Finally, regarding the Romans' attitude to the promotion of technology and productivity, Finley makes much of the "clear, almost total,
divorce between science and practice" (1965, 32). He goes on to cite
Vitruvius's monumental work on architecture and technology, in whose
ten books he finds only a single and trivial reference to means of saving effort and increasing productivity. Finley then reports the following story:

> There is a story, repeated by a number of Roman writers, that a
> man—characteristically unnamed—invented unbreakable glass and
> demonstrated it to Tiberius in anticipation of a great reward. The em-
> peror asked the inventor whether anyone shared his secret and was
> assured that there was no one else; whereupon his head was promptly
> removed, lest, said Tiberius, gold be reduced to the value of mud. I have
> no opinion about the truth of this story, and it is only a story. But is it
> not interesting that neither the elder Pliny nor Petronius nor the histo-

rian Dio Cassius was troubled by the point that the inventor turned to the emperor for a reward, instead of turning to an investor for capital with which to put his invention into production?[4] . . . We must remind ourselves time and again that the European experience since the late Middle Ages in technology, in the economy, and in the value systems that accompanied them, was unique in human history until the recent export trend commenced. Technical progress, economic growth, productivity, even efficiency have not been significant goals since the beginning of time. So long as an acceptable life-style could be maintained, however that was defined, other values held the stage. (1985, 1471)

The bottom line, for our purposes, is that the Roman reward system, although it offered wealth to those who engaged in commerce and industry, offset this gain through the attendant loss in prestige. Economic effort "was neither the way to wealth nor its purpose. Cato's gods showed him a number of ways to get more; but they were all political and parasitical, the ways of conquest and booty and usury; labour was not one of them, not even the labour of the entrepreneur" (Finley 1965, 39).

B. Medieval China Evidence

In China, as in many kingdoms of Europe before the guarantees of the Magna Carta and the revival of towns and their acquisition of privileges, the monarch commonly claimed possession of all property in his territories. As a result, particularly in China, when the sovereign was in financial straits, confiscation of the property of wealthy subjects was entirely in order. It has been claimed that this led those who had resources to avoid investing them in any sort of visible capital stocks, and that this, in turn, was a substantial impediment to economic expansion (see Balazs 1964, 53; Landes 1969, 46–47; Rosenberg and Birdzell 1986, 119–120; Jones 1987, chapter 5).

In addition, imperial China reserved its most substantial rewards in wealth and prestige for those who climbed the ladder of imperial examinations, which were heavily devoted to subjects such as Confucian philosophy and calligraphy. Successful candidates were often awarded high rank in the bureaucracy, high social standing denied to anyone engaged in commerce or industry, even to those who gained great wealth in the process (and who often used their resources to prepare their descendants to contend via the examinations for a position in the scholar bureaucracy). In other words, the rules of the game seem to have been heavily biased against the acquisition of wealth *and position* through Schumpeterian behavior. The avenue to success lay elsewhere.

Because of the difficulty of the examinations, the mandarins (scholar-officials) rarely succeeded in keeping such positions in their own families for more than two or three generations (see Marsh 1961, 159; Ho 1962, chapter 4 and appendix). The scholar families devoted enormous effort and considerable resources to preparing their children through years of laborious study for the imperial examinations, which, during the Sung dynasty, were held every three years, and only several hundred persons in all of China succeeded in passing them each time (E. A. Kracke Jr. in Liu and Golas 1969, 14). Yet, regularly, some persons not from mandarin families also attained success through this avenue (see, e.g., Marsh 1961 and Ho 1962 for evidence on social mobility in imperial China).

Wealth was in prospect for those who passed the examination and who were subsequently appointed to government positions. But the sources of their earnings had something in common with those of the Romans:

> Corruption, which is widespread in all impoverished and backward
> countries (or, more exactly, throughout the preindustrial world), was
> endemic in a country where the servants of the state often had nothing
> to live on but their very meager salaries. The required attitude of obedi-
> ence to superiors made it impossible for officials to demand higher sala-
> ries, and in the absence of any control over their activities from below
> it was inevitable that they should purloin from society what the state
> failed to provide. According to the usual pattern, a Chinese official
> entered upon his duties only after spending long years in study and pass-
> ing many examinations; he then established relations with protectors,
> incurred debts to get himself appointed, and then proceeded to extract
> the amount he had spent on preparing himself for his career from the
> people he administered—and extracted both principal and interest. The
> degree of his rapacity would be dictated not only by the length of time
> he had had to wait for his appointment and the number of relations he
> had to support and of kin to satisfy or repay, but also by the precarious-
> ness of his position. (Balazs 1964, 10)

Enterprise, on the other hand, was not only frowned on, but may have been subjected to impediments deliberately imposed by the officials, at least after the fourteenth century A.D.; and some historians claim that it was true much earlier. Balazs tells us of

> the state's tendency to clamp down immediately on any form of private enterprise (and this in the long run kills not only initiative but even the slightest attempts at innovation), or, if it did not succeed in putting a stop to it in time, to take over and nationalize it. Did it not frequently happen during the course of Chinese history that the scholar-officials, although hostile to all inventions, nevertheless gathered in the fruits of other people's ingenuity? I need mention only three examples of inventions that met this fate: paper, invented by a eunuch; printing, used by the Buddhists as a medium for religious propaganda; and the bill of exchange, an expedient of private businessmen. (p. 18)

As a result of recurrent intervention by the state to curtail the liberty and take over any accumulated advantages the merchant class had managed to gain for itself, "the merchant's ambition turned to becoming a scholar-official and investing his profits in land" (p. 32).

C. The Earlier Middle Ages Evidence

Before the rise of the cities and before monarchs were able to subdue the bellicose activities of the nobility, wealth and power were pursued primarily through military activity. Since land and castles were the medieval forms of wealth most highly valued and most avidly sought after, it seems reasonable to interpret the warring of the barons in good part as the pursuit of an economic objective. For example, during the reign of William the Conqueror (see, e.g., Douglas 1964), there were frequent attempts by the barons in Normandy and neighboring portions of France to take over each other's lands and castles. A prime incentive for William's supporters in his conquest of England was their obvious aspiration for lands.[5] More than that, violent means also served to provide more liquid forms of income (captured treasure), which the nobility used to support both private consumption and investment in military plant and equipment, where such items could not easily be produced on their own lands and therefore had to be purchased from others. In England, with its institution of primogeniture (the exclusive right of the eldest son to inherit his father's estate), younger sons who chose not to enter the clergy often had no socially acceptable choice other than warfare as a means to make their fortunes, and in some cases they succeeded spectacularly. Thus note the case of William Marshal, fourth son of a minor noble, who rose through his military accomplishments to be one of the most powerful and trusted officials under Henry II and Richard I, and became one of the wealthiest men in England (see Painter 1933).

Of course, the medieval nobles were not purely economic men. Many of the turbulent barons undoubtedly enjoyed fighting for its own sake, and success in combat was an important avenue to prestige in their society. But no modern capitalist is a purely economic man either. What I am saying here is that warfare, which was of course pursued for a variety of reasons, was also undertaken as a primary source of economic gain. This is clearly all the more true of the mercenary armies that were the scourge of fourteenth-century France and Italy.

Such violent economic activity, moreover, inspired frequent and profound innovation. The introduction of the stirrup was a requisite for effective cavalry tactics. Castle building evolved from wooden to stone structures and from rectangular to round towers (which could not be made to collapse by undermining their corners). Armor and weaponry became much more sophisticated with the introduction of the crossbow, the longbow, and, ultimately, artillery based on gunpowder. Military tactics and strategy also grew in sophistication. These innovations can be interpreted as contributions of military entrepreneurs undertaken at least partly in pursuit of private economic gains.

This type of entrepreneurial undertaking obviously differs vastly from the introduction of a cost-saving industrial process or a valuable new consumer product. An individual who pursues wealth through the forcible appropriation of the possessions of others surely does not add to the national product. Its net effect may be not merely a transfer but a net reduction in social income and wealth.[6]

D. The Later Middle Ages Evidence

By the end of the eleventh century the rules of the game had changed from those of the Dark Ages. The revival of the towns was well under way. They had acquired a number of privileges, among them protection from arbitrary taxation and confiscation and the creation of a labor force by granting freedom to runaway serfs after a relatively brief residence (a year and a day) in the towns. The free-enterprise turbulence of the barons had at least been impeded by the church's pacification efforts: the peace and the (later) truce of God in France, Spain, and elsewhere; similar changes were taking place in England (see, e.g., Cowdrey 1970; but Jones 1987, 941 suggests that some free-enterprise military activity by the barons continued in England through the reigns of the earlier Tudors in the sixteenth century). All this subsequently "gave way to more developed efforts to enforce peace by the more organized governments of the twelfth century" (Brooke 1964, 127, 350). A number of activities that were neither agricultural nor military began to yield handsome returns. For example, the small group of architect-engineers who were in charge of the building of cathedrals, palaces, bridges, and fortresses could live in great luxury in the service of their kings.

But, apparently, a far more common source of earnings was the water-driven mills that were strikingly common in France and southern England by the eleventh century, a technological innovation about which more will be said presently. An incentive for such technical advances may have been the monopoly they conferred on their owners rather than any resulting improvement in efficiency. Such monopoly rights were alike sought and enforced by private parties (Bloch 1935, 554–557; Brooke 1964, 84) and by religious organizations (see following).

The economic role of the monks in this is somewhat puzzling—the least clear-cut part of our story.[7] The Cistercian abbeys are generally assigned a critical role in the promotion of such technological advances. In some cases they simply took over mills that had been constructed by others (Berman 1986, 89). But the Cistercians improved them, built many others, and vastly expanded their use; at least some writers (e.g., Gimpel 1976, 3–6) seem to suggest that the Cistercians were the spearhead of technological advance.

Historians tell us that they have no ready explanation for the entrepreneurial propensities of this monastic order. (See, e.g., Brooke [1964, 691] and also a personal communication to me from Constance Berman. Ovitt [1987, 142–147] suggests that this may all have been part of the twelfth-century monastic drive to reduce or eliminate manual labor in order to maximize the time available for the less onerous religious labors—a conclusion with which Bloch [1935, 553] concurs.) But the evidence suggests strongly that avid entrepreneurs they were. They accumulated vast tracts of land; the sizes of their domesticated animal flocks were enormous by the standards of the time; their investment rates were remarkable; they sought to exercise monopoly power, being known, after the erection of a water mill, to seek legal intervention to prevent nearby residents from continuing to use their animal-powered facilities (Gimpel 1976, 15–16); they were fierce in their rivalrous behavior and drive for expansion, in the process not sparing other religious bodies—not even other Cistercian houses. There is a "record of pastoral expansionism and monopolies over access established by the wealthiest Cistercian houses . . . at the expense of smaller abbeys and convents . . . effectively pushing out all other religious houses as competitors" (Herman 1986, 112).

As with early capitalists, the asceticism of the monks, by keeping down the proportion of the monastery's output that was consumed, helped to provide the resources for levels of investment extraordinary for the period (pp. 40, 83). The rules of the game appear to have offered substantial economic rewards to exercise of Cistercian entrepreneurship. The order obtained relatively few large gifts, but instead frequently received support from the laity and from the church establishment in the form of exemptions from road and river tolls and from payment of the tithe. This obviously increased the *marginal* yield of investment, innovation, and expenditure of effort, and the evidence suggests the diligence of the order in pursuing the resulting opportunities. Their mills, their extensive lands, and their large flocks are reported to have brought scale economies and extraordinary financial returns (chapter 4). Puritanical, at least in earlier years, in their self-proclaimed adherence to simplicity in personal lifestyle while engaged in dedicated pursuit of wealth, they may perhaps represent an early manifestation of elements of "the Protestant ethic." But whatever their motive, the reported Cistercian record of promotion of technological progress is in diametric contrast to that of the Roman Empire.

E. Fourteenth-Century Evidence

The fourteenth century brought with it a considerable increase in military activity, notably the Hundred Years' War between France and England. Payoffs, surely, must have tilted to favor more than before inventions designed for military purposes. Cannons appeared as siege devices and armor was made heavier. More imaginative war devices were proposed: a windmill-propelled war wagon, a multibarreled machine gun, and a diving suit to permit underwater attacks on ships. A pervasive busi-

ness enterprise of this unhappy century of war was the company of mercenary troops—the condottiere—who roamed Europe, supported the side
that could offer the most attractive terms, and in lulls between fighting,
when unemployment threatened, wandered about thinking up military
enterprises of their own, at the expense of the general public (Gimpel
1976, chapter 9; see also McNeill 1969, 33–39). Clearly, the rules of
the game—the system of entrepreneurial rewards—had changed, to the
disadvantage of productive entrepreneurship.

F. Early Rent Seeking

Unproductive entrepreneurship can also take less violent forms,
usually involving various types of rent seeking, the type of (possibly) unproductive entrepreneurship that seems most relevant today. Enterprising
use of the legal system for rent-seeking purposes has a long history. There
are, for example, records of the use of litigation in the twelfth century in
which the proprietor of a water-driven mill sought and won a prohibition
of use in the vicinity of mills driven by animal or human power (Gimpel
1976, 25–26). In another case, the operators of two dams, one upstream
of the other, sued one another repeatedly at least from the second half
of the thirteenth century until the beginning of the fifteenth, when the
downstream dam finally succeeded in driving the other out of business as
the latter ran out of money to pay the court fees (pp. 17–20).

In the upper strata of society, rent seeking also gradually replaced
military activity as a prime source of wealth and power. This transition
can perhaps be ascribed to the triumph of the monarchies and the consequent imposition of law and order. Rent-seeking entrepreneurship then
took a variety of forms, notably the quest for grants of land and patents
of monopoly from the monarch. Such activities can, of course, sometimes
prove to contribute to production, as when the recipient of land given
by the monarch uses it more efficiently than the previous owner did. But
there seems to have been nothing in the structure of the land-granting
process that ensured even a tendency toward transfer to more productive proprietors, nor was the individual who sought such grants likely to
use as an argument in favor of his suit the claim that he was likely to be
the more productive user (in terms of, say, the expected net value of its
agricultural output).

Military forms of entrepreneurship may have experienced a renaissance in England in the seventeenth century with the revolt against Charles I. How that may have changed the structure of rewards to entrepreneurial activity is suggested by Hobsbawm (1969), who claims that at the end of the seventeenth century the most affluent merchants earned perhaps three times as much as the richest "master manufacturers." [8] But, he reports, the wealthiest noble families probably had incomes more than ten times as large as those of the rich merchants. The point in this is that those noble families, according to Hobsbawm, were no holdovers from an ancient feudal aristocracy; they were, rather, the heirs of the Roundheads (the supporters of the parliamentary, or Puritan, party) in the then-recent Civil War (pp. 30–32). On this view, once again, military activity would seem to have become the entrepreneur's most promising recourse.

But other historians take a rather different view of the matter. Studies reported in Thirsk (1954) indicate that ultimately there was little redistribution of property as the result of the Civil War and the Restoration. Rather it is noted that in this period the "patrician elites depended for their political power and economic prosperity on royal charters and monopolies rather than on talent and entrepreneurial initiative" (Stone 1985, 45). In this interpretation of the matter, it was rent seeking, not military activity, that remained the prime source of wealth under the restoration.

By the time the eighteenth-century Industrial Revolution ("the" industrial revolution) arrived, matters had changed once again. According to Ashton (1948, 9–10), grants of monopoly were in good part "swept away" by the Monopolies Act of 1624, and, we are told by Adam Smith (1776), by the end of the eighteenth century they were rarer in England than in any other country. Though industrial activity continued to be considered somewhat degrading in places in which industry flourished, notably in England during the Industrial Revolution there was probably a difference in degree. Thus Lefebvre (1947, 14) reports that "at its upper level the [French] nobility . . . were envious of the English lords who enriched themselves in bourgeois ways," while in France "the noble 'derogated' or fell into the common mass if [like Mirabeau] he followed a business or profession" (p. 11). (See, however, Schama [1989], who tells us that "even a cursory examination of the eighteenth-century French economy . . . reveals the nobility deeply involved in finance, business and industry—certainly as much as their British counterparts. . . . In 1765 a royal edict officially removed the last formal obstacles to their participation in trade and industry" [p. 118].) In England, primogeniture, by forcing younger sons of noble families to resort to commerce and industry, apparently was imparting respectability to these activities to a degree that, while rather limited, may have rarely been paralleled before.

The central point of all the preceding discussion seems clear—perhaps, in retrospect, self-evident. If entrepreneurship is the imaginative pursuit of position, with limited concern about the means used to achieve the purpose, then we can expect changes in the structure of rewards to modify the nature of the entrepreneur's activities, sometimes drastically. The rules of the game can then be a critical influence helping to determine whether entrepreneurship will be allocated predominantly to activities that are productive or unproductive and even destructive.

4. Does the Allocation Between Productive and Unproductive Entrepreneurship Matter Much?

We come now to the third proposition of this article.

PROPOSITION 3.   *The allocation of entrepreneurship between productive and unproductive activities, though by no means the only pertinent influence, can have a profound effect on the innovativeness of the economy and the degree of dissemination of its technological discoveries.*

It is hard to believe that a system of payoffs that moves entrepreneurship in unproductive directions is not a substantial impediment to industrial innovation and growth in productivity. Still, history permits no test of this proposition through a set of anything resembling controlled experiments, since other influences *did*, undoubtedly, also play important roles, as the proposition recognizes. One can only note what appears to be a remarkable correlation between the degree to which an economy rewarded productive entrepreneurship and the vigor shown in that economy's innovation record.

Historians tell us of several industrial "near revolutions" that occurred before *the* Industrial Revolution of the eighteenth century that are highly suggestive for our purposes (Braudel 1986, 3: 542–561; for a more skeptical view, see Coleman 1956). We are told that two of the incipient revolutions never went anywhere, while two of them were rather successful in their fashion. I shall report conclusions of some leading historians on these episodes, but it should be recognized by the reader that many of the views summarized here have been disputed in the historical literature, at least to some degree.

A. Rome and Hellenistic Egypt

My earlier discussion cited ancient Rome and its empire as a case in which the rules did not favor productive entrepreneurship. Let us compare this with the evidence on the vigor of innovative activity in that society. The museum at Alexandria was the center of technological innovation in the Roman empire. By the first century B.C., that city knew of virtually every form of machine gearing that is used today, including a working steam engine. But these seem to have been used only to make what amounted to elaborate toys. The steam engine was used only to open and close the doors of a temple.

The Romans also had the water mill. This may well have been the most critical pre-eighteenth-century industrial invention because (outside the use of sails in transportation by water) it provided the first significant source of power other than human and animal labor: "it was able to produce an amount of concentrated energy beyond any other resource of antiquity" (Forbes 1955, 2: 90). As steam did in more recent centuries, it offered the prospect of providing the basis for a leap in productivity in the Roman economy, as apparently it actually did during the eleventh, twelfth, and thirteenth centuries in Europe. Yet Finley (1965, 35–36), citing White (1962), reports that "though it was invented in the first century B.C., it was not until the third century A.D. that we find evidence of much use, and not until the fifth and sixth of general use. It is also a fact that we have no evidence at all of its application to other industries [i.e., other than grinding of grain] until the very end of the fourth century, and then no more than one solitary and possibly suspect reference . . . to a marble-slicing machine near Trier."

Unfortunately, evidence of Roman technical stagnation is only spotty, and, further, some historians suggest that the historical reports give inadequate weight to the Roman preoccupation with agricultural improvement relative to improvement in commerce or manufacture. Still, the following quotation seems to summarize the weight of opinion: "Historians have long been puzzled as to why the landlords of the Middle Ages proved so much more enterprising than the landlords of the Roman Empire, although the latter, by and large, were much better educated, had much better opportunities for making technical and scientific discoveries if they had wished to do so" (Brooke 1964, 88). It seems at least plausible that some part of the explanation is to be found in the ancient world's rules of the game, which encouraged the pursuit of wealth but severely discouraged its pursuit through the exercise of productive entrepreneurship.[9]

B. Medieval China

The spate of inventions that occurred in ancient China (before it was conquered by the barbarian Yuan dynasty in 1280) constituted one of the earliest potential revolutions in industry. Among the many Chinese technological contributions, one can list paper, (perhaps) the compass, waterwheels, sophisticated water clocks, and, of course, gunpowder. Yet despite the apparent prosperity of the Sung period (960–1270) (see, e.g., Liu and Golas 1969), at least some historians suggest that none of this spate of inventions led to a flowering of *industry*[10] as distinguished from commerce and some degree of general prosperity. And in China too, as we have seen, the rules did not favor productive entrepreneurship. Balazs (1964, 53) concludes that

> what was chiefly lacking in China for the further development of capitalism was not mechanical skill or scientific aptitude, nor a sufficient accumulation of wealth, but scope for individual enterprise. There was no individual freedom and no security for private enterprise, no legal foundation for rights other than those of the state, no alternative investment other than landed property, no guarantee against being penalized by arbitrary exactions from officials or against intervention by the state. But perhaps the supreme inhibiting factor was the overwhelming prestige of the state bureaucracy, which maimed from the start any attempt of the bourgeoisie to be different, to become aware of themselves as a class and fight for an autonomous position in society. Free enterprise, ready and proud to take risks, is therefore quite exceptional and abnormal in Chinese economic history.

C. Slow Growth in the "Dark Ages"

An era noted for its slow growth occurred between the death of Charlemagne (814) and the end of the tenth century. Even this period was not without its economic advances, which developed slowly, including the beginnings of the agricultural improvements that attended the introduction of the horseshoe, harness, and stirrup, the heavy plow, and the substitution of horsepower for oxen, which may have played a role in enabling peasants to move to more populous villages further from their fields (see White 1962, 39ff.). But, still, it was probably a period of significantly slower growth than the industrial revolution of the eleventh–thirteenth centuries (Gimpel 1976), about which more will be said presently. We have already seen that this was a period in which military violence was a prime outlet for entrepreneurial activity. While this can hardly pretend to be *the* explanation of the relative stagnation of the era, it is hard to believe that it was totally unimportant.

D. The "High Middle Ages"

A good deal has already been said about the successful industrial revolution (and the accompanying commercial revolution sparked by inventions such as double-entry bookkeeping and bills of exchange [de Roover 1953]) of the late Middle Ages, whose two-century duration makes it as long-lived as our own (see Carus-Wilson 1941; White 1962; Gimpel 1976).

Perhaps the hallmark of this industrial revolution was that remarkable source of productive power, the water mills, that covered the countryside in the south of England and crowded the banks of the Seine in Paris (see, e.g., Gimpel 1976, 3–6; Berman 1986, 81–89). The mills were not only simple grain-grinding devices but accomplished an astonishing variety of tasks and involved an impressive variety of mechanical devices and sophisticated gear arrangements. They crushed olives, ground mash for beer production, crushed cloth for papermaking, sawed lumber, hammered metal and woolens (as part of the "fulling" process—the cleansing, scouring, and pressing of woven woolen goods to make them stronger and to bring the threads closer together), milled coins, polished armor, and operated the bellows of blast furnaces. Their mechanisms entailed many forms of ingenuity. Gears were used to translate the vertical circular motion of the efficient form of the waterwheel into the horizontal circular motion of the millstone. The cam (a piece attached, say, to the axle of the waterwheel, protruding from the axle at right angles to its axis of rotation) served to lift a hammer and to drop it repeatedly and automatically (it was apparently known in antiquity, but may not have been used with waterwheels). A crank handle extending from the end of the axle transformed the circular motion of the wheel into the back and forth (reciprocating) motion required for sawing or the operation of bellows. The most sophisticated product of all this mechanical skill and knowledge was the mechanical clock, which appeared toward the end of the thirteenth century. As White (1962, 129) sums up the matter, "the four centuries following Leonardo, that is, until electrical energy demanded a supplementary set of devices, were less technologically engaged in discovering basic principles than in elaborating and refining those established during the four centuries before Leonardo." [11]

In a period in which agriculture probably occupied some 90 percent of the population, the expansion of industry in the twelfth and thirteenth centuries could not by itself have created a major upheaval in living standards.[12] Moreover, it has been deduced from what little we know of European gross domestic product per capita at the beginning of the eighteenth century that its average growth in the preceding six or seven centuries must have been very modest, since if the poverty of that later time had represented substantial growth from eleventh-century living standards, much of the earlier population would surely have been condemned to starvation.

Still, the industrial activity of the twelfth and thirteenth centuries was very substantial. By the beginning of the fourteenth century, according to Gimpel (1976), sixty-eight mills were in operation on less than one mile of the banks of the Seine in Paris, and these were supplemented by floating mills anchored to the Grand Pont. The activity in metallurgy was also considerable—sufficient to denude much of Europe of its forests and to produce a rise in the price of wood that forced recourse to coal (Nef [1934]; other historians assert that this did not occur to any substantial degree until the fifteenth or sixteenth century, with some question even about those dates; see, e.g., Coleman [1975, 42–43]). In sum, the industrial revolution of the twelfth and thirteenth centuries was a surprisingly robust affair, and it is surely plausible that improved rewards to industrial activity had something to do with its vigor.

E. The Fourteenth-Century Retreat

The end of all this period of buoyant activity in the fourteenth century (see the classic revisionist piece by Lopez [1969] as well as Gimpel [1976, chapter 91]) has a variety of explanations, many of them having no connection with entrepreneurship. For one thing, it has been deduced by study of the glaciers that average temperatures dropped, possibly reducing the yield of crops (though recent studies indicate that the historical relation between climatic changes and crop yields is at best ambiguous) and creating other hardships. The plague returned and decimated much of the population. In addition to these disasters of nature, there were at least two pertinent developments of human origin. First, the church clamped down on new ideas and other manifestations of freedom. Roger Bacon himself was put under constraint.[13] The period during which new ways of thinking brought rewards and status was apparently ended. Second, the fourteenth century included the first half of the devastating Hundred Years' War. It is implausible that the associated renewal of rewards to military enterprise played no part in the economic slowdown.

F. Remark on "Our" Industrial Revolution

It need hardly be added, in conclusion, that *the* Industrial Revolution that began in the eighteenth century and continues today has brought to the industrialist and the businessperson generally a degree of wealth and a respect probably unprecedented in human history. The fact that this period yielded an explosion of output at least equally unprecedented is undoubtedly attributable to a myriad of causes that can probably never be discovered fully and whose roles can never be disentangled. Yet the continued association of output growth with high financial and respectability rewards to productive entrepreneurship is surely suggestive, even if it can hardly be taken to be conclusive evidence for proposition 3, which asserts that the allocation of entrepreneurship *does* really matter for the vigor and innovativeness of an economy.

5. On Unproductive Avenues for Today's Entrepreneur: A Delicate Balance

Today, unproductive entrepreneurship takes many forms. Rent seeking, often via activities such as litigation and takeovers, and tax evasion and avoidance efforts seem now to constitute the prime threat to productive entrepreneurship. The spectacular fortunes amassed by the "arbitrageurs" revealed by the scandals of the mid-1980s were *sometimes*, surely, the reward of unproductive, occasionally illegal but entrepreneurial acts. Corporate executives devote much of their time and energy to legal suit and countersuit, and litigation is used to blunt or prevent excessive vigor in competition by rivals. Huge awards by the courts, sometimes amounting to billions of dollars, can bring prosperity to the victor and threaten the loser with insolvency. When this happens, it must become tempting for the entrepreneur to select his closest advisers from the lawyers rather than the engineers. It induces the entrepreneur to spend literally hundreds of millions of dollars for a single legal battle. It tempts that entrepreneur to be the first to sue others before those others can sue him. (For an illuminating quantification of some of the social costs of one widely publicized legal battle between two firms, see Summers and Cutler [1988].)

Similarly, taxes can serve to redirect entrepreneurial effort. As Lindbeck (1987, 15) has observed, "the problem with high-tax societies is not that it is impossible to become rich there, but that it is difficult to do so by way of productive effort in the ordinary production system." He cites as examples of the resulting reallocation of entrepreneurship "'smart' speculative financial transactions without much (if any) contribution to the productive capacity of the economy" (p. 15) as well as "illegal 'business areas' such as drug dealing" (p. 25).

In citing such activities, I do not mean to imply either that rent-seeking activity has been expanding in recent decades or that takeover bids or private antitrust suits are always or even preponderantly unproductive. Rather, I am only suggesting where current rent-seeking activities are likely to be found, that is, where policy designers should look if they intend to divert entrepreneurial talents into more productive channels.

The main point here is to note that threats of takeovers are sometimes used as a means to extract "greenmail" and that recourse to the courts as a means to seek to preserve rents through legally imposed imped-iments to competition does indeed occur, and to suggest that it is no rare phenomenon. This does, then, become an attraction for entrepreneurial talent whose efforts are thereby channeled into unproductive directions. Yet, to the extent that takeovers discipline inefficient managements and that antitrust intervention sometimes is legitimate and sometimes contrib-utes to productivity, it would seem that it will not be easy to change the rules in a way that discourages allocation of entrepreneurial effort into such activities, without at the same time undermining the legitimate role of these institutions. Some promising proposals have been offered, but this is not a suitable place for their systematic examination. However, a few examples will be reported in the following section.

6. Changes in the Rules and Changes in Entrepreneurial Goals

A central point in this discussion is the contention that if realloca-tion of entrepreneurial effort is adopted as an objective of society, it is far more easily achieved through changes in the rules that determine relative rewards than via modification of the goals of the entrepreneurs and pro-spective entrepreneurs themselves. I have even gone so far as to use the same terms to characterize those goals in the very different eras and cul-tures referred to in the discussion. But it would be ridiculous to imply that the attitudes of a wealth-seeking senator in Rome, a Sung dynasty man-darin, and an American industrialist of the late nineteenth century were all virtually identical. Still, the evidence suggests that they had more in common than might have been expected by the casual observer. However, even if it were to transpire that they really diverged very substantially, that would be of little use to the designer of policy who does not have centuries at his or her disposal and who is notoriously ineffective in engendering profound changes in cultural influences or in the structure of preferences. It is for this reason that I have chosen to take entrepreneurial goals as given and to emphasize modification in the structure of the rewards to different activities as the more promising line of investigation.

This suggests that it is necessary to consider the process by which those rules are modified in practice, but I believe that answers to even this more restricted question are largely beyond the powers of the historians, the sociologists, and the anthropologists into whose domains it falls. One need only review the disputatious literature on the influences that led to the revival of trade toward the end of the early Middle Ages to see how far we still are from anything resembling firm answers. Exogenous influences such as foreign invasions or unexpected climatic changes can clearly play a part, as can developments within the economy. But the more interesting observation for our purposes is the fact that it is easy to think of measures that can change these rules quickly and profoundly.[14]

For example, the restrictions on royal grants of monopolies imposed by Parliament in the Statute of Monopolies are said to have reduced substantially the opportunities for rent seeking in seventeenth- and eighteenth-century England and may have moved reluctant entrepreneurs to redirect their efforts toward agricultural improvement and industry. Even if it did not succeed to any substantial extent in reallocation of the efforts of an unchanged body of entrepreneurs from one of those types of activity to the other, if it increased failure rates among the rent seekers while not impeding others who happened to prefer productive pursuits, the result might have been the same. Similarly, tax rules can be used to rechannel entrepreneurial effort. It has, for instance, been proposed that takeover activity would be reoriented substantially in directions that contribute to productivity rather than impeding it by a "revenue neutral" modification in capital gains taxes that increases rates sharply on assets held for short periods and decreases them considerably for assets held, say, for two years or more. A change in the rules that requires a plaintiff firm in a private antitrust suit to bear both parties' legal costs if the defendants are found not to be guilty (as is done in other countries) promises to reduce the frequency with which such lawsuits are used in an attempt to hamper effective competition.

As has already been said, this is hardly the place for an extensive discussion of the design of rational policy in the arena under consideration. The objective of the preceding brief discussion, rather, has been to suggest that there are identifiable means by which the rules of the game can be changed effectively and to illustrate these means concretely, though hardly attempting to offer any generalizations about their character. Certainly, the few illustrations that have just been offered should serve to confirm that there exist (in principle) testable means that promise to induce entrepreneurs to shift their attentions in productive directions, *without any major change in their ultimate goals*. The testability of such hypotheses indicates that the discussion is no tissue of tautologies, and the absence of references to the allocability of entrepreneurship turned up in extensive search of the literature on the entrepreneur suggests that it was not entirely self-evident.

7. Concluding Comment

There is obviously a good deal more to be said about the subject; however, enough material has been presented to indicate that a minor expansion of Schumpeter's theoretical model to encompass the determinants of the *allocation* of entrepreneurship among its competing uses can enrich the model considerably and that the hypotheses that have been associated with the model's extension here are not without substance, even if none of the material approaches anything that constitutes a formal test of a hypothesis, much less a rigorous "proof." It is also easy to confirm that each of the hypotheses that have been discussed clearly yields some policy implications.

Thus clear guidance for policy is provided by the main hypothesis (propositions 1–3) that the rules of the game that specify the relative payoffs to different entrepreneurial activities play a key role in determining whether entrepreneurship will be allocated in productive or unproductive directions and that this can significantly affect the vigor of the economy's productivity growth. After all, the prevailing laws and legal procedures of an economy are prime determinants of the profitability of activities such as rent seeking via the litigative process. Steps such as deregulation of the airlines or more rational antitrust rules can do a good deal here.

A last example can, perhaps, nail down the point. The fact that Japan has far fewer lawyers relative to population and far fewer lawsuits on economic issues is often cited as a distinct advantage to the Japanese economy, since it reduces at least in part the quantity of resources devoted to rent seeking. The difference is often ascribed to national character that is said to have a cultural aversion to litigiousness. This may all be very true. But closer inspection reveals that there are also other influences. While in the United States legal institutions such as trebled damages provide a rich incentive for one firm to sue another on the claim that the latter violated the antitrust laws, in Japan the arrangements are very different. In that country any firm undertaking to sue another on antitrust grounds must first apply for permission from the Japan Fair Trade Commission. But such permission is rarely given, and, once denied, there is no legal avenue for appeal.

The overall moral, then, is that we do not have to wait patiently for slow cultural change in order to find measures to redirect the flow of entrepreneurial activity toward more productive goals. As in the illustration of the Japanese just cited, it may be possible to change the rules in ways that help to offset undesired institutional influences or that supplement other influences that are taken to work in beneficial directions.

Notes

This article originally appeared in the *Journal of Political Economy*, vol. 98, in 1990. I am very grateful for the generous support of the research underlying this paper from the Division of Information Science and Technology of the National Science Foundation, the Price Institute for Entrepreneurial Studies, the Center for Entrepreneurial Studies of the Graduate School of Business Administration, New York University, and the C. V. Starr Center for Applied Economics. I am also very much indebted to Vacharee Devakula for her assistance in the research. I owe much to Joel Mokyr, Stefano Fenoaltea, Lawrence Stone, Constance Berman, and Claudia Goldin for help with the substance of the paper and to William Jordan and Theodore Rabb for guidance on references.

1. There has, however, recently been an outburst of illuminating writings on the theory of the innovation process, analyzing it in such terms as races for patents in which the winner takes everything, with no consolation prize for a close second, or treating the process, alternatively, as a "waiting game," in which the patient second entrant may outperform and even survive the first one in the innovative arena, who incurs the bulk of the risk. For an overview of these discussions as well as some substantial added insights, see Dasgupta (1988).

2. There is a substantial literature, following the work of Jacob Schmookler, providing strong empirical evidence for the proposition that even the allocation of inventive effort, i.e., the directions pursued by inventive activities, is itself heavily influenced by relative payoff prospects. However, it is now agreed that some of these authors go too far when they appear to imply that almost nothing but the demand for the product of invention influences to any great extent which inventions will occur. For a good summary and references, see Abramovitz (1989, 33).

3. Stefano Fenoaltea comments that he knows no documented cases in which this occurred and that it was undoubtedly more common to seek advancement through adoption into an upper-class family.

4. To be fair to Finley, note that he concludes that it is not really interesting. North and Thomas (1973, 3) make a similar point about Harrison's invention of the ship's chronometer in the eighteenth century (as an instrument indispensable for the determination of longitude). They point out that the incentive for this invention was a large governmental prize rather than the prospect of commercial profit, presumably because of the absence of effective patent protection.

5. The conquest has at least two noteworthy entrepreneurial sides. First, it involved an innovation, the use of the stirrup by the Normans at Hastings that enabled William's warriors to use the same spear to impale a series of victims with the force of the horse's charge, rather than just tossing the spear at the enemy, much as an infantryman could. Second, the invasion was an impressive act of organization, with William having to convince his untrustworthy allies that they had more to gain by joining him in England than by staying behind to profit from his absence by trying to grab away his lands as they had tried to do many times before.

6. In saying all this, I must not be interpreted as taking the conventional view that warfare is an unmitigated source of impoverishment of any economy that unquestionably never contributes to its prosperity. Careful recent studies have indicated that matters are more complicated (see, e.g., Milward 1970; Olson 1982). Certainly the unprecedented prosperity enjoyed afterward by the countries on the losing side of the Second World War suggests that warfare need not always preclude economic expansion, and it is easy to provide earlier examples. The three great economic leaders of the Western world preceding the United States—Italy in the thirteenth–sixteenth centuries, the Dutch Republic in the seventeenth and eighteenth, and Great Britain in the eighteenth and nineteenth—each attained the height of their prosperity after periods of enormously costly and sometimes destructive warfare. Nevertheless, the wealth gained by a medieval baron from the adoption of a novel bellicose technique can hardly have contributed to economic growth in the way that resulted from adoption of a new steelmaking process in the nineteenth century or the introduction of a product such as the motor vehicle in the twentieth.

7. Bloch (1935) notes that the monasteries had both the capital and the large number of consumers of flour necessary to make the mills profitable. In addition, they were less likely than lay communities to undergo military siege, which, Bloch notes, was (besides drought and freezing of the waterways) one of the main impediments to adoption of the water mill, since blocking of the waterway that drove the mill could threaten the besieged population with starvation (pp. 550–553).

8. The evidence indicates that the wealth of affluent families in Great Britain continues to be derived preponderantly from commerce rather than from

industry. This contrasts with the record for the United States, where the reverse appears to be true (see Rubinstein 1980, 22–23, 59–60).

9. It has been suggested by historians (see, e.g., Bloch 1935, 547) that an abundance of slaves played a key role in Roman failure to use the water mill widely. However, this must imply that the Romans were not efficient wealth seekers. As the cliometric literature has made clear, the cost of maintaining a slave is not low and certainly is not zero, and slaves are apt not to be efficient and dedicated workers. Thus if it had been efficient to replace human or animal power by the inanimate power of the waterways, failure to do so would have cut into the wealth of the slaveholder, in effect saddling him with the feeding of unproductive persons or keeping the slaves who turned the mills from other, more lucrative, occupations. Perhaps Roman landowners *were* fairly unsophisticated in the management of their estates, as Finley (1985, 108–116) suggests, and, if so, there may be some substance to the hypothesis that slavery goes far to account for the failure of water mills to spread in the Roman economy.

10. Also, as in Rome, none of this was associated with the emergence of a systematic body of science involving coherent theoretical structure and the systematic testing of hypotheses on the basis of experiment or empirical observation. Here, too, the thirteenth-century work of Bishop Grosseteste, Walter of Henley, and Roger Bacon was an early step toward that unique historical phenomenon— the emergence of a systematic body of science in the West in, say, the sixteenth century (see Needham 1956).

11. As was already noted, science and scientific method also began to make an appearance with contributions such as those of Bishop Grosseteste and Roger Bacon. Walter of Henley championed controlled experiments and observation over recourse to the opinions of ancient authorities and made a clear distinction between economic and engineering efficiency in discussing the advisability of substituting horses for oxen. Bacon displayed remarkable foresight when he wrote, circa 1260, that "machines may be made by which the largest ships, with only one man steering them, will be moved faster than if they were filled with rowers; wagons may be built which will move with incredible speed and without the aid of beasts; flying machines can be constructed in which a man . . . may beat the air with wings like a bird . . . machines will make it possible to go to the bottom of seas and rivers" (as quoted in White [1962, 134]).

12. But then, much the same was true of the first half century of "our" Industrial Revolution, which, until the coming of the railways, was centered on the production of cotton that perhaps constituted only some 7–8 percent of national output (Hobsbawm 1969, 68). Initially, the eighteenth-century Industrial Revolution was a very minor affair, at least in terms of investment levels and

contributions to output and to growth in productivity (perhaps 0.3 percent per year) (see Landes 1969, 64–65; Feinstein 1978, 40–41; Williamson 1984).

13. The restraints imposed by the church had another curious effect: they apparently made bathing unfashionable for centuries. Before then, bathhouses had been popular as centers for social and, perhaps, sexual activity; but by requiring separation of the sexes and otherwise limiting the pleasures of cleanliness, the church undermined the inducements for such sanitary activities (see Gimpel 1976, 87–92).

14. Of course, that still leaves open the critical metaquestion, How does one go about changing the society's value system so that it will *want* to change the rules? But that is not the issue with which I am grappling here, since I see no basis on which the economist can argue that society *ought* to change its values. Rather, I am positing a society whose values lead it to favor productivity growth and am examining which instruments promise to be most effective in helping it to pursue this goal.

References

Abramovitz, Moses. 1989. *Thinking about Growth, and Other Essays of Economic Growth and Welfare.* New York: Cambridge University Press.

Ashton, Thomas S. 1948. *The Industrial Revolution, 1760–1830.* London: Oxford University Press.

Balazs, Etienne. 1964. *Chinese Civilization and Bureaucracy: Variations on a Theme.* New Haven, CT: Yale University Press.

Berman, Constance H. 1986. "Medieval Agriculture, the Southern French Countryside, and the Early Cistercians: A Study of Forty-Three Monasteries." *Transactions of the American Philosophical Society* 76, pt. 5.

Bloch, Marc. 1935. "Avènement et conquêtes du moulin à eau." *Annales d'Histoire Economique et Sociale* 7:538–563.

Braudel, Fernand. 1986. *Civilization and Capitalism, 15th–18th Century,* vols. 2, 3. New York: Harper and Row.

Brooke, Christopher N. L. 1964. *Europe in the Central Middle Ages, 962–1154.* London: Longman.

Carus-Wilson, Eleanora M. 1941. "An Industrial Revolution of the Thirteenth Century." *Economic History Review* 11 (1): 39–60.

Coleman, Donald C. 1956. "Industrial Growth and Industrial Revolutions." *Economica* 23:1–22.

———. 1975. *Industry in Tudor and Stuart England.* London: Macmillan (for Econ. Hist. Soc.).

Cowdrey, H. E. J. 1970."The Peace and the Truce of God in the Eleventh Century." *Past and Present* 46:42–67.

Dasgupta, Partha. 1988. "Patents, Priority and Imitation or, the Economics of Races and Waiting Games." *Economic Journal* 98:66–80.

de Roover, Raymond. 1953. "The Commercial Revolution of the 13th Century." In *Enterprise and Secular Change: Readings in Economic History*, ed. Frederic C. Lane and Jelle C. Riemersma. London: Allen and Unwin.

Douglas, David C. 1964. *William the Conqueror: The Norman Impact upon England*. Berkeley and Los Angeles: University of California Press.

Feinstein, C. H. 1978. "Capital Formation in Great Britain." In *The Cambridge Economic History of Europe*, vol. 8, pt. 1, ed. Peter Mathias and M. M. Postan. Cambridge: Cambridge University Press.

Finley, Moses I. 1965. "Technical Innovation and Economic Progress in the Ancient World." *Economic History Review* 18:29–45.

———. 1985. *The Ancient Economy*, 2nd ed. London: Hogarth.

Forbes, Robert J. 1955. *Studies in Ancient Technology*. Leiden, Netherlands: Brill.

Gimpel, Jean. 1976. *The Medieval Machine: The Industrial Revolution of the Middle Ages*. New York: Holt, Rinehart and Winston.

Ho, Ping-Ti. 1962. *The Ladder of Success in Imperial China, 1368–1911*. New York: Columbia University Press.

Hobsbawm, Eric J. 1969. *Industry and Empire from 1750 to the Present Day*. Harmondsworth, UK: Penguin.

Jones, Eric L. 1987. *The European Miracle: Environments, Economies, and Geopolitics in the History of Europe and Asia*. Cambridge: Cambridge University Press.

Landes, David S. 1969. *The Unbound Prometheus: Technological Change and Industrial Development in Western Europe from 1750 to the Present*. New York: Cambridge University Press.

Lefebvre, Georges. 1947. *The Coming of the French Revolution, 1789*. Princeton, NJ: Princeton University Press.

Lindbeck, Assar. 1987. "The Advanced Welfare State." Manuscript. Stockholm, Sweden: University of Stockholm.

Liu, James T. C., and Peter J. Colas, eds. 1969. *Change in Sung China: Innovation or Renovation?* Lexington, MA: Heath.

Lopez, Robert S. 1969. "Hard Times and Investment in Culture." In *The Renaissance: A Symposium*. New York: Oxford University Press (for Metropolitan Museum of Art).

Marsh, Robert M. 1961. *The Mandarins: The Circulation of Elites in China, 1600–1900*. Glencoe, IL: Free Press.

McNeill, William H. 1969. *History of Western Civilization,* rev. ed. Chicago: University of Chicago Press.

Milward, Alan S. 1970. *The Economic Effects of the Two World Wars on Britain.* London: Macmillan (for Econ. Hist. Soc.).

Murphy, Kevin M., Andrei Shleifer, and Robert Vishny. 1990. "The Allocation of Talent: Implications for Growth." Manuscript. Chicago: University of Chicago.

Needham, Joseph. 1956. "Mathematics and Science in China and the West." *Science and Society* 20:320–343.

Nef, John U. 1934. "The Progress of Technology and the Growth of Large-Scale Industry in Great Britain, 1540–1640." *Econ. Hist. Rev.* 5:3–24.

North, Douglass C., and Robert Paul Thomas. 1973. *The Rise of the Western World: A New Economic History.* Cambridge: Cambridge University Press.

Olson, Mancur, Jr. 1982. *The Rise and Decline of Nations: Economic Growth, Stagflation, and Social Rigidities.* New Haven, CT: Yale University Press.

Ovitt, George Jr. 1987. *The Restoration of Perfection: Labor and Technology in Medieval Culture.* New Brunswick, NJ: Rutgers University Press.

Painter, Sidney. 1933. *William Marshal: Knight-Errant, Baron, and Regent of England.* Baltimore, MD: Johns Hopkins University Press.

Robinson, Joan. 1933. *The Economics of Imperfect Competition.* London: Macmillan.

Rosenberg, Nathan, and L. E. Birdzell Jr. 1986. *How the West Grew Rich: The Economic Transformation of the Industrial World.* New York: Basic Books.

Rubinstein, W. D., ed. 1980. *Wealth and the Wealthy in the Modern World.* London: Croom Helm.

Schama, Simon. 1989. *Citizens: A Chronicle of the French Revolution.* New York: Knopf.

Schumpeter, Joseph A. 1912/1934. *The Theory of Economic Development.* Cambridge, MA: Harvard University Press.

Smith, Adam. 1776/1937. *An Inquiry into the Nature and Causes of the Wealth of Nations.* New York: Random House (Modern Library).

Stone, Lawrence. 1985. "The Bourgeois Revolution of Seventeenth-Century England Revisited." *Past and Present* 109:44–54.

Summers, Lawrence, and David Cutler. 1988. "Texaco and Pennzoil Both Lost Big." *New York Times* (February 14, 1988).

Thirsk, Joan. 1954. "The Restoration Land Settlement." *Journal of Modern History* 26:315–328.

Veblen, Thorstein. 1904. *The Theory of Business Enterprise.* New York: Scribner.

Veyne, Paul. 1961. "Vie de trimalcion." *Annales: Economies, Societies, Civilisa-tions* 16 (March/April): 213–247.

White, Lynn T., Jr. 1962. *Medieval Technology and Social Change.* Oxford, UK: Clarendon.

Williamson, Jeffrey G. 1984. "Why Was British Growth So Slow during the In-dustrial Revolution?" *Journal of Economic History* 44: 687–712.

5   Economic Freedom and Property Rights: The Institutional Environment of Productive Entrepreneurship

ROBERT A. LAWSON

The idea that institutions are important in determining the degree of economic productivity in a nation is hardly new. Long ago Adam Smith (1776/1937), speaking of China, wrote:

> China seems to have been long stationary, and had probably long ago acquired that full complement of riches which is consistent with the nature of its laws and institutions. But this complement may be much inferior to what, with other laws and institutions, the nature of its soil, climate, and situation might admit of. A country which neglects or despises foreign commerce, and which admits the vessels of foreign nations into one or two of its ports only, cannot transact the same quantity of business which it might do with different laws and institutions. In a country too, where, though the rich or the owners of large capitals enjoy a good deal of security, the poor or the owners of small capitals enjoy scarce any, but are liable, under the pretence of justice, to be pillaged and plundered at any time by the inferior mandarines, the quantity of stock employed in all the different branches of business transacted within it, can never be equal to what the nature and extent of that business might admit. (95: bk. 1, ch. 9, para. 15)

So, according to Smith, although the soil and climate may matter, nations that reject foreign trade or in which small businesses may be harassed by regulators, the "inferior mandarines," will not live up to their economic potential. In other words, institutions matter.

Of course, the notion that "institutions matter" is hardly unique to advocates of laissez-faire. Karl Marx (1867/1906) himself acknowledged the productive capacity of the capitalist system even while disparaging its impact on the relative standing of workers and argued for economic institutions based on socialized planning.

The debate that ensued between Marxists (and other socialists) and liberal free-market advocates was to rage for the better part of the next century. The socialist calculation debate (Hoff 1949/1981), for example, was one of the pivotal theoretical debates about the role of institutions such as private property and market pricing in the economy. Hayek's (1945) article, "The Use of Knowledge in Society," was a high-water mark in discussing the role of market institutions (specifically the role of prices) in terms of the overall functioning of the economy.

1. Modern Theories of Growth and Development

Although the political debate between totalitarian communism and liberal democracy was to continue throughout most of the twentieth century, lasting at least until the fall of the Soviet Union in 1991, the intellectual debate had receded into the background by around midcentury. A mathematical and formalization revolution had taken over the economics profession, and untidy concepts such as institutional arrangements and entrepreneurship gave way to the new "science" of development economics.[1] Development and growth economists (e.g., Solow 1956) modeled entire economies as if they were production functions: output is a function of inputs:

$$Y = F(K, L).$$

The model emphasizes the role of the *quantity* of capital (K) and labor (L) in determining the level of production (Y). In terms of economic growth, the focus therefore turned toward investment of physical capital and later human capital as the best means for increasing output.

It is certainly true that increasing inputs should increase output *ceteris paribus*, but there was little discussion about what was being held constant. Although the model was eventually extended to include technological progress, the implicit assumption was that labor and capital would always be combined in the most efficient way possible; that is, the models assumed that countries were always functioning on their production possibilities frontier.

Another line of reasoning, mostly associated with Jeffrey Sachs (2001), is that geographic and locational factors such as a temperate climate and ease of access to markets are critically important for the achievement of high income levels and growth rates. In contrast, tropical climatic conditions both erode the energy level of workers and increase the risk of disabling and life-threatening diseases such as malaria. As a result, worker productivity and the general level of development are retarded in tropical areas.

But even a casual look at the real world revealed problems with these theoretical perspectives. Countries that appeared to have high levels of inputs in terms of natural resources, such as Argentina, did not necessarily perform very well. High investment rates in the centrally planned economies likewise did not generate rapid economic development. On the other hand, the strong economic performance of resource-poor and tropical Hong Kong and Singapore appear anomalous. It seemed obvious to anyone who cared to look that the real-world pattern of economic development was based on more than just the available quantities of resources and technology or location. Nevertheless, development economics continued to recommend building roads, schools, bridges, airports, factories, and so forth without regard to whether those investments were likely to be productive in the context of the institutions in place.

Some economists did take notice of the disconnect between formal theory and reality. Bauer (1957) was almost a lone voice in the wilderness criticizing the development literature's emphasis only on quantifiable inputs and outputs.

> The character of a society is governed by its historical development, by national and ethnic characteristics, by the political system, and by *institutional arrangements*, to mention some of the more obvious influences. (1957, 125–126, emphasis added)

Recent researchers have rediscovered the role of institutions as a cause of economic development. Acemoglu, Johnson, and Robinson (2001, 2004) argue that differences in institutions have been important in determining the pattern of economic development and that after control-ling for these institutional differences, geographical location loses much of its explanatory power. Rodrick, Subramanian, and Trebbi (2004) also strongly reinforce this view.

One problem for the early theorists and empirical researchers alike is that institutional quality is quite difficult to measure quantitatively. Fortunately, today we have many measures of these institutional factors at our disposal.

2. Measuring Economic Freedom

One such measure is the Economic Freedom of the World (EFW) index produced by Gwartney and Lawson (2004). The foundation of economic freedom and hence of the EFW index is the proposition that individuals own themselves; they are not owned by the government. Be-cause of this self-ownership, the protection of individuals and their prop-erty against aggression by others is at the core of economic freedom. Of course, ownership also implies the right to enter markets and exchange goods and services with others at mutually agreeable terms. Thus the four cornerstones of economic freedom are (1) private ownership, (2) personal choice, (3) voluntary exchange, and (4) free entry into markets. The EFW index is designed to measure the degree to which a nation's institutions and policies are consistent with these four cornerstones.

The EFW index was based initially on seventeen components such as government expenditures as a share of GDP (Gwartney, Lawson, and Block 1996) but has recently been expanded to include thirty-eight components. Country ratings for each of the thirty-eight components are placed on a zero-to-ten scale and then used to derive area and overall ratings for the 123 countries covered by the index. The overall index is divided into five major areas: (1) size of government, (2) legal structure and security of property rights, (3) access to sound money, (4) exchange with foreigners, and (5) regulation of credit, labor, and business.

The components of Area 1 indicate the extent to which countries rely on individual choice and markets rather than on the political process to allocate resources and goods and services. Taken together, the compo-nents measure the degree of a country's reliance on personal choice and markets rather than government budgets and political decision making.

Protection of persons and their rightfully acquired property is a central element of both economic freedom and a civil society. Area 2 focuses on this element. The key ingredients of a legal system consistent with economic freedom are rule of law, security of property rights, an independent judiciary, and an impartial court system.

Security of property rights, protected by the rule of law, is essential to economic freedom. Freedom to exchange, for example, is meaningless if individuals do not have secure rights to property, including the fruits of their labor. Failure of a country's legal system to provide for the security of property rights, enforcement of contracts, and the mutually agreeable settlement of disputes will undermine the operation of a market-exchange system.

Money oils the wheels of exchange. An absence of sound money undermines gains from trade. Sound money is essential to protect property rights and, thus, economic freedom. Inflation erodes the value of property held in monetary instruments. When governments use money creation to finance their expenditures, they are, in effect, expropriating the property and violating the economic freedom of their citizens.

In order to earn a high rating in Area 3, a country must follow policies and adopt institutions that lead to low (and stable) rates of inflation and avoid regulations that limit the use of alternative currencies, should citizens want to use them.

In our modern world of high technology and low costs for communication and transportation, freedom of exchange across national boundaries is a key ingredient of economic freedom. The vast majority of our current goods and services is now either produced abroad or contains resources supplied from abroad. Of course, exchange is a positive-sum activity.

Responding to protectionist critics and special-interest politics, virtually all countries adopt trade restrictions of various types. Tariffs and quotas are obvious examples of roadblocks that limit international trade. Because they reduce the convertibility of currencies, controls on the exchange rate also retard international trade. The volume of trade is also reduced by administrative factors that delay the passage of goods through customs. Sometimes these delays are the result of inefficiency, whereas in other instances they reflect the actions of corrupt officials seeking to extract bribes. In order to get a high rating in Area 4, a country must allow people the freedom to trade with people in other nations.

When regulations restrict entry into markets and interfere with the freedom to engage in voluntary exchange, they reduce economic freedom. Area 5 of the index focuses on this topic. Regulatory restraints that limit the freedom of exchange in credit, labor, and product markets are included.

Countries that use a private banking system to allocate credit to private parties and refrain from controlling interest rates receive higher ratings for the regulation of credit markets component.

Many types of labor-market regulations infringe on the economic freedom of employees and employers. Among the more prominent are minimum wages, dismissal regulations, centralized wage setting, extensions of union contracts to nonparticipating parties, unemployment benefits that undermine the incentive to accept employment, and military conscription. The labor-market regulation component is designed to measure the extent to which these restraints upon economic freedom are present across countries.

Like the regulation of the credit and labor markets, the general regulation of business activities inhibits economic freedom. The regulation of business components is designed to identify the extent to which regulatory restraints and bureaucratic procedures limit competition and the operation of markets. In order to score high in this portion of the index, countries must allow markets to determine prices and refrain from regulatory activities that retard entry into business and increase the cost of producing products. They also must refrain from playing favorites—from using their power to extract financial payments and to reward some businesses at the expense of others.

Of course, a government may do a pretty good job in some areas—for example, access to sound money and freedom of international exchange—and at the same time impose regulations that restrict economic freedom in other areas. The EFW area ratings can help identify the consistency of a country's policies with economic freedom in each of the five areas.

Table 5.1 reports the overall EFW ratings for the 123 countries for 2002. Hong Kong and Singapore occupy the top two positions as usual.

TABLE 5.1
Economic freedom index ratings and rankings, 2002

Rank	Countries	EFW index	Rank	Countries	EFW index	Rank	Countries	EFW index
1	Hong Kong	8.7	44	France	6.8	86	Argentina	5.8
2	Singapore	8.6	44	Lithuania	6.8	86	Cote d'Ivoire	5.8
3	New Zealand	8.2	44	Malta	6.8	86	Indonesia	5.8
3	Switzerland	8.2	44	Peru	6.8	86	Senegal	5.8
3	United Kingdom	8.2	44	South Africa	6.8	90	Albania	5.7
3	United States	8.2	44	Uruguay	6.8	90	China	5.7
7	Australia	7.9	50	Thailand	6.7	90	Nigeria	5.7
7	Canada	7.9	51	Cyprus	6.6	90	Pakistan	5.7
9	Ireland	7.8	51	Dominican Rep.	6.6	94	Barbados	5.6
9	Luxembourg	7.8	51	Israel	6.6	94	Cameroon	5.6
11	Estonia	7.7	51	Philippines	6.6	94	Ecuador	5.6
11	Finland	7.7	51	Slovak Rep.	6.6	94	Mali	5.6
11	Netherlands	7.7	51	Uganda	6.6	94	Nepal	5.6
14	Denmark	7.6	51	Zambia	6.6	94	Pap. New Guinea	5.6
14	Iceland	7.6	58	Bolivia	6.5	100	Madagascar	5.5
16	Austria	7.5	58	Malaysia	6.5	100	Malawi	5.5
16	Unit. Arab Em.	7.5	58	Mexico	6.5	100	Turkey	5.5
18	Belgium	7.4	61	Ghana	6.4	103	Benin	5.4
18	Botswana	7.4	61	Guatemala	6.4	103	Chad	5.4
18	Kuwait	7.4	61	Guyana	6.4	103	Romania	5.4

Rank	Country	Value	Rank	Country	Value	Rank	Country	Value
18	Oman	7.4	61	Honduras	6.4	103	Syria	5.4
22	Chile	7.3	61	Kenya	6.4	107	Colombia	5.3
22	Germany	7.3	61	Namibia	6.4	107	Niger	5.3
22	Hungary	7.3	61	Nicaragua	6.4	107	Rwanda	5.3
22	Sweden	7.3	61	Poland	6.4	107	Ukraine	5.3
22	Taiwan	7.3	69	Bahamas	6.3	111	Sierra Leone	5.2
27	El Salvador	7.2	69	Belize	6.3	112	Gabon	5.1
27	Mauritius	7.2	69	India	6.3	112	Togo	5.1
27	Panama	7.2	69	Tanzania	6.3	114	Russia	5.0
27	Portugal	7.2	69	Tunisia	6.3	115	Burundi	4.9
31	Bahrain	7.1	74	Brazil	6.2	115	Congo, Rep. of	4.9
31	Costa Rica	7.1	74	Egypt	6.2	117	Guinea-Bissau	4.8
31	South Korea	7.1	74	Paraguay	6.2	118	Algeria	4.6
31	Spain	7.1	74	Slovenia	6.2	118	Venezuela	4.6
31	Trinidad & Tob.	7.1	78	Bulgaria	6.0	120	Central Afr. Rep.	4.5
36	Italy	7.0	78	Fiji	6.0	121	Congo, Dem. R.	4.4
36	Japan	7.0	78	Haiti	6.0	122	Zimbabwe	3.4
36	Jordan	7.0	78	Iran	6.0	123	Myanmar	2.5
36	Latvia	7.0	78	Sri Lanka	6.0			
36	Norway	7.0	83	Bangladesh	5.9			
41	Czech Rep.	6.9	83	Croatia	5.9			
41	Greece	6.9	83	Morocco	5.9			
41	Jamaica	6.9						

The other nations in the top ten are New Zealand, Switzerland, United Kingdom, United States, Australia, Canada, Ireland, and Luxembourg. At the bottom of the list are the Republic of Congo, Guinea-Bissau, Algeria, Venezuela, Central African Republic, the Democratic Republic of Congo, Zimbabwe, and, in last place, Myanmar.[2]

3. Economic Freedom and Economic Performance

There are many reasons to expect that freer economies will grow more rapidly than those that are less free. Chief among these reasons are the roles played by competition, entrepreneurship, and investment in the economy.

Competition. Open markets—free entry into occupations and businesses—are an integral part of economic freedom. If business firms do not cater to the preferences of potential consumers and supply them with quality products at a low cost, they soon will be replaced by rivals who can provide customers with more value for their money.

Entrepreneurship. Freer economies provide greater opportunity for entrepreneurial discovery. Our modern living standards reflect the discovery of better ways of doing things—the development of new technology or the introduction of new products or lower-cost production methods. In recent decades, heart transplants, laser surgeries, miracle drugs, microwave ovens, CD and now DVD players, cellular phones, and personal computers have all dramatically changed the way we live and work. Innovations such as these do not just happen. They have to be discovered and undertaken by someone, and this process often involves the cooperative efforts of numerous parties. We do not know where the next ingenious idea will come from. More than any other form of economic organization, a free market economy makes it possible for a wide range of people to try out their innovative ideas and see if they can pass the market test. If they do, they will improve living standards. On the other hand, if they fail the market test, they will soon be brought to a halt. This experimentation and discovery process is a powerful force for economic progress.

Investment. Investors have a choice, and economic theory indicates that private investment will tend to flow toward economic environments that are more attractive for productive activities. Free economies will at-

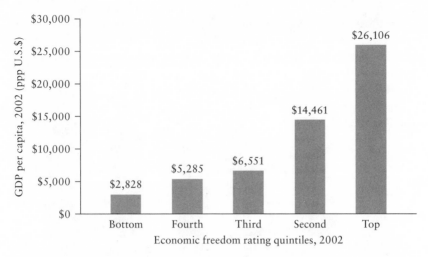

FIGURE **5.1**   Economic freedom and GDP per capita

tract more investment, which in turn will promote economic growth. On the other hand, high taxes, excessive regulation, biased enforcement of contracts, lack of legal recourse, insecure property rights, and monetary instability will deter both investment and therefore growth.

Economic Freedom, Income, and Growth. Figure 5.1 shows the economic freedom ratings related to GDP per capita. The chart organizes the world into five quintiles, ordered from the countries with the least economic freedom to the countries with the most. As economic freedom increases, so does average income.

The level of economic development at any point in time is, of course, the result of the accumulation of capital and technology over a long period of time. Figure 5.2 illustrates the correlation between economic growth (rates of change in GDP per capita) between 1980 and 2002 relative to the average level of the economic freedom index since 1980.

Of course, these simple correlations are not conclusive and cannot substitute for more serious scholarly work. Many scholars have used the economic freedom index to study differences in income and economic growth among countries around the world. Berggren's (2003) survey article cites most of the relevant literature.

One of the first such studies was by Easton and Walker (1997), who added economic freedom to the standard empirical neoclassical model. Their results suggested that an increase of one standard deviation

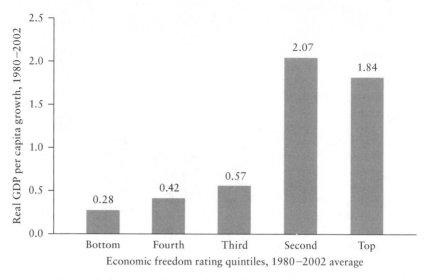

FIGURE **5.2**   Economic freedom and economic growth

in the economic freedom index corresponded to an increase in GDP per capita of more than $1,500 and that the difference in income associated with moving from the bottom of the economic freedom index to the top was approximately $7,200. Hanke and Walters (1997) found similar results.

Most studies conclude that the *level of economic freedom* positively affects growth, and it is also very clear that *increases in the level of economic freedom* over time correlate with faster economic growth.[3]

Gwartney and colleagues (1999) concluded that "a country that improved its economic freedom by moving from the bottom one-sixth of the countries up to the average could expect its long-term growth rate to increase by approximately 1.4 percentage points." More recently, Gwartney and colleagues (2004) found that the long-run level of economic freedom is positively related to both income levels and economic growth:

> A one-unit increase in the square of EFW enhances per capita GDP by slightly more than $500. This implies, for example, that an increase in the mean 1980–2000 EFW rating from 5.0 (approximately the levels of Argentina and Colombia) to 6.0 (approximately the level of South Korea) enhances 2000 per capita GDP by about $5500. (p. 214)

Moreover,

> A one-unit increase in a country's [average] EFW rating increases the growth of per capita GDP by about 1.24 percentage points. The average annual growth of per capita GDP during 1980–2000 for the 99 countries of this study was only 1.32 percent, so a 1.24 percentage point increase in long-term growth would be substantial. (p. 231)

Gwartney and colleagues (2004) also found that even while holding constant the average level of economic freedom, *increasing the level* of economic freedom during the period also correlates positively with growth: "a one-unit increase in EFW [during the period] increases overall growth during the period by an additional 0.68 of a percentage point" (pp. 226–227).

Given the emphasis in the formal literature on changes in the level of economic freedom (as opposed to simply the level itself), it is worthwhile to take a look at some of the countries with strong records of economic reform toward liberalization. The following countries have registered substantial gains in economic freedom during the last couple of decades.[4]

- Botswana increased its rating from 5.1 in 1985 to 6.0 in 1995 and 7.4 in 2002.
- Chile's rating improved from 3.6 in 1975 to 5.8 in 1985 and 7.5 in 1995. Chile's 2002 rating was 7.3, more than three points above its 1975 level.
- China's rating rose from 3.8 in 1980 to 4.3 in 1990 and 5.8 in 2000. China's 2002 rating was 5.7, almost two full points above its rating in 1980.
- El Salvador improved its rating substantially during the 1990s, moving from 4.5 in 1990 to 6.8 in 1995 and 7.3 in 2000 (and 7.2 in 2002).
- Ghana's rating increased from 2.5 in 1985 to 5.1 in 1995 and 6.4 in 2002.
- Iceland increased its rating from 5.1 in 1985 to 7.3 in 1995 and 7.6 in 2002.
- India's rating has improved substantially since 1990. After stagnating between 4.1 and 4.9 throughout the 1970–1990 period, India's rating rose to 5.5 in 1995, 6.2 in 2000, and 6.3 in 2002.

- Ireland's rating jumped between 1985 and 1995. It rose from 6.2 in 1985 to 7.0 in 1990 and 8.2 in 1995. During the last few years, Ireland's rating has receded slightly to 7.8 in 2002.
- New Zealand's rating improved substantially between 1985 and 1995. It rose from 5.9 in 1985 to 7.3 in 1990 and 8.5 in 1995, before receding slightly to 8.2 in 2002.
- Uganda has improved its rating from 2.6 in 1990 to 4.9 in 1995 and to 6.6 by 2002. Thus its rating jumped by more than four points during the 1990s.
- United Kingdom was a big gainer during 1980–1995, when its rating rose from 6.1 in 1980 to 7.0 in 1985 and 7.7 in 1990 and 8.2 in 1995, where it has remained during the last several years.

This group is quite geographically and economically diverse. It contains the world's two most populous countries, India and China. It includes some of the world's poorest economies, such as Uganda, as well as some that are relatively well off, such as Ireland. This diversity is an indication of the breadth of economic liberalization around the world.

Only a few countries have experienced outright declines in their EFW rating since 1980. Zimbabwe and Venezuela stand out among this short list. Astoundingly, Venezuela's index rating has declined by more than two full points since 1980.

In terms of economic performance, it is clear that those countries taking the largest strides toward economic freedom have performed well economically. China and more recently India, of course, have posted the strongest growth rates in the world in recent years. According to the World Bank, China has increased per capita income from $550 in 1975 to more than $4,000 in 2002.[5] In Europe, Ireland is the continent's fastest-growing economy, and as a result average income has increased from $7,700 to more than $32,000. Botswana is the fastest-growing country in Africa during the last twenty years—its GDP per capita has grown to $7,200 from about $1,500. Meanwhile in Venezuela, the people on average are poorer today than they were a generation ago. GDP per capita has fallen from about $6,500 to $4,800. Zimbabwe has exhibited a similarly regrettable pattern.

The larger point of these findings is that economic growth and productivity do not simply happen by themselves. People are constantly looking to "better their own conditions," and if allowed to do so in an economically free environment they will naturally make strides to improve their material well-being. However, the sad fact is that all too often government stands in the way.

In all such studies the question that inevitably has to be asked is whether economic freedom is really the *cause* of higher incomes or faster growth or of both. Statistical analysis, of course, can show only correlation. Is it possible that countries with higher incomes or faster rates of growth are choosing to pursue more economic freedom? That is, could the economic performance of the economy be dictating the amount of economic freedom instead of the other way around? Although statistics can never answer these questions definitively, they can be used to provide hints at the answer. Gwartney and colleagues (1999), for instance, found that increases in economic freedom precede faster economic growth but that faster economic growth does not precede increases in economic freedom. Heckelman (2000) found that economic freedom overall as well as several components of economic freedom precede growth. Dawson's (2003) work suggests, however, that causation (again in the sense of which comes first) is possibly from growth to economic freedom or that they both cause each other in a sort of harmonious circle. In a more complete growth model, however, Gwartney and colleagues (2005) find that the direction is unidirectional only from economic freedom to growth. Overall these studies indicate that it is more likely that increasing economic freedom is causing economic growth and that growth is not causing increases in economic freedom.

Economic Freedom and Entrepreneurship. Economic growth is the aggregate result of entrepreneurial activity occurring at the microeconomic level. Measuring entrepreneurship directly is quite difficult, and there are few good studies at the international level. Sobel, Clark, and Lee (2005), however, do look directly at entrepreneurial activity among Organisation for Economic Co-operation and Development (OECD) nations, finding that

> for the countries in our sample, we calculate the average business failures per 10,000 firms, and the average total entrepreneurial activity score, for the half of the countries with the most (highest) economic freedom and the half with the lowest economic freedom. . . . Those countries with the highest economic freedom scores had not only a

12 percent higher level of total entrepreneurial activity (the percentage difference in the index score), but they also have a rate of business failure that is almost twice as high as the countries with the lowest economic freedom scores. More freedom is not only correlated with more entrepreneurship, but also with a higher rate of business failure. Economic freedom means not only the freedom to enter and succeed, but also the freedom to fail.

Also, Kreft and Sobel (2005) argue that entrepreneurial activity is higher among the states of the United States with more economic freedom. They conclude that

> taken as a whole, the results from the previous two sections have significant policy implications for state and local development agencies. To encourage economic growth, localities must encourage entrepreneurial activity, and to do so, they must focus on creating an environment consistent with economic freedom, rather than focusing efforts on bringing in more venture capital to the area. Again, a state's economic freedom consists of an environment of low taxes, low regulations, and secure private property rights, where these factors collectively work to produce economic freedom.

Economic Freedom and Investment.[6] As suggested earlier, one important underlying reason why freer economies grow more rapidly than their less-free counterparts is because people have the incentive to invest more in freer economies. In fact, countries that adopt institutions and follow policies more consistent with economic freedom have substantially higher investment rates.

During 1980–2000, economies with EFW ratings of less than 5 attracted only $845 of investment per worker, compared with $3,319 for those with EFW ratings between 5 and 7, and a whopping $10,871 for those economies with EFW ratings of more than 7. Thus the investment rate per worker of the persistently free economies was more than twelve times the figure for the least-free group.

Foreign direct investment is mostly undertaken by private investors and therefore is perhaps a better indicator of how institutional quality influences the choices of private decision makers. The average annual rate of foreign direct investment per worker in the persistently free economies was $3,117, compared with $444 for the middle group and only $68 for the least-free group. The foreign direct investment per worker of the persistently free economies was more than forty-five times the figure for the least-free group.

The most standard way to measure investment is as a share of GDP. During 1980–2000, private investment averaged 18 percent of GDP in countries with EFW ratings of more than 7 but 14.2 percent for the middle group and just 9.6 percent for the least-free group. Thus the private investment rate as a share of GDP of the economically free economies was almost twice that of the least economically free group.

Economic freedom not only influences the level of investment but also influences its productivity. Gwartney and Lawson (2004) find that

> holding initial per capita GDP, tropical location, coastal population, changes in human capital, and public investment constant, a one percentage point increase in the private I/GDP ratio increased the growth of per capita GDP during 1980–2000 by 0.33 percentage points in countries with EFW ratings of more than 7. But in countries with EFW ratings between 5 and 7, a percentage point increase in the private I/GDP ratio enhanced growth by only 0.27 percentage points, and in the least free group growth was enhanced by only 0.19 percentage points. Thus the productivity of investment—the impact of a unit change of private I/GDP on growth—was more than 70 percent higher in the more free economies than for the group with the least economic freedom.

Economic freedom enhances the incentive of people to finance the investments necessary to spur economic growth; furthermore, the investments undertaken will be more productive in a freer economic environment.

Economic Freedom and Other Measures of Social Progress.[7] Economists are sometimes criticized, not without some justification, for being overly interested in monetary matters such as income levels and economic growth. "Surely there are more important things in life than just money," the critics will say. Of course, the critics are right; there is more to life than money. However, the economists' reasonable response is that most of these other important things (music, leisure, literature, health, etc.) are probably easier to acquire if you have more money, so there is no necessary conflict between economic growth and the good life.

A second line of criticism argues that economic freedom may lead to growth but that it still hurts the poor or creates unacceptably large

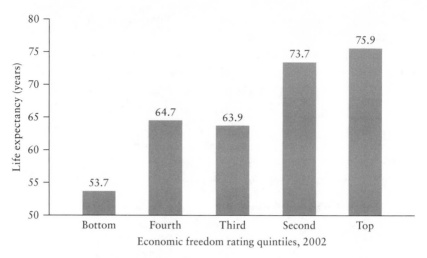

FIGURE **5.3**   Economic freedom and life expectancy

disparities in the distribution of income. This criticism is essentially the classic Marxian argument.

Because of these criticisms it is certainly worthwhile to examine directly the performance of freer economies in providing citizens with other measures of the good life. Although the literature looking at the relationship between economic freedom and other social outcomes is less extensive than the literature looking at growth and income, what research we have does show that economic freedom leads to better results in many dimensions.

Figure 5.3 illustrates the large improvements in life expectancy associated with greater economic freedom. The difference in life expectancy between the top quintile and the bottom quintile in economic freedom is more than twenty years—this is quite literally the difference between getting to know your grandchildren or not.

Despite considerable hand-wringing about the deleterious effects of markets on the distribution of income, there is simply no evidence that economic freedom creates greater income inequality. As seen in Figure 5.4, the bottom tenth of the income distribution earns about 2.0 to 2.5 percent of total income regardless of the level of economic freedom.

However, there is clear evidence that low-income people in freer countries are better off than their counterparts in less-free countries.

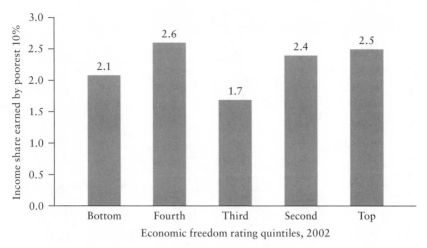

FIGURE **5.4**   Economic freedom and income share of the poor

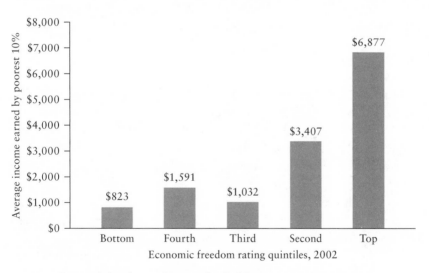

FIGURE **5.5**   Economic freedom and income level of the poor

Figure 5.5 shows the average income level of the poorest tenth of the population by economic freedom quintile. Clearly, economic freedom and the economic prosperity it brings work to the advantage of the poor.

Among the scholarly literature, Grubel (1998) finds that freer economies perform better on the UN Human Development Index, which

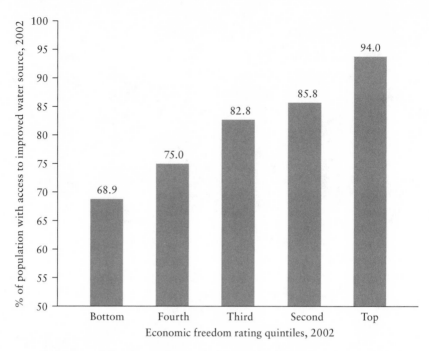

FIGURE **5.6**   Economic freedom and access to improved water

is based on life expectancy, literacy, poverty, and income distribution. Furthermore, in a very sophisticated study, Scully (2002) concludes that "the amount of economic freedom across nations has the attribute of increasing the rate of economic progress and *improving the distribution of market income*" (emphasis added).

Health and environmental outcomes appear to be better with more economic freedom, too. Figure 5.6 shows the correspondence between economic freedom and access to improved water sources. Along similar lines, Norton (1998) finds that economic freedom correlates positively with better environmental results.

4. Conclusions

It has long been argued that "institutions matter" in determining the level of entrepreneurship and ultimately economic progress. However, theoretical disagreements about exactly which institutions are needed for economic progress as well as difficulties in accurately measuring different types of institutions have clouded the debate.

By the middle part of the last century, formal economic theory placed almost no emphasis on economic institutions such as private property, taxation, regulation, and so forth or on the role of entrepreneurs as determinants of economic progress. In the end, events occurring in the real world, such as the breakup of the Soviet bloc, and recent innovations in the measurement of institutions, such as the EFW index, have forced both institutions and entrepreneurs back to the forefront of the discussion.

After more than a decade of research, the empirical evidence is overwhelmingly clear: societies that organize themselves with private property, rule of law, and free markets outperform, on almost every measurable margin, societies that are less economically free.

Notes

1. In the same way, the concept of entrepreneurship was largely drummed out of microeconomics because it was too nebulous a concept to work within the new formal models. Kirzner (1997) was one of the few economists left trying to keep that flame alive.

2. The EFW index is calculated in five-year intervals from 1970 through 2000 and annually since 2000 as data availability allows; see the Web site http://www.freetheworld.com for information from past years. Because some data for earlier years may have been updated or corrected, readers are always encouraged to utilize the data from the most recent annual report to assure the best-quality data. There is also a "chain-linked" economic freedom index available. For researchers doing time-series or longitudinal studies of economic freedom, these chain-link data are most appropriate for that purpose.

3. There is some debate about whether it is the level or changes in the level of economic freedom that affect growth (see de Haan and Sturm 2000).

4. This section is based in part on "Chapter 1: Economic Freedom of the World, 2002" in Gwartney and Lawson (2004). These EFW index ratings use the "chain-link" version of the index. This procedure eliminates possible distortions arising from the unavailability of data for some components of the EFW index during various years.

5. These data are from the World Bank, *World Development Indicators 2004* CD, and are expressed in constant 1995 purchasing power parity (U.S. dollars).

6. This section is largely based on "Chapter 2: Economic Freedom, Investment and Growth" in Gwartney and Lawson (2004).

7. This section is based in part on "Chapter 1: Economic Freedom of the World, 2002" in Gwartney and Lawson (2004).

References

Acemoglu, Daron, Simon Johnson, and James A. Robinson. 2001. "The Comparative Origins of Colonial Development: An Empirical Investigation." *American Economic Review* 91 (5): 1369–1401.

———. 2005. "Institutions as the Fundamental Cause of Long-Run Growth." In *Handbook of Economic Growth*, ed. Philippe Aghion and Steve Durlauf. Amsterdam, Netherlands: North-Holland.

Bauer, P. T. 1957. *Economic Analysis and Policy in Underdeveloped Countries.* Durham, NC: Duke University Press.

Berggren, Niclas. 2003. "The Benefits of Economic Freedom: A Survey." *The Independent Review* 8 (2): 193–211.

Dawson, John W. 2003. "Causality in the Freedom-Growth Relationship." *European Journal of Political Economy* 19 (3): 479–495.

de Haan, Jakob, and Jan-Egbert Sturm. 2003. "Does More Democracy Lead to Greater Economic Freedom? New Evidence for Developing Countries." *European Journal of Political Economy* 19 (3): 547–563.

Easton, Stephen T., and Michael A. Walker. 1997. "Income, Growth, and Economic Freedom." *American Economic Review* 87 (2): 328–332.

Friedman, Milton. 1962. *Capitalism and Freedom.* Chicago: University of Chicago Press.

Grubel, Herbert G. 1998. "Economic Freedom and Human Welfare: Some Empirical Findings." *Cato Journal* 18 (2): 287–304.

Gwartney, James D., Randall G. Holcombe, and Robert A. Lawson. 2004. "Economic Freedom, Institutional Quality, and Cross-Country Differences in Income and Growth." *Cato Journal* 24 (3): 205–231.

———. 2005. "Institutions and the Impact of Investment on Growth." Working paper.

Gwartney, James, and Robert Lawson. 2004. *Economic Freedom of the World: 2004 Annual Report.* Vancouver, Canada: Fraser Institute. http://www.freetheworld.com (accessed April 9, 2007).

Gwartney, James, Robert Lawson, and Walter Block. 1996. *Economic Freedom of the World: 1975–1995.* Vancouver, Canada: Fraser Institute.

Gwartney, James D., Robert A. Lawson, and Randall G. Holcombe. 1999.

"Economic Freedom and the Environment for Economic Growth." *Journal of Institutional and Theoretical Economics* 155 (4): 643–663.

Hanke, Steve H., and Stephen J. K. Walters. 1997. "Economic Freedom, Prosperity, and Equality: A Survey." *Cato Journal* 17 (2): 117–146.

Hayek, F. A. 1945. "The Use of Knowledge in Society." *The American Economic Review* 35 (4): 519–530.

Heckleman, Jac C. 2000. "Economic Freedom and Economic Growth: A Short-Run Causal Investigation." *Journal of Applied Economics* 3 (1): 71–91.

Hoff, Trygve J. B. 1949/1981. *Economic Calculation in the Socialist Society*. Indianapolis, IN: Liberty Press.

Kirzner, Israel. 1997. "Entrepreneurial Discovery and the Competitive Market Process: An Austrian Approach." *Journal of Economic Literature* 35 (1): 60–85.

Kreft, Steven F., and Russell S. Sobel. 2005. "Public Policy, Entrepreneurship, and Economic Freedom." *Cato Journal* 25 (3): 595–616.

Marx, Karl. 1867/1906. *Capital: A Critique of Political Economy*. New York: Modern Library.

Norton, Seth W. 1998. "Property Rights, the Environment, and Economic Well-Being." In *Who Owns the Environment?* ed. Peter J. Hill and Roger E. Meiners. Lanham, MD: Rowman & Littlefield.

Rodrick, Dani, Arvind Subramanian, and Francesco Trebbi. 2004. "Institutions Rule: The Primacy of Institutions over Geography and Integration in Economic Development." *Journal of Economic Growth* 9 (2): 131–165.

Sachs, Jeffrey D. 2001. "Tropical Underdevelopment." NBER Working Paper no. w8119.

Scully, G. W. 2002. "Economic Freedom, Government Policy, and the Trade-Off between Equity and Economic Growth." *Public Choice* 113 (1–2): 77–96.

Smith, Adam. 1776/1937. *An Inquiry into the Nature and Causes of the Wealth of Nations*. New York: Modern Library.

Sobel, Russell S., J. R. Clark, and Dwight R. Lee. 2005. "Freedom, Barriers to Entry, Entrepreneurship, and Economic Progress." West Virginia University working paper.

Solow, Robert M. 1956. "A Contribution to the Theory of Economic Growth." *The Quarterly Journal of Economics* 70 (1): 65–94.

II   *Failures in Entrepreneurial Development*

6   The African Development Conundrum

GEORGE B. N. AYITTEY

1. Introduction: The African Paradox

Economic conditions in Africa have deteriorated alarmingly, which is paradoxical given the continent's vast development potential and immense untapped mineral wealth. As an old continent, it is the source of strategic minerals, such as tantalite, vanadium, palladium, uranium, and chromium. It has the bulk of the world's gold, cobalt, diamonds, and manganese. Compared with the Asian continent, Africa is not overpopulated. Therefore, it "has enormous unexploited potential in resource-based sectors and in processing and manufacturing. It also has hidden growth reserves in its people—including the potential of its women, who now provide more than half of the region's labor force" (World Bank/ UNDP 2000a, 12).

Africa could well be the next and final frontier for roaring market-based capitalism. Yet, paradoxically, a continent with such abundance and potential is inexorably mired in steaming squalor, misery, deprivation, and chaos. The Congo River basin is extremely rich in minerals, but its people are yet to derive any substantial benefit from that wealth. Instead, they have slipped with indecent haste back to near–Stone Age existence. Provision of basic social services—such as education, health care, sanitation, clean water, and roads—is nonexistent. Freelance banditry and pillage are the daily fare. No one is in control of anything—not even rebel groups of his or her own people.

When Ghana gained its independence in 1957, its $200 income per capita was the same as South Korea's. Ghana's economic potential was enormous: rich endowments of minerals (gold, diamonds, bauxite, manganese), cash crops (cocoa, coffee, kola nuts), and timber. In addition, Ghana had a well-educated population and a relatively larger professional and educated class than many other African countries. But fifty years later, South Korea's income per capita was about thirty times that of Ghana: $12,200 versus $420.

Nigeria also stood at the same stage of development with South Korea in 1960, but in 2007, Africa's most-populous nation seems uncharitably mired in convulsive violence and grinding poverty with nearly the same per capita income as in 1960—as if the economy hibernated. Even with the inception of civilian rule in May 1999 after decades of villainous military rule, more than ten thousand people had died in deadly ethnic and religious clashes by 2003. The army continued to massacre hundreds of civilians with impunity. On February 2, 2002, fighting in two neighborhoods between members of the Yoruba and Hausa ethnic groups claimed the lives of more than one hundred people in Lagos. "By all accounts, the fighting began in Idi Araba on Saturday afternoon after a Yoruba youth defecated in front of a house owned by Hausas" (*New York Times*, February 8, 2002). "Every occurrence of violence erodes the legitimacy of the state and its leaders, leaving democracy to stand alone and exposed to those who want to subvert it further or destroy it altogether," said a hopelessly weak and frustrated President Oluegun Obasanjo (*New York Times*, February 8, 2002).

Independence did not bring the prosperity promised by the nationalist leaders. Poverty levels instead increased sharply in the postcolonial period. Most Africans today are worse off than they were at independence in the 1960s.

A. Bleak Prospects

Africa's postcolonial economic performance remains dismal, and prospects for the new millennium are, to put it bluntly, bleak. Sub-Saharan Africa, consisting of forty-eight countries, is the least-developed region of the Third World. Since 1990, the United Nations Development Program (UNDP) has ranked 162 countries in terms of their progress on human development, using the Human Development Index (HDI). It determines the overall achievements in a country in three basic dimensions of human development—life expectancy, educational attainment, and income per capita in purchasing power parity (ppp) U.S. dollars (UNDP 2001, 14). Each year, however, African countries compete for the lowest rankings. In 2001, the twenty-eight countries at the bottom of the rankings were from sub-Saharan Africa (UNDP 2001, 142). Compared with other regions in the Third World, sub-Saharan Africa lags far behind in terms of economic performance. Not only have already-low incomes fallen, but also per capita GDP growth over the period 1975–1999 averaged −1 percent. Madagascar and Mali now have per capita incomes of $799 and $753 (1999 ppp U.S.$)—down from $1,258 and $898 (1999 ppp U.S.$) twenty-five years ago." In sixteen other sub-Saharan African countries per capita incomes were also lower in 1999 than in 1975" (UNDP 2001, 12). Table 6.1 shows the comparative performance of sub-Saharan Africa in stark terms.

Sub-Saharan African GNP per capita dropped steadily from $624 in 1980 to $513 in 1998. A similar trend was registered for all of Africa: a drop from $749 in 1980 to $688 in 1998 (World Bank/UNDP 2000b, 35). Prognosis for the new millennium is widely acknowledged to be disheartening.

The United Nations Conference on Trade and Development's (UNCTAD) report, *Least Developed Countries, 2002*, noted that both the extent and depth of poverty have increased dramatically in sub-Saharan Africa: "The proportion of people in 29 African countries living below $2 per day increased from 82 percent in the late 1960s to 87.5 percent in the late 1990s. For those in extreme poverty—under $1 per day—

TABLE 6.1
Africa's comparative economic performance, 1975–1999

Region	GDP per capita	Annual growth of GDP per capita, 1975–1999	Annual growth of GDP per capita, 1990–1999
Least-developed countries	$1,170	0.2	0.8
East Asia and Pacific	3,950	6.0	5.9
Latin America and Caribbean	6,880	0.6	1.7
South Asia	2,280	2.3	3.4
Sub-Saharan Africa	1,640	−1.0	−0.4

SOURCE: UNDP (2001, 181).

the increase was from 55.8 percent to 64.9 percent" (*Africa Recovery*, September 2002).

On July 8, 2003, the UN issued a stern warning about worsening economic and social conditions in black Africa just as U.S. President George W. Bush began a five-day tour of the continent. In its *Human Development Report* (2003), the UNDP warned that at the prevailing rates black Africa would take another 150 years to reach some of the development targets agreed to by UN members for 2015.

> Unless things improve it will take sub-Saharan Africa until 2129 to achieve universal primary education, until 2147 to halve extreme poverty and until 2165 to cut child mortality by two thirds. For hunger no date can be set because the region's situation continues to worsen. (*Financial Times*, July 9, 2003)

In 1995, the population of Africa was estimated to be 580 million. Of that population, according to the World Bank,

- 291 million people had average incomes of less than one dollar a day in 1998
- 124 million of those up to age thirty-nine were at risk of dying before forty
- 43 million children were stunted as a result of malnutrition in 1995
- 205 million were estimated to be without access to health services in 1990–1995
- 249 million were without safe drinking water in 1990–1995
- more than two million infants die annually before their first birthday (World Bank 2001, xiii)

These statistics paint a grim picture of the rapidly deteriorating socioeconomic conditions in Africa. Independence from colonial rule was not supposed to further impoverish the continent, given its wealth in natural resources.

B. The Paucity of Economic Success Stories

Western economic analysts over the decades have tried in vain to focus on Africa's economic success stories in order to avoid painting too negative a portrait of Africa for reasons of political correctness. Multilateral lending institutions, such as the World Bank and the International Monetary Fund, also engage in this sport.

To be sure, there are economic success stories in Africa, but they are distressingly few. In 2001, this tiny coterie included Benin, Botswana, Equatorial Guinea, Guinea, Lesotho, Madagascar, Mauritius, Mozambique, Seychelles Islands, and Uganda. Never mind what criteria were used and their appropriateness. Whatever the case, this situation suggests that most of the fifty-four African countries are economic basket cases. The real danger in focusing on the tiny number of success stories is that doing so ignores the much, much larger sordid picture. Even then, the economic success stories are themselves "small country" examples and are unlikely to serve as "regional powerhouses" to pull their neighbors or the rest of the continent out of its economic doldrums. Having Nigeria, Sudan, Congo (DRC), Ethiopia, or Angola as a success story would be more meaningful and strategic than, say, Lesotho and Equatorial Guinea. Most unsatisfactorily, the list of economic success stories keeps changing. Gambia, Nigeria, Ghana, Tanzania, and Zimbabwe have vanished from the success list that the World Bank trumpeted in 1994.

A number of African countries have initiated economic reforms aimed at increasing the role of the private sector and at moving to a market economy. State-owned enterprises have been privatized, and various state controls have been removed. In addition, steps have been taken to restore and maintain macroeconomic stability through the devaluation of overvalued national currencies and the reduction of inflation rates and budget deficits.

In addition, African countries have improved their regulatory frameworks for foreign direct investment (FDI), making them far more open, permitting profit repatriation, and providing tax and other incentives to attract investment. For example, twenty-six of the thirty-two least-developed countries in Africa covered in a 1997 survey had a liberal or relatively liberal regime for the repatriation of dividends and capital (UNCTAD, 1997). Reforms have also been made in other areas that are important for the FDI climate, such as trade liberalization, the strengthening of the rule of law, improvements in legal and other institutions, as well as in telecommunications and transport infrastructure (World Economic Forum 1998, 20).

The reforms in the regulatory framework for FDI have been buttressed in many countries by the conclusion of, or accession to, international agreements dealing with FDI issues. More than fifty African countries have concluded bilateral investment treaties (BITs) with other countries, aimed at protecting and promoting FDI and clarifying the terms under which FDI can take place between partner countries. Egypt, for instance, had signed fifty-eight BITs by January 1, 1999, more than any other developing country (the Republic of Korea had signed forty-nine and Argentina forty-four BITs). By January 1999, African countries had concluded 335 BITs, the majority of which had been signed since the beginning of the 1990s. The treaties contribute to the creation of a more secure environment for foreign investors in the continent.

Yet all these reforms in the policy framework for FDI have not been enough to spur economic growth, overcome the negative image of Africa, and attract foreign investors. Perhaps it takes time, but instead of addressing those issues that create the negative image—such as ending insane civil wars—many African governments have established investment promotion agencies and engage in PR campaigns to change this image in the hope that the PR campaigns would attract the investors. In the Southern African Development Community (SADC), for example, all fourteen member states have established such agencies. But much of this effort is likely to prove futile.

Investment promotion agencies cannot be effective when SADC members do not follow the rules of their own organization and have failed to erase the negative image that afflicts their own region. Foreign investment does not occur in a vacuum but rather in a stable environment where the rule of law prevails. Southern African government agencies seeking to attract foreign investment had not done much to end the violent political crisis in Zimbabwe that could destabilize the entire region.

President Festus Mogae of Botswana had persistently complained that the Zimbabwean crisis was hurting the region's economy. Foreign investors fled South Africa when two white Zimbabwean farmers were murdered on April 18, 2000. According to the *Wall Street Journal* (May 4, 2000), "the South African bond market witnessed an outflow of R1.8 billion ($263 million)" (p. A16). And "the Kenyan shilling hit a six-month low against the dollar with traders citing fears of a Zimbabwe contagion as the primary cause" (*Washington Times*, May 6, 2000). It was clear that the economic interests and needs of an entire region were being held hostage by one despot's megalomaniac thirst for power.

Finally, on January 14, 2002, leaders of the fourteen-member SADC gathered in Blantyre, Malawi, to discuss the political crisis in Zimbabwe that was spiraling out of control. Opposition supporters in Zimbabwe were being brutalized and killed by government-backed thugs. And Zimbabwe's Parliament was considering passing a draconian bill that would severely restrict press freedoms. So how could SADC leaders call Mugabe to order when most of them do not respect these freedoms in their own countries?

2. Who Ruined Africa?

The causes of Africa's lack of development have always evoked heated debates. On one hand are those people who portray Africa as a victim of powerful external forces and conspiracies. This group may be described as "externalists." On the other hand are those people who believe that the causes of Africa's crisis lie mostly within—in the nature of government or governance. This group may be described as "internalists."

A. The Externalists

Disciples of the externalist school include most African leaders, scholars, and intellectual radicals. For decades the externalist position held sway, attributing the causes of almost every African problem to such external factors as Western colonialism and imperialism, the pernicious effects of the slave trade, racist conspiracy plots, exploitation by avaricious multinational corporations, an unjust international economic system, inadequate flows of foreign aid, and deteriorating terms of trade.

In his book, *The Africans*, African scholar and history professor Ali Mazrui examined the African crisis, claiming that almost everything that went wrong in Africa was the fault of Western colonialism and imperialism. "The West harmed Africa's indigenous technological development in a number of ways" (Mazrui 1986, 164). He attributed Africa's collapsing infrastructure (roads, railways, and utilities) to the "shallowness of Western institutions," "the lopsided nature of colonial acculturation," and "the moral contradictions of Western political tutelage" (p. 202). In fact, "the political decay is partly a consequence of colonial institutions without cultural roots in Africa" (p. 199). Therefore, self-congratulatory Western assertions of contributing to Africa's modernization are shallow: "The West has contributed far less to Africa than Africa has contributed to the industrial civilization of the West" (p. 164). Decay in law enforcement and mismanagement of funds were all the fault of Western colonialism, too. "The pervasive atmosphere in much of the land is one of rust and dust, stagnation and decay, especially within those institutions which were originally bequeathed by the West" (p. 210). They signal "the slow death of an alien civilization" (p. 204) and Africa's rebellion "against westernization masquerading as modernity" (p. 211). Western institutions are doomed "to grind to a standstill in Africa" or decay. "Where Islam is already established, the decay of western civilization is good for Islam since it helps to neutralize a major threat" (p. 19).

Since independence, almost every African malaise was ascribed to the operation or conspiracy of extrinsic agents by African leaders. The leadership was above reproach and could never be faulted. President Mobutu even blamed corruption on European colonialism. Asked who introduced corruption into Zaire, he retorted: "European businessmen were the ones who said, 'I sell you this thing for $1,000, but $200 will be for your (Swiss bank) account'" (*New African*, July 1988). "President Danial Arap Moi accused the IMF and other development partners of denying Kenya development funds, thus triggering mass poverty" (*Washington Times*, June 3, 1999). According to the chairman of Ghana's ruling NDC, Issifu Ali, whatever economic crisis the nation is going through has been caused by external factors. "He said the NDC has since 1982 adopted pragmatic policies for the progress of Ghana, adding that the macro-economic environment of 1999 has been undermined by global economic developments" (*Independent*, November 18, 1999). According to the *Zimbabwe Independent*, "Mugabe rejects the criticism of those who blame the government for the economic crisis. It is, he says, the fault of greedy Western powers, the IMF, the Asian financial crisis and the drought" (April 27, 1999, 25).

Of course, African leaders blame everybody except themselves. Robert Mugabe of Zimbabwe blames British colonialists, racists, and "snakes" (whites) for ruining his economy. The New Economic Partnership for African Development (NEPAD) claims that Africa's impoverish-

ment has been accentuated by the legacy of colonialism and other historical legacies, such as the Cold War and the unjust international economic
system. Colonialism subverted the "traditional structures, institutions
and values," creating an economy "subservient to the economic and political needs of the imperial powers" (NEPAD 2001, para. 21). Colonialism, according to NEPAD, retarded the development of an entrepreneurial and middle class with managerial capability. At independence, Africa
inherited a "weak capitalist class," which explains the "weak accumulation process, weak states and dysfunctional economies" (para. 22). More
recent reasons for Africa's dire condition include "its continued margin-
alization from globalization process" (para. 2).

B. The Internalists

Internalists are the new and angry generation of Africans who are
fed up with African leaders who refuse to take responsibility for their own
failures and instead use colonialism and other external factors as conve-
nient alibis to conceal their own incompetent management. Internalists
believe that although it is true that colonialism and Western imperialism
did not leave Africa in good shape, Africa's condition has been made
immeasurably worse by internal factors: misguided leadership, misgovernance, systemic corruption, capital flight, economic mismanagement, declining investment, collapsed infrastructure, decayed institutions, senseless civil wars, political tyranny, flagrant violations of human rights, and
military vandalism.

UN Secretary General Kofi Annan, himself an African, lashed out
at African leaders at the Organization of African Unity (OAU) summit
in Lome, Togo, in July 2000. He pointedly told them that they are to
blame for most of the continent's problems. "Instead of being exploited
for the benefit of the people, Africa's mineral resources have been so mis-
managed and plundered that they are now the source of our misery" (*Daily
Graphic*, July 12, 2000). At a press conference in London in April 2000,
Kofi Annan "lambasted African leaders who he says have subverted democracy and lined their pockets with public funds, although he stopped
short of naming names" (*African-American Observer*, April 25–May 1,
2000). Ordinary people are speaking out, too. Said Akobeng Eric, a Ghanaian, in a letter to the *Free Press*, "A big obstacle to economic growth

in Africa is the tendency to put all blame, failures and shortcomings on outside forces. Progress might have been achieved if we had always tried first to remove the mote in our own eyes" (March 29–April 11, 1996).

Angry at deteriorating economic conditions in Ghana, thousands of Ghanaians marched through the streets of the capital city, Accra, to denounce the ruling regime of President Rawlings. "If Jerry Rawlings says the current economic crisis is due to external forces and therefore, beyond his control, then he should step aside and allow a competent person who can manage the crisis to take over," Atta Frimpong demanded (*Ghanaian Chronicle*, November 29, 1999). Appiah Dankwah, another protestor, blamed the NDC government for mismanaging the resources of the nation.

In Zimbabwe, the people did not buy President Mugabe's claim that "Britain, greedy Western powers, the IMF, the Asian financial crisis and the drought" were responsible for the country's economic mess (*Zimbabwe Independent*, April 27, 1999, 25). They rejected his request for constitutional revisions to give him more draconian powers in a February 15, 2000, referendum, handing him his first political defeat in twenty years of virtually unchallenged rule.

3. The Real Causes of Africa's Economic Decline

After African nations won independence, they rejected capitalism as a Western colonial institution in one monumental syllogistic error. Colonialism was evil, and because the colonialists were capitalists, it, too, was evil. Socialism, the antithesis of capitalism, was adopted.

Every effort was made to eradicate the vestiges of colonialism and protect the new nations against foreign exploitation. Names of cities and towns were changed. A plethora of state controls were instituted to ensure state participation in the economy as well as control of the commanding heights of the economy. The leadership, with few exceptions, demanded great powers to eradicate poverty and fight the colonialist enemy. The results were the establishment of defective political and economic systems in which enormous power was concentrated in the hands of the state and ultimately one individual and economic systems of "statism" or dirigisme, heavy state participation or direction of economic activity. Even pro-Western countries such as Ivory Coast, Kenya, Malawi, Nigeria, and Togo were dirigiste and one-party states or military dictatorships. These monstrous systems were created by African leaders and elites themselves. They bore no affinity to the indigenous systems or even the hated colonial systems.

No effort was made to build on Africa's indigenous institutions; only Botswana did this. Foreign systems and paraphernalia were blindly aped and transplanted into Africa. Thus not *organic* development but rather "development by imitation" took place. American farmers use tractors; so, too, must African. London has double-decker buses; so, too, must Lagos. Rome has a basilica; so, too, must Yamassoukro (Ivory Coast). France once had an emperor; so Bokassa of the Central African Republic spent $25 million to crown himself "emperor." The United States has a space program; so Nigeria is spending $39 million to develop one for weather forecasting. The continent is littered with the carcasses of failed foreign systems.

To initiate development, it was widely held that the African state needed wide-ranging powers to marshal the resources from the rural area and to channel them into national development. Extensive powers were conferred upon African heads of state by rubber-stamp parliaments. If a piece of land was needed for highway construction, it was simply appropriated by the state, and if an enterprise was needed, it was established by the government without any consultation with the people it was intended to benefit. In this way, *all* African governments, regardless of their ideological predilections, came to assume immense powers.

The drift toward state interventionism and development planning, however, was accentuated by the socialist ideology. After independence, many African elites and intellectuals argued for an ideology to guide the government on the road to development. The choice almost everywhere was socialism. The dalliance and fascination with socialism emerged during the struggle for political independence and freedom from colonial rule in the 1950s.

In Africa, these arguments were buttressed by the continent's special circumstances and historical experience. Markets were simply assumed to be nonexistent or severely underdeveloped. Even where they existed, they were rejected as an allocative mechanism because Africa's peasants were assumed to be unresponsive to market or price incentives. Bound by the chains of tradition, these peasants produced only the bare minimum to feed themselves (subsistence agriculture).

Perhaps the most compelling need for development planning, in the eyes of African leaders, was Africa's colonial legacy. Colonial objectives were not to develop Africa but rather to undertake only such forms of development that were compatible with the interests of European metropolitan powers. Because they were mostly industrialized, the colonies were envisaged to function as nonindustrial appendages to the metropolitan economy: consumers of European manufactured goods and providers of minerals and agricultural and sylvan commodities. As a result, the development of the colonial economies was perniciously "skewed": overspecialized in one or two main cash crops (monoexport culture), making African economies highly vulnerable to oscillations in commodity prices on the world market.

Specialization in cash crops, it was argued, also destroyed Africa's ability to feed its people and supply their other needs internally. Most domestic industries collapsed from competition: from cheaper and probably better imported manufactures. Because of collusion among foreign firms and discrimination from colonial banks, the modern sector was completely in foreign hands. Thus most of the surplus profit generated by the economy flowed overseas and was not invested in the colony. Local industrialization was flatly discouraged.

True African development, according to these leaders, required a carefully planned and massive transformation of African economies. Such an investment could be undertaken only by the state. This belief set the stage for massive state interventionism in the 1950s and 1960s in Africa. In Francophone Africa, industries were nationalized, tariff barriers were erected, and the state assumed near-total control of the national economy. Rather interestingly, the World Bank, the U.S. Agency for International Development (USAID), the State Department, and even development experts from Harvard University supported these arguments and channeled much aid to African governments (Bandow 1986).

A wave of socialism swept across the continent as almost all the new African leaders succumbed to the contagious ideology, copied from the East. The proliferation of socialist ideologies that emerged in Africa ranged from the "Ujamaa" ("familyhood" or "socialism" in Swahili) of

Julius Nyerere of Tanzania to the vague amalgam of Marxism, Christian socialism, humanitarianism, and "Negritude" of Leopold Senghor of
Senegal to the humanism of Kenneth Kaunda of Zambia to the scientific
socialism of Marien N'Gouabi of Congo (Brazzaville) to the Arab-Islamic
socialism of Muammar Gadhafi of Libya, the "Nkrumaism" (conscien-
cism) of Kwame Nkrumah of Ghana, and the "Mobutuism" of Mobutu
Sese Seko of Zaire. Only a few African countries were pragmatic enough
to eschew doctrinaire socialism.

Although there was a general disposition among African leaders
to erase the "exploitative, capitalistic tendencies of colonial structures,"
there were sharp individual differences between them on the need for the
ideology. Kwame Nkrumah of Ghana, generally regarded as the "father of
African socialism," was convinced that "only the socialist form of society
can assure Ghana of a rapid rate of economic progress without destroying
that social justice, that freedom and equality, which are a central feature
of our traditional way of life" (Government of Ghana 1963, 1).

Nyerere of Tanzania, on the other hand, misread the communalism
of African traditional life as readiness for socialism, which he was first
exposed to during his schooling in Scotland. The money economy was, in
his purview, foreign to Africa, and it "can be catastrophic as regards the
African family social unit." As an alternative to "the relentless pursuit of
individual advancement," Nyerere insisted that Tanzania be transformed
into a nation of small-scale communalists ("Ujamaa") (Nyerere 1962).

Accordingly, in 1973 Tanzania undertook massive resettlement programs under Operation Dodoma, Operation Sogeza, Operation Kigoma,
and many others. Peasants were loaded into trucks, often forcibly, and
moved to new locations. Many lost their lives in the process, and to prevent others from returning to their old habitats, abandoned buildings
were destroyed by bulldozers. By 1976, some thirteen million peasants
had been forced into eight thousand cooperative villages, and by the end
of the 1970s, about 91 percent of the entire rural population had been
moved into government villages (Zinsmeister 1987). All crops were to be
bought and distributed by the government. It was illegal for the peasants
to sell their own produce.

In the rest of Africa, planned socialist transformation of Africa
meant the institution of a plethora of legislative instruments and controls.
All unoccupied land was appropriated by the government. Roadblocks

and passbook systems were employed to control the movement of Africans. Marketing boards and export regulations were tightened to fleece the cash crop producers. Price controls were imposed on peasant farmers and traders to render food cheap for the urban elites.

Under Nkrumah, socialism as a domestic policy in his Seven-Year Development Plan was to be pursued toward "a complete ownership of the economy by the state." A bewildering array of legislative controls and regulations was imposed on imports, capital transfers, industry, minimum wages, the rights and powers of trade unions, prices, rents, and interest rates. Some of the controls had been introduced by the colonialists, but they were retained and expanded by Nkrumah. Private businesses were taken over by the Nkrumah government and nationalized. Numerous state enterprises were acquired.

Even in avowedly capitalist countries such as Ivory Coast and Kenya, the result was the same: government ownership of most enterprises and a distrust of private-sector initiative and foreign investment.

Problems emerged soon after independence. State controls created artificial shortages and black markets, providing opportunities for rent-seeking activities and illicit enrichment. Import and exchange controls were the most lucrative. Ministers demanded 10 percent commission before issuing an import license. Everyone was chasing scarce commodities to buy at government-controlled prices and to resell on the black market to make a profit—a process known in Ghana as *kalabule*. Neglected, peasant agriculture fell into decline, and food production per capita fell, diminishing Africa's capacity to feed itself.

A. The Failure of Statism/Socialism

Everywhere in Africa, statism and development planning failed miserably to engineer development. In their wake, economic atrophy, repression, and dictatorship followed with morbid staccato. As Mabogunje (1988) asserted, "It is generally agreed that the false start in all African countries has been due largely to the high level of governmental and bureaucratic domination of the economy with its consequences of inefficiency, profligacy and inappropriate control" (p. 25).

Ghana's Seven-Year Development Plan achieved little, if any, by way of development. The indictment of Killick (1978) was more scathing:

The 7-Year Plan, then, was a piece of paper, with an operational impact close to zero. Why? It could be argued that this was due to defects in the plan itself, to shortages of staff to monitor and implement it, and to the intervention of factors beyond Ghana's control, especially the falling world cocoa prices of the early and mid-sixties. [But] in retrospect, we see an almost total gap between the theoretical advantages of planning and the record of the 7-Year Plan. Far from providing a superior set of signals, it was seriously flawed as a technical document and, in any case, subsequent actions of government bore little relation to it. Far from counteracting the alleged myopia of private decision-takers, government decisions tended to be dominated by short-term expediency and were rarely based upon careful appraisals of their economic consequences. The plan was subverted, as most plans are, by insufficient political determination to make it work. (p. 143)

Similarly in Tanzania, Nyerere's social transformation was also a crushing fiasco. According to Japheth M. M. Ndaro, director of the Institute of Development Planning at Dodoma, during the period 1961–1970, the inhabitants of Dodoma devised and adopted strategies that did not conform with the political slogan of nation building that was dominant in the early 1960s. In some parts of the district, the concept of *ujamaa* actually stifled local initiative. "All in all, the Arusha Declaration of 1967 and the *Ujamaa* Policy of 1968, which marked an important milestone in the development of the country as a whole, did not inspire the people of Dodoma to engage in development initiatives that were alien to their socio-cultural environment" (as quoted in Taylor and Mackenzie 1992, 178).

Industrial output across Africa has been declining, with some regions experiencing *deindustrialization*. The state enterprises established under Africa's various development plans were hopelessly inefficient:

> There are countless examples of badly chosen and poorly designed
> public investments, including some in which the World Bank has par-
> ticipated. A 1987 evaluation revealed that half of the completed rural
> development projects financed by the World Bank in Africa had failed.
> A cement plant serving Cote d'Ivoire, Ghana and Togo was closed in
> 1984 after only four years of operation. A state-run shoe factory in Tan-
> zania has been operating at no more than 25 percent capacity and has
> remained open only thanks to a large government subsidy. (World Bank
> 1989, 27)

Indeed, in a speech at the International Conference on Privatization on February 17, 1987, in Washington, DC, a former president of the African Development Bank, Babacar N'Diaye, himself admitted that

> It is now generally accepted that over time the majority of public sector enterprises or *entities* have not performed efficiently. Instead of accumulating surpluses or supplying services efficiently, a good number of these enterprises have become a drain on the national treasuries." (*African Business*, June 1987)

In short, the state-led development approach that spurned market processes impeded Africa's economic progress in the postcolonial period. Heavy-handed state interventionism undermined both agricultural and industrial development, producing negative growth rates, commodity scarcities, and rising prices. These in themselves provided the grist for *more* state interventionism to control prices and commodity shortages. But state controls created black markets and exacerbated the shortage situations, setting the stage for a vicious cycle of state interventions to correct problems created by previous state interventions.

B. The Evolution of the Vampire State

Very quickly African nationalist leaders discovered they could use the enormous economic and political power they had accumulated to enrich themselves, crush their political rivals, and perpetuate themselves in office. Over time, the defective economic and political systems metastasized into a monstrosity—a "vampire state." In a vampire state, the government has been hijacked by a phalanx of unrepentant gangsters and thugs who employ the machinery of the state to enrich themselves, their cronies, and tribesmen. All others are excluded. The richest persons in Africa are heads of state and ministers. And quite often, the chief bandit is the head of state himself. Thus government is totally divorced from the people and perceived by those running it as a vehicle not to serve but rather to fleece the people. The African state was reduced to a mafialike bazaar where anyone with an official designation can pillage at will.

The primordial instinct of the ruling bandits is to loot the national treasury, perpetuate themselves in power, and brutally suppress all dissent and opposition. And worse, the loot is not invested in their own countries but rather is stashed in Swiss and foreign bank accounts. According to a United Nations estimate, in 1991 alone more than $200 billion in capital was siphoned out of Africa by the ruling elites (*New York Times*, February 4, 1996). Note that this amount was more than half of Africa's foreign debt of $320 billion. A UN *Report on Global Corruption* says that up to $30 billion in aid for Africa, twice the GDP of Ghana, Kenya, and Uganda combined, has ended up in foreign bank accounts (*New Vision*, April 15, 2000).

"Many people in government have the biggest accounts in foreign banks. Critics of the Moi government say there is more money from Kenyans in foreign banks than the entire Kenyan foreign debt, which is about $8 billion. Kenya's situation is not unique to the country. It is a reality found throughout Africa" (*Washington Times*, August 3, 1995). Nairobi businessman Peter Wamai charged that "if they are serious about eradicating poverty, they should start by returning the money that has been stolen" (*Washington Times*, June 3, 1999).

The situation in Kenya so deteriorated that eighty-four members of Parliament vowed to oust the Moi regime and replace it with an all-party interim government. In a July 28, 1999, statement, signed by members of Parliament and read by lawyer and opposition member of Parliament George Kaptain, they said: "Corruption within the top leadership of the government had reached endemic levels and the only solution is for Mr. Moi's regime to be kicked out" (*Washington Times*, July 30, 1999).

The ruling elite take over and subvert every key institution of government to serve their needs of self-aggrandizement and self-perpetuation in power, not the needs of the people: the civil service, judiciary, military, media, and banking. Key positions in these institutions are handed over to the president's tribesmen, cronies, and loyal supporters. Meritocracy, rule of law, property rights, transparency, and administrative capacity vanish. Even various commissions with lofty ideals that are supposed to be nonpartisan and neutral are taken over and debauched: press/media commission, human rights commission, and commission on civic education.

As a result, state institutions and commissions become paralyzed. Laxity, ineptitude, indiscipline, and lack of professionalism thus flourish in the public sector. Of course, Africa has a police force and judiciary system to catch and prosecute the thieves. But the police are themselves highway robbers, under orders to protect the looters, and many of the judges are themselves crooks. As a result, there are no checks against brigandage. The worst is the military—the most trenchantly perverted institution in Africa. In civilized society, the military is supposed to defend the territorial integrity of the nation and the people against external aggression. In Africa, the military is instead locked in combat with the very people it is supposed to defend.

Thus what exists in many African countries is a cabal of criminals and murderers whose members have monopolized both economic and political power as well as subverted state institutions to advance only their interests and to exclude everyone else's. It is this "apartheid-like" system that lies at the root of Africa's incessant woes and instability. Thus one word, *power*, explains why Africa is in the grip of a never-ending cycle of wanton chaos, horrific carnage, senseless civil wars, and collapsing economies: the struggle for power, its monopolization by one individual or group, and the subsequent refusal to relinquish or share it. Because politics constitutes the gateway to fabulous wealth in Africa, the competition for political power has always been ferocious. The "winner takes all" competition forces people to fight to "their very last man"—even if doing so means destroying the country. Political defeat could mean exile, jail, or starvation. Those who win power capture the state and proceed to transform it into their own personal property.

Over time, the vampire state metastasizes into a "coconut republic" and implodes, sucking the country into a vortex of savage carnage and heinous destruction: Somalia, Rwanda, Burundi, Zaire, Sierra Leone, Liberia, Togo, and Sudan. The process varies, but its onset follows two predictable response patterns. First, those exploited by the vampire state are eventually driven to exercise the "exit option": leave or reduce their exposure to the formal economy by smuggling and taking their activities to the underground economy or the black market. This process deprives the state of tax revenue and foreign exchange. Over time, the formal economy progressively shrinks, and the state finds it increasingly difficult to raise revenue as taxes are massively evaded, leading the ruling vampire elites to resort to printing money and inflate the economy.

Second, those excluded from the spoils of political power eventually rise up in a rebel insurgency or secede (Biafra in 1967). And it takes only a small band of determined ragtag malcontents to plunge the country into mayhem. In 1981, Yoweri Museveni, the current president of Uganda, started out with only twenty-seven men in a guerrilla campaign against Milton Obote. Charles Taylor, now the president of Liberia, set out with 150 rebels; the late Mohamed Farah Aidid of Somalia began with 200 rebels; and Paul Kagame of Rwanda set out with fewer than 250.

The adamant refusal of African despots and the ruling vampire elites to relinquish or share political power is what triggers an insurgency. The blockage of the democratic process or the refusal to hold elections plunged Angola, Chad, Ethiopia, Mozambique, Somalia, and Sudan into civil war. The manipulation of the *electoral process* by hardliners destroyed Rwanda (1993) and Sierra Leone (1992). The subversion of the *electoral process* in Liberia (1985) eventually set off a civil war in 1989 and instigated civil strife in Cameroon (1991), Congo (1992), Togo (1992), and Kenya (1992). The annulment of *electoral results* by the military started Algeria's civil war (1992) and plunged Nigeria into political turmoil (1993). Similarly, the manipulation of the *electoral process* precipitated Ivory Coast's crisis in 2000 and Togo's in 2005, as well as the current crisis in Zimbabwe.

The struggle over political power degenerates into civil strife or war. Chaos and carnage ensue. Infrastructure is destroyed. Food production and delivery are disrupted. Thousands are dislocated and flee, becoming internal refugees and placing severe strains on social systems of the resident population. Food supplies run out. Starvation looms.

The Western media bombard the international community with horrific pictures of rail-thin famine victims. Unable to bear the horror, the conscience of the international community is stirred to mount eleventh-hour humanitarian rescue missions. Foreign relief workers parachute into the disaster zone, dispensing high-protein biscuits, blankets, and portable toilets at hastily erected refugee camps. Refugees are rehabilitated, repatriated, and even airlifted. At the least sign of complication or trouble, the mission bogs down and is abandoned. That is, until another mafia African state implodes, and the same macabre ritual is repeated year after year. It seems that nothing—absolutely nothing—has been learned by all sides from the meltdowns of Somalia, Liberia, and Rwanda. As long as the politics of exclusion is practiced in Africa, there will be more civil strife, wars, and state collapse.

C. Western Culpability—The Failure of Western Aid

In destroying their economies, African tyrants received much help from the West—not so much out of willful intent or malice but rather out of sheer naiveté. In the postcolonial period, various Western governments, development agencies, and multilateral financial institutions have provided generous assistance to support Africa's development efforts. According to the Organisation for Economic Co-operation and Development (OECD), "the net disbursement of official development assistance (ODA), adjusted for inflation between 1960 and 1997 amounted to roughly $400 billion. In absolute magnitude, this would be equivalent to almost six Marshall Aid Plans" (Eberstadt 1998, B4).

The consensus among African development analysts is that foreign aid programs and multilateral lending to Africa have failed to spur economic growth, arrest Africa's economic atrophy, or promote democracy. The continent is littered with a multitude of black elephants (basilicas, grandiose monuments, grand conference halls, and showy airports) amid institutional decay, crumbling infrastructure, and environmental degradation.

The UN agrees: in 1999 it declared that "70 countries—all aid recipients—are now poorer than they were in 1980. An incredible 43 were worse off than in 1970. Chaos, slaughter, poverty and ruin stalked Third World states, irrespective of how much foreign assistance they received" (*Washington Post*, November 25, 1999).

The African countries that received the most aid—Liberia, Zaire, and Somalia—have slid into virtual anarchy. Another large Western aid recipient, Kenya, teeters on the brink of an economic collapse, while its government "inflicts unspeakable abuses of human rights on its own citizens while aid pays the bills" (Maren 1997, 11).

In a 1995 letter to U.S. Secretary of State Warren Christopher, the U.S. House of Representatives' International Relations Committee chairman, Benjamin Gilman—a Republican—and Lee H. Hamilton, a ranking Democratic member, wrote:

> Zaire under Mobutu represents perhaps the most egregious example of the misuse of U.S. assistance resources. The U.S. has given *Mobutu* nearly $1.5 billion in various forms of aid since Mobutu came to power in 1965. Mobutu claims that during the Cold War he and his fellow

African autocrats were concerned with fighting Soviet influence and were unable to concentrate on creating viable economic and political systems. The reality is that during this time Mr. Mobutu was becoming one of the world's wealthiest individuals while the people of Zaire, a once-wealthy country, were pauperized. (*Washington Times*, July 6, 1995)

Somalia is probably the most execrable example of a recipient of Western patronage gone berserk. Huge amounts of economic and disaster relief aid were dumped into Somalia, transforming the country into a graveyard of aid. But it was the massive inflow of food aid in the early 1980s that did much to shred the fabric of Somali society. Droughts and famines are not new to Africa, and most traditional societies developed indigenous methods of coping. The flood of cheap food aid destroyed these methods, and Somalia became more and more dependent on food imports. "The share of food import in the total volume of food consumption rose from less than 33 percent on average for the 1970–1979 period to over 63 percent during the 1980–1984 period, which coincides with Western involvement in the Somalia economy and food-aid programs" (Maren 1997, 171).

According to UNCTAD, "Despite many years of policy reform, barely any country in the region has successfully completed its adjustment program with a return to sustained growth. Indeed, the path from adjustment to improved performance is, at best, a rough one and, at worst, disappointing dead-end. Of the fifteen countries identified as 'core adjusters' by the World Bank in 1993, only three (Lesotho, Nigeria and Uganda) are now classified by the IMF as 'strong performer'" (UNCTAD 1998, xii). The World Bank itself evaluated the performance of twenty-nine African countries to which it had provided more than $20 billion in funding to sponsor structural adjustment programs (SAPs) over a ten-year period, 1981–1991. Its report, *Adjustment Lending in Africa*, released in March 1994, concluded that only six African countries had performed well: Gambia, Burkina Faso, Ghana, Nigeria, Tanzania, and Zimbabwe. Six out of twenty-nine gives a failure rate in excess of 80 percent. More distressing, the World Bank concluded that "no African country has achieved a sound macro-economic policy stance." Since then, the World Bank's list of "success stories" has shrunk. Gambia, Nigeria, and Zimbabwe were struck off the list on account of political turmoil. Even on Ghana, the World Bank's own Operations Evaluation Department noted in its December 1995 report that, "although Ghana has been projected as a success story, prospects for satisfactory growth rates and poverty reduction are uncertain" (World Bank 1995, 6).

In 1998, the West began touting Guinea, Lesotho, Eritrea, and Uganda as the new "success stories"—but not for long. The conflict in eastern Guinea, the senseless Ethiopian-Eritrean war, the eruption of civil strife after an army takeover in Lesotho in 1998, and the eruption of civil wars in western and northern Uganda have eclipsed their stardom.

"The West's record of aid for Africa in the past decade [1980s] can only be characterized as one of failure," declared Sir William Ryrie, executive vice president of the International Finance Corporation, a World Bank subsidiary (*Financial Times*, June 7, 1990). Nicholas Eberstadt wrote: "Western aid today may be compromising economic progress in Africa and retarding its development of human capital. . . . Western aid directly underwrites current policies and practices; indeed, it may actually make possible some of the more injurious policies, which would be impossible to finance without external help" (Eberstadt 1988, 100).

Many Africans would agree. David Karanja, a former Kenyan member of Parliament, for example, was blunt: "In fact, foreign aid has done more harm to Africa than we care to admit. It has led to a situation where Africa has failed to set its own pace and direction of development free of external interference" (*New African*, June 1992).

4. Fixing Africa

Private investment is the way out of Africa's economic miasma and grinding poverty. Africa needs investment in agriculture, manufacturing, education, health care, telecommunications, and infrastructure. But the continent has remained unattractive to investors. In fact, UNCTAD concluded that "Africa has lost attractiveness as [a] market for Foreign Direct Investment (FDI) as compared to other developing regions during the last two decades" (*African Observer*, November 30–December 13, 1998). This is yet another irony—or paradox.

Rates of return on investment in Africa are among the highest in the world. "Since 1990, the rate of return in Africa has averaged 29 percent; since 1991, it has been higher than in any other region, including developed countries as a group, and in many years by a factor of two or more" (UNCTAD 1999, 12). Net income or profit from British direct investment in sub-Saharan Africa (not including Nigeria) increased by 60 percent between 1989 and 1995 (Bennell 1997, 132). Furthermore, in 1995 Japanese affiliates in Africa were more profitable (after taxes) than in the early 1990s and were even more profitable than Japanese affiliates in any other region except for Latin America, the Caribbean, and west Asia. Earlier studies by UNCTAD also confirmed the high rate of return of foreign affiliates of transnational corporations in Africa (UNCTAD 1995). But foreign investors have stayed away from Africa. "Too often, Africa has been associated only with pictures of civil unrest, starvation, deadly diseases and economic disorder, and this has given many investors a negative picture of Africa as a whole" (UNCTAD 1999, 12).

For much of the time since 1970, foreign direct investment into Africa has increased only modestly—from an annual average of almost $1.9 billion in 1983–1987 to $3.1 billion in 1988–1992 and $6 billion in 1993–1997. Whereas inflows to developing countries as a group almost quadrupled, from less than $20 billion in 1981–1985 to an average of $75 billion in 1991–1995, inflows into Africa only doubled during that period. As a result, Africa's share in total inflows to developing countries dropped from more than 11 percent in 1976–1980 to 9 percent in 1981–1985, to 5 percent in 1991–1995, and to 4 percent in 1996–1997 (UNCTAD 1999, 13). "Net private direct investment in sub-Saharan Africa dwindled to $3.9 billion in 2002—a paltry sum and worse than in six of the seven previous years. . . . Even rich Africans do not invest in Africa: An estimated 40 percent of the continent's privately held wealth is stashed offshore" (*Economist*, January 17, 2004).

A. Enabling Environment

Investment does not occur in a vacuum but rather in an environment. Various government legislations, policies (taxes, duties, and subsidies), institutions, and attitudes shape this environment. Thus politics, law, ecology, and culture all form part of what may be called the "development environment."

When this environment is such that it encourages people to greater effort, it is described as "enabling" or "conducive" to productive effort. An "enabling environment" includes

- Security of persons and property
- System of incentives
- Rule of law
- Basic functioning infrastructure
- Stability: economic, political, and social
- Basic freedoms: intellectual, political, and economic

It should be obvious to even the most casual observer that the requirements for an "enabling environment" have not been met in most African countries. African governments have recklessly banished the rule of law and wreaked mayhem across the continent, scattering human debris and wanton devastation in their wake. Even Julius Nyerere, former president of Tanzania and spokesman for African leaders, noted in a speech at the University of Edinburgh on October 9, 1997, "The necessary conditions for attracting foreign direct investment are simply not there yet in most African countries" (*PanAfrican News*, September 1998). It was an astonishing statement to come from Julius Nyerere, an avowed African socialist and deeply suspicious of private capital. The tragedy is that his domestic record and legacy were riddled with massive economic failures and policy blunders that left Tanzanians worse off than they were at independence in 1962. With an income per capita of $210, Tanzania is among the seven poorest nations in the world.

The first requirement of an enabling environment, *security of persons and property*, derives from the commonsensical fact that a person's first interest is survival. No farmer, regardless of his level of education, would go to his farm and double output when bombs go off in the middle of the night and his own life is in danger. Nor would any entrepreneur or investor establish a company that can be arbitrarily seized by gun-toting bandits.

In most places in Africa, people live in fear of their lives and property. In 1996, civil war and strife raged in at least seventeen African countries: Algeria, Angola, Burundi, Central African Republic, Chad, Congo, Djibouti, Egypt, Mozambique, Liberia, Rwanda, Senegal, Sierra Leone, Somalia, Sudan, Uganda, and Zaire. These senseless wars uprooted millions of peasants and caused severe dislocations in agricultural production. By that year, Africa's refugee count, including internally displaced persons and returnees, had reached twenty-two million—about one-third of the world's total. The costs of these wars are impossible to calculate, but most experts believe that Africa's agricultural production would increase by as much as 30 percent if the civil wars would end.

The second requirement is a *system of incentives*. There are two ways of inducing greater productive effort from people. One is to provide them with incentives. For example, people may be praised, honored, or rewarded for certain patriotic acts. The other way is to remove disincentives that discourage them. Nothing rewards people better than enjoying the fruits of their own labor. People do not engage in economic activity for altruistic reasons. Peasant farmers do not break their backs in the hot sun to produce maize because of patriotism. They do so because they want to earn a living, feed their families, and survive. If market prices rise, the rise gives farmers the incentive to produce more. Thus the market's price mechanism operates as a system of incentives. By rising and falling, prices perform an important economic function. The "signals" that prices transmit influence the allocation of resources. Anything that interferes with the operation of the price mechanism, therefore, not only reduces the effectiveness of incentives but also leads to distortions in the allocation of resources. Price controls, security checkpoints (or roadblocks), and poor road conditions that impede the free movement of goods are examples of such interference. The removal of these impediments may induce greater production.

The importance of a freely functioning price system cannot be overemphasized. Such a system was always the rule in traditional Africa, where prices on village markets fluctuated freely. Traditional African chiefs seldom fixed prices or interfered with the free-market system.

The third requirement is the *rule of law*. A well-functioning legal system offers security of persons and property. It also ensures that the laws of the land are obeyed by all. In other words, the law "rules," taking precedence over the whims or caprices of individuals. For example, the law may say that it is larceny to acquire property by stealing it from someone else. Anyone guilty of such a felony, whether that person is a doctor, a chief, or even the president of the country, shall be prosecuted and punished for all to see. Embezzlement or theft of public funds falls into this category because the victim is the taxpayer. And when one's security is threatened or one's property is stolen, one does not "take the law into one's own hands" but rather follows established procedure to seek a redress, usually by hauling the culprit, even if it is the government, into a court of law. When these conditions are met, the rule of law, which means respecting and following established ways of doing things, is said to prevail.

The rule of law is important for economic development because the constitution and the system of laws define the parameters or the legal framework within which economic activity or competition takes place. If the parameters are constantly being shifted or violated, confusion, uncertainty, or even chaos may result. Economically, it is difficult to make investment plans when laws are suddenly abrogated and new decrees are issued without notice and take immediate effect. People cannot be expected to follow the rules when the authorities themselves flout the law or apply it capriciously to favor one person over another. It would not be fair to a competitor to see a rival company blatantly violating the law while the authorities look the other way. And yanking a company's license to operate simply because the president of the country dislikes the owner's political views or ethnicity can have a chilling effect on business investment and innovation.

To ensure that the rule of law prevails, the most fundamental prerequisite is the existence of an independent and impartial judiciary. The judges must not all be appointed by the president or hail from his ethnic group. And judges must be free to deliberate on issues without fear of incurring government displeasure and even to reach verdicts against the government without fear of being abducted and murdered—as happened to three Ghanaian judges in 1982.

The rule of law does not exist in many African countries where the leaders themselves and their ministers flout the law. African governments arbitrarily seize people's private property with impunity. People cannot obtain relief from the court system because the judiciary is just another organ of the kleptocratic government, which appoints judges and justices of the peace. The police, the military, and security forces that are supposed to protect the citizens are themselves the abductors, the killers, and the thieves.

Looting and arbitrary seizures of property by undisciplined soldiers have become rampant in much of Africa, discouraging not only foreign but also domestic investment. Fed up, an irate Bedford N. Umez, a Nigerian professor of government at Lee College in Texas, said: "Even wild animals protect their own territories. These wild beasts, as we call them, use their own common sense to hunt together, share the price of their bounties together and, most important, protect their territories together. Not so the embezzlers of our public funds. A man who denies himself, his parents and his children good roads, hospitals, education, clean air and water by providing such amenities to his enemies [the rich countries] needs help—he is sick in the head (*African News Weekly*, October 7–13, 1996).

"Nigeria is the most corrupt nation in the world," according to Transparency International (*Houston Chronicle*, July 28, 1996). Between 1970 and the early 1980s, when oil prices collapsed, $100 billion in oil money flowed into Nigerian government coffers. Nigerians are now asking what happened to the "oil money." According to the *Washington Post* (July 21, 1992), "corruption robs Nigeria's economy of an estimated $2 billion to $3 billion each year" (p. A16).

In the most pernicious types of kleptocracy, such as Angola, Kenya, Nigeria, and Zaire, the heads of state and their entourages systematically looted the wealth of the countries. Corruption in modern Africa has several deleterious effects on economic development.

Corruption drives away foreign investors: "Government contracts in Nigeria, say international businessmen, are among the most expensive in the world 'mainly because of excessive margins built into such contracts for personal interests.' Those personal interests can be seen as attending expensive schools in Britain, or parked outside plush government villas: a Maserati or Lamborghini is quite normal for an army chief" (*Economist*, August 21, 1993). "In Cameroon, foreign investors are particularly discouraged that the justice system is the most corrupt of all government departments," said Severin Tchonkeu, publisher of the independent French-language newspaper, *L'Expression*. "It is often easier now to bribe a judge for a favorable judgment than to pay a lawyer to argue a case. Lawyers are retained only in the most complicated cases, where several judges and Justice Ministry officials need to be bribed" (*Washington Times*, November 5, 1998).

The fourth requirement of an enabling environment is a *basic functioning infrastructure*. Some basic infrastructure, such as roads, schools, electricity, water, and telephone services, is essential to economic development, and it must function reliably. A factory will have difficulty with production if there are frequent interruptions in the power supply. And if factory owners must install their own power generators, water supply, or mobile telephone systems, the cost of production will increase and be passed on to the consumer in the form of higher prices. Such prices would place the business at a competitive disadvantage, making it difficult to compete with imports.

Infrastructure has crumbled in many African countries. The educational system is a shambles. Roads are potholed. Hospitals lack basic supplies, and patients are often asked to bring their own bandages and blankets. When the late president Mobutu Sese Seko of Zaire fell ill, he flew to France for treatment. "Zimbabwe's phone system is so notoriously bad [that] many businesses use messengers and personal visits instead" (*Economist*, March 2, 1996). In Nigeria, "besides the collapse of the fuel distribution system, the telephone network is decaying. The electrical grid is failing. Almost no part of Lagos—the steaming, teeming financial and commercial capital—gets electricity all day, and vast tracts of the city of 8 million never get power at all" (*Washington Post*, June 9, 1998).

Caution needs to be sounded on building infrastructure because ego and delusions of grandeur often enter the equation. The late president Felix Houphouet-Boigny of Ivory Coast built a new capital at his hometown, Yamassoukro, with wide, tree-lined streets and a basilica. More goats use the streets than cars. The late president Mobutu Sese Seko transformed his village hometown, Gbadolite, into the "Versailles of the Jungle," complete with an airport large enough to accommodate the Concorde. Such infrastructure, built specifically at the whim of the president, hardly serves any useful economic purpose because it is used only occasionally by the president and the ruling elite.

The fifth requirement is *economic, political, and social stability*. People and businesses need a stable world in which to conduct and plan their daily activities. People cannot make production decisions or increase agricultural production when bombs go off in the middle of the night and everything is in chaos. Stability has several aspects: political, economic (monetary, price), and social.

A political system is stable if, after an election, the system returns, not necessarily with the same head of state but at least to the same bedrock of principles on which it was founded: democracy, rule of law, accountability, freedom of expression, and so on. That is, the system must have the capability to sustain itself year after year without violent and chaotic change. Political stability is not assured by having one buffoon declare himself president-for-life and keep all power to himself. That kind of "stability" is artificial because groups excluded from power sharing and decision making will plot to overthrow or battle the government for inclusion. These activities result in violence and civil strife—hardly the environment that encourages development.

Economic stability is also required for development. Both producers and consumers need assurances that the economic system will not suddenly be overthrown and replaced with a convoluted one, that banks will continue to exist and function, and that the currency they have stashed under their mattresses will continue to have value. Peasant farmers need to be assured that markets will still be there and that the farmers will not be uprooted and forcibly resettled on government farms or ordered to sell their produce to government agencies.

Monetary stability means that the currency, the banks, and the monetary system as a whole continue to function smoothly without major upheavals. It means that Amna will not find that the *zonga* is no longer legal tender because overnight the government replaced it with a new currency without giving people time to exchange the old for the new currency.

In Africa, stability, especially political stability, has been elusive. Groups excluded from power agitate for inclusion, and excluded groups may resort to civil disobedience. Chaos and strife ensue. The chaos may even be deliberate: "'Don't be deceived by the chaos,' said one experienced Western businessman. 'Mobutu likes it this way. With hyperinflation it's easy for foreigners to make money, and it's the cut from foreigners that fills his pockets. With no roads, the army can never topple him. With no communications, the opposition can never organize. With total corruption, it's every man for himself and people can be picked off one by one'" (*Vanity Fair*, November 1994).

A peculiar form of stability prevails in many African countries— stability wrought by impoverishment and repression. In Zimbabwe, according to Paul Taylor, an American journalist, "There's [a] big enough patronage base in the civil service and parastatal companies, which together account for about 35 percent of the economy, for the Mugabe government to keep a firm grip on power. Ministers get rich, political opponents get weary, the masses get poorer. The country is stable" (*Washington Post*, April 9, 1995).

To rebuff any threats to their authority, insecure African regimes invest heavily in the military and security forces. The salaries of such forces consume a huge portion of the budget. But the tax base is small. To generate the revenue, the government slaps a tax on anything that moves. The regime may seek foreign aid or loans, but much of it is used to pay the salaries of civil servants and to import consumer goods and weapons for the military. If access to foreign credit is tight, the regime may simply print the necessary money to finance government expenditures and political campaigns. For example, "In the 1992 election campaign, Moi's cronies established a network of 'political banks' that siphoned money out of the Central Bank and pumped it into the ruling party's campaign. This brazen abuse of the monetary system to finance the campaign almost doubled the money supply in six months, creating 100 percent inflation" (*Atlantic Monthly*, February 1996).

And how much confidence do Africans have in the banking system? "No sense putting money in the bank," says Hilal El-Jamal, a refrigerator merchant in Ghana. "Dig a hole and bury it, or better, build something with it" (*West Africa*, May 8–14, 1995). Economists estimate that 50 percent of Ghana's money supply lies outside the banks.

In Nigeria, the banking system is on the verge of collapse. Most banks are unable to meet their obligations to customers. Depositors often are not allowed to withdraw amounts in excess of 1,000 *naira* ($110), regardless of their credit balances. In June 1995 hundreds of irate depositors took action. At the Onitsha Branch of the Mercantile Bank at Owerri Road in Lagos, they held the staff hostage and demanded to withdraw their money from the bank. "The bank manager maintained that there was not enough cash on hand to satisfy this great number of customers. In response, the depositors blocked all entrances to the bank and would not permit staff members to leave" (*African News Weekly*, June 2, 1995). Depositors were infuriated by a notice on the door of the Ikolaje/Idi-Iroko Community Bank stating that "we have been forced to close shop as a result of external auditors certification. . . . A team of auditors had examined the bank's records and found them wanting" (*African News Weekly*, June 9, 1995).

The sixth requirement for an enabling environment is *basic freedoms*: intellectual, political, and economic. People must have some measure of freedom to make decisions. At the individual level, farmers, for example, must be free to determine what type of crops to cultivate, how much of their produce to consume with their family, where the surplus must be sold, and at what price. The government cannot make these decisions for millions of farmers. Similarly, consumers must be free to determine for themselves what products to purchase and at what prices. If an item is too expensive, consumers may decline to purchase it, buy a substitute, or produce the item themselves. Consumers know what is best for them. Consequently, economic actors must have the freedom to make these decisions for themselves.

People must have the freedom to express themselves, their beliefs, thoughts, and ideas; the freedom to live where and when they choose; the freedom to practice a religion of their own choice; the freedom to produce and market goods of their choice; the freedom to belong to or form any association—trade, religious, economic, or political; the freedom from arbitrary arrest; and the freedom from tyrannical rule or despotism. These freedoms may be grouped into intellectual, economic, and political freedoms as well as human rights. On each type, Africa scores worse than do other regions in the Third World.

According to New York–based Freedom House, of Africa's fifty-four countries, only eight have a free press. Of the twenty countries throughout the world where the press is most shackled, nine are in Africa: Algeria, Burundi, Egypt, Equatorial Guinea, Libya, Nigeria, Somalia, Sudan, and Zaire. Countries in the "not free" category include Angola, Cameroon, Central African Republic, Chad, Eritrea, Ghana, Guinea, Ivory Coast, Kenya, Liberia, Mauritania, Rwanda, Sierra Leone, Swaziland, Togo, and Tunisia (Freedom House 2003).

A similar situation exists for political freedoms. Of the fifty-four African countries, only sixteen are democratic: Benin, Botswana, Cape Verde Islands, Ghana, Kenya, Madagascar, Malawi, Mali, Mauritius, Namibia, Sao Tome & Principe, Senegal, Seychelles, South Africa, and Zambia. Political tyranny is still the order of the day.

Economic freedom has also been elusive in Africa. The Heritage Foundation and the *Wall Street Journal* annually compile an Index of Economic Freedom. According to their 2001 index:

> Sub-Saharan Africa remains the most economically unfree—and by far the poorest—area in the world. Of the 42 sub-Saharan African countries graded, none received a free rating. Only five (12 percent

regionally) received a rating of mostly free—a decline from last year's seven—while 29 were rated mostly unfree and two were rated repressed. (Angola, Burundi, Democratic Republic of Congo, Sierra Leone, Somalia and Sudan were excluded from the study because of the unreliability of available data caused by political instability, outright civil war, or lack of central government) (Heritage Foundation 2002).

There were some improvements in 2004. According to the Heritage Foundation and the *Wall Street Journal* Index of Economic Freedom (2004), nine African countries came to be classified as mostly free (Botswana, Uganda, South Africa, Cape Verde Islands, Morocco, Mauritania, Tunisia, Namibia, and Mauritius). Zimbabwe was the worst African performer, ranking 153rd out of 155 countries. However, no African country received a free rating.

In sum, the greatest obstacle to Africa's development is the absence of an enabling environment. Note that this obstacle is human-made—created by African governments themselves. As such it can be removed only by human action from within Africa. To establish an enabling environment, Africa's vampire states must be reformed. This reform entails political pluralism, market liberalization, decentralization or diffusion of power, respect for the rule of law, and the adoption of power-sharing arrangements. The politics of exclusion must be replaced by the politics of inclusion. The elites should seek their wealth in the private sector by actually producing something. Government does not produce wealth; it only redistributes it. In addition, state institutions must be reformed so that transparency, accountability, and professionalism prevail.

B. The Acrobatics on Reform

African despots are loath to relinquish control or power. They would rather destroy their economies and countries than give up economic and political power. This power allows them to allocate or extract resources to build personal fortunes and to dispense patronage to buy political support. Their business empires will collapse if economic reform strips them of state controls. Economic liberalization may also undermine their ability to maintain their political support base and thus prove suicidal. Thus they profit from their own mismanagement of the economy.

The second reason for clinging to power is the fear that their gory past misdeeds may be exposed should they step down from power. So they stay in office at all costs, regardless of the consequences for the economy or the country. Witness the tortuous acrobatics of President Hosni Mubarak of Egypt as he waffles over the implementation of democracy. Thus the country is sentenced to perpetual misery because no meaningful reform is possible unless the "obstacle" is removed.

In short, most African leaders lack the competence and credibility to institute real reform. Nor are they interested in it. They implement only the minimum cosmetic reforms that would ensure continued flow of Western aid. Africans deride the posturing, tricks, and acrobatics as "Babangida Boogie": one step forward, three steps back, a sidekick, and a flip to land on a fat Swiss bank account.

More scandalous perhaps has been the ready supply of Western dance partners. The Kenyan version of this ritual dance, the *Moi massamba,* was well-described by the *Economist* (August 19, 1995): "Over the past few years, Kenya has performed a curious mating ritual with its aid donors. The steps are: One, Kenya wins its yearly pledges of foreign aid. Two, the government begins to misbehave, backtracking on economic reform and behaving in an authoritarian manner. Three, a new meeting of donor countries looms with exasperated foreign governments preparing their sharp rebukes. Four, Kenya pulls a placatory rabbit out of the hat. Five, the donors are mollified and aid is pledged. The whole dance then starts again" (p. 37).

Ask African leaders to develop their countries, and they will develop their pockets. Ask them to establish better systems of governance, and they will set up a "Ministry of Good Governance" (Tanzania). Ask them to curb corruption, and they will set up an "Anti-Corruption Commission" with no teeth and then sack the commissioner if he gets too close to the fat cats (Kenya). Ask them to establish democracy, and they will empanel a coterie of fawning sycophants to write the electoral rules, hold fraudulent elections with opposition leaders either disqualified or in jail, and return themselves to power (Ivory Coast, Rwanda). Ask them to reduce state hegemony in the economy and place more reliance on the private sector, and they will create a Ministry of Private Enterprise (Ghana). Ask them to privatize inefficient state-owned enterprises, and they will sell them off at fire-sale prices to their cronies. In 1992, in accordance with World Bank loan conditions, the government of Uganda began a privatization effort to sell off 142 of its state-owned enterprises. However, in 1998, the process was halted twice by Uganda's own Parliament because, according to the chair of a parliamentary select committee, Tom Omongole, it had been "derailed by corruption," implicating three senior ministers who had "political responsibility" (*East African*, June 14, 1999). The sale of these 142 enterprises was initially projected to generate 900 billion Ugandan shillings (Ushs) or $500 million. However, by the autumn of 1999 the revenue balance was only 3.7 billion Ushs.

Now their recalcitrance has been turned into extortion. Ask them to move a foot, and they will demand foreign aid in order to do so. In 2003, some thirty thousand ghost names were discovered on the payroll of Ghana's Ministry of Education, costing the government $1.2 million a month in salaries heisted by living workers. When Ghana demanded foreign aid to purge these ghost names, Japan coughed up $5 million. Foreign aid has done nothing to help reform African governance.

Accordingly, the reform process has stalled through vexatious chicanery, willful deception, strong-arm tactics, and vaunted acrobatics. In 1990, only four of the fifty-four African countries were democratic. This tiny number grew to sixteen in 2004. Thus political tyranny is still the order of the day.

5. How to Develop Africa

To develop Africa, two fundamental distinctions are necessary. The first is between African elites and the African peasants or people. The leaders (drawn from the elite class), not the people, have been the problem, and criticizing failed leaders does not mean one hates black people. The slate of postcolonial African leaders has been a disgusting assortment of "Swiss-bank socialists," military *fufu*-heads, quack revolutionaries, crocodile liberators, and brief-case bandits whose single-minded purpose was to impose themselves on their people and raid the national treasury. The exceptions have been few.

The second distinction is even more important—between modern Africa and traditional Africa, with a transitional informal sector between them. The vast majority of the African people live in the informal and traditional sectors. Africa cannot be developed by ignoring the two sectors; nor can the two sectors be developed without understanding how they work. But these were precisely the two sectors that African leaders and elites neglected. Traditional Africa works—albeit at a low level of efficiency—and has sustained its people for centuries. Modern Africa, the abode of the parasitic elite minority, is, by contrast, dysfunctional, lost, and collapsing. It has been the source of most of Africa's problems, engulfing the informal and traditional sectors, causing disruptions and dislocations, and claiming innocent victims. These three Africas do not operate by the same principles and logic.

Traditional or rural Africa is the home of the real people of Africa—the peasant majority who produce the real wealth of Africa: agricultural produce, cash crops (cocoa, coffee, tea, etc.), timber, minerals, sculpture, and other artifacts. They lack formal education, but they have raw native intelligence and skills. African natives have always been free enterprisers, going about their daily economic activities on their own volition. They do not queue before their rulers' palaces or huts for permission to engage in trade, fishing, or agriculture. They produce surpluses that are sold on free village markets, where prices are determined by bargaining, not by dictates from the tribal government. Their traditional societies are generally peaceful and stable. They live in harmony not only with others but also with their natural environment, including wildlife. They run their societies with their own unique political and economic institutions.

A careful study of their "primitive" societies reveals an astonishing degree of functionality: participatory forms of democracy, rule of customary law, and accountability. Their system of government was so open that some allowed participation by foreign merchants. No modern country, even the United States, can boast of such an open government. Africa's traditional rulers were no despots, despite their characterization as such by European colonialists in order to justify various pacification campaigns.

The ruler was surrounded by various councils, bodies, and institutions to prevent abuses of power and corruption. Furthermore, the ruler was held accountable for his actions at all times and could be removed at any time if he was corrupt or failed to govern according to the will of the people. "Under most traditional African constitutions, bad or ineffective rulers were more readily removed from office than most modern constitutions allow. Divine kingship does not absolve a ruler from removal if he fails to live up to his responsibilities or constitutional duties. Important decisions were made only after necessary discussions and consultations had been made. Akan kings had no right to make peace or war, make laws, or be directly involved in important negotiations such as treaties without the consent of their elders and/or elected representatives" (Boamah-Wiafe 1993, 169).

Modern Africa, by contrast, is a meretricious fandango of imported or borrowed institutions that is little understood by the elites themselves. The end product is a mass of confusion and an internally contradictory system that bears no affinity to either the indigenous system or the colonial state. It is a ludicrous monstrosity that was created by the ruling elites themselves after independence by copying and grafting here and there from foreign systems they hardly comprehended. Over time, it evolved into the present-day bizarre politico-economic system that admits of no rule of law, no accountability, no democracy of any form, and even no sanity. There is utter institutional chaos and misgovernance. Here common sense has been murdered, and arrogant lunacy rampages with impunity. At the helm of the affairs of the state is a "hardened coconut" who has debauched all key institutions of government—the military, judiciary, civil service, banking, and law enforcement. "Government" resembles a mafia or a gangster state that evolves into a coconut republic and eventually implodes.

From the 1970s until the twenty-first century, considerable effort and resources were invested in cajoling the ruling vampire elites to reform the African mafia state and the modern sector. They were bribed with foreign aid to reform their abominable political systems. The World Bank and the IMF popped in with structural adjustment loans to help reform decrepit state-controlled economies. Buzzwords such as *reliance on the private sector, market economies, accountability, transparency,* and *governance* all punctuated the air. But as we saw earlier, much of this drive fizzled after billions of dollars were spent. The democratization process stalled, and economic liberalization went kaput.

It should be clear that the modern sector is beyond redemption and nonreformable by the ruling vampire elites. They are simply not interested in reform. In fact, it would be economically and politically suicidal for them to do so. But the refusal of the ruling elite to implement real reform will continue to produce never-ending crises on the continent. In fact, for much of the past forty years or so, the bulk of the energies of gangster African governments has been absorbed in damage control and crisis management—managing scandals and such crises as budget crisis, debt crisis, foreign exchange crisis, AIDS crisis, agricultural crisis, and environmental crisis, affording governments little time to devote to real African development. When one is shuttling back and forth between creditors in ragged clothes, begging for alms, one has little time to craft a new vision for Africa.

At some point, even those most recklessly optimistic about Africa would have to come to terms with the law of diminishing returns: pumping more and more aid to reform Africa's dysfunctional modern sector to induce gangster regimes to implement reforms will yield less and less in results. The rogue African state should be left to the fate it deserves—implosion and state collapse. Greater returns can be achieved elsewhere by channeling aid to the traditional and informal sectors where the majority of the African people live. The future of Africa does not lie, for the moment, in the crisis-laden modern sector. Nor does it ride on the backs of dysfunctional elites who are incapable of learning from their own horrendous mistakes. Rather, it rides on the backs of the peasants, their cutlasses, and other "primitive" implements. The real challenge of economic development is how to use or improve upon their existing institutions and technology to lift them out of poverty. It entails approaching them with humility, appreciating the contributions they can make, studying their traditional system, asking them what sort of assistance they need, and devising new initiatives and simple technologies that fit into their cultural and socioeconomic environment. It requires going to the villages and living with the peasants. In short, it requires a completely new mentality and willingness to give the peasants a better deal in the current economic and political dispensation.

Unfortunately, few have been able to meet this challenge in Africa, despite a swarm of foreign aid workers and development experts working in partnership with various African governments. African governments and elites held the peasants in contempt and castigated their native institutions. Few were willing to live in the villages. And if they ever visited the villages, they arrogantly marched off to "educate" and "teach" the peasants about "modern and scientific" farming techniques and to feed them empty revolutionary slogans. This old development approach, characterized by "elite dysfunctionalism," got Africa nowhere. That approach was geared toward wiping out peasants and the traditional system because they were "backward" and imitating symbols of modernity either to "prove something" or to "impress" foreigners. The peasants or the urban poor were an eyesore and did not fit into this modernization scheme.

From the outside, few of the multitudes of development experts and foreign aid workers were in a position to help the peasants. For one thing, they had to work through corrupt elite-run governments to reach the peasants, with frustrating results. The cultural gap was another obstacle. Few understood the peasants' cultural practices and beliefs and the complexities of the traditional system. Thus one often encounters a situation where foreign aid workers, in noble humanitarian endeavors, are trying to help people they do not understand. Innocent but tragic miscalculations often occur.

To take Africa to the next level, a completely new approach or paradigm is required. The new paradigm turns the old one completely upside down. It shatters myths, places the peasant full-square at the center, and starts from the bottom up rather than the top down. Furthermore, it seeks to liberate the peasant from the chains of tyranny, mismanagement, misgovernance, ignorance, disease, and abject poverty. Instead of marching off to the villages to "teach" the peasants, perhaps it is rather the peasants who can teach the dysfunctional elites a thing or two about agriculture and governance. After all, the peasants have been farming for centuries. Elitism is just a new phenomenon, emerging after independence. And the elite had better be humble enough to learn from the peasants because there is a treasure trove of useful knowledge embedded in the peasants' traditional system that the elite can discover and use.

A. Africa's Indigenous Economic System

There is still much misconception among both foreign observers and African leaders about Africa's indigenous economic system. Africa's traditional economic system was not "primitive communism" or "socialism" (see Ayittey 1991, especially ch. 8). Many tribal societies had no state planning or direction of economic activity; nor were there state enterprises or widespread state ownership.

The means of production were privately owned. Huts, spears, and agricultural implements were all private property. The profit motive was present in most market transactions. Free enterprise and free trade were the rule in indigenous Africa. The natives went about their economic activities on their own initiative and free will. They did not line up at the entrance of the chief's hut to apply for permits before engaging in trade or production. What and how much they produced were their own decisions to make. The African woman who produced *kenkey*, *garri*, or *semolina* decided to produce those goods herself. No one forced her to do so. Nor did anyone instruct fishers, artisans, craftspeople, or even hunters what to produce.

In modern parlance, those who go about their economic activities on their own free will are called "free enterprisers." By this definition, the *kente* weavers of Ghana, the Yoruba sculptors, the gold-, silver-, and blacksmiths, as well as the various indigenous craftspeople, traders, and farmers were free enterprisers. The natives have been so for centuries. The Masai, Somali, Fulani, and other pastoralists who herded cattle over long distances in search of water and pasture also were free enterprisers. So were the African traders who traveled great distances to buy and sell commodities—a risk-taking economic venture.

The extended family system offered them the security they needed to take the risks associated with entrepreneurial activity. Many development experts overlooked these positive economic aspects of the much-maligned extended family system. Although this system entailed some "sharing" (which was not forced or proportionate), it also provided the springboard for Africans to launch themselves into highly risky ventures. If they failed, the extended family system was available to support them. By the same token, if they were successful, they had some obligation to the system that supported them. The Fanti have this proverb: *Obra nyi woara abo* (Life is as you make it within the community).

Even in commerce, African states lacked state controls and ownership. In the Gold Coast, for example, gold mining was open to all subjects of the states of Adanse, Assin, Denkyira, and Mampong. Chiefs did benefit from mining: some chiefs taxed mining operations at the rate of one-fifth of the annual output, and in some states, all gold mined on certain days was ceded to the throne. But the mines were in general not owned and operated by the chiefs. Any villager could mine or pan for gold on any unoccupied land. Foreign entities needed mining concessions from the chiefs.

Much of the indigenous economic system still exists today where African governments have not destroyed it through misguided policies and civil wars. Female traders still can be found at the markets. They still trade their wares for profit. And in virtually all African markets today, one still bargains over prices.

B. Indigenous Africa Under Colonial Rule

When Africa was colonized, the colonialists sought to control indigenous economic activities to their advantage. Africa's colonial history is replete with successes and failures of these policies. For example, on the Gold Coast (now Ghana), European mining companies sought legislative curtailment of indigenous mining operations without success. The two operated side by side throughout the colonial era.

Notably absent during that era were state or colonial government enterprises. A few large European companies dominated the field, but no indigenous economic activity was reserved exclusively for the colonial government or European companies. Nor would the colonial administrations have been successful had they attempted such repression, which would have entailed an extraordinary expenditure of resources. Africa then had not developed the communications and transportation networks needed for effective control of the natives, and their economic activities and costs were one reason why the British adopted the policy of "indirect rule"—administration through the chiefs.

For the most part, the natives were free to go about their economic activities. In western Africa, European settlement was confined to the urban enclaves, and the rural areas were left almost intact. In central and southern Africa, the story was a little different. The plunder and barbarous atrocities against the natives in King Leopold's Congo need no belaboring. In southern Africa, where the climate was more congenial to European settlement, there were widespread land seizures, massive dislocation of the natives, and restrictions on their movements and places of residence. Pass laws in apartheid South Africa and land seizures in Angola, Namibia, Mozambique, and Zimbabwe can be recalled. Nonetheless, despite the formidable odds, the natives could open shops and compete with the European firms. Many did and were successful. There

were rich African shopkeepers as well as timber merchants, transport owners, and farmers during the colonial period. African natives have always
welcomed foreigners and foreign firms, provided the foreigners were willing to play fair. And given the opportunities and access to capital, African
natives showed themselves capable of competing with the foreigners.

C. The Golden Age of Peasant Prosperity

The period 1880–1950 may be characterized as the golden age of
peasant prosperity in Africa. Although colonialism was invidious, one of
its little-known and -acknowledged "benefits" was the peace it brought to
Africa. The slave trade and competition over resources had fueled many
of the tribal wars in precolonial Africa—just as competition over mineral
resources, in particular diamonds, fueled wars in Angola, Congo, Liberia,
and Sierra Leone in the twenty-first century. The slave trade generates
intense emotional reaction among blacks. Unfortunately, however, there
is much confusion and mythology about African participation in that
abominable trade.

The abolition of the slave trade in the 1840s eliminated a casus
bellum and made apparent the need to provide an alternative to the trade
in human cargo. Toward this end, cash crops were introduced into Africa.
About this time, the Industrial Revolution was gathering momentum in
Europe. Factories needed raw materials and markets for manufactured
products. Colonies could provide both: raw materials and markets. Tribal
wars and rivalries virtually came to halt, although they flared up occasionally. Their amelioration gave Africa a much-needed atmosphere of
peace for productive economic activity. In addition, skeletal forms of infrastructure (roads, railways, bridges, schools, post office, etc.) were laid
down during this period, greatly facilitating the movement of goods and
people. This infrastructural development really gave production and economic expansion a tremendous boost. The secret to economic prosperity
in Africa is not hard to find. A mere three words unveil this secret: *peace,
infrastructure*, and *economic freedom*.

It is instructive to note that the economic system used by the natives of Africa to engineer their economic prosperity in the 1880–1950
period was their own indigenous system. Except for a few places in Africa,
notably in the Portuguese colonies, plantation agriculture was unknown.
Cash crops were grown by peasant farmers on their own individual plots,

using traditional farming methods and practices. In other words, the natives prospered using their own existing indigenous system with only minor modifications and improvements. For example, the cultivation of cocoa was not mechanized; it was a highly labor-intensive undertaking. Transportation of cocoa in the early twentieth century was by human portage, which gave rise to the pricing of cocoa by the "head load." The building of roads and the introduction of motor vehicles tremendously improved the transportation of cocoa and boosted exports, and there were other improvements as well: insecticides, spraying machines, and so on. But the basic system of land tenure and the peasants' discretion over what crops to grow and so on were unchanged. African peasants were generally not forced to cultivate any cash crops. Forced labor in the French, Belgian, and Portuguese colonies was mainly for construction purposes.

The fundamental point is that African natives had the economic freedom to decide for themselves what crops they could cultivate—cash crops or food crops—and what to do with the proceeds. This economic freedom was a notable feature of their indigenous economic system. Indeed, Kendall and Louw (1986)—two white South Africans—noted: "The freedom that characterized tribal society in part explains why black South Africans responded so positively to the challenges of a free market that, by the 1870s, they were out-competing whites, especially as farmers" (p. 4).

Although this freedom was circumscribed under colonialism in central and southern Africa, the peasants prospered during the colonial era. Why, then, were they unable to continue prospering after independence? The answer is obvious: their economic freedom was somehow snatched from them.

D. The Onset of Economic Repression and Destruction

The move away from economic freedom came first in South Africa, where, according to Kendall and Louw (1986):

> Black success had tragic consequences. White colonists feared black competition and this fear, combined with the whites' desire for cheap labor, resulted in a series of laws that systematically denied blacks access to the marketplace and stripped them of any meaningful form of land ownership. (p. 4)

Kendall and Louw (1986) continued:

> The truth is that white farmers felt threatened by blacks. Not only were
> blacks better farmers but they were also competing with white farmers
> for land. Moreover, they were self-sufficient and hence not available to
> work on white farms or in industry, particularly in the Transvaal gold
> mines where their labor was badly needed. As a result a series of laws
> was passed that robbed blacks of almost all economic freedom. The
> purpose of these laws was to prevent blacks from competing with whites
> and to drive them into the work force. (p. 12)

In 1869, 1876, and 1884 the Cape Assembly passed a series of
Location Acts (the first set of apartheid laws) that sought to protect white
farmers from black competition and to force blacks to become wage laborers by working for white farmers. Then came the Native Land Act of
1913; the rest is history.

In the rest of Africa, the turn toward statism and the attendant
restrictions on economic freedom came after independence. Support services and infrastructure were not provided by new elites. Traditional Africa was castigated by the elites as "backward and primitive." Peasant
agriculture was neglected in favor of industry. Chiefs and Africa's traditional rulers were stripped of their power and authority. Foreign ideologies were imposed on the peasants, and their economic freedom was
wrenched from them while their economic prosperity was taxed and
squandered by vampire elites through a series of edicts, state controls,
and decrees.

After independence, many African governments not only nationalized European companies, ostensibly to prevent "foreign exploitation,"
but also barred the natives from many economic fields. For example, after Ghana gained its independence, mining operations were monopolized
by the state, and indigenous gold mining was declared illegal. In fact,
"Anyone caught indulging in illegal gold prospecting, popularly known
as 'galamsey' (gather them and sell), will be shot, a PNDC representative announced to a workers' rally in the Western Region" (*West Africa*,
March 1, 1982).

In many other African countries, the natives were squeezed out
of industry, trade, and commerce, and the state emerged as the domi-
neering, if not the only, player. Indigenous operators were not tolerated.
Indeed, there was a time when the director of the Club du Sahel, Anne de

Lattre, would begin her meetings with the frightening remark, "Well, there is one thing we all agree on: that private traders should be shot" (*West Africa*, January 26, 1987). The prices that the peasants received for their produce were dictated by governments, not determined by market forces in accordance with African traditions. African chiefs do not fix prices. Bargaining over prices has always been the rule in village markets. When the peasants violated government-imposed price controls, brutalities were heaped upon them.

In Ghana, price controls and various legislative instruments quickly became tools for the systematic exploitation of the peasant farmers. One undeclared intention was to milk the agricultural sector and transfer resources to the state. Another was to fix the prices of agricultural produce and to render food cheap for the urban elites—the basis of political support for African governments. Elsewhere in Africa, government policies to make food available at reasonable prices to the elites flouted not only economic laws but also common sense. Agricultural marketing boards were established, to which farmers were required to sell their produce at artificially low prices set by the government.

In Ghana, the Marxist Rawlings regime denounced indigenous markets, which had been in existence for centuries, as dens of economic profiteers and saboteurs. The regime slapped stringent price controls onto hundreds of goods during the 1981–1983 period. Not content with the commodity shortages occasioned by the price controls, the regime employed price inspectors and established the Price Control Tribunal to hand down stiff penalties to violators. For example, an Accra trader, Umaro Shaibu, was jailed for four years by the Price Control Tribunal in Accra for selling a bottle of Sprite for 7 *cedi*s instead of 1.50 *cedi*s (*West Africa*, February 28, 1983). How did traders respond to these inanities?

> The brisk trading activities around Accra Central Market and the Orion Cinema Palace areas have slowed down considerably, following the coming into effect yesterday of the government's price control exercise in the Accra-Tema metropolitan areas. Most stores in this area did not open for normal business and only a handful of the large number of people, who previously sold various items on the pavements and sidewalks, could be seen. The few stores which opened for business had almost empty shelves unlike the situation last week and some stores had mounted notice boards reading "stock-taking." (*Daily Graphic*, January 18, 1982)

The *Daily Graphic* (state-owned) reported that a section of market women and traders in Cape Coast would not "heed appeals." It said a market survey there had shown that traders would rather withdraw their goods than bring prices down (*West Africa*, January 25, 1982). The authorities, in turn, responded by wreaking destruction "as a warning to traders who had decided to withdraw their wares instead of reducing prices" (*West Africa*, February 1, 1982).

Markets were burned down and destroyed at Accra, Kumasi, Koforidua, and other cities when traders refused to sell at government-dictated prices. In February 1982, "the Tamale Central Market was set ablaze, causing the destruction of large quantities of foodstuffs, drugs, and imported spare parts. Then John Ndeburge, the Northern Regional Secretary, set up a five-member committee of inquiry to investigate the circumstances leading to the incineration of the market" (*West Africa*, March 8, 1982). Imagine deploying air force personnel and a police strike force to destroy tables and enforce price controls. Economic lunacy was on the rampage.

Worse, the little food that there was in Ghana was being destroyed! When doing that failed to intimidate the market traders, the military government launched house-to-house searches for goods (*West Africa*, February 15, 1982). "The Rawlings government also declared that it would conduct unannounced searches of traders and stated that if any were found with hoarded goods they would be taken away to be shot by firing squad" (Herbst 1993, 26). Economic lunacy was running amok. And the results of all these inanities?

Between January 1982 and April 1983, prices of locally produced goods rose by more than 600 percent. The price of a bag of maize, for example, went from 500 *cedis* in January 1982 to 4,000 *cedis* in April 1983; and for nine months, bread disappeared completely from the markets (*West Africa*, July 11, 1983).

Having jailed the traders and destroyed their markets, the government of Ghana discovered it had to feed them. But there was no food to feed the food traders it had jailed for allegedly selling or buying above government-fixed prices. Thirty prisoners died in Sunyani prison for lack of food; thirty-nine inmates died at another prison (*West Africa*, July 15, 1983). Imagine. For the economy as a whole, "GNP per capita declined from $483 in 1979 to $447 in 1981 while by 1983 living standards had fallen steadily to some 16 percent of 1972 levels" (*West Africa*, July 15, 1983).

This bizarre experiment in economic folly was repeated in Zimbabwe. In October 2001, President Robert Mugabe announced that Zimbabwe was abandoning market-based economic policies and returning to socialist/statist policies. He imposed price controls on basic foods, warning that the controls would be strictly enforced and that the government would seize firms that shut down, withheld their goods, or engaged in illegal profiteering. Mugabe railed: "Let no one on this front expect mercy. The state will take over any businesses that are closed. We will reorganize them with workers and, at last, that socialism we wanted can start again. Those tired of doing business here can pack up and go" (*Washington Times*, October 16, 2001).

Mugabe's government ordered price cuts of 5 percent to 20 percent on corn meal, bread, meat, cooking oil, milk, salt, and soap. Three days later, "Bread, cooking oil and margarine were unobtainable across the country; bread shortages were also experienced in Harare. A main bakery chain in Harare said the set prices did not take into account transportation, power and other costs; the chain had put 200 of its workers on shorter working hours as production was cut" (*Washington Times*, October 16, 2001).

The Mugabe government never learned, believing that *more* of the *wrong* economic medicine would cure the food shortage crisis. To halt the surging costs of staples such as bread, the government imposed more-stringent price controls. The result? "The main effect has been a decline in supply from producers unwilling to settle for below-market prices" (*New York Times*, November 10, 2001). "Already, some farmers have been switching to more lucrative crops like soybeans and the pepper plant, from which paprika is derived. If the price of corn is held down too much, many more will abandon it, setting up much bigger shortages next year, the officials say" (*New York Times*, July 18, 2001).

By 2005, Zimbabwe's economy was teetering toward collapse. There were shortages of nearly everything—from fuel, milk, and cooking oil to even mealie meal, the national staple. "At one downtown grocery, tubes of much-prized American toothpaste are kept in a locked case" (*New York Times*, May 21, 2005). On May 18, 2005, about ten thousand traders were arrested in a police operation in Harare. Paramilitary units armed with batons and riot shields smashed up stalls of street traders as the units targeted the huge informal sector. The official statement claimed that the raids were aimed at black-market profiteers who were hoarding commodities. "Police will leave no stone unturned in their endeavor to flush out economic saboteurs," Police Chief Superintendent Oliver Mandipaka told the state media (*New York Times*, May 24, 2005). The police chief said informal business operators had been arrested and fined for operating without licenses or for possessing scarce staple items such as maize meal, sugar, and petrol intended for resale on the black market. The police destroyed thirty-four flea markets, netted Z$900 million ($100,000) in fines, and seized Z$2.2 billion in goods. President Mugabe blamed the West for the nation's economic crisis.

It's déjà vu all over again; nothing was learned from Ghana's disastrous experimentation with misguided statist policies and destruction of markets. Price-fixing and state controls were intended to extract resources from the peasants for national development. But in most African countries, these resources were spent to develop the urban areas for the elites.

Botswana was the only black African country in the postcolonial period that did not persecute its peasants but rather went back and built upon their indigenous roots. This policy paid off handsomely. In elegant brevity, *Newsweek* (July 23, 1990) put the issue poignantly: "Botswana built a working democracy on an aboriginal tradition of local gatherings called *kgotlas* that resemble New England town meetings; it has a record $2.7 billion in foreign exchange reserves" (p. 28).

6. Conclusion: How the West Can Help

Western aid policies toward Africa have failed miserably over the decades to reverse the continent's economic decline. Although other factors such as design flaws and bureaucratic red tape played a significant role, the policies themselves were structured on false premises. Most aid programs were crafted in Western capitals with little input from the people they were intended to benefit; aid was used to support grandiose prestige projects with little economic value; and aid funds were sometimes looted, among other reasons.

Western donors often exercised little prudence in backing wrongheaded projects. For example, Tanzania's ill-conceived Ujaama socialist experiment received much Western support. *The New York Times* reported that "at first, many Western aid donors, particularly in Scandinavia, gave enthusiastic backing to this socialist experiment, pouring an estimated $10 billion into Tanzania over 20 years. Yet, today as Mr. Nyerere leaves the stage, the country's largely agricultural economy is in ruins, with its 26 million people eking out their living on a per capita income of slightly more than $200 a year, one of the lowest in the world" (*New York Times*, October 24, 1990).

Western donors have displayed a baffling inability to make a distinction between African *people* and African *leaders*. It is always important to make this distinction because leaders and people are not synonymous. The leaders, not the people, have been the problem. And leadership failure is not tantamount to failure of Africans as people. The vast majority of African leaders neither represent nor are chosen by the peasants (the people). Unfortunately, there are many Western organizations and governments that seek to establish "solidarity" or a "relationship of deep friendship" with the African people. But somehow these Western organizations and governments rather naively believe that they can best help the African people by working with or forming partnerships with African leaders. Thus the Western approach to African problems often tends to be "leader-centered."

The mistake that the West often makes is investing its faith in some "Abraham Lincoln" who will transform his African society. Of course, it would be desirable to have a democratic African country based on the free-market system. But these are the outcomes of often long and arduous processes.

The Bush administration's Millennium Challenge Account, by which the U.S. would increase its foreign aid programs by 50 percent to $15 billion a year, must avoid three fundamental pitfalls of Clinton's Africa policy. First, President Clinton relied almost exclusively on black Americans for counsel in the formulation of U.S. Africa policy. Although African American legislators may mean well, they lack an operational understanding of Africa's current woes.

Second, the Clinton administration's Africa policy was "leader-centered." It sought to develop warm, cozy relationships—euphemistically called "partnerships"—with "new leaders" of Africa. By focusing almost exclusively on such Lincoln wannabes, Western governments set themselves up to be suckered by hucksters who parrot "democracy" not because they believe in it but rather because they know that is what unlocks the floodgates of Western aid.

Third, a market economy cannot be established without secure property rights, the free flow of information, the rule of law, and mechanisms for contract enforcement. Because these processes or foundations are missing in most African countries, so are the free markets.

Western donors must fundamentally alter policy toward Africa by depoliticizing and deracializing Africa policy. The problems that Africa faces today have little to do with the slave trade, colonialism, or racism but rather more to do with bad leadership and bad governance, originating from the establishment of defective economic and political systems.

A new approach must be adopted that places less emphasis on the rhetoric of African leaders and more emphasis on institution building. Leaders come and go, but institutions endure. Six institutions are critical: an independent central bank, an independent judiciary, an independent and free media, an independent electoral commission, an efficient civil service, and a neutral and professional armed or security force.

Africa remains mired in grinding poverty and social destitution. A cacophonous chorus of rock stars, antipoverty activists, and heads of state is calling on rich countries to do more for Africa—cancel its $350 billion crippling foreign debt and double aid to the continent. British Prime Minister Tony Blair made this goal the centerpiece of Britain's presidency of the G-8 meeting in Gleneagles, Scotland, in July 2005. The G-8 leaders agreed to write off $40 billion of poor nations' debts and pledged to double aid to Africa to $50 billion by 2010. Two years later, only 10 percent of those pledges have been fulfilled. Will any of these plans help Africa?

Skepticism and dissension abound. Wrangling over financing modalities will ensue. Years will go by, and then, a decade later, another round of grand initiatives to help Africa will be unveiled. In 1985, the UN held a special session on Africa to boost aid to Africa. In March 1996, the $25 billion Special Initiative for Africa was launched by the UN. In September 2005, the plight of Africa took center stage at a UN conference in New York. Expect another UN conference in 2015.

Helping Africa is a noble cause but has become a theater of the absurd—the blind leading the clueless in political posturing. Neither party sees that Africa's begging bowl leaks horribly. Nigerian President Olusegun Obasanjo said corrupt African leaders have stolen at least $140 billion (£95 billion) from their people since independence (*London Independent*, June 14, 2002). The World Bank estimates that 40 percent of wealth created in Africa is invested outside the continent. In August 2004, an African Union report claimed that Africa loses an estimated $148 billion annually to corrupt practices, a figure that represents 25 percent of the continent's gross domestic product. "Mr. Babatunde Olugboji, Chairman of the Independent Advocacy Project, made this revelation in Lagos while addressing the press on the survey scheduled to be embarked upon by the body to determine the level of corruption in the country even though Transparency International has rated Nigeria as the second most corrupt nation in the world" (*Vanguard*, August 6, 2004). Rather than clean up their own houses, African leaders prefer to badger the West for more money. And the West, burdened by racial oversensitivity and guilt over the iniquities of the slave trade and colonialism, obliges.

African leaders don't use their heads, and more tragic is the fact that Western donors who set out to help Africa don't use theirs, either. Said the *Economist* (January 17, 2004): "For every dollar that foolish northerners lent Africa between 1970 and 1996, 80 cents flowed out as capital flight in the same year, typically into Swiss bank accounts or to buy mansions on the Cote d'Azur" (p. 12). The West may think it is helping reform Africa, but instead it is compounding Africa's woes.

References

Ayittey, George B. N. 1991. *Indigenous African Institutions*. Dobbs Ferry, NY: Transnational Publishers.

Bandow, Doug. 1986. "The First World's Misbegotten Economic Legacy to the Third World." *Journal of Economic Growth* 1 (4): 17.

Bennell, Paul. 1997. "Foreign Direct Investment in Africa: Rhetoric and Reality." *SAIS Review* (Summer/Fall): 127–139.

Boamah-Wiafe, Daniel. 1993. *Africa: The Land, People, and Cultural Institutions*. Omaha, NE: Wisdom Publications.

Eberstadt, Nicholas. 1988. *Foreign Aid and American Purpose*. Washington, DC: American Enterprise Institute.

———. 2000. "Pursuit of Prosperity South of the Sahara." *Washington Times* (August 27).

Freedom House. 2003. "Map of Press Freedom." http://www.freedomhouse
.org/template.cfm?page=251&year=2003 (accessed May 31, 2007).

Government of Ghana. 1963. *The Seven-Year Development Plan 1963–1970*.
Accra: Government of Ghana.

Herbst, Jeffrey. 1993. *The Politics of Reform in Ghana*. Berkeley and Los
Angeles: University of California Press.

Heritage Foundation/*Wall Street Journal*. n.d. *Index of Economic Freedom*.
Washington, DC: Heritage Productions.

Kendall, Frances, and Leon Louw. 1986. *After Apartheid: The Solution*. San
Francisco: Institute of Contemporary Studies.

Killick, Tony. 1978. *Development Economics in Action: A Study of Economic
Policies in Ghana*. London: Heinemann.

Mabogunje, A. 1988. *Africa after the False Start*. Paper presented to 26th Congress of the International Geographical Union, Sydney, Australia.

Maren, Michael. 1997. *The Road to Hell: The Ravaging Effects of Foreign Aid
and International Charity*. New York: Free Press.

Mazrui, Ali. 1986. *The Africans*. London: BBC Publications.

NEPAD. 2001. "The New Partnership for Africa's Development." http://www
.nepad.org/2005/files/documents/inbrief.pdf (accessed May 31, 2007).

Nyerere, Julius K. 1962. *Ujaama: The Basis of African Socialism*. Dar es
Salaam, Tanzania: Government Printer.

Taylor, D. R. Fraser, and Fiona Mackenzie. 1992. *Development from Within:
Survival in Rural Africa*. New York: Routledge.

United Nations Conference on Trade and Development (UNCTAD). 1994.
Adjustment in Africa: Reforms, Results and the Road Ahead. New York:
Oxford University Press.

———. 1995a. *Foreign Direct Investment in Africa*. United Nations Publication
no. E.95.II.A.6. Geneva, Switzerland: United Nations.

———. 1995b. *Ghana: Is Growth Sustainable? Operations Evaluations Department*. Report no. 99. Washington, DC: World Bank Publications.

———. 1997. "Investment Opportunities in Pre-Emerging Markets." Geneva,
Switzerland: United Nations Publications.

———. 1999. *Investment Policy Review of Egypt*. Mimeo. Geneva, Switzerland: UNCTAD.

———. *World Development Report*. n.d. New York: Oxford University
Press.

United Nations Development Program (UNDP). 2001. *Human Development
Report*. New York: United Nations.

World Bank. 1989. *Sub-Saharan Africa: From Crisis to Self-Sustainable
Growth*. Washington, DC: World Bank.

World Bank/UNDP (1997). *African Economic and Financial Data*. Washington, DC: World Bank.

————. 1998. *Trade and Development Report, 1998*. United Nations Publication no. E.98.II.D.6. Geneva, Switzerland: United Nations.

————. 2000a. *Can Africa Claim the 21st Century?* Washington, DC: World Bank.

————. 2000b. *African Development Indicators 2000*. Washington, DC: World Bank.

World Economic Forum (WEF). 1998. *Africa Competitiveness Report 1998*. Cologne, Germany, and Geneva, Switzerland: World Economic Forum.

Zinsmeister, Karl. 1987. "East African Experiment: Kenyan Prosperity and Tanzanian Decline." *Journal of Economic Growth* 2 (2): 28.

ALVARO VARGAS LLOSA

1. The Principles of Oppression

People have been striving for freedom since the dawn of civilization. Thanks to cuneiform inscriptions, we know that around 2400 B.C.
a man known by the name of Urukagina led a people's revolution against
the oligarchic state in Lagash, one of the city-states of Sumer, in Mesopotamia, accusing special interests—priests, administrators, the governor—
of acting for their own benefit and either usurping the property of others
or simply enslaving them. "The priest no longer invaded the garden of a
humble man," says the document that conveys his reforms and gave the
human race the first recorded word for liberty: *amagi* (literally "a return
to the mother," referring to an idyllic past in which the gods wanted
people to be free). He banned the authorities, both ecclesiastical and civil,
from seizing property from commoners, did away with most of the tax
collectors, curtailed the power of judges to rule in favor of oligarchs trying to exploit the weak, and got the government out of proceedings such
as divorce. Although Lagash thrived, Urukagina's reign succumbed to a
rival king after a decade. It stands as perhaps the first case of reform along
classical liberal lines (to use a much more recent paradigm) and a very
early example of struggle against collectivism, plunder, and conquest.[1]
    I bring this fact to light because the precedent indicates that people
from various cultures and geographical areas that we would not associate
with the idea of liberty today have attempted throughout the ages to

vindicate individual sovereignty, private property, and peaceful cooperation as guiding principles of civilization. It should come as no surprise
that in what is today known as "Latin America" we can also find, in pre-
Columbian times, significant manifestations of the free spirit.

Although much more research is needed, archaeologists have recently determined that the city of Caral, built as early as 2627 B.C. and
located in the Supe River valley of Peru, probably thrived on exchange
and not on war, as the absence of weapons, mutilated remains, and battle-
ments suggests. It appears that the inhabitants traded their cotton and
fruit crops with fishing communities of the coast in return for food.[2]

Long before the classic period of Maya civilization, taken to have
started in the third century A.D., trade was a mainstay in various locations in the Yucatán Peninsula and the surrounding areas. Later, before the establishment of Tenochtitlán as the capital of what is known as
the "Aztec Empire" in Mexico, Tlatelolco emerged as a vibrant mercan-
tile center.[3] In Peru, the Inca Empire devoted considerable energy to eliminating trade precisely because it had been a tradition among many of the
cultures that came under the domination of Cuzco's *Quechua* tribes. Anyone who visits a market fair among the Indian communities of the Andes,
the South of Mexico, or Guatemala will detect a powerful commercial
spirit among people who are in many ways remote from the mainstream,
Western culture.[4]

A century and a half after Spain and Portugal conquered what is
known today as "Latin America," because of the lack of free trade, smuggling came to represent as much as two-thirds of all colonial commerce,
mainly by the French, the Dutch, and the English (a reason, incidentally,
why Buenos Aires prospered).[5] Clearly, Latin Americans were finding
creative ways to get around the oppressive laws in order to survive on
trade—something similar to what millions of poor people working in the
underground or informal economy are doing today.

After the various republics came into existence, numerous attempts at liberal reform took place, the most important of which happened in Argentina in the mid-nineteenth century under the intellectual
inspiration of Juan Bautista Alberdi, an admirer of the founders of the
United States—with the result that that country enjoyed seven decades
of impressive wealth creation, attracting millions of immigrants from Europe. In contemporary times, Chile, after having gone through traumatic

experiences in the second half of the twentieth century, has become something of a showcase for free-market reform, even if there are still many changes that need to take place.

The various manifestations of the spirit of liberty among Latin Americans throughout the ages, however, do not detract from the fact that oppression, from near-totalitarianism under systems such as that of the Inca state to much milder types of authoritarian democracy today, has been the dominant feature of the region's social order.

In a recent book, I describe the system underlying the many vicissitudes and transformations that have occurred in the last five hundred years—and that I do not underestimate—as a mix of corporatism, state mercantilism, privilege, wealth transfer, and political law.[6] By "corporatism" I mean the tendency to look at society not as a group of sovereign individuals but rather as a group of "corporations" that in effect usurps individual rights—and with which the state chooses to deal unequally according to its needs. "State mercantilism" refers to a state of affairs reminiscent of premodern Europe in which competition takes place primarily in the political, not the economic, market. "Privilege" means privilege resulting from legal discrimination. "Wealth transfer" involves the decoupling of the productive and the distributive functions, an act of force that ultimately hurts production. Finally, *political law* is the term by which I describe the law as a child and instrument of the political system rather than as a set of abstract principles and norms resulting from the evolutionary process of society, safeguarding life, liberty, and property.

These have been, in varying degrees according to the period and the specific country or region in question, the essential traits of the political and economic system in Latin America through the pre-Columbian, colonial, and republican eras. There have been attempts at reform—particularly in the mid-nineteenth century, the early twentieth century, and the late twentieth century—but in most cases, despite some decentralization of power and the removal of a number of obstacles to trade, the basic rules continued to sustain privilege.

2. The Myths of Underdevelopment

Latin America's poverty disproves many theories regarding the causes of development. Those theories attribute development to the abundance of natural resources, the terms of trade, the ratio of labor to land, education, and the available stock of capital.

Venezuela is the world's fifth-largest producer of oil, and yet 53 percent of its population is in poverty today (2005). In fact, the proportion of the population that is poor has increased from 43 percent in 1998 to what it is today, even though the international price of a barrel of oil has gone from $15 to more than $50 in that same period.[7] This reality, and indeed Venezuela's condition despite almost eighty years of reaping large profits from oil exports, indicates that natural resources and terms of trade are not per se a determining factor in economic development.

Argentina, a vast territory with some of the most fertile land in the hemisphere, has a population density of only eleven people per square kilometer[8] and yet has managed to go from being one of the twelve most-developed nations of the world in the early twentieth century to producing only slightly more than $100 billion a year in goods and services nowadays, almost seven times less than Spain, a country with a similar population.[9] Population density, then, cannot be a major factor in explaining Latin America's underdevelopment.

If education alone was the decisive factor, the disparity between Argentina and Spain would be hard to explain because Argentina had during most of the twentieth century a higher level of education and a much more intense cultural life than the mother country. Until Spain's modernization in the last quarter of the twentieth century, that country was known as provincial and archaic, while Buenos Aires was a vibrant, cosmopolitan city that attracted many Spanish intellectuals unable to pursue their work at home.

Spain has made a leap forward in cultural terms in the last three decades, and Argentina has lost its vigor of yesteryear, but no one who is familiar with both countries could state that a significant change in the respective levels of education preceded the change in economic fortunes or that there is a proportionality between the economic gap that today separates them and the educational disparity between the two nations. Numerous studies indicate that expenditure on education, both public and private, was lower in Spain than in most other nations in the Organisation for Economic Co-operation and Development (OECD) throughout the 1980s and 1990s, a period in which that country's economy grew at a faster rate than did the economies of most other members of the

European Union (Spain's economy has been steadily catching up with the rest of Europe; its per capita GDP today represents more than 85 percent of the European Union's average per capita GDP).[10]

Is the stock of available capital a more significant factor of development? In the 1990s, a decade in which most Latin American countries undertook what purported to be free-market reform, more than $400 billion worth of investment flowed into that region. However, per capita GDP growth averaged a mere 1.5 percent during those years, and there was no significant reduction in poverty.[11] Similarly, in the 1970s, the era of petrodollars in which many of the loans that would later become "the debt problem" were incurred by Latin America, per capita GDP growth in the region averaged 0.5 percent annually.[12] As Peter Bauer noted thirty-five years ago, "even though increased capital may be a necessary concomitant of economic growth, it is not a sufficient condition for it." His conclusion that "it is nearer the truth to say that capital is created in the process of development than that development is a function of capital accumulation" appears to be confirmed by these facts.[13]

If natural resources, the terms of trade, the ratio of labor to land, education, and the stock of capital do not per se explain the level of development of a country, what is the key factor? Although some of these elements, especially the accumulation of capital, are actual symptoms and manifestations of development, the causes of this process, as many scholars have understood for some time, have to do with the prevailing institutional environment, that is, the rules that govern social interaction and the structure of rewards and punishments within which human activity takes place, as expressed both in the norms and laws of the particular society in question and in the values that inform people's conduct.[14] If the institutional environment is impersonal and tends to decentralize power, providing citizens with a certain amount of security regarding their property and the contracts into which they choose to enter with others, the result tends to be sustained economic growth and therefore long-term prosperity. If the rules limit the capacity of the authorities or of third parties to invade the sovereign sphere of the individual by the use of superior force, the effect will usually be a framework that creates incentives for creative initiative as well as for saving and investing, thereby triggering an increase in productivity. Recent studies have concluded that GDP per capita is twice as high in nations with the strongest protection of property

($23,796) as in those providing only a moderate amount of protection ($13,027). By the same token, in those countries where there is little protection, GDP per capita drops considerably ($4,963).[15]

3. Parasitic Entrepreneurship

As William Baumol has suggested, entrepreneurship can be constructive or parasitical, according to how the rules that govern economic life determine the payoffs to different entrepreneurial activities.[16] That is why certain periods in history—for instance, the Industrial Revolution— show an explosion of entrepreneurship, while others—such as medieval China—show stagnation. In the case of Latin America, although there have been exceptional periods, the norm has been an environment in which parasitic rather than constructive entrepreneurship was rewarded because success and failure were functions of competition in the political, not the economic, market. Stanislav Andreski was referring precisely to this type of system when he described the traditional institutions in most Latin American countries as constituting "a parasitic involution of capitalism," defined as a "tendency to seek profits and alter market conditions by political means in the widest sense of the word."[17]

Historically, there is evidence to show that ordinary people have an instinct for property and private enterprise, making true Richard Pipes's claim that even before the rise of the state in its modern form, "in most countries property took the form of possession, claims to which rested not on documented legal title but on prolonged tenure, which custom acknowledged as proof of ownership."[18] In modern times, many studies have been conducted in Latin America on the topic of how poor people have made numerous legal arrangements of their own in order to bring security to their possessions and a measure of predictability to their social interactions in the face of the failure of the state to provide either despite its size and its pervasiveness throughout society.[19] However, under corporatism, state mercantilism, privilege, wealth transfer, and political law, it has not been possible for the spirit of enterprise to flourish in a constructive way and to realize its full potential—a potential expressed, for instance, in the fact that Latin Americans who have migrated to more-developed countries are able to generate sufficient capital to send back home more than $40 billion every year.[20] Both historically and in contemporary times, the parasitic system has stifled development in the region.

During colonial times, Latin Americans had little access to landed property or to trade. The church owned more than one-half of the land in Mexico[21] and was in control of one-quarter of all the buildings in Mexico City and Lima (all church-held land had originally belonged to the Indians). The Spanish Council of the Indies was the almighty entity exercising political control over the colonies, and the House of Trade (Casa de la Contratación) governed all commercial exchange under monopoly conditions that prevented the colonies from trading with other countries. The *consulados* (associations of merchants with political clout) were given exclusive licenses on both sides of the Atlantic to engage in commerce. After the revenues were not enough to cover the financial needs of the Crown, the state, as the logic of such a system dictated, traded directly and exclusively in certain products such as salt, pepper, quicksilver, and gunpowder.

In the case of Brazil, the mercantilist system operated more gradually than in the Spanish colonies. In the early period, the political and economic organization was not too centralized: colonization, at least before the reforms of the eighteenth century, was more of a business venture undertaken by private interests with some support from the Crown. But in the eighteenth century, the discovery of gold led Portugal to establish a much more centralized form of rule.[22] One of the consequences of this establishment was the constitution of trading monopolies,[23] while the Crown reserved an important proportion of mining revenues for itself. Local manufacture was severely restricted: it became illegal to produce goods that could be supplied from the metropolis.[24]

In republican times, again official institutions prevented most Latin Americans from gaining access to property and from engaging in free commercial activities. Through the use of violence, discriminatory legislation, elite-dominated municipalities that replaced the local and village colonial governments, and plain encroachment, the land was quickly appropriated by the privileged few.[25]

In countries that were still primarily rural, agriculture was dominated by the high concentration of property and the high marginal product of labor, an environment in which there was little incentive to revolutionize technology. When the Brazilian authorities offered cheap land in the nineteenth century, coffee plantations surged all the way to São Paulo. An opportunity opened for many new landowners to prosper. But public policy, especially legislation promulgated in the 1850s, prevented small-scale agriculture and favored huge estates under control of a few *fazendeiros* (influential landowners) who employed masses of low-wage laborers and immigrants under *parceria* or sharecropping arrangements. In Peru, meanwhile, local politicians and wool traders helped to create powerful haciendas (large estates) by encroaching on Indian community lands. By the end of the nineteenth century, there were 705 estates, and the number tripled by the early twentieth century, covering most of the Peruvian fertile land.[26] Around that same time, 95 percent of the rural population in Mexico owned no land at all, and one-fourth of all the land of that large country was in the hands of two hundred families.[27]

In the twentieth century, revolution became the response to that iniquitous state of affairs. The result was not the deliverance of the masses but rather new forms of parasitism. The Mexican revolution undertook reform in the countryside early on and continued to expropriate land until the 1970s, distributing it through the *ejido* (communal farm) system at various stages.[28] Vast tracts of land were handed out to peasants, but the peasants were not given full ownership rights, and they were organized into movements that came to fit perfectly the corporatist structure masterminded by the state (the Confederación Nacional Campesina created by Lázaro Cárdenas is a case in point). After 1950, other countries implemented their own land reforms, from Guatemala in 1952 and Bolivia in 1953 to Peru in the early 1970s. The methods varied—Bolivia legalized invasions, Peru expropriated land from the *hacendados* (landowners) and turned it into hundreds of government-run cooperatives—but the result was generally the same, except that in Bolivia peasants were better at withstanding their government's intrusions and reserving a little space for private initiative.[29]

Revolution and agrarian reform did not entail full property rights exercised by millions of private owners but rather an arrangement by which the state became the real owner.[30] This new form of concentration of property—and the fact that much of the land untouched by the transfer was so small that almost no economies of scale could take place—explains in part why in the three decades after World War II agriculture grew at only one-half the rate of industry, the new (and only temporary) star of the Latin American economy under the policies of subsidized industrialization.[31] It was only when, as happened in Peru after 1976, the government-run cooperatives began to sell the land on an illegal basis to peasant associations that some peasants became landowners. But because the parceling of land was illegal, transaction costs were high and access to credit, investment, and transfers of rights was severely limited on these small, undercapitalized, low-production plots. That is why, despite informal privatization, Peru's land reform was followed by a drop of 2.3 percent in agricultural output per capita from 1971–1973 until 1981–1983.

4. Economic Nationalism

Not just the countryside experienced government interference and severe limits to property rights and free exchange. The phrase that catches the spirit (and the letter) of the twentieth century in terms of institutional arrangements is "economic nationalism." Its leaders and intellectuals sought to explain underdevelopment as the result of unjust terms of trade between cheap primary exports coming out of the "periphery" (underdeveloped) nations in exchange for expensive manufactured goods coming from the "center" (developed) nations. Because rich countries "monopolized" capital and technology, it was thought, poor countries were at a "structural" disadvantage because with their low-priced primary exports they did not earn enough foreign exchange with which to pay for the capital and technology they needed in order to maintain appropriate levels of investment and with which to buy the manufactured goods that rich countries also "monopolized." [32] Consequently, the way to "correct" these unjust terms of trade was to erect all sorts of barriers against imports, to channel resources, through the use of subsidies and legal discrimination, toward certain industries, and to nationalize certain areas of the economy outright.

Economic nationalism had two decisive phases. The first one took place in the 1930s, and the second, really an expansion of the first but standing on much more systematic and ideological ground, came after World War II. Latin America's export economy was devastated by the 1930s world crisis. In most countries, the disruption of exports, the contraction of foreign capital, and the rise in domestic public spending were followed by a decisive move in the direction of economic nationalism. The gold standard was dropped, devaluation ensued, multiple exchange rates were adopted, capital controls set in, tariffs were erected against foreign products, and other types of import control emerged. After the 1930s, politicians gained control of monetary policy, finding it useful in times of recession and unemployment, and saw the use of tariffs in a new strategic light.

Brazil experienced the Estado Novo (New State) under Getulio Vargas, who rose to power in 1930; Mexico came under the grip of Lázaro Cárdenas in 1934; more than seven decades of free trade and liberalism in Argentina came to an end with military rule in 1930; and the era of the social-democratic Radical Party dawned in Chile. These regimes engaged in, and symbolized, import substitution, an attempt to boost domestic production by protecting the economy from imports through the use of tariffs and nontariff barriers, exchange rate manipulation, and subsidies. Not all countries in Latin America pursued the same policies with equal vigor. The Southern Cone countries, such as Brazil, Argentina, and Chile, were much more radical than smaller countries such as those in Central America. Mexico, geographically much closer to the second group, belongs, in terms of political economy, to the first group.[33]

After World War II, import substitution gained new momentum and followed a logic of its own, an inertia dragging the Latin American governments toward ever-increasing intervention in the economy. If the government was going to play a key role in directing investment toward particular industries, then it might as well take direct ownership of those areas or exercise indirect control through cooperatives. If the government was going to decide what products were to be imported freely and what foreign products the domestic consumers were going to be scared away from, then it might as well establish state trading monopolies. If particular activities were to be encouraged outside the sphere of state enterprises, then strict industrial and commercial licensing needed to be imposed. If unfavorable terms of trade and the developed world's "monopoly" of capital had been at the root of underdevelopment, and import substitution was the answer to the condition of the Third World, then capital and exchange controls (including differential rates) were indispensable. If governments artificially expanded the monetary base by printing money in order to boost public spending, price controls were necessary to stem the effect of inflation. If credit was essential for greasing the industrial machinery, then credit had to be subsidized. If expanding demand was an objective with a view to spurring production, then extensive collective bargaining, in many cases by trade, would help ensure that workers had enough money to buy products with.

Brazil, Argentina, and Mexico were the engines of economic nationalism across the region. In Argentina, Juan Domingo Perón became an emblem of these policies, which, as had previously been the case with Vargas in Brazil, were accompanied by intense corporatism reminiscent of Italian fascism—including labor codes, functional representation, and the incorporation of mass social movements into the orbit of the state. In Mexico, other PRI governments consolidated the legacy of Lázaro Cárdenas. In Brazil, Juscelino Kubitschek de Oliveira gave new impetus to industrialization. By the end of the 1960s, these three nations accounted for 80 percent of industrial production, while five others—Chile, Colombia, Peru, Uruguay, and Venezuela—produced 17 percent of Latin America's industrial goods.[34]

This second phase of import substitution was supported by considerable foreign investment. As happens when investment is concentrated in a particular area and the government realigns the economy through a selective allocation of resources, many Latin American countries experienced years of industrial growth between the 1940s and the 1970s. But the basic economics of this model, whose statistical results did not reflect comparable improvements in standards of living and in consumption levels, was flawed. By 1972, the share of agriculture in the region's GDP as a whole had fallen to 15.4 percent, but that activity, which had a very low productivity, employed more than 40 percent of the population.[35] By 1970, the infant mortality rate in Latin America was three times higher than in OECD countries.[36] The policies of economic nationalism incubated a crisis that was subdued by massive foreign lending in the 1970s but eventually exploded in the 1980s. Between the 1970s and 1990, Argentina's per capita income was reduced by one-quarter.[37] What incentive could there be for efficiency and for the use of new technology in companies that operated in highly protected markets? How could high prices and costs resulting from trade barriers and other government guarantees given to domestic industries be sustained indefinitely? How could an economy that was living in a cloud, a fictitious environment, keep importing the ever-increasing quantity of capital goods and even raw materials needed to feed industrialization? How could the foreign exchange pressures caused by these imports allow for the acquisition of first-rate technologies in order to be competitive beyond reduced domestic markets? How could agriculture survive in nations where everything was geared toward industry, including subsidies and price controls favoring urban workers against the Argentinean pampas (green plains), the Brazilian land, or the Mexican *ejidos*? How could industrialization be sustained without a solid agricultural base, unless massive food imports were ordered? And if rural areas were going to be depopulated as a result of the urban drive, how could these highly regulated economies absorb millions of new workers?

Economic nationalism—Latin America's version of populism—was a new way of doing what had been done before, that is, of draining the resources of ordinary people so as to sustain a structure in which only parasites living off the government (directly or indirectly) could succeed. The larger public was left with a simple choice: to "skin or be skinned," in Andreski's apt phrase.[38] That is in great part the source of the social unrest, the political instability, and the moral abdication that the outside world tends to associate with Latin America.

By the mid-1980s, public spending represented the equivalent of 61 percent of Mexico's GDP. In Venezuela, by that time the government was consuming more than 50 percent of the national wealth. In Peru, economic nationalism and populism reached new heights with Velasco Alvarado in the 1970s and with Alan García in the late 1980s; by 1990, government-owned companies were generating an annual deficit of $2 billion. In Brazil, by 1980 the government owned some 560 companies and consumed more than 40 percent of the nation's wealth. The result of all this was poverty and underdevelopment. A revolution with hundreds of thousands of casualties had taken place at the start of the 20th century in Mexico, in the name of the peasants. What did Mexico have to show for it toward the end of the century? By then, 60 percent of those in extreme poverty were part of the rural population despite the fact that no more than one-quarter of the population lived in the countryside.

The decades of economic nationalism also saw an expansion of foreign aid coming from wealthy nations. The failures of economic nationalism to obtain the desired results were often blamed on "dependency," a byword that came to justify large transfers from rich countries to poor countries in order to compensate the latter for the primary responsibility the former were supposed to have for their underdeveloped condition.

Latin America's underdevelopment is a testament to how unproductive most of the foreign aid reaped on poor countries has been. In the past fifty years, rich nations have given poor nations as much as $2.3 trillion in aid (in today's dollars), and so far not one of the countries that has overcome underdevelopment has been a primary recipient of that money, whether in Asia, southern Europe, Australasia or, more recently, eastern and central Europe. Chile, the only country that appears to be on the path to development in Latin America, has received negligible foreign aid.[39] Just as welfare programs in Latin America have not helped the poor,[40] foreign aid has failed to aid the larger population.

5. The Mirage of Reform

In the late 1980s and during the 1990s, important reforms took place across Latin America. Hyperinflation, economic stagnation, the ensuing struggle between different factions dependent on the parasitical system, and the symbol of Chile's relative success opened up the opportunity for free-market reform across the region. However, despite some early successes, especially in reducing inflation, attracting foreign investment, and spurring the economy by lowering some barriers to trade, a great opportunity was missed. What really took place in those years was crony capitalism, not the decentralization of power through the desocialization of the economy, the spread of property, and the elimination of barriers to entry in all markets.

Leaving aside Chile, whose reforms started earlier under General Augusto Pinochet's military dictatorship and went further than those of other countries, Bolivia, Mexico, Peru, Argentina, El Salvador, Brazil, Colombia, and others experienced many transformations between 1985 and 2000. With varying degrees of depth and emphasis, the process started as an effort to rein in monetary and fiscal policy, and to free most prices, and continued with some liberalization in areas such as trade and the financial system, as well as the privatization of state-owned companies. But many reforms were eventually undone or offset with interventionist, centralizing measures, so that the net result was not a free economy. Negligible reform took place in one crucial area—the judiciary. Without strong institutions and safeguards that protect property and enforce contracts, the transition to a free-market economy is seriously hampered, in no small part because the culture created by the interventionist environment over the years is one of mistrust, predation, and dependency. During this period, Latin America showed the world that a private economy is not synonymous with a free economy and that oftentimes privatizing assets can lead to new and perverse forms of privilege and parasitism.

In effect, reform meant replacing inflation with new taxes, high tariffs with regional trading blocs, government monopolies with private monopolies, price controls with regulatory bodies. Ultimately, the windfall obtained by governments thanks to the sale of state assets created new commitments that they had a hard time meeting after the proceeds from privatization ceased to come in. Thus "free-market" reform translated into high levels of expenditure, more government debt, and more taxes. The most dramatic consequences of this were felt by Argentineans at the end of 2001, when the government defaulted on its debt, and the ensuing crisis saw the devaluation of the peso by 300 percent, the confiscation of people's savings, and the pauperization of millions of people overnight.

In Latin America as a whole, GDP per capita experienced no growth between 1989 and 2004 (−0.1 percent a year on average[41]). Figure 7.1 charts the average growth rate for the region and selected countries from 1980 to 2001.[42] This period includes the recession that hit most countries in the region between 1998 and 2002, but even if we take the decade of the 1990s alone we find that annual GDP growth per capita was minimal.[43] In the decade leading to the year 2000, Mexico's annual GDP growth per capita averaged about one-third the annual rate of growth in the 1940–1980 period,[44] leading many to disparage "neoliberalism" and to evoke the good old days of economic nationalism and populism. After all the efforts made to privatize companies and to liberalize some areas of the economy, Latin America was left with a foreign debt reaching a combined amount of almost $1 trillion, with states that still consumed at least one-third of the wealth of their respective nations, with a multitude of taxes, regulations, and regulatory bodies, with large informal economies that evaded the law in order to survive but were not sufficiently productive because they did not enjoy the protection of the law, and with institutions torn apart by corruption and discredited before the eyes of the people. Countries such as Bolivia and Ecuador, where ethnic conflicts and social violence have toppled many governments since the year 2000, illustrate the depth of frustration with flawed and insufficient reform.

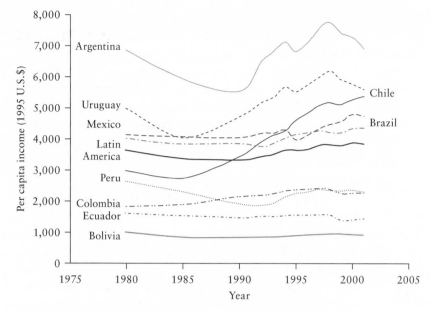

FIGURE **7.1**   Per capita income in Latin America, 1980–2001

According to the Economic Commission for Latin America and the Caribbean (ECLAC), government spending was not reduced in any Latin American country in the 1990s; in some, it expanded considerably as a proportion of GDP, as was the case in Brazil (where the proportion of the national wealth consumed by the government rose by more than 30 percent[45]). What use was it for Argentina to have its economy grow by more than 50 percent during the decade of the 1990s if fiscal spending— including expenditures by local governments—grew by almost 100 percent? (In that country's period of splendor, at the end of the nineteenth century, the combined public spending for all levels of governments did not exceed 10 percent.)

If one looks at many specific areas of reform, one finds that the result was not the transfer of power to the citizens but quite the opposite: New forms of concentration of power in the hands both of the bureaucracy and of government cronies replaced the old, populist model. Citizens in some cases obtained better services from some of the privatized companies, but these benefits were offset by high prices and tariffs due to monopoly conditions. The consumer in many cases was able to exercise few new options in the marketplace, except for access to new imports, and the producer was unable to overcome many barriers set up for the protection of the privileged minority.

Table 7.1 and Figure 7.2 show the evolution of the Fraser Institute's Economic Freedom of the World index for six Latin American countries between the years 1970 and 2002 (the most recent year for which comprehensive data are available) as well as for the United States during that same period. In the 0 to 10 ratings, 10 is most free.

Tax reform saw a reduction in income and corporate taxes, but because of new commitments on the part of governments thanks to the windfall from the proceeds of privatization, new taxes eventually came into being—affecting areas such as financial transactions in Brazil and Peru (in this country the sales tax also rose significantly). Taxation discriminated between big and small businesses and between industry and agriculture. Assembly plants in Mexico and the advertising industry in Argentina benefited from exemptions for which others had to pay dearly.

Trade reform had similar flaws. Although tariffs were initially reduced by between one-half and two-thirds in the region, trading blocs such as the South American Common Market or the Community of Andean Nations imposed high tariffs on goods coming from outside. Thus Argentina saw its tariffs actually go up for most items during a period when that country was supposed to have liberalized trade. Again, certain goods and services—for example, dairy products in Peru, automobiles in Argentina, footwear in Mexico—received extraordinary government protection. To make matters worse, yet another regional entity came into existence in 2005—the South American Community of Nations—with the stated objective of achieving integration. Already most of its

TABLE 7.1

Economic freedom: Latin America and the United States

	1970	1975	1980	1985	1990	1995	2000	2001	2002
Argentina	4.4	2.8	3.9	3.5	4.4	6.7	7.2	6.5	5.8
Brazil	4.8	4.0	3.7	3.2	3.9	4.1	5.9	5.9	6.2
Mexico	6.0	5.3	5.1	4.3	5.7	6.2	6.3	6.3	6.5
Peru	4.6	3.8	3.9	2.9	3.6	6.2	6.9	6.9	6.8
Venezuela	7.3	6.2	6.7	6.2	5.6	4.3	5.8	5.7	4.6
U.S.	7.0	7.1	7.4	7.5	8.1	8.3	8.6	8.3	8.2

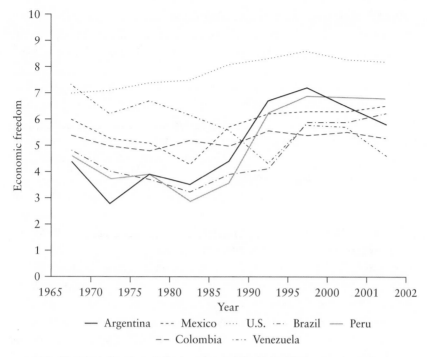

FIGURE **7.2**   Economic freedom: Latin America and the United States

members—notably Brazil and Argentina, Peru and Chile, Colombia and Venezuela—are engaged in bitter squabbles over trade and border issues.

Financial reform had similar interventionist dimensions. Curbs on interest rates were removed, many capital controls lifted, and bank reserve ratios lowered, but various governments gave lending guarantees to privatized banks, with the result that a virtual oligopoly came into existence in many countries. Irresponsible lending practices were inevitable in such conditions. In Mexico, taxpayers were left to foot a bill of $70 billion in the nation's biggest financial collapse via the government's "Fobaproa" contingency fund that was created to protect savings.

Investment reform lured many foreign companies into Latin America, but the constant changes in the rules and the failure to reform other sectors meant that as soon as other regions with lower costs came up on the horizon they decided to leave. Mexico's high level of taxation and the heavy costs imposed by the government's ownership of the energy sector persuaded a few hundred foreign companies that China was a better deal after 2000. In Argentina, the current president, Néstor Kirchner, has blamed foreign investors for the energy shortages brought about by price controls imposed through the regulatory bodies, with the result that foreign investment has not picked up since the mid-1990s. Argentina once again has a government-owned energy company.

Labor legislation is an area where almost no reform took place, which is why even during the period of considerable foreign investment and high growth, unemployment continued to hit double digits. Argentina's laws are particularly restrictive, going back in some cases to the time of Juan Domingo Perón, who took his cue in this and other respects from Mussolini's corporatist legislation.

By contrast, reform was much more consistent in Chile. That country enjoys today much greater freedom of trade, with the average tariff at 6 percent but, in practice, because of a number of free trade agreements, no higher than 3 percent, with very few exceptions. Ownership has been spread in many ways, especially through the privatization of the pension system, which has boosted domestic savings and, more important, given ordinary citizens a taste of property and capital and therefore a stake in the preservation of the economic and social order. Government expenditures, although high, do not exceed 25 percent of GDP, and Chile is the country that offers by far the most security in Latin America for contractual agreements. The result of these reforms is that the informal economy represents no more than one-fifth of the total size of the economy—between one-half and one-third of the proportion in other countries of the region. Chile boasts an annual investment rate equalling 22 percent of its GDP, against rates of between 12 and 16 percent in the rest of the continent, and exports more than 45 percent of its production, a much larger share than that of its neighbors. With 18 percent of the population still in poverty, clearly the country needs further reform, but it is an exception in the region and could overcome underdevelopment in a generation if it continues to transform itself. Chile is the only country showing a substantial increase in productivity between 1982 and 2002. Whereas per capita GDP has increased by 14 percent in Brazil and by 10 percent in Mexico, has remained the same in Argentina, and actually has decreased in Venezuela, in Chile it doubled in that period.[46]

The foundations for this success were laid in the late 1970s and throughout the 1980s, under a brutal military dictatorship that systematically violated human rights and concentrated political power but had the good sense to leave economic matters to a group of young, free-market-oriented economists (whose achievements ironically paved the way for the return of democracy after a solid middle class started to demand participation in the running of the country). The privatization of the economy started in 1974 with the return to their owners of 202 companies expropriated by the socialist government of Salvador Allende. By 1981, the number of state-owned companies was reduced from 620 to 76, and after a crisis in the early 1980s that slowed down the pace of reform the process continued until virtually all companies previously owned by the government were transferred. (Codelco, the massive copper-mining state concern, was one of the few companies kept in government hands because the military obtains a constitutionally mandated annual rent from the proceeds of its sales.)

Unlike in many other Latin American countries, the privatization process was not dominated by the creation of legal monopolies, and the ownership base increased significantly. In the first two decades of reform, more than 100,000 Chileans were able to own stock in privatized companies, more than 400,000 housing units (one-fifth of the total houses in the country) were transferred to their tenants, and about 150,000 titles to farms (one-half the total farmland of the country) were given to small farmers.[47] And, even more significantly, the privatization of the social security system, which gave workers the choice of opting out of the state pension and owning individual accounts, became so attractive that more than 95 percent of the working force took up the offer. The private system, which has earned individual account holders an annual rate of return of 10 percent, has in effect created an ownership society in which account holders own in total the equivalent of more than 70 percent of the country's GDP. Thanks to those savings—and to other measures such as the elimination of income tax on domestic investment—that country has maintained investment levels that are almost 50 percent higher (in relative terms) than those in the rest of the region. This vital reform is one of the reasons why Chile's economy was able to grow at an average rate of 7.2 percent between 1985 and 1997.[48]

Reform slowed down after that period until it was taken up again by socialist President Ricardo Lagos in some respects (especially trade). However, many other areas, such as taxation and labor markets, need further reform if Chile is going to maintain the pattern of success and go beyond its current GDP per capita of just under $11,000 (based on purchasing power parity).

6. The Justice System

One of the areas least talked about with regard to Latin America's reforms in the past decade is the judicial system. It is often said that the judicial system is the "Cinderella" of Latin America's state because it is forced to operate with low budgets. Most countries allocate no more than 2 percent of their national budget to the judicial system, and almost all of that money is spent on salaries. But the resources that politicians allocate to the courts and judges bear little relation to the importance they assign to them, which is why all governments and the special interests attached to them devote considerable time and resources to controlling and corrupting them.[49]

"Justice is like a snake—it only bites the barefoot," said Archbishop Arnulfo Romero before perishing in the midst of El Salvador's civil war in the 1980s. The phrase captures the essence of the judicial system in the region. It is an arm of the government, not a limit on political power or a safeguard for the protection of individual rights. The problem lies in the confusion between law and legislation. It is generally assumed that the norms and laws dictated by Congress or by the bureaucracy are legitimate sources of law, whatever they establish. This confusion is part of an old tradition. It existed in pre-Columbian times and was compounded by both the colonial and the republican eras.

When Latin America was conquered by Spain and Portugal, most of Europe had long ceased to understand law as an evolutionary process stemming from the customs of the people, as something that jurists "discovered" rather than created—a practice that had been alive in different periods, including, partly, in Rome and in some medieval cities and that was still alive in England. Under Spain and Portugal, the law was essentially an instrument of the Crown, a top-down rather than a bottom-up process. The *audiencias*, as the courts of law were known, were closely linked to either the Crown or the church, the two greatest powers. In the nineteenth century, after gaining independence, Latin America's republics imported legal codes from Europe, especially from France and Spain, where legislation, not law, was the guiding principle of government. Under the succession of coups and countercoups that marked Latin America's nineteenth century, those codes were reformed time and again to suit the interests of those in power. In the twentieth century, under democratic rule, the judicial system, guided by ever-changing codes that reflected the interests of the newly dominant classes, continued to discriminate against ordinary citizens and to subject their decisions to considerations of power politics or influence rather than justice.

The confusion between law and legislation is so entrenched in the region that, even as sweeping changes were taking place in the economy in the 1990s, there was no profound judicial reform in any country, internationally funded programs and bureaucratic reviews notwithstanding. The countries where the justice system is less corrupt and less vulnerable to the meddling of politicians are also the ones where strong civilian institutions have long been in place (Costa Rica being a case in point) and where ethical standards and the separation of powers have been traditionally greater (such as Uruguay).[50] The rest continue to have weak judicial systems and have engaged in either no reform at all or very limited reform.

Table 7.2 and Figure 7.3 show the evolution of the legal structure and the security of property rights for six Latin American countries between the years 1975 and 2002 (the most recent year for which comprehensive data are available) as well as for the United States during that period. The figures, based on the Economic Freedom of the World index, indicate the consistency of a nation's legal structure with the protection of property rights, the enforcement of contracts, the independence of the judiciary, and the rule of law. In the 0 to 10 ratings, 10 means most reliable legal institutions and most secure property rights.

Lack of serious reform does not mean that those in positions of

TABLE 7.2

Legal system and security of property rights: Latin America and the United States

	1970	1975	1980	1985	1990	1995	2000	2001	2002
Argentina	N/A	1.6	4.2	4.6	6.0	5.5	5.4	3.6	3.2
Brazil	N/A	5.4	5.9	5.7	6.2	5.8	5.4	4.9	4.9
Colombia	N/A	3.3	4.0	3.4	3.4	2.8	3.5	3.4	3.3
Mexico	N/A	4.1	6.3	5.4	6.8	5.3	4.2	3.6	4.2
Peru	N/A	1.1	3.8	2.2	2.9	4.8	3.9	4.2	4.0
Venezuela	N/A	2.8	6.2	5.3	5.7	3.8	3.7	1.9	1.6
U.S.	N/A	7.9	8.3	8.3	8.3	8.8	9.2	8.7	8.2

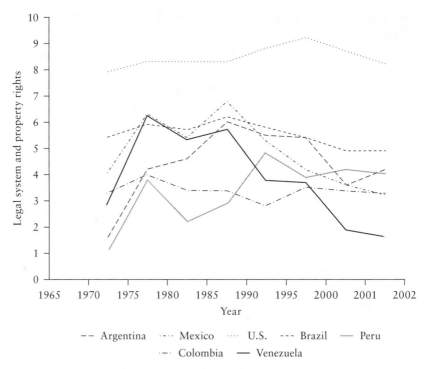

FIGURE **7.3**   Legal system and security of property rights: Latin America and the United
States

power did not entertain lively discussions—sometimes even acting on
them—about everything from changing the way judges are appointed to
increasing budgets, updating technology, reshuffling the structure of the
courts, elevating the level of training, or decentralizing the judicial network. But in the new millennium Latin America is left with opinion polls
that consistently put the judicial system at the top of the list of the most
corrupt, inefficient, and untrustworthy institutions. The economic implications of inadequate judicial institutions are considerable. Conservative
estimates by multilateral bodies point to a 15 percent negative incidence
of such a factor in economic growth due to lack of investor trust.[51]

The problem does not lie in the way judges are appointed because
no matter what mechanism is used, the power of government is such that
judges are subservient to those who run it or to the prosecutors acting
in its name (what Richard Pipes calls "telephone justice" with reference
to Russia's courts of law). It is of no real consequence by how much the

budget is increased, how many new courts there are and how they divide the load, how many computers are made available, how sophisticated the level of training is, or how many judges work from the provinces as opposed to the capital city. The real problem lies in the lack of independence vis-à-vis the government and its arm, political law, in the high costs of access to the courts for ordinary citizens, and in the sheer inefficiency of the judiciary. By not attacking these factors, or by doing so partially, all attempts at judicial reform have failed. Brazil's new 1988 Constitution embraced what looked like ambitious judicial reform, carried out with much enthusiasm in the following years. The result of greater access to the courts was that pending cases increased ten times in the subsequent decade.[52] In the case of Ecuador, there are more than a half-million backlogged cases, lasting a little less than two years on average.[53]

Decisions continue to be made not on the basis of justice but rather on the basis of the legislation controlled by politicians and of how much relative power the parties involved wield even at the low end of the scale. Ultimately, the Latin American justice system, like the rest of the public sector but to much worse effect, depends on the incentives that judges have to be fair or unfair, and it is often the case that those incentives work against what is right because the courts are an extension of power as a source of legal discrimination. Because the benefits of judicial reform are not immediate, the incentive for decision makers to reverse the situation is null. It does not matter that ordinary citizens at large reject the system that victimizes them, because the weakness of civil society, in part related to the inadequacy of the judiciary, means the issue of real reform is subject to the incentives or disincentives of the elites. The elites attempted the transition from economic nationalism to private enterprise because the cost of the former system had become unbearable. There was no equivalent pressure to overhaul the justice system. In fact, the continuing subservience of judges to the powerful is one of the very reasons why the elites managed to turn "free-market" reform in the 1980s and 1990s into a reshuffling of power rather than a reversal of the status quo.

7. The Backlash

Latin America did not draw the right conclusions from the poor results obtained by the process of reform in the 1990s. The first decade of the new millennium has seen the return of populism, albeit with less impetus than in the past, thanks to the widespread belief that what failed in the previous decades were free markets rather than corporatism, state mercantilism, privilege, wealth transfer, and political law. The accumulated inflation between May 2003 and March 2005 in Argentina, under President Néstor Kirchner, was 11 percent, more than the accumulated inflation in the eight years from 1993 to 2001. The Argentinean government expanded the money supply considerably between 2003 and 2005, kept an artificially high exchange rate to please industrialists close to power, created new state-owned corporations (including one in the energy sector), increased funds for social programs and public works, mounted a very strong campaign against foreign utility companies, and chose to write off much of the debt it owed to bondholders. Thanks to a rebound effect from the previous recession and to the high prices of the country's commodities in the world markets, there has been some economic growth, as has happened so often in the past, but the result of this has been to temporarily conceal the hard realities that come with populism.

In other countries, such as Mexico, the opening of the political system and the greater freedom enjoyed by the press since the transition to democracy in 2000 have not been accompanied by major institutional reform; populism has begun to gain considerable ground as a response to the lack of reformist zeal on the part of the authorities. Millions of Mexicans who are supporting old-style populism do not seem to have learned the lessons from the fact that South Korea, a nation that was underdeveloped three decades ago and has less than half their population, enjoys a per capita income that is 50 percent higher thanks to a number of free-market reforms undertaken in this period. In Peru, a country that borders Chile, almost no reform has taken place since the transition to democracy in the year 2001, and the timid efforts to privatize government-owned companies have been met with violent resistance, with the effect that there are still forty-eight companies in state hands related to major sectors of the economy; none of the principal political actors is proposing to privatize them.

The cumulative effect of statism in most Latin American countries has been the creation of dual societies in which a small segment of the population is able to partake in the opportunities of globalization and to make the most of the technological advances that the information era makes rapidly available, while a much larger segment is clearly operating below its potential, unable to translate its entrepreneurial capacity into a process of sustained wealth creation. This state of affairs is ultimately bad for everyone but the ruling elite: the legal enterprises cannot grow and pay high salaries to more people so that they can buy goods and services from midsize and small companies, and these, in turn, because of a depressed market, are obliged to sell their products to public employees (the reason why so many informal vendors cluster around government buildings seeking to attract the only customers with money in their pockets). In Peru, for instance, only 2 percent of all private companies are legal, and they produce 60 percent of the wealth, while the other 98 percent of all enterprises, operating outside of the law, produce little.[54]

These realities are usually lost on the macroeconomic statistics that tend to be disproportionately impacted by primary exports and other variables that benefit from a positive international context and oftentimes translate into misleadingly healthy aggregate figures. The problems are compounded by protectionism in developed nations. It is estimated that farm subsidies in OECD countries (i.e., rich countries) add up to almost $350 billion—a sum that is ironically the equivalent of six and one-half times all the foreign aid handed out by these nations precisely in the name of development![55] However, it would be disingenuous of Latin American countries to devote their main efforts to obtaining the elimination of protectionism in developed nations rather than to reforming their own institutions. After all, many countries have been able to develop themselves, or to make significant progress, without waiting for others to address their own flaws. Even if other countries eliminated protectionism, Latin America would be unable to make the most of the new opportunities without first having undergone profound domestic reform.

8. The Next Attempt

What is needed at this stage in Latin America is probably akin to what took place in eighteenth-century England when Whig reformers decided to undo much of the statute book—and the agencies attached to those laws and norms—legated by previous generations. By the third quarter of the eighteenth century, more than eighteen thousand norms had been repealed—some four-fifths of the laws passed since Henry III.

The process was dictated by the principle of individual liberty—most of the norms that undermined individual liberty were done away with, to the effect that the power of the state over the citizens was dramatically reduced. The result was a long period of prosperity that we now partly associate with the Industrial Revolution.[56]

A recent study in Argentina indicated that the accumulation of laws in that country is such that 85 percent of them are not even enforceable because they contradict or overlap each other and in many cases remain in the statute book even though they have already been tacitly repealed. The result of this legislative labyrinth is that citizens simply do not know what the law of the land is, finding it so complex and meddlesome that they often choose to disregard it. According to a study conducted by the Law School of the University of Buenos Aires, there are currently twenty-six thousand norms, but no more than four thousand are really applicable.[57] This situation is the result of a legislative process (including decrees emanating from the executive branch) that has survived all regime changes since Argentina gained its independence from Spain, despite the many times in which democratically elected governments or military juntas have promised a clean break with the past.

Any serious reform process geared toward the liberation of the individual from the phenomenal accumulation of state power in Latin America, the release of the creative energy that is constrained by the prevailing institutional environment, and the establishment of the rule of law will entail a thorough purgation of the legislation and of the bodies generated by it. This process will allow the official institutions to be much more closely in touch with reality—that is, with the ways and means of ordinary people who have generated parallel institutions in their struggle to survive. After the institutions are stripped of their authoritarian and socialistic dimensions, they will cease to expropriate the belongings of ordinary people, to stifle their entrepreneurial spirit through barriers to entry and coercive redistribution of wealth, and to relegate them to a second-class status in which they have very limited access to the courts. The result should be a bridging of the gap that today separates the law from reality and the restoration of a social order governed by peaceful cooperation.

Here are some examples of laws that need to be eliminated or, at the very least, to be replaced with norms that essentially purge corporatism, state mercantilism, privilege, wealth transfer, and political law from the system. The current legislation in most countries can be divided (rather simplistically) into five major categories: business, finance, labor, social issues, and, finally, justice and law and order.

In the first category (business), a number of laws limit entrepreneurship through the use of permits and licenses; crowd out potential new businesses by sanctioning and supporting government-owned companies; create shortages and ultimately make goods and services expensive through the use of price controls or "pro-consumer" laws; hinder economies of scale through antitrust action; hurt production through the coercive redistribution of wealth via subsidies and tariffs; and benefit certain industries at the expense of others with the excuse of "promoting" the development of strategic sectors. All of these actions in turn generate government bodies sustained through high taxes that penalize income, savings, and investment as well as consumption and commerce.

In the second category (finance), a number of laws allow the government to generate debt, a practice that has led to a combined foreign debt in Latin America of close to $1 trillion. Other laws restrict competition in the banking system, impose arbitrary fractional reserves, or make it difficult to participate in the stock exchange through barriers to entry and mandatory high commissions. The same is true of the insurance market, where similar restrictions drive up the price of the service.

In the third category (labor), a number of laws violate freedom of contract and association between employers and employees, giving monopoly powers to certain unions and forcing collective bargaining by trade, which severely hampers the market's capacity to generate jobs even when investment is high.

In the fourth category (social legislation), education and health continue to suffer from the heavy presence of the government both through the direct provision of the service—generally under the control of politicized unions that dictate policy—and through laws that place many obstacles in the way of private provision.

In the final category (justice and law and order), we find many laws that create special jurisdictions—and therefore privilege—as well as norms that give the political authorities a strong say in the judiciary. Other legal instruments—especially the civil and penal codes and the respective procedural rules—invade all spheres of an individual's and a family's life through a labyrinthine web of mandates and restrictions disguised as the protection of public health, the environment, and social peace.

Until these and many other types of legal intrusions on the part of the government are repealed or severely curtailed, until, that is, many areas that now absorb the energy of lawmakers are left, in Burke's words, to "wise and salutary neglect," it will be impossible for more than 400 million Latin Americans to translate their rich cultural legacy and entrepreneurial potential into prosperity. Something of the spirit of Urukagina, the first free-market reformer in recorded history, needs to impregnate the popular and intellectual discussion so that decision makers can begin the process of "undoing" much of what has been done over the last few centuries and liberate society from the constraints that today impede development even as other regions of the world—less well endowed by nature and with less impressive histories—are moving in the right direction.

Notes

1. There are many interesting accounts of Urukagina's reforms in Lagash; see Kramer (1956; 1963).

2. Shady Solís, Haas, and Creamer (2001).

3. James (2001).

4. Carlos Antonio Mendoza Alvarado, who has conducted extensive research on Indian markets in Guatemala, states that "indigenous markets are institutions stemming from the Guatemalan Maya culture, based on free and voluntary exchange by their members, and on the value of their word (oral contracts), constituting meeting places where information is also exchanged and intercultural relations take place" (1999, p. 5).

5. In the first years of the eighteenth century, no more than 14.5 percent of the ships that departed from Callao in Peru were destined for Panama, the viaduct for legitimate trade with Spain. See Clayton (1985), p. 190.

6. Vargas Llosa (2005).

7. Page 5 of the *Reporte Social* published by the Instituto Nacional de Estadística (INE), the official Venezuelan body in charge of publishing statistics, and posted on its Web site (www.ine.gov.ve), indicates that poverty went up from 43 percent to 54 percent of the population in the first four years of Hugo Chávez's government (1999–2003). The president of INE told Venezuelan newspapers at the end of 2004 that the proportion of the population living in poverty remained at around 53 percent. See Oppenheimer (2005).

8. Olson (1996).

9. "Pocket World in Figures: 2005 Edition," pp. 110, 216.

10. For an analysis of expenditures on health and education in Spain and other European countries in the 1980s and 1990s, see Neira and Iglesias (2001).

11. McQuerry (2002).

12. Taylor (2000).

13. Bauer (1970), p. 127.

14. For a discussion of the role played by formal and informal institutions in development, see North (1990).

15. Hoskins and Eiras (2002), p. 40.

16. Baumol (1990), pp. 894, 899.

17. Andreski (1969), p. 77.

18. Pipes (1999), pp. 97–98.

19. One case study was conducted in some barrios (shantytowns) of Caracas, Venezuela; see Karst, Schwartz, and Schwartz (1973).

20. "Remittances: Key Source of Capital for Latin America and the Caribbean," Multilateral Investment Fund, Inter-American Development Bank, 2005. http://www.iadb.org/NEWS/DISPLAY/issuebriefs/2004/remitt.cfm?Language=English (accessed April 11, 2007).

21. Wiarda (2001), p. 133.

22. The period in which Portugal came under Spain's control, between 1580 and 1640, did see a greater measure of centralized administration.

23. Small traders and the Jesuits reacted strongly, and an authoritarian crackdown ensued. Politics and the economy became more controlled than ever before in the colony. See Russell-Wood (1975), pp. 13–29.

24. Prado (1967), p. 54.

25. In Venezuela, according to John Lynch, "independence reaffirmed the power of the land-owning class. The colonial aristocracy did not survive in its entirety, but its ranks were replenished by new, plebeian entrants. Estates confiscated by royalists were restored to their owners or descendents, while the republican Government confiscated the property of its enemies" (1973, p. 222).

26. Drinot (2000), vol. 1, p. 161.

27. Burns and Charlip (2002), p. 201.

28. Powelson and Stock (1990), pp. 35–37.

29. Ibid., pp. 141–142.

30. Some countries, such as Brazil, did not engage in full-scale land reform, so concentration of property was perpetuated according to the old legacy. The response was the massive "landless" peasant movement, which in the 1980s engaged in violence against, and was the object of violence by, the big owners.

31. Muñoz Gomá (2001), p. 53.

32. For a good dissection of Raúl Prebisch's argument, see Bauer (1976), pp. 234–271.

33. Alan M. Taylor attributes later differences in the depth of economic distortions between the Southern Cone and Central America to the differing extents of these early capital controls. See Taylor (2000), pp. 133–134.

34. Burns and Charlip (2002), p. 238.

35. "Social Change in Latin America in the Early 1970s."

36. United Nations Development Program (2001).

37. International Monetary Fund (2000), p. 81.

38. Andreski (1969), p. 11.

39. "Economist Urges America to Do More to Fight Poverty," *San Francisco Chronicle*, May 8, 2005.

40. It is estimated that in Peru, less than one-third of the money related to the most important welfare program, Vaso de Leche (Glass of Milk), reaches the poor children it is supposed to reach. See José Luis Sardón, "Un Vladimiro Montesinos cada año," *Lima*, May 20, 2004. www.libertaddigital.es (accessed April 11, 2007).

41. "IMF Wants Further Economic Liberalization in Latin America," *Wall Street Journal*, February 9, 2005.

42. Sources: ECLAC, *Statistical Yearbook of Latin America for Latin America and the Caribbean*, 2000; ECLAC, *Balance Preliminar de las Economías de América Latina y el Caribe*, 2001.

43. Ian Vásquez (2002) estimates that GDP per capita grew at an annual average of 1.5 percent in the 1990s.

44. Damian (2000).

45. Yeats (2003), p. 154.

46. Heston, Summers, and Aten (2002).

47. Fontaine (1990), pp. 95–113.

48. Piñera (2004).

49. The government of President Menem, for instance, increased the number of Supreme Court justices from five to nine, obtaining the control of a key institution. Corruption plagued his government, based to a large extent on rule by decree, but the subservience of the Supreme Court prevented the judiciary from acting as a safeguard against the government's unethical practices and political excesses.

50. Laurence Whitehead has referred to Chile's advantages over other Latin American countries regarding judicial institutions in their increasing role as substitutes for the government's other branches in a privatized economy. He argues that the "neoliberal" trend might be reversed if the legal system is not strong

enough to support the demands of the market economy. See Whitehead (2000), pp. 266–267, 270–271.

51. Prillaman (2000), p. 3.

52. Buscaglia, Dakolias, and Ratliff (1995), p. 23. Buscaglia and Ratliff (2000, p. 57) also indicate that between 1973 and 1985 the median delay in first-instance Brazilian courts experienced a change of 4 percent, whereas between 1986 and 1997 the median delay experienced a change of 38.1 percent.

53. Buscaglia, Dakolias, and Ratliff (1995), p. 9.

54. Mansueti (2003).

55. Organisation for Economic Co-operation and Development (2003).

56. Nock (1991), p. 279.

57. "No sirve el 85 por ciento de las leyes que hoy rigen en el país," *La Nación*, Buenos Aires, Argentina, June 12, 2005.

References

Andreski, Stanislav. 1969. *Parasitism and Subversion: The Case of Latin America*. New York: Schocken Books.

Bauer, Peter T. 1976. *Dissent on Development*. Cambridge, MA: Harvard University Press.

Baumol, William. 1990. "Entrepreneurship: Productive, Unproductive, and Destructive." *The Journal of Political Economy* 98 (5), pt. 1 (October): 893–921.

Burns, Bradford E., and Julie A. Charlip. 2002. *A Concise Interpretive History*. Englewood Cliffs, NJ: Prentice Hall.

Buscaglia, Eduardo, Maria Dakolias, and William Ratliff. 1995. *Judicial Reform in Latin America: A Framework for National Development*. Stanford, CA: Hoover Institution Press.

Buscaglia, Eduardo, and William Ratliff. 2000. *Law and Economics in Developing Countries*. Stanford, CA: Hoover Institution Press.

Clayton, L. A. 1985. "Trade and Navigation in the Seventeenth-Century Viceroyalty of Peru." In *Readings in Latin American History*, vol. 1, *The Formative Centuries*, ed. Peter J. Bakewell, John J. Johnson, and Meredith D. Dodge. Durham, NC: Duke University Press.

Damian, Araceli. 2000 *Adjustment, Poverty, and Employment in Mexico*. Hampshire, UK: Ashgate.

Drinot, Paulo. 2000. "Peru, 1884–1930: A Beggar Sitting on a Bench of Gold." In *An Economic History of Twentieth-Century Latin America* (3 vols.), ed. Enrique Cárdenas, Jose Antonio Ocampo, and Rosemary Thorp, vol. 1. Houndsmill, UK: Palgrave in association with St. Anthony's College, Oxford.

"Economist Urges America to Do More to Fight Poverty." 2005. *San Francisco Chronicle* (May 8).

Fontaine, Arturo. 1990. "The War of Ideas in Chile." In *Fighting the War of Ideas in Latin America*, ed. John Goodman and Ramona Morotz-Baden. Dallas, TX: National Center for Policy Analysis.

Heston, Alan, Robert Summers, and Bettina Aten. 2002. *Penn World Tables 6.1*. Philadelphia: Center for International Comparisons, University of Pennsylvania.

Hoskins, Lee, and Ana I. Eiras. 2002. "Property Rights: The Key to Economic Growth." In *2002 Index of Economic Freedom*, ed. Gerald P. O'Driscoll Jr., Kim R. Holmes, and Mary Anastasia O'Grady. Washington, DC: Heritage Foundation and Dow Jones.

"IMF Wants Further Economic Liberalization in Latin America." 2005. *Wall Street Journal* (February 9).

Instituto Nacional de Estadística (INE). 2005. *Reporte Social*. www.ine.gov.ve (accessed April 11, 2007).

International Monetary Fund. 2000. *International Financial Statistics Yearbook*. Washington, DC: International Monetary Fund.

James, N. 2001. *Aztecs and Maya: the Ancient Peoples of Middle America*. Charleston, SC: Tempus.

Karst, Kenneth L., Murray L. Schwartz, and Audrey J. Schwartz. 1973. *The Evolution of the Law in the Barrios of Caracas*. Los Angeles: Latin American Center, University of California.

Kramer, Samuel Noah. 1956. *From the Tablets of Sumer: Twenty-Five Firsts in Man's Recorded History*. Indian Hills, CO: Falcon's Wing Press.

———. 1963. *The Sumerians: Their History, Culture, and Character*. Chicago: University of Chicago Press.

Lynch, John. 1973. *The Spanish American Revolutions, 1808–1826*. New York: W. W. Norton.

Mansueti Alberto, with José Luis Tapia and Instituto de Libre Empresa. 2003. *La Salida* (e-book). Lima, Peru: Instituto de Libre Empresa.

McQuerry, Elizabeth. 2002. "In Search of Better Reform in Latin America." *Econ. South* 4 (2).

Mendoza Alvarado, Antonio. 1999. *Aproximación al funcionamiento de los mercados indígenas de Guatemala: Consideraciones económicas sobre el mercado de Tecpán*. Guatemala City, Guatemala: Universidad Francisco Marroquín.

Multilateral Investment Fund, Inter-American Development Bank. 2005. "Remittances: Key Source of Capital for Latin America and the Caribbean." http://www.iadb.org/NEWS/DISPLAY/issuebriefs/2004/remitt.cfm?Language=English (accessed April 11, 2007).

Muñoz Gomá, Oscar. 2001. *Estrategias de desarrollo en economías emergentes: Lecciones de la experiencia latinoamericana.* Santiago de Chile, Chile: Facultad Latinoamericana de Ciencias Sociales.

Neira, Isabel, and Ana Iglesias. 2001. "Comparación internacional del gasto público en sanidad y educación de España con los países de la OCDE, 1982–1996." *Estudios Económicos de Desarrollo Internacional, AEEAED* 1 (2).

Nock, Albert J. 1991. "Liberalism, Properly So Called." In *The State of the Union: Essays in Social Criticism.* Indianapolis, IN: Liberty Press.

"No sirve el 85 por ciento de las leyes que hoy rigen en el país." 2005. *La Nación* (June 12).

North, Douglass. 1990. *Institutions, Institutional Change and Economic Development.* Cambridge: Cambridge University Press.

Olson, Mancur, Jr. 1966. "Distinguished Lecture on Economics in Government: Big Bills Left on the Sidewalk: Why Some Nations Are Rich, and Others Poor." *Journal of Economic Perspectives* 10 (2): 3–24.

Oppenheimer, Andres. 2005. "The Oppenheimer Report: Poverty Figures Undermine Chávez's Success Claim." *Miami Herald* (March 31).

Organisation for Economic Co-operation and Development. 2003. "Producer and Consumer Support Estimates: OECD Database, 1986–2003." http://www.oecd.org/document/58/0,2340,en_2649_37401_32264698_1_1_1_37401,00.html (accessed April 11, 2007).

Piñera, José. 2004. "Retiring in Chile." *New York Times* (December 1).

Pipes, Richard E. 1999. *Property and Freedom.* New York: Alfred A. Knopf.

"Pocket World in Figures: 2005 Edition." 2005. *Economist.*

Powelson, John P., and Richard Stock. 1990. *The Peasant Betrayed: Agriculture and Land Reform in the Third World.* Washington, DC: Cato Institute.

Prado, Caio, Jr. 1967. *História econômica do Brasil.* São Paulo, Brazil: Editôra Brasiliense.

Prillaman, William. 2000. *The Judiciary and Democratic Decay in Latin America: Declining Confidence in the Rule of Law.* Westport, CT: Praeger.

Russell-Wood, A. J. R. 1975. "Preconditions and Precipitants of the Independence Movement in Portuguese America." In *From Colony to Nation: Essays on the Independence of Brazil,* ed. A. J. R. Russell-Wood. Baltimore, MD: Johns Hopkins University Press.

Sardón, José Luis. 2004. "Un Vladimiro Montesinos cada año." *Lima* (May 20). www.libertaddigital.es (accessed April 11, 2007).

Shady Solís, Ruth, Jonathan Haas, and Winifred Creamer. 2001. "Dating Caral, a Preceramic Site in the Supe Valley on the Central Coast of Peru." *Science* 292 (April 27): 723–726.

"Social Change in Latin America in the Early 1970s, Economic Commission for Latin America." Robinson Rojas Archive. http://www.rojasdatabank.org.

Taylor, Alan M. 2000. "Latin America and Foreign Capital in the Twentieth Century." In *Political Institutions and Economic Growth in Latin America: Essays in Policy, History, and Political Economy*, ed. Stephen Haber. Stanford, CA: Hoover Institution Press.

United Nations Development Program. 2001. *Human Development Report 2001.* http://hdr.undp.org/reports/2001/en/.

Vargas Llosa, Alvaro. 2005. *Liberty for Latin America: How to Undo Five Hundred Years of State Oppression.* New York: Farrar, Straus & Giroux.

Vásquez, Ian. 2002. *Una política exterior de Estados Unidos para América Latina.* Washington, DC: Cato Institute.

Whitehead, Laurence. 2000. "Privatization and the Public Interest: Partial Theories, Lopsided Outcomes." In *Liberalization and Its Consequences: A Comparative Perspective on Latin America and Eastern Europe*, ed. Werner Baer and Joseph L. Love. Cheltenham, UK: Edward Elgar.

Wiarda, Howard J. 2001. *The Soul of Latin America.* New Haven, CT: Yale University Press.

Yeats, Guillermo M. 2003. *Las perversas reglas de juego en América Latina.* Buenos Aires, Argentina: LexisNexis Abeledo-Perrot.

8   Entrepreneurship or Entremanureship?
     Digging Through Romania's Institutional
     Environment for Transition Lessons

PETER J. BOETTKE, CHRISTOPHER J. COYNE, AND PETER T. LEESON

1. Introduction

Since the fall of communism, countries transitioning to the market economy have had very different experiences. In some cases, such as Estonia, Hungary, and Poland, transition has been relatively successful. In these countries, market institutions have been adopted, placing the countries on a path of economic growth and development. In contrast, other countries, such as Russia and Romania, have yet to turn the corner. These countries have been unable to exploit the technologies and beneficial liberal institutions found in other parts of the world. As such, these countries have remained stuck in a trap of underdevelopment, noncooperative behavior, and unhealthy institutions. In this chapter we focus on assessing and understanding the institutional environment faced by entrepreneurs in Romania. In addition to understanding the specific issues challenging Romania, we seek to draw some general lessons applicable to all of the postcommunist transition countries.

A. Brief Economic History of Romania

The Treaty of Adrianopole in 1829 marks the beginning of the modern economic history of Romania. Ending the Ottoman economic domination, the treaty opened the way for Romania's integration into the international economic system. Starting as a primarily agrarian economy,

Romania developed trade, economic infrastructure, and the foundations of industrialization over the next century. Important political successes during this period served to strengthen these developments. For instance, Moldavia and Wallachia were unified in 1859, and Romania gained formal independence in 1877. During this period, Romania established itself as one of the world's major exporters of grain and meat.

Romania's economic development during the interwar period is commonly referred to as the "Romanian miracle." In the wake of World War I, Transylvania, Basarabia, and Bucovina united with Romania in 1918. Despite losses incurred due to the war, the economy grew quickly during this period. The process of industrialization that preceded the war continued in the postwar period. Romania established itself as a major oil exporter, although agriculture remained the most significant source of income.

The communist period (1947–1989) destroyed both Romania's market economy and its social structure. Soviet economic exploitation slowed the country's recovery from the losses incurred in World War II. Furthermore, communist projects, such as land collectivization, forced industrialization, and economic planning, destroyed the progress that was made during the industrialization process.

B. Romania's Current Situation

Romania is a lower-middle-income, developing nation in transition from a centrally planned economy to a market economy.[1] Its population is around 22.3 million, making it one of the largest countries in central Europe. The population is roughly equally divided between urban and rural areas, with slightly fewer inhabitants (about 3 percent fewer) in the latter.

Although it has progressed somewhat since the collapse of Ceaușescu's communist regime in 1989, Romania continues to struggle economically and faces a long uphill journey before it reaches the level of development obtained by relatively successful reforming economies such as Estonia, Hungary, and Poland. To provide one gauge of Romania's progress relative to that of other postcommunist transition countries, Table 8.1 shows the average annual change in real per capita GDP for transition countries during the 1991–2003 period.

TABLE 8.1
*Average annual change in real per capita GDP (U.S.$ 2000
base year) for postcommunist transition countries,
1991–2003*

Country	Average annual growth rate (%)
Poland	3.26
Albania	2.70
Estonia	1.91
Hungary	1.57
Slovak Republic	1.04
Czech Republic	0.86
Armenia	0.83
Belarus	0.54
Bulgaria	0.48
Latvia	0.41
Kazakhstan	0.29
Romania	0.15
Turkmenistan	−0.24
Lithuania	−0.45
Uzbekistan	−0.89
Macedonia FYR	−1.32
Russia	−1.50
Kyrgyzstan	−3.19
Ukraine	−4.03
Georgia	−5.33
Moldova	−6.07
Tajikistan	−6.39

SOURCE: World Bank (2004).

Romania is in the middle of the pack, ranking twelfth out of twenty-two transition countries. It has not fared nearly as well as some transition countries such as Poland, Estonia, and Hungary, but it has outperformed others such as Russia and Ukraine.

Currently, Romania's per capita GDP (purchasing power parity) is approximately $7,000, and nearly 45 percent of its population lives below the poverty line (World Bank 2004; Central Intelligence Agency 2004). Inflation has been a persistent problem in Romania, reaching its peak of more than 250 percent in 1993. Inflation remains a problem and in 2003 was approximately 15 percent (Central Intelligence Agency 2004).

Some privatization has occurred since 1989. However, many of these efforts have stalled. Thus although the private sector has grown, the weight of large loss-making public enterprises remains high. In 2001, the private sector employed 62.8 percent of the workforce, primarily in commerce and services (37.5 percent), agriculture and forestry (17.3 percent), industry (17.3 percent), and construction (3.4 percent). Public companies, however, still account for more than 40 percent of enterprise investment and 75 percent of all tangible assets. In the agricultural sector, despite some progress, the problem of property titles is not yet fully clarified. This, coupled with limited progress in privatizing agricultural companies, holds back the consolidation of fragmented land holdings and the development of a viable land market (Central Intelligence Agency 2004).

The Heritage Foundation/*Wall Street Journal* Index of Economic Freedom (2005) has placed Romania in the category of "Mostly Unfree" every year since 1995. Excessive regulation, bureaucracy, taxation, and rapidly changing laws have created a difficult environment for entrepreneurs and continue to pose serious obstacles to business start-ups and growth (Heritage Foundation/*Wall Street Journal* 2005). Although this fact is widely recognized both inside and outside of Romania, little has been done to improve the business climate. On the contrary, new legislation that deals with issues such as taxation and regulation tends to exacerbate the problem rather than fix it. We will explore this point in greater detail in subsequent sections.

Politically, Romania is a constitutional democracy and has a multiparty, bicameral parliamentary system. In 2000, the center-left Social Democratic Party (PSD) became Romania's leading party. In the December 2004 presidential elections, the opposition center-right alliance, consisting of the National Liberal Party (PNL) and the Democratic Party (PD), won a surprising victory over the ruling PSD. The current president is Traian Basescu. The Social Democratic Party holds about 37 percent of the seats in both the Senate and the Chamber of Deputies (Central Intelligence Agency 2004). Political corruption is rampant in Romania. In 2002, it was ranked the third-most corrupt country in Europe after Russia and Albania (Transparency International 2003).

C. Framework and Methodology

This chapter critically analyzes the current institutional environment in Romania.[2] Specifically, we seek to understand how the institutional environment influences entrepreneurship and innovation. For the analysis that follows, we use the notion of entrepreneurship developed by Israel Kirzner (1973). Kirzner emphasized alertness to profit opportunities as the main characteristic of entrepreneurship. We combine this notion of entrepreneurship with the dichotomy of entrepreneurial activity put forth by William Baumol (1990, 2002).

Baumol noted that entrepreneurs are present in all cultural settings. These entrepreneurs exploit profit opportunities that they observe in their specific institutional setting. The reason why one observes economic development in some areas and economic stagnation in others is because profit opportunities are tied to different ends in different settings. More specifically, although entrepreneurs are present in all settings, the institutional environment, which directs their alertness, differs across societies. Baumol made the distinction between productive, positive-sum activities, and unproductive zero- or negative-sum activities. The payoff to each of these types of activity is directly dependent on the formal and informal institutions present in a society. Some institutional regimes channel entrepreneurial activity into economically destructive avenues, whereas other frameworks direct this activity in a way that creates wealth.

In the following analysis we combine general information regarding the institutional payoffs in Romania with original data gathered from original fieldwork in order to better understand the situation in Romania. Our fieldwork consisted of approximately thirty in-depth, guided, face-to-face interviews with Romanian entrepreneurs and political agents in three major geographic regions of the country—Bucharest, Arad, and Olt—representing both urban and rural perspectives in roughly equal proportions.[3] Political subjects were selected on the basis of relevance and availability. Thus those available political agents who seemed most likely to have insights related to the government's role in shaping Romania's climate of entrepreneurship received priority. Interviews with entrepreneurs were selected primarily by reference from other subjects, although some were selected at random.[4] All interviews were conducted during a two-month period from May 2003 through July 2003.

In the following section we first consider the institutional environment in Romania. We focus specifically on understanding how this environment influences the relative payoffs that entrepreneurs face. The first subsection (2.A) considers how the current institutional environment directs entrepreneurial activity toward what Baumol termed "unproductive activities." Subsection 2.B discusses how entrepreneurs engage in productive activities. In many cases, in order to undertake productive activities, entrepreneurs must incur additional costs to avoid other unproductive agents. We explore how these additional costs impact entrepreneurs looking to engage in productive activities.

Although studies often focus on entrepreneurs as a general category, in the case of Romania it is important to consider urban and rural entrepreneurs as distinct groups. Our fieldwork indicated that entrepreneurs in both the rural and urban settings face the same administrative and bureaucratic barriers. However, in addition to these common barriers, rural entrepreneurs face additional challenges. As such, Section 3 focuses on understanding the specific barriers that face rural entrepreneurs in Romania. The chapter concludes with some specific policy suggestions.

2. The Entrepreneurial Environment in Romania

A. Understanding the Cause of Unproductive Activities

Our fieldwork identified Romania's unstable legal and judicial institutions as the primary cause of corruption in its political institutions.[5] Excessive and uncertain regulations raise the relative payoff to unproductive activities. An economic adviser to the Romanian president with whom we spoke indicated that "it is easier to take money from others than by producing."[6] The problem of instability is compounded by the random and ineffective enforcement of regulations. To illuminate this situation relative to other transition countries, consider the transparency scores shown in Table 8.2.

A lower score indicates a greater level of opacity. The total opacity score is a composite of five subcategories: corruption, legal and judiciary opacity, economic/policy opacity, accountability/corporate governance, and regulatory opacity. Because we are considering the impact of regulations on entrepreneurship, this component of the total score is also presented in Table 8.2. Of the European transition countries considered in the study, Romania ranks above only Russia in total score and the regulatory component.

Based on our fieldwork in Romania, we observed that administrative incapacity characterizes both the central and local governments. The inability to carry out basic functions effectively presents a continuing problem. Appropriate resources—both financial and human—do

TABLE 8.2
PricewaterhouseCoopers opacity index for 2001

Country	Total opacity score	Regulatory component
Czech Republic	71	62
Hungary	50	47
Lithuania	58	66
Poland	64	72
Romania	71	73
Russia	84	84

SOURCE: http://www.irisprojects.umd.edu/anticorruption/Files/PWC_OpacityIndex.pdf (accessed May 21, 2007).

not support the high velocity of regulatory changes, with the end result being an incoherent legal framework. A 2000 study by the World Bank of corruption in Romania provides insight into the extent of the general legal environment in the country.[7] Of the results reported, 86 percent of respondents claimed that "constant changes in laws and regulations" are a main obstacle to doing business (p. 11).

In order to provide some means of considering Romania relative to other comparable countries, Table 8.3 presents the data for several global indicators that characterize the general environment for selected transition countries in 2002. (The details of these indicators can be found in Appendix Table 8.1.)

As Table 8.3 indicates, for all of the indicators considered, Romania ranks in the bottom one-third. Indeed, in corruption, Romania ranks twelfth out of thirteen, and in the category of "Rule of Law and Government Effectiveness," Romania ranks eleventh out of fourteen. These relatively low scores are in line with the findings of our fieldwork. In general, the environment in Romania poses serious barriers to productive entrepreneurship. Corruption is widespread, the judiciary is ineffective, and the quality of the government provision of goods and services is relatively low.

Romania's volatile laws are largely the product of "emergency ordinances"—immediately active executive decrees issued by the Romanian president on a frequent basis.[8] The Romanian Constitution states that the government may de facto legislate through direct ordinances that do not require an "organic law."[9] The Constitution also states that emergency ordinances may be used only "in exceptional cases." Ordinances go into effect immediately and are approved retrospectively by the

TABLE 8.3
Global indicators for selected transition countries, 2002

Country	ECONOMIC FREEDOM		RULE OF LAW		CORRUPTION		GOVERNMENT EFFECTIVENESS	
	Index	Rank	Score	Rank	Score	Rank	Score	Rank
Albania	3.24	8	−0.37	14	2.5	13	−0.47	14
Bulgaria	3.28	10	0.62	9	4.0	5	−0.06	10
Croatia	3.29	11	0.19	10	3.8	7	0.19	9
Czech Rep.	2.29	3	1.12	3	3.7	8	0.70	4
Estonia	1.73	1	1.35	1	5.6	2	0.78	2
Hungary	2.23	2	1.21	2	4.9	3	0.78	2
Latvia	2.49	5	0.86	5	3.7	9	0.67	5
Lithuania	2.35	4	0.96	4	4.8	4	0.61	6
Macedonia	3.35	12	−0.10	12	NA	NA	−0.39	12
Poland	2.60	6	0.67	8	4.0	5	0.61	7
Romania	3.48	13	0.04	11	2.6	12	−0.33	11
Russia	3.74	14	−0.30	13	2.7	11	−0.40	13
Slovakia	2.76	7	0.76	7	3.7	9	0.40	8
Slovenia	3.25	9	0.81	6	6.0	1	0.82	1

Parliament. In theory, emergency ordinances must be approved by the Parliament prior to going into effect. However, in practice, emergency ordinances go into effect in the same manner as regular ordinances. The end result is the complete absence of a check on executive legislation. Utilizing emergency ordinances has become standard practice in all situations. For instance, several emergency ordinances were used between 1999 and 2002 to reschedule the debts of or exempt from taxes several state companies (Coyne and Leeson 2004, 240; Open Society Institute 2002, 489).

To understand the magnitude of these ordinances, consider that between 1997 and 2000 alone, 684 emergency ordinances were issued—nearly 43 percent of all laws created during this period. In 2000, emergency ordinances actually accounted for the majority—more than 56 percent—of all laws created in Romania that year.[10] Given the rapid change in laws, it is nearly impossible to comply with the law even when one desires to do so. This is supported by the *2002 Corruption Perception Report*, which found that 53 percent of Romanians surveyed indicated that they would "break the law to get things done."[11] The rapidly changing law also erodes norms of trust. The aforementioned survey indicated that 54 percent of the respondents said they had "trust in other people," but only 23 percent said they had "trust in institutions" that comprise society (Transparency International 2003, 280). The logic here is straightforward. Trust in institutions requires stability and predictability. When these characteristics are lacking, so, too, will be trust in the institutions necessary for the creation of impersonal exchange and economic growth. In theory, well-functioning legal institutions can facilitate exchange and lower transaction costs, but dysfunctional legal institutions may have the opposite effect. Indeed, in such situations individuals may incur greater costs as they seek to avoid corruption and other negative externalities generated by an unstable legal system.

The unstable legal institutions in Romania create an environment of arbitrary enforcement and widespread corruption. The World Bank (2000) report discussed earlier illuminates the environment facing Romanian citizens. Approximately two-thirds of those surveyed believed that "all" or "most" public officials are corrupt (2000, vi). Of those surveyed, 42 percent of households and 28 percent of established enterprises experienced corruption in a twelve-month period (pp. viii, 7). Further, 50 percent of households and 44 percent of enterprises "think that bribery is part of everyday life" (p. 4). The types of corruption identified by the report include permits for building repair, construction and real estate, driving licenses, and loan applications.

Our fieldwork in both the urban and rural areas confirms the characterization portrayed by the data cited earlier. In all cases, entrepreneurs indicated that regulations were both plentiful and rapidly changing. As one entrepreneur indicated, "changes are so fast that no one, including public functionaries, know[s] what the law requires on any given day." [12] This situation is strongly reinforced by the lack of an efficient court system. Another entrepreneur noted that one "cannot use the state courts; they do not exist for me." [13] An entrepreneur in Visina Noua told us that he has never used state courts for dispute settlement because "whether you are guilty or not, you have to pay." [14] The ineffectiveness of state courts also hampers productive entrepreneurs. The absence of a courts system that is effective in protecting property and enforcing contracts in an efficient manner limits the expansion of one's network of clients, lenders, and suppliers. [15]

The uncertainty created by legal instability, excessive regulation, and corruption impacts entrepreneurs in a multitude of ways. For instance, those alert to a potential business opportunity must pay bribes at several levels of government to obtain the appropriate permits, licenses, and authorizations. Therefore, corruption is extremely damaging to economic progress on two fronts. In addition to impacting current enterprises, it also raises the cost of acting on potential business opportunities in the first place. In terms of Baumol's framework, the payoff to productive activities is lowered by the very presence of expensive bribes. Productive profit opportunities that would be exploited under a more favorable institutional setting remain untapped. Moreover, bribes continue after the business is up and running. As one entrepreneur summarized the situation, "I'm upset about paying bribes but I've adapted to them. I want to make money." [16] Our interviews confirmed that entrepreneurs have come to view corruption and the uncertain legal environment as part of their normal daily lives.

Assuming that entrepreneurs can overcome the barriers caused by bribes, the lack of stability and predictability of the legal environment makes it difficult to develop a long-term business plan. Given the high turnover of laws, the regulations in place today may very well be drastically different in future periods. This makes it extremely difficult for entrepreneurs not only to decide whether to pursue a potential profit opportunity but also to forecast the future business environment. As one entrepreneur put it, the "law changes so often, you can't formulate a long-term business plan." [17] In addition to these problems, the lack of stability and predictability of the legal environment makes it difficult to obtain funding. Most formal lending institutions require some forecast of expected profitability over the long term. Generating a forecast, however, is virtually impossible, given that legal factors affecting potential profitability change frequently.

Given the ease in changing laws and in earning an income via bribes and corruption, we see entrepreneurial activities directed toward these activities instead of toward productive ones. Returning to the World Bank survey cited earlier, 42 percent of enterprises responded that state officials engage in "skewing parliamentary votes in favor of certain private interests" (2000, x). Because changing the law is relatively easy, it makes sense for entrepreneurs to engage in activities that shift the legal environment to their own personal gain. Therefore, a large amount of resources is dedicated to rent seeking in order to obtain privileges from those in positions of power. One entrepreneur we interviewed in Visina Noua described this problem particularly well: "The sole profitable business in this environment is to have a connection in the government and make money from cheating and stealing." [18]

The situation in Romania can be viewed as a vicious circle. One unproductive activity—for example, a new law or regulation—creates several more opportunities for other unproductive activities—for example, inspectors using the new law to extract bribes. In fact, the constant creation of new laws and regulations often raises the returns from entering civil service above those of entering wealth-creating enterprises such as business. As one entrepreneur we spoke with indicated, several of his associates left successful businesses that they were running to become regulators and inspectors because they could earn more by engaging in unproductive activities as compared with productive ones. [19] Unproductive activities thus have a negative cumulative effect, reinforcing the current stagnation that characterizes the Romanian economy. Our

TABLE 8.4
Doing business in 2004

Country	Informal economy (% of GNI, 2003)	STARTING A BUSINESS			REGISTERING PROPERTY		
		Number of procedures	Time (days)	Cost (% of income per capita)	Number of procedures	Time (days)	Cost (% of property per capita)
Albania	34.1	11	47	32.2	7	47	3.8
Bulgaria	36.9	10	32	10.3	9	19	2.4
Croatia	33.4	12	49	14.4	5	956	2.5
Czech Rep.	19.1	10	40	10.8	4	122	3.0
Estonia	NA	6	72	7.5	4	65	0.5
Hungary	25.1	6	52	22.9	4	79	6.8
Latvia	39.9	7	18	17.6	10	62	2.1
Lithuania	30.3	8	26	3.7	3	3	0.9
Macedonia	NA	13	48	11.6	6	74	3.7
Poland	27.6	10	31	20.6	6	204	1.6
Romania	34.4	5	28	7.4	8	170	1.9
Russia	46.1	9	36	6.7	6	37	0.8
Slovakia	18.9	9	52	5.7	5	22	3.1
Slovenia	27.1	10	61	12.3	6	391	2.0
OECD Avg.	16.8	6	25	8.0	4	34	4.9

SOURCE: World Bank report.

fieldwork made it evident that entrepreneurship is alive and well in Romania. However, given the institutional environment, entrepreneurial alertness is currently directed toward unproductive ends.

B. Understanding the Barriers Facing Productive Entrepreneurs

In the previous subsection we considered the reasons why entrepreneurs in Romania would direct their efforts toward unproductive ends. We concluded that oftentimes the institutional environment in Romania yields relatively higher payoffs from engaging in such activities. However, it is important to note that productive activities still exist and are being undertaken. However, these productive activities are often stifled by unproductive activities and involve the expenditure of resources to evade the unproductive activities of other individuals. In this subsection we seek to explore the barriers facing those entrepreneurs who are alert to profit opportunities that are linked to productive activities.

Our interviews and experience in Romania indicated that tax evasion is the most common form of evasive activity. Tax evasion is largely a result of the opaque and rapidly changing Romanian tax code. Romania ranks 100 out of 102 countries in the 2003–2004 *Global Competitiveness Report*, which ranks countries according to business leaders' beliefs about how difficult the tax system is on business decisions. In the same report, entrepreneurs cited tax regulations as "the most problematic factor for doing business" in Romania. Although the volume of tax evasion is hard to measure, the Executive Opinion Survey, which asked Romanian business leaders about the frequency of bribes paid in connection with annual tax payments, placed Romania among the top thirty-two nations in this regard (World Economic Forum 2003–2004).

Regarding the formally required authorizations, approvals, and licenses, many entrepreneurs try to evade the legal process altogether. In order to provide a comparison of the number of procedures and costs associated with establishing a business across transition countries, Table 8.4 shows data from the World Bank report, *Doing Business in 2004*.

Relative to those in other transition countries considered, the number of official procedures and costs required to start a business in Romania is relatively low. However, caution should be used when interpreting these results. The number of procedures, time, and costs presented represent only the "official" information given in government documents. Our fieldwork indicated that there are additional costs, namely in the form of bribes, that the *Doing Business* database does not capture. Although the total number of official procedures, time, and costs required to start a business may be relatively low, the additional costs that entrepreneurs actually experience make the process more arduous. We will return to this point in Section 3 when we consider the barriers facing rural entrepreneurs.

The evasion of laws and regulations has resulted in a large informal sector in Romania.[20] Romania received a score of 4 (with 1 being the best and 5 being the worst) in the 2004 Index of Economic Freedom in the category of "Informal Market." According to the aforementioned *Doing Business in 2004* report, the size of Romania's informal economy in 2004 was 34.4 percent of 2003 gross national income (see Appendix Table 8.2). Due to corruption and an unstable legal system, entrepreneurs who are productive must hold many of their assets outside the law. The costs of engaging within the system are simply too high. As a result, they do not have access to the mechanisms that a formal legal system would provide them.

Although the informal economy allows entrepreneurs to engage in productive activities, it is far from the ideal situation. This is largely due to the fact that there are substantial costs involved with operating in the informal sector. As Hernando de Soto writes, "informality is not the best of all possible worlds . . . it involves tremendous costs, that people try to offset . . . in all kinds of novel but inadequate ways, that lawbreaking is not . . . desirable" (1989, 152). Returning to the situation facing Romanian entrepreneurs acting in the informal sector, the range of choices available to those in the informal sector, whether they are clients, suppliers, financiers, or courts, is severely limited.

Productive entrepreneurs are also negatively impacted by Romania's latest labor laws (2003 Code). These labor laws make it extremely difficult to hire short-term labor and make the process of firing employees arduous. The excessive taxation of labor causes many entrepreneurs to report the minimum wage on the books while paying employees the remainder, and majority, of their salaries off the books.[21] Rapid changes in tax law make it difficult for entrepreneurs to calculate their tax liability for the purposes of forecasting liabilities. Many of the entrepreneurs we spoke with understate their revenues in order to avoid paying taxes. As one entrepreneur indicated, he doesn't feel guilty about evading taxes because "if you don't steal the money, state officials will." [22] Bribes and other side payments made to avoid the unproductive activities of regulators and bureaucrats cannot be formally recorded and tracked by entrepreneurs. This is the case despite the fact that bribes constitute a major business expense for entrepreneurs.[23] In this environment it is extremely difficult to effectively keep accounts of the actual costs and revenues of various business activities.

3. The Predicament of Rural Entrepreneurs

The analysis provided earlier focused on the general institutional environment facing all entrepreneurs in Romania. However, our fieldwork provided additional and specific insights regarding rural entrepreneurship in Romania. This is an important consideration because nearly half (about 45 percent) of the Romanian population lives in rural areas (United Nations 2004). The collapse of the communist regime led to the closing of many state-owned industries. As a result, many Romanians who had been employed in these industries were unable to find adequate opportunities. As a result, they eventually migrated to rural areas. This was especially the case in the late 1990s, as illustrated by the internal migration patterns in Table 8.5.

Given the percentage of the population inhabiting rural areas, it is critical to consider unique barriers faced by rural entrepreneurs. Indeed, although rural entrepreneurs face the same barriers as urban entrepreneurs, they face an additional set of barriers above and beyond the set faced by urban entrepreneurs. The following subsections seek to explore the unique challenges faced by rural entrepreneurs in Romania.[24]

TABLE 8.5

Structure of urban and rural internal migration flows due to permanent residence change (rates per 1,000 inhabitants)

	1991	1992	1993	1994	1995	1996	1997	1998	1999	2000
From rural to urban	10.7	9.4	6.9	6.6	5.9	5.9	5.6	4.9	4.7	3.9
From urban to rural	2.5	3.8	3.4	4.7	5.8	6.7	7.7	7.7	8.3	8.1

SOURCE: Maníu et al. (2002, 28).

A. Physical Distance and Dependence on the Political Center

Physical distance from major cities is one of the main additional barriers faced by rural entrepreneurs. Distance is a barrier because one has to travel to these cities to obtain the appropriate approvals, licenses, and paperwork from administrative centers. This additional time and travel raise the costs of following the laws and regulations required to start and maintain a business. As a result, many rural entrepreneurs join the underground economy or look to better-connected individuals from urban areas who specialize in obtaining the necessary forms and so forth. These intermediaries engage solely in assisting productive entrepreneurs in evading the barriers erected by the dysfunctional formal legal structure. As a result, the official and unofficial fees paid by rural entrepreneurs are comparatively higher than those paid by their urban counterparts. In order to understand the distance from the political center of Bucharest, consider the map of Romania.

Along these lines, one entrepreneur we interviewed cited five major licenses and permits he needed to obtain before he could open his business. These licenses and permits included rechartering his company statute, environmental protection, sanitary/animal, police, fire, and worker protection standards.[25] These registrations and approvals could be obtained only by going to the Chamber of Commerce in Arad. It took him seven trips to Arad, approximately fifty miles from his home, and one and one-half months to obtain all the paperwork to open his business. The entrepreneur estimated that each permit took about three hours to obtain, and he indicated that the office in Arad is open only until 11 A.M. each day. Further, there is the additional cost of lost business when an entrepreneur has to travel long distances to obtain permits and licenses.

It may appear that physical distance from the political center is a potential benefit because there is less opportunity for the central government to monitor and interfere with local activities. However, our fieldwork indicated that physical distance does not allow entrepreneurs to escape the barriers caused by corruption and excessive regulation. In contrast, our discussions with rural and urban entrepreneurs indicated that excessive inspections and the need to bribe were especially high in the rural areas. Due to the relatively smaller number of enterprises and

Map of Romania
SOURCE: *CIA World Factbook* (2004).

entrepreneurs in each local bureau's jurisdiction as compared with the number in the urban areas, inspections tend to occur in these rural places more often. The frequency of inspections requires entrepreneurs to build relationships with inspectors so that they can minimize the bribes that need to be paid. Several entrepreneurs indicated to us that this is a time-consuming process.

Physical distance is part of the larger problem of dependence on the political center in major cities. Understanding the connection and dependence of the local rural areas on the political center is a critical part of understanding the entrepreneurial environment facing rural entrepreneurs. Currently, the local level (villages and towns) is under the control of both the county and national levels. The main source of control by the political center over the local level is the tax and public budgetary system. For instance, according to one of the mayors interviewed, the local taxes in his commune cover only 15 percent of the local budget.[26] The other 85 percent comes from national-level redistribution and EU funds. Financing local budgets through country-level redistributions and EU funds results in arbitrary budgeting based largely on special interest group and political pressures.

Another example of the barriers facing rural entrepreneurs is business financing. All of the rural entrepreneurs we interviewed financed their businesses either from their own resources or from money borrowed from friends and family. The rare occurrence of loan financing for rural entrepreneurs is at least partially due to the lack of access opportunities in rural areas. Bank loans and EU funds can usually be obtained only at the county level, although in some cases they are available in neighboring towns. The level of information regarding financing opportunities is low. Further, in order for an entrepreneur to be considered, political connections are usually required. One entrepreneur that we interviewed indicated that EU funds are impossible to obtain "because you must have important political connections and be willing to bribe these connections in order to get them." [27] Unfortunately, many of those living in rural areas do not have the connections required to obtain such funds.

The impact of the local level's dependence on the political center is that rural entrepreneurs assume that the local political levels are powerless to generate meaningful political, social, and economic change.[28] Many have given up hope for change and have learned to live with the barriers they face on a daily basis. To a large extent, this involves undertaking activities to evade existing regulations and laws.

B. Dysfunctional Property Rights in Land and Government Restrictions

Another key factor contributing to the additional barriers faced by rural entrepreneurs is the current land ownership structure. Under communism, the industrial organization of Romania's agricultural sector was collectivization, with state determination of production targets and resource allocation. Households were allowed private plots of land for self-subsistence, but in total these private holdings were relatively small as compared with the state-controlled land. With the collapse of the communist regime, land reforms were conducted in the early 1990s. Property titles have been distributed slowly, resulting in the lack of an active market in land. To better understand this, consider that by the end of the 1990s almost one-quarter of the property titles had yet to be distributed (Romanian Ministry of Agriculture 1999).

A key reason for the sluggish distribution of land titles was the structure of ownership dictated by the land reform laws. In *The Other Path* (1989) and *The Mystery of Capital* (2000), de Soto indicated the importance of aligning de facto and de jure property rights. In the case of Romania, instead of recognizing the de jure property rights, the 1991 Land Law (Law No. 18/1991) called for the distribution of property based on the pre-1949 property structure.[29] This contributed to the lack of speed in distributing titles because of the time involved in tracking down the relevant parties. Moreover, the means of distribution dictated in the law led to a high number of decisions being challenged in court.

Using the pre-1949 structure as a benchmark ignored the basic fact that many of the former landowners had died or moved away—either to the city or to another country. The law did not specify how the land in such cases was to be divided among remaining relatives. As a result, conflicts between family members needed to be resolved by the courts. Given the court system's general inefficiency, this has been a long and arduous process. Indeed, some of the distribution decisions are still being contested to this day.

In addition to legal inefficiencies, the bureaucratic and administrative incapacity hampers the assignment of titles. As Cartwright (2001) points out, even when a settlement was reached, in many cases it took years for some to receive formal title to their land. In addition to the dysfunction caused in the general land market, a lack of formal title prevents those in rural areas from using their property as collateral for loans, machinery, and so forth.

4. Conclusion

This chapter has focused on understanding the institutional environment facing entrepreneurs in Romania. Romania's inability to turn the corner is due largely to an institutional environment providing a relatively large payoff to unproductive activities. Furthermore, even when productive activities are present, entrepreneurs must invest a great deal of resources in evading other unproductive agents.

Based on this analysis, we can put forth some policy suggestions, first for Romania and then for postcommunist transition countries in general. At the national level, the number of rules and regulations must be reduced. Abolishing the use of emergency ordinances is particularly important in this regard. The logic here is straightforward. Although there is no doubt that an environment conducive to productive entrepreneurship requires stable rules, at some point increases in the number of rules yield diminishing returns in terms of productive activities. Too many rules and too much administration produce counterproductive results.

Another key implication is that future reforms should seek to align the de facto with the de jure. As de Soto writes, "It is simpler and cheaper to bring the formals and informals together by changing the law than by trying to change the characteristics of the people" (1989, 187). This is especially important to keep in mind at the rural level as it relates to the distribution of property titles and the structure of land ownership. Another key implication is that reforms should aim at reducing local and rural dependence on the political centers located in major cities. This requires decentralizing political control so that local levels play a more active role in reforms.

Romania joined the European Union in 2007. It is not yet clear whether Romania's EU accession is enough incentive to generate real and lasting reforms.[30] The possibility has been met with skepticism. As the *Economist* noted, "it [the EU] is going to let the country in largely on trust, knowing that reforms promised today will be implemented only in years, even decades, to come."[31] Ultimate success will depend on Romania's ability to commit to markets and the capitalist methods that recognize the entrepreneur as the driver of the wealth-creation process.

Our analysis of Romania provides some general lessons that should be kept in mind when considering other postcommunist transition countries. Although these countries have broken away from the original communist leaders, they have not broken away from the system that those leaders left behind. The corruption, government ineffectiveness, and gross resource misallocation caused by communist regimes remain.

Understanding the specifics of these systems is the key to understanding the impediments to the reallocation of resources in these countries.

It is widely agreed that, in a society characterized by well-defined and enforceable property rights, economic freedom, and the rule of law, productive entrepreneurs tend to allocate resources toward their highest-valued use. In communist societies, the entrepreneurial function was not allowed to legally operate in this manner. Only by recognizing the impediments to productive entrepreneurship, which are ultimately grounded in the old communist system, can one understand potential solutions.

Another implication is that it is critical to recognize the disconnect between official figures and the existence of a black market in transition countries. In most communist countries, a thriving black market developed, allowing entrepreneurs and citizens to engage in mutually beneficial exchanges. As our analysis of Romania illustrates, these black markets still exist in most, if not all, of the transition economies. Legalizing these black markets is perhaps the fastest means toward transition to a market economy. Black markets are real and existing markets that are deeply embedded in the society of the country in question. It is critical to remember that those people engaged in black markets are not inherently villainous but rather are deemed so by the legal system. The "black market" is simply the market that has turned "black" because activity in that market has been criminalized. The best means of understanding the existence and functioning of black markets is to engage in further fieldwork.

Finally, our analysis also highlights the importance of focusing on the specific conditions present throughout the country rather than focusing on a one-size-fits-all policy. In Romania, there are many differences between the situation faced by rural entrepreneurs and that faced by urban entrepreneurs. This may or may not be the exact case in other transition countries. The key point is that the policies of communist regimes had differing impacts on different sections of the country in question.

APPENDIX TABLE 8.1
Community overview and development indicators

Visina Noua, Olt County

Location	Part of the Visina commune in the Danube plain; village situated approximately 7.5 miles from Corabia and approximately 25 miles from Caracal
Population	Approximately 4,800
Roads	Unpaved except the main street, which is paved with asphalt
Water quality	Poor—there is no public water network
Heating	Based on wood
Electricity & phones	Existing public networks
Gas network	Nonexistent—cooking is based on household gas reserve
Crime	Low
Cultural activities	Pottery workshop for youth, local cable TV network, church, bar
Employment	Mainly in agriculture; production plants in the neighboring towns have been closed
Local economy	Agricultural companies and trading companies in the village
Schools	Primary school in the village; distance to closest secondary school is approximately 10 miles
Hospitals	Closest hospital is approximately 10 miles
Public transportation	Public bus lines to the town; closest railway station is approximately 1.5 miles

Buteni, Arad County

Location	Administrative center of the Buteni commune (composed of three other villages) in the western Carpathians; village situated approximately 3.5 miles from Sebis and approximately 42 miles from Arad
Population	Approximately 5,800, including the three other villages
Roads	Paved
Water quality	Good—public network exists
Heating	Based on wood
Electricity & phones	Existing public networks
Gas network	Nonexistent—cooking is based on household gas reserve
Crime	Low
Cultural activities	Local cable TV network, cultural house, sports facilities, churches, bar
Employment	Mainly in services and small industries in the village and in the neighboring towns
Local economy	Small industries, agricultural companies, and trading companies in the village
Schools	Primary school in the village; distance to closest secondary school is approximately 3.5 miles
Hospitals	Closest hospital is approximately 3.5 miles
Public transportation	Public and private bus lines to the town; closest railway station is approximately 3 miles

Definition and source of indicators

Variable	Definition	Source
Economic freedom	Index of 50 independent variables divided into 10 broad factors of economic freedom, including trade policy, fiscal burden of government, government intervention in the economy, monetary policy, capital flows and foreign investment, banking and finance, wages and prices, property rights, regulation, and informal market activity. Scores range from 1 (Free) to 5 (Repressed). The higher the score on a factor, the greater the level of government interference in the economy and the less economic freedom a country enjoys.	Heritage Foundation/*Wall Street Journal* (2005); http://www.heritage.org/research/features/index/
Rule of law	Index of aggregate measures of the perceptions of the rule of law, effectiveness of judiciary and incidence of crime. The score range is 2.5 maximum (indicating the least violence and instability) and −2.5 minimum (indicating the most violence and instability). Scores are provided for 1996, 1998, 2000, and 2002.	Kaufmann et al. (2003)
Corruption	Index of survey data on perception of corruption. The score range is 10 (highly clean) to 0 (highly corrupt).	Transparency International (2003); http://www.globalcorruptionreport .org/download/ gcr2003/24_Data_ and_research.pdf
Government effectiveness	Index of aggregate measures of perceptions of such indicators as the quality of public service provision, bureaucracy, and civil service independence from the political process. The score range is 2.5 maximum (indicating the most effective) and −2.5 minimum (indicating the least effective). Scores are provided for 1996, 1998, 2000, and 2002.	Kaufmann et al. (2003)
Doing business indicators	Database of statistics of business environment, including magnitude of informal economy, time and cost of starting a business, registering property, enforcing contracts, etc.	World Bank, *Doing Business in 2004*; http://rru.worldbank. org/DoingBusiness/

Notes

The financial assistance of the Earhart Foundation, Oloffson Weaver Foundation, United States Agency for International Development, and the Mercatus Center is acknowledged. We are grateful to Paul Aligica for his assistance with the fieldwork in Romania.

1. Economies are divided by the World Bank according to GNI per capita. As of 2004, the groups are low income, $825 or less; lower-middle income, $826–$3,255; upper-middle income, $3,256–$10,065; and high income, $10,066 or more. As of 2004, Romania's GNI per capita was $2,920.

2. Institutions can be understood as the formal and informal rules governing human behavior and the enforcement of these rules through the internalization of certain norms of behavior, the social pressure exerted on the individual by the group, or the power of third-party enforcers who can use the blunt instrument of the threat of force on violators of the rules.

3. Interviews were conducted by Christopher Coyne and Peter Leeson under the auspices of a project considering barriers to entrepreneurship for the United States Agency for International Development (USAID). Both were present for all interviews. Peter Boettke was the project director. Bucharest is the capital city of Romania and provides a sample of entrepreneurs in the urban environment. Our interviews of rural entrepreneurs took place in the village of Buteni in Arad County in the western Carpathians and in Visina Noua in Olt County in the Danube plain. Community overviews of Buteni and Visina Noua can be found in Appendix Table 8.1.

4. Subjects ranged in age from twenty-nine to approximately sixty-five and included both males and females.

5. Section 2 draws on Coyne and Leeson (2004, 239–246).

6. Interview with Vladimir Pasti, Bucharest, May 26, 2003.

7. "Diagnostic Surveys of Corruption in Romania." http://www1.worldbank .org/publicsector/anticorrupt/romenglish.pdf (accessed May 30, 2007).

8. The problem of "Emergency Ordinances" was discussed with Cristian Boureanu, former adviser to the minister of finance, Bucharest, May 28, 2003; and Entrepreneur 13, Visina Noua, June 1, 2003.

9. The Romanian Constitution differentiates between (1) constitutional law— dealing with revisions to the Constitution, (2) organic law—regulations for areas of special interest, and (3) ordinary law.

10. Romanian Ministry of Justice Legislative Database. http://www.guv.ro (accessed April 13, 2007). See also Stan (2002).

11. Report available at http://www.globalcorruptionreport.org/download/ gcr2003/24_Data_and_research.pdf (accessed April 13, 2007).

12. Interview with Entrepreneur 7, Bucharest, May 27, 2003.

13. Interview with Entrepreneur 1, Bucharest, May 19, 2003.

14. Interview with Entrepreneur 13, Visina Noua, June 1, 2003.

15. The state of the courts and its impact on the entrepreneurial process were discussed in interviews with Entrepreneur 1, Bucharest, May 19, 2003; Entrepreneur 4, Bucharest, May 22, 2003; Entrepreneur 7, Bucharest; May 27, 2003; Entrepreneur 8, Bucharest, May 27, 2003; Cristian Boureanu, Bucharest, May 28, 2003; Entrepreneur 13, Visina Noua, June 1, 2003; Entrepreneur 16, Visina Noua, June 2, 2003; and Entrepreneur 18, Visina Noua, June 3, 2003.

16. Interview with Entrepreneur 1, Bucharest, May 19, 2003.

17. Interview with Entrepreneur 1, Bucharest, May 19, 2003.

18. Interview with Entrepreneur 16, Visina Noua, June 2, 2003.

19. Interview with Entrepreneur 1, Bucharest, May 22, 2003.

20. Romania received a score of 4 (with 1 being the best and 5 being the worst) in the 2004 Index of Economic Freedom in the category of "Informal Market" (Heritage Foundation/*Wall Street Journal* 2005).

21. The impact of tax law and tax evasion on the entrepreneurial process was discussed in interviews with Entrepreneur 1, Bucharest, May 19, 2003; Entrepreneur 7, Bucharest, May 27, 2003; Entrepreneur 8, Bucharest, May 27, 2003; Entrepreneur 12, Visina Noua, June 1, 2003; Entrepreneur 13, Visina Noua, June 1, 2003; Entrepreneur 16, Visina Noua, June 2, 2003; Entrepreneur 18, Visina Noua, June 3, 2003; and Entrepreneur 26, Visina Noua, June 3, 2003.

22. Interview with Entrepreneur 1, Bucharest, May 19, 2003.

23. According to the *Global Competitiveness Report* (2003–2004), Romania ranked 70/102 in terms of the commonness of paying bribes connected to annual tax payments.

24. The challenges facing rural entrepreneurs are also discussed in Aligica et al. (2003).

25. Interview with Entrepreneur 24, Buteni, June 14, 2003.

26. Interview 22: Aurel Dinga, Buteni, June 13, 2003.

27. Entrepreneur 19, Visina Noua, June 3, 2003.

28. The relationship between the political center and the rural periphery was discussed with Entrepreneur 12, Visina Noua, June 2, 2003; Entrepreneur 13, Visina Noua, June 1, 2003; Entrepreneur 19, Visina Noua, June 3, 2003; Entrepreneur 20, Visina Noua, June 4, 2003; and Entrepreneur 24, Buteni, June 14, 2003.

29. Prior to the rise of the communist regime, Romania had a system of private property rights in land. In May 1949 the Central Committee of the Romanian Communist Party called for the collectivization of agriculture.

30. Although not the focus of this chapter, it is also not clear that the Euro-

pean Union will be a net benefit for member countries. Although the EU may represent an "easier" way to get market-friendly reforms and policies passed, policy harmonization may also make the policy path more burdensome to businesses.

31. "Brussels Beckons," *Economist* (November 4, 2004).

References

Aligica, P., P. Leeson, and C. Coyne. 2003. *Extending the Analysis—Romania Lessons from the Investors Roadmap.* Washington, DC: Mercatus Center and United States Agency for International Development.

Baumol, W. J. 1990. "Entrepreneurship: Productive, Unproductive and Destructive." *The Journal of Political Economy* 98:893–921.

———. 2002. *The Free-Market Innovation Machine.* Princeton, NJ: Princeton University Press.

Cartwright, A. L. 2001. *The Return of the Peasant: Land Reform in the Post-Communist Romania.* Burlington, VT: Ashgate.

Central Intelligence Agency. 2004. *CIA World Factbook.* https://www.cia.gov/cia/publications/factbook/index.html (accessed April 13, 2007).

Coyne, C. J., and P. T. Leeson. 2004. "The Plight of Underdeveloped Countries." *Cato Journal* 24 (3): 235–250.

de Soto, H. 1989. *The Other Path.* New York: Harper & Row.

———. 2000. *The Mystery of Capital.* New York: Basic Books.

Heritage Foundation/*Wall Street Journal.* 2005. "Index of Economic Freedom." Washington, DC: Heritage Foundation.

Kaufmann, D., A. Kraay, and M. Mastruzzi. 2003. *Governance Matters III: Governance Indicators for 1996–2002.* World Bank Policy Research Working Paper 3106. http://web.worldbank.org/WBSITE/EXTERNAL/WBI/EXTWBIGOVANTCOR/0,contentMDK:20773686~menuPK:1976990~pagePK:64168445~piPK:64168309~theSitePK:1740530,00.html (accessed April 13, 2007).

Kirzner, I. M. 1973. *Competition & Entrepreneurship.* Chicago: University of Chicago Press.

Maníu, M. T., E. Kallai, and D. Popa. 2002. "Explaining Growth: Country Report: Romania (1990–2000)." Global Research Project, June. http://www.cerge-ei.cz/pdf/gdn/grp_final_romania.pdf (accessed April 13, 2007).

Open Society Institute. 2002. "Corruption and Anti-Corruption Policy in Romania." http://www.eumap.org/reports/2002/corruption/international/sections/romania/2002_c_romania.pdf (accessed April 13, 2007).

Rapacki, R. 2001. "Economic Performance 1989–1999 and Prospects for the

Future." In *Poland into the New Millennium*, ed. G. Blazyca, G. Rapacki, and R. Rapacki, pp. 107–141. London: Edward Elgar.

Romanian Ministry of Agriculture. 1999. *National Plan for Agricultural Development*. Bucharest, Romania: Romanian Ministry of Agriculture

South Eastern Europe Democracy Support. 2002. *South Eastern Europe Public Agenda Survey*. Stockholm, Sweden: International Institute for Democracy and Electoral Assistance.

Stan, L. 2002. "Comparing Regime Governance: A Case Study." *Journal of Communist Studies and Transition Politics* 18:77–109.

Transparency International. 2003. *Global Corruption Report 2003*. Berlin, Germany: Transparency International.

United Nations. 2004. *World Urbanization Prospects: The 2003 Revision Population Database*. http://esa.un.org/unup/ (accessed April 13, 2007).

World Bank. 2000. "Diagnostic Surveys of Corruption in Romania." http://www1.worldbank.org/publicsector/anticorrupt/romenglish.pdf (accessed April 13, 2007).

———. 2004. "World Development Indicators." http://www.worldbank.org/data/onlinedatabases/onlinedatabases.html (accessed April 13, 2007).

World Economic Forum. 2003–2004. *The Global Competitiveness Report 2003–2004*. Geneva, Switzerland: World Economic Forum.

9   Sweden's Slowdown: The Impact of Interventionism on Entrepreneurship

DAN JOHANSSON

Economic development can be viewed as a process of creative destruction combining a positive side—the introduction and expansion of enterprises—with a negative one—the contraction and exit of enterprises (Schumpeter 1942, ch. 7). Entrepreneurs are crucial in this process: they start firms to commercialize innovations—representing new knowledge or new combinations of old knowledge. By doing this, they challenge the established structures, thereby inducing and driving the course of creative destruction (Schumpeter 1934).

Both the positive and negative sides are important: the establishment and expansion of firms are required to take the innovations to the market and to attract resources to the production and expansion of profitable innovations. The contraction and exit of firms are needed to sort out failed innovations and to set resources free from established firms that are no longer competitive. Long-run economic growth is probably enhanced when both sides are balanced.

Today, many western European countries suffer from high and persistent unemployment and relatively slow economic growth. One explanation is that these countries suffer from a heavy regulatory burden impinging on entrepreneurship and economic dynamism. This explanation is in line with evidence presented by many scholars, who all conclude that the success and prosperity of nations are due to institutions and institutional changes that enable and promote productive entrepreneur-ship and economic flexibility.[1]

This chapter discusses this explanation for Sweden, perhaps the country with the most developed welfare state. Sweden has long been admired by many for its ambition to combine the efficiency of the market economy with "equality" and a fair distribution of incomes and wealth facilitated by a large public sector financed by the world's highest taxes. The question to be explored is whether these policies and institutions have impinged on the positive side of the process of creative destruction. Empirical evidence on the lack of entrepreneurship and on the lack of new and small firms is presented, and the empirical findings are related to the institutional setup.

1. Swedish Entrepreneurship in an International Perspective

The *Global Entrepreneurship Monitoring (GEM)* report measures entrepreneurship by surveying how large a fraction of the adult popula-tion (eighteen to sixty-four years of age) has started or has taken some action to start a new business.[2] In Sweden, about 3.7 percent of the adults answered affirmatively in 2004 (Figure 9.1). This was the sixth-smallest share among the thirty-four countries included in the survey that year and below the share of Sweden's Nordic neighbors (with a similar culture, a common history, and so forth). Among the Nordic countries, Iceland is at the top, reporting a share of 13.6 percent, followed by Norway (7.0 percent), Denmark (5.3 percent), and Finland (4.4 percent). Ireland and the United Kingdom, two of the more successful western European countries concerning economic performance in the last decades, report relatively high numbers, 7.7 and 6.3 percent, respectively. The United States reports 11.3 percent—about three times as high a share as that of Sweden.

The highest numbers are reported in Peru, Uganda, and Ecuador. A large share of entrepreneurship in these countries is due to necessity entrepreneurship. Individuals "are pushed into entrepreneurship because all other options for work are either absent or unsatisfactory" (Acs, Arenius, Hay, and Minniti 2005, 18). This is distinguished from oppor-tunity entrepreneurship, defined as individuals exploiting a perceived

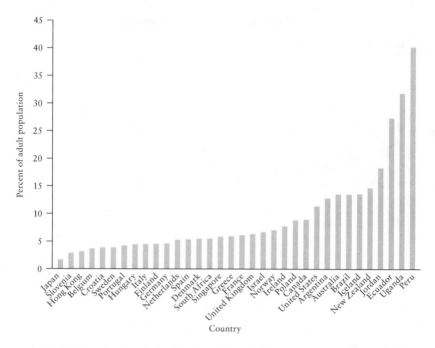

FIGURE **9.1**   Total entrepreneurial activity by country, 2004
SOURCE: Acs et al. (2005).

business opportunity. Sweden is not a country where people are pushed into necessity entrepreneurship, but Swedish policies do prevent much opportunity entrepreneurship.

Sweden also reports among the fewest self-employed in the Organisation for Economic Co-operation and Development (OECD), about one-tenth of the total labor force (Figure 9.2). That figure is more than in Norway (7.3 percent) and Denmark (8.8 percent) but less than in Iceland (16.6 percent) and Finland (12.9 percent). It is also more than in the United States (7.6 percent) but less than in the United Kingdom (12.7 percent) and Ireland (17.5 percent).

In line with these results, Sweden diverges in the number of enterprises in different size classes. Table 9.1 presents the density of firms (defined as the number of firms per million inhabitants) in different size classes for countries in the European Union (and Iceland) in 1997 (the latest available year). The countries are listed in descending order of average rank: the country with the highest density of firms is ranked first

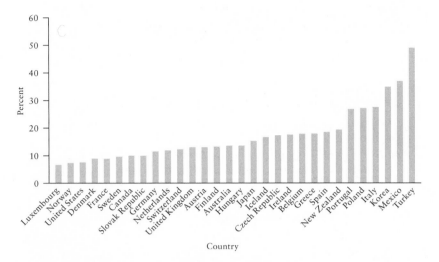

FIGURE **9.2**   OECD self-employment rates as percentage of total civilian employment, 2003
SOURCE: OECD (2005a).
NOTE: Data for Belgium are from 1999, for Greece from 2002, for Iceland from 2002, and for the Netherlands from 2002.

and the country with the lowest density of firms is ranked last. Sweden has the fourth-lowest rank (rank 13) in the smallest (0) and the fifth-lowest rank in the second-smallest (1–9) size classes. Sweden is also ranked below average in the other size classes, with ranks of 11, 9, and 9 in the 10–49, 50–249, and 250+ size classes, respectively. Notably, Sweden has the second-lowest average rank of all countries.

The number of firms in a country has a dynamic effect on economic performance. For instance, Nickell (1996), Nickell, Nicolitsas, and Dryden (1997), and Lever and Niewenhuijsen (1999) find a positive relationship between the number of firms in an industry and productivity growth. Within Sweden, Davidsson, Lindmark, and Olofsson (1994a, 1994b, 1996) and Fölster (2000) report that the number of entrepreneurs has a positive effect on regional economic growth.

There are indications that today's situation, with relatively few entrepreneurs and firms, especially small firms, is the outcome of a long process. Figure 9.3 presents the number of Swedish firms in different size classes in the manufacturing industry—the most deregulated industry that is most exposed to international competition. Hence the manufacturing industry is an indicator of the competitiveness of a country and

TABLE 9.1
Density of firms in EU countries, 1997

	NUMBER OF EMPLOYEES										Average rank
	0	Rank	1–9	Rank	10–49	Rank	50–249	Rank	250+	Rank	
Luxembourg	1,868	9	2,078	7	498	1	105	1	18	2	4.5
Iceland	4,811	1	3,339	2	334	4	34	12	34	1	4.8
Portugal	209	15	5,903	1	373	3	59	3	7	13	5.5
Germany	1,424	11	2,162	6	424	2	53	4	16	3	5.8
Spain	3,487	5	2,384	5	279	5	37	10	6	14	6.3
U.K.	3,621	4	1,802	8	264	9	40	7	11	5	7.0
Italy	3,475	6	2,839	4	278	6	26	14	7	12	7.5
Netherlands	1,362	12	1,611	10	276	7	60	2	13	4	7.8
Greece	3,759	2	3,066	3	154	15	21	15	0	16	8.8
Denmark	1,552	10	1,232	13	271	8	47	5	9	7	9.0
France	2,013	8	1,690	9	227	12	40	8	8	10	9.3
Belgium	3,633	3	1,223	14	220	13	31	13	10	6	10.8
Finland	2,140	7	1,577	11	202	14	36	11	8	11	10.8
Ireland	776	14	1,035	15	252	10	47	6	8	8	11.3
Sweden	1,133	13	1,334	12	231	11	38	9	8	9	11.3
Austria	105	16	178	16	37	16	7	16	1	15	16.0

SOURCE: European Commission (2001) and author calculations.

NOTE: The density of firms is the number of firms per million inhabitants. The size classes are defined according to the number of employees. Data for Denmark, Greece, France, Iceland, Ireland, Italy, Luxembourg, Netherlands, Portugal, and Sweden are from 1996. To be defined as having one employee, a firm must pay a salary to a person. Firms without any employees are, for instance, firms in a startup phase and dormant firms.

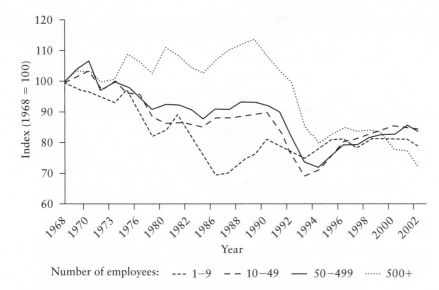

FIGURE **9.3** Density of Swedish manufacturing firms, 1968–2002
SOURCES: Johansson (1997) and updatings.
NOTE: Swedish statistics did not correspond fully with European statistics until Sweden joined the European Union in 1993. Therefore, the size classes in Figure 9.3 differ from those in Table 9.1. Firms without any employees are excluded here owing to statistical problems.

its institutions. The number of firms has decreased profoundly in all size classes. In the size classes with fewer than five hundred employees, the decline started in the beginning of the period. The number of large-sized firms (five hundred and more employees) increased first but started to decrease in the early 1990s, resulting in the largest decrease of all size classes by the end of the period. This development can partly be explained by a natural transformation of the economy from agriculture via industry to services. However, considering the high total unemployment in Sweden, some of this decrease has to be explained by destruction without any corresponding transformation.[3]

Sweden also lacks high-growth firms, "gazelles." Delmar and Davidsson (2000) and Davidsson and Henrekson (2002) found that Swedish high-growth firms only modestly contribute to job creation. In fact, adjusted for mergers and acquisitions, they lost jobs during 1987–1996.[4] This is a remarkable difference compared with the United States and the United Kingdom, where a few very fast-growing firms have generated the bulk of new jobs. In both the United States and the United Kingdom, high-technology firms, in particular, have been shown to be growing fast

(Birch and Medoff 1994; Kirchhoff 1994; Storey 1994; Birch, Haggerty, and Parsons 1995). A microlevel analysis of the Swedish and U.S. biomedical and polymer cluster also shows that new Swedish firms have grown much slower than their U.S. counterparts (Braunerhjelm and Carlsson 1999; Braunerhjelm, Carlsson, Cetindamar, and Johansson 2000). In a comparison of two similar medical-equipment innovations launched in a Swedish and a U.S. firm, Fridh (2002) found that the U.S. innovation became a commercial winner very quickly, whereas it took a very long time for the Swedish innovation to be brought to industrial-scale production.

The lack of "gazelles" seems to have been a problem for a long time. As early as the beginning of the 1980s, Utterback and Reitberger (1982) and Utterback, Meyer, Roberts, and Reitberger (1988) documented a low propensity to grow among Swedish technology-based firms. In a later study of all technology-based firms that entered the Swedish economy during 1975–1993, Rickne and Jacobsson (2000) found that the new technology-based firms had a small effect on employment and growth. Out of all new technology-based firms, no single firm employed more than three hundred people in 1993.

A recent study of business start-ups among the whole science and technology labor force, defined as persons with at least three years of higher education (university) in science, technology, or medicine, shows their contribution to employment and growth to be small and declining. During the last eleven years, only 3.5 percent have started a new business. Among those, firm growth has low priority. In fact, people highly educated in science, technology, or medicine prefer employment and further education before starting a business of their own. Even when facing unemployment, they often prefer to become unemployed before becoming entrepreneurs. A major reason for this is that employees are embraced by the social security systems, such as income insurance, whereas self-employed people are not. Hence many hesitate to jeopardize their social security benefits for uncertain (and, if successful, heavily taxed) entrepreneurial incomes (Delmar, Wennberg, Wiklund, and Sjöberg 2005).

2. Policies, Institutions, and Entrepreneurship

It is a common misconception that Sweden has always been a well-developed welfare state. During most of the last century, the Swedish economy was quite market-oriented; for instance, Sweden had a lower ratio of total tax revenues to GDP than the United States and the United Kingdom until the end of the 1950s. Under the rule of the Social Democratic Party, which came into power in 1932 and has stayed in power since then with the exception of eleven years (1976–1982 and 1991–1994) and from September 2006, the Swedish economy became more centrally planned as institutions gradually transformed to become more centralized. With a few exceptions, such as the organization of wage bargaining and Keynesian demand policy, the strongly centralized characteristics of Swedish institutions were not created or accentuated until the late 1960s and the beginning of the 1970s.

The growth of total tax revenues to GDP is one indication of the gradual transformation of Swedish institutions from a highly decentralized market economy to the centrally planned welfare state because taxes finance the welfare state. Figure 9.4 shows that tax revenues as a percent of GDP started to increase steadily shortly after the Social Democrats came into power. In 1930, total tax revenues to GDP were 10 percent; in 1940, they were 15 percent and in 1950 about 20 percent. In 1960, total

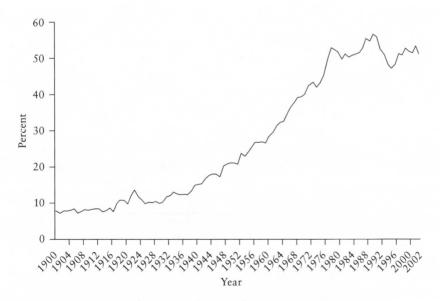

FIGURE **9.4** Total tax revenues as percentage of GDP, 1900–2002
SOURCE: Swedish National Tax Board (2004).

tax revenues had increased to 28 percent, which was about the same level as in most other Western countries. A decade later, in 1970, total tax revenues were up to 40 percent, one of the highest levels in the world. It took just six years to increase total tax revenues another 10 percentage points to 50 percent in 1976.[5] The total tax revenues to GDP peaked at 56.5 percent in 1989. Since then they have decreased somewhat and amounted to 51 percent in 2002. In comparison, total tax revenues to GDP are less than 30 percent in the United States, less than 40 percent on average in the OECD, and slightly more than 40 percent on average in the EU 15 (OECD 2004).

Until 1970, Swedish institutions did not diverge from those of other Western countries enough to allow talk of a unique Swedish model. Then, during the 1970s, large and centralized institutions that dominated society began to characterize the Swedish institutional setup. According to Lindbeck (1997, 12) important features of Swedish institutions were:

1. a large public-spending sector and high taxes, reflecting ambitious welfare state arrangements and large-scale interventions in the economic lives of individuals and households;
2. a strongly interventionist stabilization policy, originally designed to "fine-tune" full employment, with so-called active labor market policy as an important tool;
3. government interventions to influence aggregate saving and credit supply, as well as their allocation by public-sector saving, capital market regulations, taxes, and subsidies;
4. increased centralization within the public sector;
5. centralized wage bargaining at a national level;
6. highly centralized decision making in the private sector, where a small group of large firms predominates on the production side, and holdings of financial assets, including shares, are highly concentrated in a few large institutions—three or four banks, a half-dozen insurance companies, and a few investment corporations. These centralist structures have, however, been combined with
7. a pronounced free-trade regime.

The fast expansion of the welfare state led to recurrent economic crises. Beginning in the 1970s, Sweden frequently ran into problems of rapid labor-cost increases, budget deficits, deficits in foreign affairs, increasing unemployment, and decreasing growth. The problems were generally met with devaluations of the Swedish currency, which temporarily "solved" them. The crises also induced a number of deregulations:

- Capital markets were deregulated in steps and were freed by the end of 1987. The capital market regulations were extensive and included (among other things) restrictions on the right to hold foreign currency and to move financial capital abroad. Credits were in practice rationed. Banks and other credit institutions were obliged to hold part of their assets in government bonds and bonds issued to finance construction at an interest below the market interest rate (for further details, see, for instance, Jonung 1994).
- Deregulation of a number of product markets was undertaken. The market for telecommunications was opened up for entrepreneurs in 1993. The government had owned many firms, including some of the largest in the Swedish economy. The government has also started to privatize many of these firms, and to a larger extent these firms operate under conditions of profit maximization. One example is Telia, the largest network carrier in Sweden, which was (partly) privatized in the mid-1990s.[6]
- A number of tax reforms have been carried out to lower the extremely high marginal taxes on capital and income. In the 1970s and 1980s, many income earners faced real tax rates above 100 percent because of the combined effect of high marginal taxes and high inflation rates (about 10 percent). A major reform was carried out in the beginning of the 1990s. The intention was to make the tax system more neutral, reducing the large distortions inherent in the earlier system. The objective was to keep the total tax share and the large public sector at the same level while limiting the devastating marginal effects. This was basically done through a decrease of the marginal taxes (down from about 85 percent for a high-income earner to about 57 percent), which was financed by a broadened tax base.
- Increased mobility due to the deregulation of capital markets also induced significant decreases of corporate taxes and taxes on capital incomes, a "requirement" that also came with

Sweden's joining the European Union. Corporate tax rates are down from 50 to 28 percent, and capital income taxes are 30 percent today (they were about 85 percent in the 1970s and 1980s).

- Since 1991, parts of the public sector have been privatized, and today private firms produce some of the goods and services earlier produced by the public sector alone under a regime of no competition. Still, private entrepreneurship is profoundly constrained by regulations in these markets.
- Some of the rigidities in the labor markets have been removed; for instance, tenure-priority rules in cases of employment reduction have been eased. These changes were introduced in 1997. Wage bargaining is now also more decentralized than before.
- In the beginning of the 1990s, economic policy was reoriented from the prime goal of full employment to the prime goal of price stability. To ensure this, the Bank of Sweden was made more independent. In addition, a number of institutional changes were made to discipline government spending to avoid large and persistent budget deficits. For instance, a spending limit on government expenditures was introduced. Since then, inflation rates have fallen from about 10 percent to close to zero.

Despite reforms, research identifies three institutional areas that still have a major negative impact on new firm formation and firm growth: the access of private entrepreneurs to some markets, the incentives for entrepreneurship provided by the tax system, and the regulation of the labor market.

3. Entrepreneurial Access to Markets

In Sweden, large parts of the service sector are more or less closed to entry by private firms by law or regulation. First, the government has monopolized large parts of the production of services that could be produced privately, such as health care and child care. The potential markets for private-business production of services monopolized by government are large, in total about 30 percent of GDP.[7] Recently, the markets for the public production of these private goods have partly been opened up for private competition. However, most impediments to private competition remain, and private firms produce just a fraction of the total output of these services (Werenfels Röttorp 1998; Jordahl 2002). Second, the high tax pressure combined with still-high marginal taxes on labor income makes it impossible or very expensive for most income earners to buy consumer-related services, such as repair services. Thus the tax system prevents entrepreneurial activities in the market for household-related private services and the development of specialized markets for these types of services. The high payroll taxes and social security fees (about 32 percent) on labor aggravate the situation further. According to Davidsson and Henrekson (2002), the hourly wage of the buyer has to exceed that of the seller by a factor of 2.7–4.1 to make it profitable to buy the service. In the United States, the same factor is 1.4–1.9. As a consequence, this type of service production is very small in Sweden compared with in the United States. The employment share of personal and household-related services is about 40 percent higher in the United States than in Sweden (Davis and Henrekson 1999, 2005). Highly productive and skilled employees substitute household services for ordinary work because they cannot afford to hire professional workers. Because many services must be produced within households, these policies limit the division of labor and specialization. Limiting specialization has particularly negative effects for rapidly expanding industries with a shortage of skilled and experienced employees.

4. Taxes and Entrepreneurial Incentives

Since the mid-1960s, in all but a few years, Sweden has had the highest ratio of total tax revenues to GDP in the world.[8] Surprisingly, not until recently have researchers estimated the effective tax rate for entrepreneurs over time (Du Rietz and Johansson 2003a, 2003b).[9] The objective of these calculations is to study how the effective tax rate for private entrepreneurs has been affected by changes in the tax system in the period from 1970 to 2002. All relevant capital taxes are taken into account: the corporate tax, the marginal income tax on dividends and capital gains, and the wealth tax. The effect of inflation is included in the calculations as well. Because the Swedish tax system is (chiefly) based on nominal taxation, the real rate of return and the inflation compensation are taxed. As a consequence, the effective tax rates increase with inflation.

Due to the complexity of the tax system, a number of assumptions have had to be made: the firm is assumed to yield an annual pretax real rate of return of 10 percent, the equity value is $1.3 million in 2002 (which is assumed to be the same in real terms throughout the whole time period), and the entrepreneur is a high-income earner (earning $46,300 in 2002, which is also assumed to be constant in real terms throughout the period). To avoid complicating the estimations further, it is assumed that the entrepreneur does not use debt as a supplementary source to finance his or her business. As a result, the effective tax rate level can be expected to be somewhat higher than if a common debt level of 20–40 percent had been chosen. Furthermore, the average overall tax rate for all owners (suppliers of finance) is lower than our tax rate because the effective tax rate is lower for tax-exempt institutions and insurance companies. The relatively lower tax rate on debt finance is due to the fact that companies are allowed to deduct the nominal cost of interest and to the fact that there is no double taxation on interest income, as there is on dividends and capital gains (see Du Rietz and Johansson 2003a, 2003b for further details).

The effective tax rate was extremely high in the 1970s and 1980s (Figure 9.5). The tax rate surpassed 100 percent from the mid-1970s to 1985 and in 1990. It peaked at 140 percent in the beginning of the 1980s, whereas it declined to about 50 percent in the 1990s due to the combined effect of the 1990–1991 tax reform and lower inflation. It was relatively lower in 1994 (38 percent), when dividends were temporarily exempted from taxation and when capital gains were taxed at a reduced rate of 12.5 percent. The nominal-based tax system caused the high real effective tax rate in the 1970s and 1980s because high inflation combined with high marginal tax rates. As a result, on nominally profitable projects often the entire real rate of return was taxed away.

A comparison with Södersten's (1993) estimates of effective tax rates for households also assuming a pretax real rate of return of 10 percent indicates that taking account of debt diminishes the overall household effective tax rates, particularly in the early 1980s (Table 9.2). Yet Södersten's (1984, 135) conclusion, "at the inflation rate actually experienced in 1971–1980, the wedge between the pre-tax and post-tax rates of return corresponds to more than 100 percent of the pre-tax rate of return," is in agreement with our estimated effective tax rates for the same period.

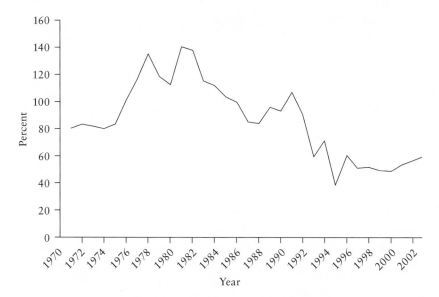

FIGURE **9.5**   Effective tax rate for a private entrepreneur, 1970–2002
SOURCE: Du Rietz and Johansson (2003a).
NOTE: The effective tax rate is calculated as the sum of the capital taxes—the effective corporate income tax, the dividend and capital gains tax, and the wealth tax. Consideration is given to inflationary effects. The pretax real rate of return is assumed to be 10 percent every year.

Södersten's calculations also show that for about three decades, beginning in the 1960s, the tax system distorted sources of funding and ownership. Individuals and households were taxed more heavily than any other owner, debt was favored at the expense of retained earnings, and new share issues were strongly disfavored. The tax system consequently favored large, real-capital-intensive, well-established firms financed by debt and with institutional owners. Tax-exempt institutions and insurance companies financing their investments with debt faced substantial negative taxes for decades. In other words, the Swedish tax system has long disfavored young, small, independent, and less-capital-intensive (for instance, service) firms. These are exactly those firms that the last decade's research shows are the most important for firm and industry growth (Birch 1979, 1981, 1987; Audretsch 2002). Compared internationally, the distortions created by the Swedish tax system were extreme. For instance, in 1980 the average effective marginal tax rate on corporate profits surpassed 100 percent for a Swedish household, whereas it was less than 60 percent for a U.S. household and about 40 percent for a British household (King and Fullerton 1984; Fukao and Hanazaki

TABLE 9.2

Effective marginal tax rates for different combinations of owners and sources of finance, various years

	Debt	New share issues	Retained earnings
1960			
Households	27.2	92.7	48.2
Tax-exempt institutions	−32.2	31.4	31.2
Insurance companies	−21.7	41.6	34.0
1970			
Households	51.3	122.1	57.1
Tax-exempt institutions	−64.8	15.9	32.7
Insurance companies	−45.1	42.4	41.2
1980			
Households	58.2	136.6	51.9
Tax-exempt institutions	−83.4	-11.6	11.2
Insurance companies	−54.9	38.4	28.7
1985			
Households	46.6	112.1	64.0
Tax-exempt institutions	−46.8	6.8	28.7
Insurance companies	−26.6	32.2	36.3
1991			
Households	31.7	61.8	54.2
Tax-exempt institutions	−9.4	4.0	18.7
Insurance companies	14.4	33.3	31.6
1994			
Households	32.0/27.0*	28.3/18.3*	36.5/26.5*
Tax-exempt institutions	−14.9	21.8	21.8
Insurance companies	0.7	32.3	33.8
2001			
Households	29.7/24.7*	61.0/51.0*	44.1/34.1*
Tax-exempt institutions	−1.4	23.6	23.6
Insurance companies	19.6	47.2	44.7

SOURCE: Södersten (1993) and updatings.

NOTE: All calculations are based on the actual asset composition in manufacturing; calculations conform to the general framework developed by King and Fullerton (1984). The average holding period is assumed to be 10 years, and the real pretax rate of return is assumed to be 10% at actual inflation rates. A negative tax rate implies that the rate of return after tax is greater than before tax. For instance, a tax rate of −64.8 percent for a debt-financed investment owned by a tax-exempt institution in 1970 means that the real rate of return after tax is 16.48 percent.

*Excluding the wealth tax (abolished on unlisted shares in 1992).

1987).[10] The 1991 and 1994 tax reforms reduced the distortions. However, in 1995, changes were made that once again increased them.

The high Swedish ratio of total tax revenues to GDP, in effect, has made it difficult for individuals to save. Marginal taxes on labor income have been high, even in low-income brackets, particularly in the 1970s and 1980s. Taxes on wealth, current returns to capital, capital gains, and inheritances are high by international standards. Many industrial countries do not tax wealth at all, yet Sweden taxes wealth exceeding two million SEK (about $250,000) at an average rate of 1.5 percent.[11] During the 1970s and 1980s, many income earners paid 80–85 percent in tax on current returns and capital gains. Starting in 1992, the inheritance tax rate (above a basic allowance of about $9,000 for children) was 10 percent on taxable inheritances between $0 and about $40,000, 20 percent on taxable values between $40,000 and about $75,000, and 30 percent on taxable values above $75,000.[12] The inheritance tax was higher in the 1970s and 1980s. It was abolished as of January 1, 2005.

Swedish policy has brought about a situation in which private wealth per capita is among the lowest in the OECD. For instance, in the mid-1990s financial wealth net per capita was estimated to be about $13,000 in Sweden, $45,000 in Germany, $95,000 in Japan, $12,000 in Spain, and $75,000 in the United States (Pålsson 1998). Numerous studies demonstrate a positive relationship between private wealth and new firm formation and firm growth (Holtz-Eakin, Joulfain, and Rosen 1994; Lindh and Ohlsson 1996; Blanchflower and Oswald 1998). The Swedish policy, therefore, has most probably had a negative effect on new-firm formation and firm growth.

The bulk of Swedish total savings is carried out within the system for compulsory savings for pensions, a pay-as-you-go system. This system has accumulated huge funds, the so-called AP funds, as a buffer toward an expected decrease in private savings when they were introduced and as a buffer toward unexpected events. The funds are not owned by individuals and are administered by officials appointed by the government. The investment policy was restrictive, favoring government bonds, investments in residential property, and large firms yielding a low interest set by the government. One reason why this investment policy was chosen was that the government wanted to borrow cheaply to cover budget deficits and to stimulate house building through subsidized loans.[13] Today, these restrictions have been eased but not abolished. Since 1995, the pension system has been reorganized, and individuals have the right to invest a minor part of compulsory savings in a variety of funds. However, individuals are not allowed to invest these savings in self-owned firms.

The high taxes on private income and wealth have also made it difficult for entrepreneurs to accumulate private wealth from their business activities. Hence the policy is expected to lead to a relative absence of entrepreneurs who act as business angels, using their industrial knowledge to invest (part of) their wealth in new ventures in need of competent venture capital. This has probably barred the development of well-functioning and diversified venture-capital markets (Eliasson 2003). The fact that active venture capitalists who provide both competence and capital are taxed more heavily than passive investors who provide only capital makes the situation worse (Braunerhjelm 2000).

The negative effects on industrial development from these institutional impediments are probably large. Research has demonstrated that a large and competent venture-capital market made possible the rapid development of the U.S. computing and communications industry, as well as the modern U.S. biotechnology industry. Almost all major enterprises within the biotechnology, semiconductor, and computer hardware industries were funded by venture capital in their early stages of development (Brav and Gompers 1997; Gompers and Lerner 2001). Institutional changes in the early 1980s were necessary for the creation and growth of the venture-capital market in the United States. Among other things, taxes on capital gains were significantly reduced, and the taxation on options to employees changed (Fenn, Liang, and Prowse 1995; Zider 1998). Stock options to employees have been a very successful instrument for the remuneration of employees in the United States. The Swedish tax system makes compensation by option schemes less useful (Henrekson and Rosenberg 2000).

A peculiar feature of the Swedish tax system is that foreign owners are favored as compared with Swedish owners. A number of researchers (for instance, Henrekson and Jacobsson 2005) argue that such distortions have had a profoundly negative effect on ownership and the efficiency of firms in Sweden.

The effects of the tax system were strengthened by the capital market regulations that rationed credit to firms between World War II and the end of the 1980s. These regulations favored the house-building industry and large established firms with good contacts with banks and other creditors. Also, the market for foreign capital was heavily regulated.

5. Labor Market Legislation

In the early 1970s, a number of laws were introduced to the Swedish labor market that broke a long tradition by which the employers and the labor unions made agreements through negotiations without interference from the government. The new legislation was the result of a profound radicalization of the unions and the Social Democratic Party (and of the "whole" society). According to the OECD (1994), which surveyed labor market legislation in eighteen countries, Sweden was the second most regulated, with only Greece being more regulated. The rigidities in the labor market imposed by regulators can be regarded as one of the major problems of the Swedish economy today. In particular, the Swedish Employment Security Act (*Lagen om anställningsskydd*, LAS), which was introduced in 1974, hindered the labor market for new and rapidly expanding firms. LAS regulates the period of notice before a dismissal, requires objective grounds for dismissal, and contains time limits on temporary employment and strict tenure rules at dismissals.

For a number of reasons, the burden of rigid labor market legislation can be expected to fall most heavily on new, small, entrepreneurial, and high-growth firms. Davidsson, Lindmark, and Olofsson (1996), Fritsch (1996), Reynolds (1999), and Johansson (2005) show that net job creation results from a turmoil process of entry, expansion, contraction, and exit of firms. Davidsson, Lindmark, and Olofsson (1996) estimate that a net increase of one job requires that seven to ten gross jobs be created. The bulk of adjustment does not take place between firms but rather within firms and establishments. Gross flows are larger in young, small, and highly specialized firms and in firms showing high productivity growth. The rates at which employees quit and at which employers settle job positions decline with the employer's age, size, and capital intensity (Brown and Medoff 1989). These findings suggest that the entry and growth of firms require flexibility in labor contracts and that this is particularly important for new, small, less-capital-intensive, and high-growth firms.[14] Hence laws that impose rigidities on the labor market have negative effects on firm dynamics and economic growth. The negative effects are probably worsened by the fact that the rigidities hit the firms most important for economic renewal most severely.

Rigid labor market legislation also increases transaction costs for hiring because it becomes more important to match employees and jobs correctly when hiring new staff (Nooteboom 1993). This should affect small entrepreneurial firms more severely for at least three reasons: (1) employees in small firms have fewer opportunities to find an alternative job within the firm if the initial match turns out poorly. Employers, therefore, would probably have to evaluate potential employees more thoroughly. (2) It is likely that the absolute costs for employing new staff are about the same over the size distribution of firms. Thus the relative costs (in relation to profits, sales, and so forth) are higher for small firms. (3) Many large firms have been able to adjust the rules stipulated in LAS by local agreements with the unions.

Labor market legislation that imposes increased transaction costs for hiring is one explanation for the lack of high-growth firms in Sweden. It is simply impossible for Swedish firms to grow as fast as U.S. high-performing firms because of the time and costs it takes Swedish firms to screen and select employees. They abstain from recruiting rather than raise their employment-risk exposure. In spite of ample opportunities for growth, NUTEK (1996) reports that about fifty thousand firms in Sweden in the mid-1990s chose not to grow. The labor market legislation was one reason, particularly among small-sized firms. Labor market legislation was also one main reason why firms with one employee avoided hiring one additional person (NUTEK 2005).

The egalitarian wage policy carried out in Sweden from the mid-1960s to 1983, when centralized wage bargaining broke down (Hibbs 1990; Edin and Holmlund 1995), probably also had a negative effect on new and small firms. Wages are reported to increase with age, capital intensity, and the size of employers (Brown and Medoff 1989; Brown, Hamilton, and Medoff 1990; Davis and Haltiwanger 1991, 1996). An egalitarian wage policy that increases wages in the lower tail of the wage distribution and decreases wages in the upper tail of the wage distribution will disfavor new, less-capital-intensive, and small firms and will favor old, more capital-intensive, and large firms. Davis (1992) shows that the Swedish wage structure was extremely compressed in an international comparison.

6. Growth and Employment

Two facts about Swedish economic growth are usually stressed in the public debate. First, the Swedish economy grew on average faster than that of any other economy in the world for the one-hundred-year period between 1870 and 1970, eventually with the exception of Japan. Such

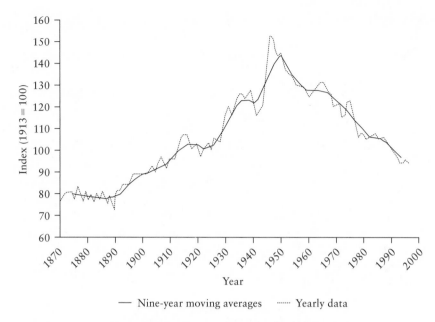

—— Nine-year moving averages   ······ Yearly data

FIGURE **9.6**   Swedish GDP per capita versus average for sixteen industrialized countries, 1870–1997 (constant prices)
SOURCE: Krantz (2004).
NOTE: Sweden grows relatively faster when the slope is positive and relatively slower when the slope is negative. The data are for Australia, Austria, Belgium, Canada, Denmark, Finland, France, Germany, Italy, Japan, Netherlands, Norway, Sweden, Switzerland, the United Kingdom, and the United States.

exceptional growth made Sweden, which had been one of the poorest and most underdeveloped countries in Europe, one of the technologically most advanced and richest countries in the world. Second, Swedish economic growth has lagged behind that of other countries since the beginning of the 1970s (see, for instance, Lindbeck 1997). Krantz (2004) argues that the slowdown of Swedish economic growth occurred about two decades earlier than previously thought (soon after World War II); see Figure 9.6. He suggests that less-market-oriented institutions are the cause.

Private employment has also developed poorly since 1950 (Figure 9.7). In spite of an increase in the population with close to two million persons, private employment has barely increased with about 155,000 persons. Since World War II, practically all employment growth has taken place in the public sector: up to about 770,000 employees. The development of employment is in line with Krantz's analysis.

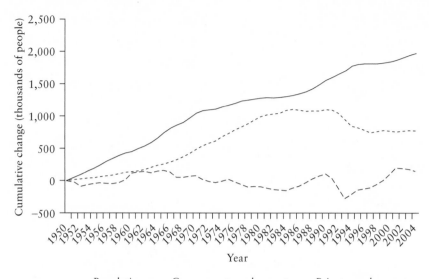

FIGURE **9.7** Cumulative change in Swedish population, government employment, and private employment, 1950–2004 (thousands)

SOURCES: Davidsson and Henrekson (2002) and update received directly from Magnus Henrekson.

The slow economic growth has made Sweden's relative income fall compared with that of other countries. In 1970, Sweden was ranked as the fourth-highest-income country in the OECD (Table 9.3). Three decades later, Sweden is ranked below the median at place fourteen—a drop of ten positions. Besides France and New Zealand, no other country has fallen so many positions. The development is striking compared with Ireland, which has improved its ranking from twenty-first place to fourth.

7. Concluding Remarks

The lagging of Swedish economic growth, the inability of the Swedish economy to generate private jobs, and Sweden's fall in the ranking of the richest countries coincide with the deterioration of the conditions for private entrepreneurship. Research has showed new, small, and fast-growing firms to be decisive for employment and economic growth. Swedish institutions and policies have placed these firms at a disadvantage. The

TABLE 9.3
Country rankings of GDP per capita by percent of OECD average (current ppp)

	1970			1990			2003	
Rank	Country	Index	Rank	Country	Index	Rank	Country	Index
1	Switzerland	154	1	Luxembourg	143	1	Luxembourg	191
2	United States	148	2	United States	137	2	United States	133
3	Luxembourg	131	3	Switzerland	133	3	Norway	131
4	Sweden	115	4	Canada	114	4	Ireland	118
5	Canada	108	5	Japan	110	5	Switzerland	115
6	Denmark	106	6	Norway	109	6	Denmark	109
7	France	106	7	France	108	7	Austria	108
8	Australia	104	7	Iceland	108	7	Canada	108
8	Netherlands	104	9	Sweden	106	9	Netherlands	107
10	New Zealand	101	10	Austria	104	9	Australia	107
11	United Kingdom	98	11	Denmark	103	11	United Kingdom	106
12	Belgium	95	12	Belgium	102	12	Iceland	105
12	Germany	95	12	Italy	102	12	Belgium	105
14	Austria	91	14	Finland	101	14	Sweden	102
15	Italy	89	15	Germany	100	15	Finland	101
15	Norway	89	15	Netherlands	100	15	Japan	101
17	Finland	86	15	Australia	100	17	France	98
18	Japan	85	18	United Kingdom	99	18	Germany	96
19	Iceland	83	19	New Zealand	84	19	Italy	94
20	Spain	67	20	Spain	74	20	Spain	87
21	Ireland	56	21	Ireland	70	21	New Zealand	82
22	Greece	53	22	Portugal	59	22	Greece	72
23	Portugal	47	23	Greece	57	23	Portugal	66
24	Mexico	37	24	Mexico	32	24	Mexico	34
25	Turkey	28	25	Turkey	29	25	Turkey	24

SOURCES: OECD (1996, 2005b).

NOTE: Countries that were not members of the OECD in 1970 (Korea, Czech Republic, Hungary, Poland, and Slovak Republic) are excluded for reasons of comparison.

institutions preventing or obstructing new-firm formation and small-firm growth were mainly introduced in the 1970s: increased taxes, expansion of the public sector closed to private entrepreneurship, and rigid labor market legislation. A number of researchers conclude that Swedish economic policy has made the Swedish economy less flexible and that it has had a conserving effect on the industrial structure. Myhrman (1994) dubs the Swedish economy "the petrified economy." One consequence is a lack of the variety in Swedish industrial structure that would be required for creating strong dynamics (Eliasson 1991).

Legally imposed restrictions and prohibitions on private entrepreneurship in large parts of the economy, unfavorable taxes for private entrepreneurship, and a labor market policy impinging on the will to hire people are major explanations of the lack of entrepreneurship and firm dynamics in Sweden. Considering the importance of entrepreneurship and new and small firms, Swedish policies have had a negative impact on economic performance. To begin growing more rapidly and to return to being among the richest countries in the world, Sweden will have to make far-reaching pro-market reforms, especially with regard to small firms and entrepreneurship.

Notes

I am grateful for comments from Niclas Berggren and Benjamin Powell, and financial support from Sparbankssteftelsen Alfa is gratefully acknowledged.

1. For instance, North and Thomas (1973), Olson (1982, 1990), Rosenberg and Birdzell (1986), North and Weingast (1989), Mokyr (1990), De Long and Schleifer (1993), de Vanssay and Spindler (1994, 1996), Knack and Keefer (1995), Barro (1997), de Haan and Siermann (1998), Kasper and Streit (1998), Norton (1998), Olson, Naveen, and Swamy (2000), Berggren (2003), and Acemoglu, Johnson, and Robinson (2004), to mention a few.

2. "GEM estimates the overall level of involvement in entrepreneurial activity by calculating the total entrepreneurial (TEA) index. The TEA index is essentially the sum of nascent entrepreneurs (people in the process of starting a new business) and new businesses. Nascent entrepreneurs are those individuals, between the ages of 18 and 64 years, who have taken some action toward creating a new business in the past year. In order to qualify in this category, these individuals must also expect to own a share of the business they are starting and the business must not have paid

any wages or salaries for more than three months. This measure allows GEM to calculate the level of start-up activity in a specified country. Owners-managers of firms are classified as a start-up if the entrepreneurs report that they are active as an owner-manager of a new firm that has paid wages or salaries for more than three months, but less than 42 months. This measure allows GEM to calculate the new business prevalence rates in a specified country" (Acs, Arenius, Hay, and Minniti 2005, 16).

3. In May 2005 open unemployment was reported to be 5.2 percent (Statistics Sweden), and about 3.1 percent of the labor force participated in different kinds of labor market programs (National Labour Market Board). However, government "hides" unemployment through generous rules for sick leave, early retirement, and so forth. Taking this into account, the total unemployment could be as high as 20–25 percent (Confederation of Swedish Enterprise).

4. That means that the job expansion of the fastest-growing firms was entirely due to mergers and acquisitions of other firms and not due to growth of the "original" business.

5. The single largest increase in the twentieth century occurred between 1975 and 1976, when the total tax revenues to GDP rose 5 percentage points.

6. Government is still the largest shareholder.

7. The costs for schooling, childcare, and care of the elderly exceed 10 percent of GDP. The health-care sector is almost as large. Public-sector purchases of goods and services (besides education, health, and welfare services) also exceed 10 percent of GDP.

8. Except for a few years when Denmark has had the highest ratio and Sweden the second highest.

9. One obvious reason is that the economic theory dominating the economics departments in Sweden does not identify entrepreneurs as important for economic growth (Johansson 2004; Bianchi and Henrekson 2005). On the whole, there are very few studies on the effects of policies and institutions on firm dynamics, entrepreneurship, industrial structure, and so forth; Davis and Henrekson (1997, 1999, 2005), Henrekson and Johansson (1999), Fölster (2000, 2002), Davidsson and Henrekson (2002), Henrekson and Jakobsson (2005), and Henrekson (2005) are notable exceptions.

10. The calculations assume the real pretax rate of return to be 10 percent, actual inflation rates are used, and corporate as well as personal income taxes are taken into account.

11. There are exceptions; for instance, the wealth tax on net worth of companies not listed on the stock exchange was abolished in 1992.

12. The exchange rate $1 = 7.88 SEK is used.

13. The consequence has been huge losses to the pensioners compared with a situation in which the resources had been professionally managed, losses that now have to be covered by increased charges or reduced benefits or both.

14. Compare Haltiwanger (2000), who surveys the empirical literature and concludes that the reallocation of labor and capital contributes significantly to aggregate economic growth, implying the importance of flexibility.

References

Acemoglu, Daron, Simon Johnson, and James Robinson. 2004. *Institutions as the Fundamental Cause of Long-Run Growth*. NBER Working Paper no. 10481.

Acs, Zoltan, Pia Arenius, Michael Hay, and Maria Minniti. 2005. *Global Entrepreneurship Monitor: 2004 Executive Report*. Wellesley, MA: Babson College; London: London Business School.

Audretsch, David. 2002. "The Dynamic Role of Small Business Firms: Evidence from the US." *Small Business Economics* 18 (1–3): 13–40.

Barro, Robert. 1997. *Determinants of Economic Growth: A Cross-Country Empirical Study*. Cambridge, MA: MIT Press.

Berggren, Niclas. 2003. "The Benefits of Economic Freedom." *The Independent Review* 8 (Fall): 193–211.

Bianchi, Milan, and Magnus Henrekson. 2005. "Is Neoclassical Economics Still Entrepreneurless?" *Kyklos*, forthcoming 58 (3): 353–377.

Birch, David. 1979. "The Job Generation Process." In *MIT Program on Neighbourhood and Regional Change*. Cambridge, MA: MIT.

———. 1981. "Who Creates Jobs?" *The Public Interest* 65 (1): 3–14.

———. 1987. *Job Creation in America: How Our Smallest Companies Put the Most People to Work*. New York: Free Press.

Birch, David, Andrew Haggerty, and William Parsons. 1995. *Who's Creating Jobs?* Boston: Cognetics.

Birch, David, and James Medoff. 1994. "Gazelles." In *Labor Markets, Employment Policy and Job Creation*, ed. Lewis Solmon and Alec Levenson, 159–165. Boulder, CO, and London: Westview Press.

Blanchflower, David, and Andrew Oswald. 1998. "What Makes an Entrepreneur?" *Journal of Labor Economics* 16 (1): 26–60.

Braunerhjelm, Pontus. 2000. *Knowledge Capital and the New Economy*. Dordrecht, Netherlands: Kluwers Academic Publishers.

Braunerhjelm, Pontus, and Bo Carlsson. 1999. "Industry Clusters in Ohio and in Sweden, 1975–1995." *Small Business Economics* 12 (4): 279–293.

Braunerhjelm, Pontus, Bo Carlsson, Dilek Cetindamar, and Dan Johansson. 2000. "The Old and the New: The Evolution of Polymer and Biomedical

Clusters in Ohio and Sweden." *Journal of Evolutionary Economics* 10 (5): 471–488.

Brav, Alon, and Paul Gompers. 1997. "Myth or Reality? The Long-Run Underperformance of Initial Public Offerings: Evidence from Venture and Nonventure-Backed Companies." *Journal of Finance* 52:1781–1821.

Brown, Charles, James Hamilton, and James Medoff. 1990. *Employers: Large and Small.* New York: Holmes and Meier.

Brown, Charles, and James Medoff. 1989. "The Employer Size Effect." *Journal of Political Economy* 97 (5): 1027–1059.

Davidsson, Per, and Magnus Henrekson. 2002. "Determinants of the Prevalence of Start-Ups and High-Growth Firms." *Small Business Economics* 19 (2): 81–104.

Davidsson, Per, Leif Lindmark, and Christer Olofsson. 1994a. *Dynamiken i Svenskt Näringsliv.* Lund, Sweden: Studentlitteratur.

———. 1994b. "New Firm Formation and Regional Development in Sweden." *Regional Studies* 28 (4): 395–410.

———. 1996. *Näringslivsdynamik Under 90-talet.* Stockholm, Sweden: NUTEK.

Davis, Steven. 1992. "Cross-Country Patterns of Change in Relative Wages." *NBER Macroeconomics Annual* 7:239–292.

Davis, Steven, and John Haltiwanger. 1991. "Wage Dispersion between and within US Manufacturing Plants." *Brookings Paper on Economic Activity: Microeconomics,* 115–180.

———. 1996. "Employer Size and the Wage Structure in US Manufacturing." *Annales d'Economie et de Statistique* (41–42) (January–June): 323–367.

Davis, Steven, John Haltiwanger, and Scott Schuh. 1996. *Job Creation and Destruction.* Cambridge, MA: MIT Press.

Davis, Steven, and Magnus Henrekson. 1997. "Industrial Policy, Employer Size and Economic Performance in Sweden." In *The Welfare State in Transition,* ed. Richard Freeman, Birgitta Swedenborg, and Robert Topel, 353–397. Chicago: University of Chicago Press.

———. 1999. "Explaining National Differences in the Size and Industry Distribution of Employment." *Small Business Economics* 12 (1): 59–83.

———. 2005. "Tax Effects on Work Activity, Industry Mix and Shadow Economy Size: Evidence from Rich-Country Comparisons." In *Labour Supply and Incentives to Work in Europe,* ed. Ramon Goméz-Salvador, Ana Lamo, Barbara Petrongolo, Melanie Ward, and Etienne Wasmer, 44–104. Aldershot, UK: Edward Elgar.

De Haan, Jakob, and Clemens Siermann. 1998. "Further Evidence on the Relationship between Economic Freedom and Economic Growth." *Public Choice* 95 (3–4): 233–246.

Delmar, Frédéric, and Per Davidsson. 2000. "Where Do They Come From? Prevalence and Characteristics of Nascent Entrepreneurs." *Entrepreneurship & Regional Development* 12 (1): 1–23.

Delmar, Frédéric, Karl Wennberg, Johan Wiklund, and Karin Sjöberg. 2005. "Self-Employment among the Swedish Science and Technology Labor Force: The Evolution of Firms between 1990 and 2000." Report A2005:001. Östersund: Swedish Institute for Growth Policy Studies.

De Long, Bradford, and Andrei Schleifer. 1993. "Princes and Merchants: European City Growth before the Industrial Revolution." *Journal of Economics* 36 (2): 671–702.

De Vanssay, Xavier, and Zane Spindler. 1994. "Freedom and Growth: Do Constitutions Matter?" *Public Choice* 78 (3–4): 359–372.

———. 1996. "Constitutions, Institutions and Economic Convergence: An International Comparison." *Journal of Studies in Economics and Econometrics* 20 (3): 1–19.

Du Rietz, Gunnar, and Dan Johansson. 2003a. *Missing Entrepreneurs and Slow Economic Growth: Detrimental Effects of High Taxes.* Mimeo. Stockholm, Sweden: Ratio Institute.

———. 2003b. "Skatterna, Företagandet och Tillväxten." *Ekonomiska Samfundets Tidskrift* 56 (2): 75–86.

Edin, Per-Arne, and Bertil Holmlund. 1995. "The Swedish Wage Structure: The Rise and Fall of Solidarity Policy." In *Differences and Changes in Wage Structures*, ed. Richard Freeman and Lawrence Katz, 307–343. Chicago: University of Chicago Press.

Eliasson, Gunnar. 1991. "Deregulation, Innovative Entry and Structural Diversity as a Source of Stable and Rapid Economic Growth." *Journal of Evolutionary Economics* 1 (1): 49–63.

———. 2003. "The Venture Capitalist as a Competent Outsider." In *Talouden tutkimus ja päätöksenteko—kirjoituksia rakennemuutoksesta, kasvusta ja talouspolitiikasta* [Economic Research and Decision Making—Essays on Structural Change, Growth and Economic Policy], ed. Kari Alho, Jukka Lassila, and Pekka Ylä-Anttila, 111–142. Helsinki, Finland: Taloustieto Oy.

European Commission. 2001. *Enterprises in Europe: Sixth Report.* Luxembourg: Office for Official Publications of the European Communities.

Feldt, Kjell-Olof. 1991. *Alla Dessa Dagar—i Regeringen 1982–1990.* Stockholm, Sweden: Norstedt.

Fenn, George, Nellie Liang, and Stephen Prowse. 1995. *The Economics of the Private Equity Market.* Washington, DC: Board of Governors of the Federal Reserve System.

Fölster, Stefan. 2000. "Do Entrepreneurs Create Jobs?" *Small Business Economics* 14 (2): 420–448.

———. 2002. "Do Lower Taxes Stimulate Self-Employment?" *Small Business Economics* 19 (2): 135–145.

Fridh, Ann-Charlotte. 2002. "Dynamic and Growth: The Health Care Industry." PhD thesis, Royal Institute of Technology, Stockholm, Sweden.

Fritsch, Michael. 1996. "Turbulence and Growth in West Germany: A Comparison of Evidence by Regions and Industries." *Review of Industrial Organization* 11 (2): 231–251.

Fukao, Mitsuhiro, and Masaharu Hanazaki. 1987. "Internationalization of Financial Markets and the Allocation of Capital." *OECD Economic Studies* 8:35–92.

Gompers, Paul, and Josh Lerner. 2001. *The Money of Invention: How Venture Capital Creates New Wealth*. Cambridge, MA: Harvard University Press.

Haltiwanger, John. 2000. "Aggregate Growth: What Have We Learned from Microeconomic Evidence?" Economics Department Working Paper no. 267. Paris: OECD.

Henrekson, Magnus. 2005. "Entrepreneurship: A Weak Link in the Welfare State." *Industrial and Corporate Change* 14 (3): 437–467.

Henrekson, Magnus, and Ulf Jakobsson. 2005. "The Swedish Model of Corporate Ownership and Control in Transition." In *Who Will Own Europe? The Internationalisation of Asset Ownership in Europe*, ed. Harry Huizinga and Lars Jonung, 207–246. Cambridge: Cambridge University Press.

Henrekson, Magnus, and Dan Johansson. 1999. "Institutional Effects on the Evolution of the Size Distribution of Firms." *Small Business Economics* 12 (1): 11–23.

Henrekson, Magnus, and Nathan Rosenberg. 2000. *Akademiskt Entreprenörskap: Universitet och Näringsliv i Samverkan*. Stockholm, Sweden: SNS Förlag.

Hibbs, Douglas, Jr. 1990. "Wage Dispersion and Trade Union Action in Sweden." In *Generating Equality in the Welfare State: The Swedish Experiment*, ed. Inga Persson, 181–200. Oslo: Norwegian University Press.

Holtz-Ekin, Douglas, David Joulfain, and Harvey Rosen. 1994. "Sticking It Out: Entrepreneurial Survival and Liquidity Constraints." *Journal of Political Economy* 102 (1): 53–75.

Johansson, Dan. 1997. "The Number and the Size Distribution of Firms in Sweden and Other European Countries." Licentiate thesis, Stockholm School of Economics, Stockholm, Sweden.

———. 2004. "Economics without Entrepreneurship or Institutions: A Vocabulary Analysis of Graduate Textbooks." *Econ. Journal Watch* 1 (December): 515–538.

———. 2005. "The Turnover of Firms and Industry Growth." *Small Business Economics* 24 (5): 487–495.

Jonung, Lars. 1994. "The Rise and Fall of Credit Controls: The Case of Sweden, 1939–1989." In *Monetary Regimes in Transition*, ed. Michael Bordo and Forrest Capie, 346–370. Cambridge: Cambridge University Press.

Jordahl, Henrik. 2002. *Vad har hänt med de enskilda alternativen?* Stockholm, Sweden: Reforminstitutet.

Kasper, Wolfgang, and Manfred Streit. 1998. *Institutional Economics*. Cheltenham, UK: Edward Elgar.

King, Mervyn, and Don Fullerton, eds. 1984. *The Taxation of Income from Capital: A Comparative Study of the United States, the United Kingdom, Sweden and West Germany*. Chicago: University of Chicago Press.

Kirchhoff, Bruce. 1994. *Entrepreneurship and Dynamic Capitalism*. London: Praeger.

Knack, Stephen, and Philip Keefer. 1995. "Institutions and Economic Performance: Cross-Country Tests Using Alternative Institutional Measures." *Economics and Politics* 7 (3): 207–227.

Krantz, Olle. (2004). "Economic Growth and Economic Policy in Sweden in the 20th Century: A Comparative Perspective." Working Paper no. 32. Stockholm, Sweden: Ratio.

Lever, Marcel, and Henry Nieuwhuijsen. 1999. "The Impact on Productivity in Dutch Manufacturing." In *Innovation, Industry Evolution and Employment*, ed. David Audretsch and Roy Thurik, 111–128. Cambridge: Cambridge University Press.

Lindbeck, Assar. 1997. *The Swedish Experiment*. Stockholm, Sweden: SNS Förlag.

Lindh, Tomas, and Henry Ohlsson. 1996. "Self-Employment and Windfall Gains: Evidence from the Swedish Lottery." *Economic Journal* 106 (439): 1515–1526.

Mokyr, Joel. 1990. *The Lever of Riches: Technological Creativity and Economic Progress*. Oxford, UK: Oxford University Press.

Myhrman, Johan. 1994. *Hur Sverige blev rikt*. Stockholm, Sweden: SNS Förlag.

Nickell, Stephen. 1996. "Competition and Corporate Performance." *Journal of Political Economy* 104 (4): 724–746.

Nickell, Stephen, Daphne Nicolitsas, and Neil Dryden. 1997. "What Makes Firms Perform Well?" *European Economic Review* 41 (3–5): 783–786.

Nooteboom, Bart. 1993. "Firm Size Effects on Transaction Costs." *Small Business Economics* 5 (3): 283–295.

North, Douglass, and Robert Thomas. 1973. *The Rise of the Western World: A New Economic History*. Cambridge: Cambridge University Press.

North, Douglass, and Barry Weingast. 1989. "Constitutions and Commitment:

The Evolution of Institutions Governing Public Choice in Seventeenth-Century England." *Journal of Economic History* 49 (4): 803–832.

Norton, Seth. 1998. "Poverty, Property Rights, and Human Well-Being: A Cross-National Study." *Cato Journal* 18 (2): 233–246.

NUTEK. 1996. *Småföretagen i Sverige 1996.B 1996:11.* Stockholm, Sweden: NUTEK Företag.

———. 2005. *Den första anställningen: Hinder och möjligheter för soloföretag att en anställa en första person. R 2005:1.* Stockholm, Sweden: NUTEK.

OECD. 1994. "Labor Standards and Economic Integration." *OECD Employment Outlook.* Paris: OECD.

———. 1996. *National Accounts,* vol. 1. Paris: OECD.

———. 2004. *Revenue Statistics of OECD Member Countries.* Paris: OECD.

———. 2005a. *OECD Factbook 2005: Economic, Environmental and Social Statistics.* Paris: OECD.

———. 2005b. *National Accounts,* vol. 1. Paris: OECD.

Olson, Mancur, Jr. 1982. *The Rise and Decline of Nations: Economic Growth, Stagflation, and Social Rigidities.* New Haven, CT: Yale University Press.

———. 1990. *How Bright Are the Northern Lights? Some Questions about Sweden.* Lund, Sweden: Lund University Press.

Olson, Mancur, Jr., Sarna Naveen, and Anand Swamy. 2000. "Governance and Growth: A Simple Hypothesis Explaining Cross-Country Differences in Productivity Growth." *Public Choice* 102 (3–4): 342–364.

Pålsson, Anne-Marie. 1998. "De svenska hushållens sparande och förmögenheter 1986–1998." Mimeo. Department of Economics, Lund University, Lund, Sweden.

Reynolds, Paul. 1999. "Creative Destruction: Source or Symptom of Economic Growth?" In *Entrepreneurship, Small and Medium-Seized Enterprises and the Macroeconomy,* ed. Zoltan Acs, Bo Carlsson, and Charlie Karlsson, 97–135. Cambridge: Cambridge University Press.

Rickne, Annika, and Staffan Jacobsson. 2000. "New Technology-Based Firms in Sweden. A Study of Their Impact on Industrial Renewal." *Economics of Innovation and New Technology* 8 (2): 197–223.

Rosenberg, Nathan, and Luther Birdzell. 1986. *How the West Grew Rich: The Economic Transformation of the Industrial World.* London: Tauris.

Schumpeter, Joseph. 1934. *The Theory of Economic Development.* London: Transaction Publishers.

———. 1942. *Capitalism, Socialism and Democracy.* New York: Harper & Row.

Södersten, Jan. 1984. "Sweden." In *The Taxation of Income from Capital: A Comparative Study of the United States, the United Kingdom, Sweden and*

West Germany, ed. Mervyn King and Don Fullerton, 87–148. Chicago: University of Chicago Press.

———. 1993. "Sweden." In *Tax Reform and the Cost of Capital: An International Comparison*, ed. Dale Jorgenson and Ralph Landau, 270–299. Washington, DC: Brookings Institution.

Storey, David. 1994. *Understanding the Small Business Sector*. London: Routledge.

Swedish National Tax Board. 2004. *Tax Statistical Yearbook of 2003*. Stockholm, Sweden: Fritzes.

Utterback, James, Marc Meyer, Edward Roberts, and Göran Reitberger. 1988. "Technology and Industrial Innovation in Sweden: A Study of Technology-Based Firms Formed between 1965 and 1980." *Research Policy* 17 (1): 15–26.

Utterback, James, and Göran Reitberger. 1982. *Technology and Industrial Innovation in Sweden: A Study of New Technology-Based Firms*. Cambridge, MA: Center for Policy Alternatives, MIT; Stockholm, Sweden: STU.

Werenfels Röttorp, Monica. 1998. "Den offentliga sektorns förnyelse—vad har hänt under de senaste 15 åren?" In *På svag is: hur får vi upp den offentliga sektorn på fast mark?* ed. Håkan Lundgren. Stockholm, Sweden: Timbro.

Zider, Bob. 1998. "How Venture Capital Works." *Harvard Business Review* (November/December): 131–139.

III   *Reform and Success in Entrepreneurial Development*

10   China's March Toward the Market

In 1957, Peter Bauer wrote, "I regard the extension of the range
of choice, that is, an increase in the range of effective alternatives open to
people, as the principal objective and criterion of economic development;
and I judge a measure principally by its probable effects on the range of
alternatives open to individuals" (Bauer 1957, 113). The institutional
infrastructure is an important determinant of the effective alternatives
open to individuals and, hence, the wealth of nations. To understand the
process of development, one must examine the effect of alternative institutions on incentives and behavior—especially the behavior of private
entrepreneurs.

China's economic liberalization, which was announced in December 1978 during the Third Plenum of the Eleventh Party Congress Central
Committee, has improved the investment climate and greatly expanded
the choices available to millions of people. Private property rights and access to capital markets, however, continue to be restricted. The legacy of
central planning remains in the form of state-owned banks, state-owned
enterprises (SOEs), capital controls, and the lack of competitively determined interest rates. Nevertheless, China has made substantial progress
in moving toward a market system.

When China's paramount leader, Deng Xiaoping, permitted new
ownership forms to evolve and opened China to the outside world, he
created a strong incentive for the growth of the nonstate sector, which

includes township and village enterprises (TVEs), urban collectives, privately owned firms, and foreign-invested enterprises (FIEs)—also known as "foreign-funded enterprises" (i.e., joint ventures or wholly owned foreign subsidiaries). In 1978, the nonstate sector produced less than one-third of industrial output value; today it accounts for more than two-thirds of industrial output, more than 70 percent of national output, and is the dominant force in the highly market-oriented coastal provinces (EAAU 1997, 355). The rapidly expanding private sector is now officially recognized as an important part of China's socialist market system. By the end of 2004, there were more than 3.8 million privately owned enterprises, and FIEs and private firms conducted about 60 percent of China's foreign trade (Jiang 2005, 1; Zhang 2005, 1). China has quickly moved from being a largely closed economy in the 1950s, 1960s, and 1970s to being the world's third-largest trading nation and the largest recipient of foreign direct investment (FDI), having attracted $60.6 billion in 2004. Figure 10.1 shows the rapid growth of foreign trade during the reform era, especially after 1990.

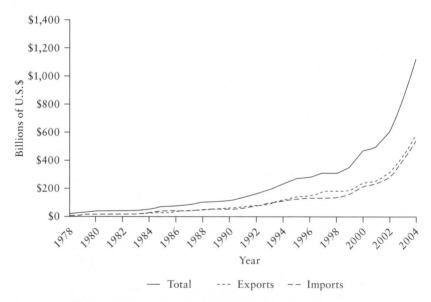

FIGURE **10.1**   China's opening to the outside world
SOURCE: PRC General Administration of Customs, *China's Customs Statistics.*

In December 2001, China was admitted to the World Trade Organization (WTO), with a firm commitment to continue its trade liberalization policies.

The growth of trade and the expansion of the nonstate sector have increased the standard of living dramatically, especially in the coastal provinces. As one observer notes, "The economic reforms have created new opportunities, new dreams, and to some extent, a new atmosphere and new mindsets. The old control system has weakened in many areas, especially in the spheres of economy and lifestyle. There is a growing sense of increased space for personal freedom" (Zha 1995, 202).

During the reform period, real per capita income has more than quadrupled, from $157 in 1978 to $1,150 in 2004 (Figure 10.2). Progress is even more striking when one adjusts for differences in relative prices between the United States and China. The World Bank (2004, 27) found that, in terms of purchasing power parity, real per capita income (gross domestic product) rose from $440 in 1980 to $4,475 in 2002—a tenfold increase.

This chapter will examine the process of development in China and compare prereform and postreform institutions, incentives, and performance. The shortcomings of the current system will be addressed,

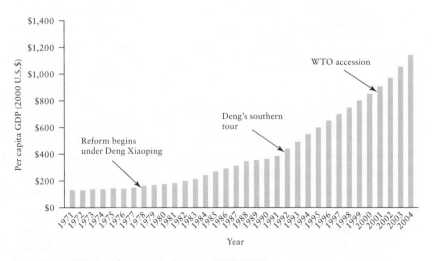

FIGURE **10.2** China's real per capita income, 1971–2004
SOURCE: World Bank, *World Development Indicators.*

and recommendations will be made for further reform. The real challenge will be to allow civil liberties to emerge alongside economic freedom, so that private property rights, broadly construed, are protected under the rule of law. Development, in Bauer's sense, will then be sustainable.

1. The Institutional Environment Before 1978

Under central planning, private entrepreneurs were outlawed, and individual choices were severely constrained. All economic decisions became political decisions, and coercion took the place of consent as the organizing principle of economic and social life.

When Mao Zedong declared victory in 1949 and established the People's Republic of China, he chose Soviet-style central planning as his model. The consensus of development experts at the time was that state-led development was superior to market-led development. The strategy was to use the power of government to nationalize industry and rapidly build up capital-intensive industries. In 1953, Mao issued his first five-year plan, and in 1955 he collectivized agriculture.

To implement his "heavy industry model," Mao had to suppress all market prices, including the interest rate and exchange rate. Ministries were set up to administer the planned economy, and in 1958 the Ministry of International Trade was given complete monopoly power. That development strategy distorted economic decisions and assumed that centrally directed investment and import-substitution are superior to private property and free markets. In reality, China's development model wasted scarce capital and increased costs by ignoring the principle of comparative advantage.[1]

Under Mao's command economy, China achieved relatively high growth rates, *but the level of development was low*. During the period 1952–1977 (Mao died in 1976), national income grew in real terms by an average of 5.74 percent per year, but per capita GNP was only $52 in 1952 and $210 in 1975. Given the difficulty—or impossibility—of measuring economic development in the absence of market prices, one should take the nearly 6 percent growth rate with a grain of salt. As Warren Nutter and other economists demonstrated in the case of the former Soviet Union, centrally planned economies under single-party rule have a strong incentive to overstate output, to produce products of low quality, and to spur the growth of heavy industry at the expense of consumer goods (i.e., generate forced saving).

What Nutter (1962, 283) said about Soviet statistics readily applies to China under central planning: (1) "Published statistics come from only one source: the state"; (2) "The suppliers of data to the central authorities—the economic and administrative units—have a stake in the figures they report, since their performance is judged on the basis of them"; (3) "Statistics are grist for the propaganda mill. The drive to proselytize prevents Soviet leaders from viewing and dispensing facts in a passive and detached manner." Consequently, "Soviet statistics are selective and of varying reliability." Of course, those criticisms are in addition to the problem of trying to value outputs without competitively determined prices. Moreover, Soviet growth—like China's growth under Mao—was achieved through the use of force and at the cost of great human suffering and waste of resources.[2]

During the era of central planning, China's growth reflected the low starting base, forced saving, and an excessive focus on heavy industry to the detriment of consumer goods. Growth was extremely inefficient because of the lack of market-determined prices to guide employment and investment decisions in line with consumers' preferences (Lin, Cai, and Li 1996, 5, 62–64).

The growth of China's total factor productivity (TFP), a measure of efficiency, was at best only 0.5 over the period 1952–1981 and under more realistic assumptions was stagnant or negative (Lin, Cai, and Li 1996, 83). The failure to increase the growth of TFP under central planning should not be surprising. State ownership and control of economic life deprived individuals of the freedom necessary to improve their standard of living. People could not freely trade, invest, travel, or work where they wanted. Private entrepreneurs could not legally enter business or divert resources from heavy industries to the uses that consumers preferred.

Incentives for efficient production were also weakened by the "iron rice bowl" approach to the distribution of income and by the fact that people's work units (*danwei*) made all major decisions. In this "three no difference" system, "it made no difference whether one worked more or less, no difference whether the work was done well or poorly, and no difference whether one worked or didn't" (Lin, Cai, and Li 1996, 139).

Having political connections, not producing for the market, became the dominant strategy for getting ahead.

The politicization of economic life and human suffering that occurred during the period of central planning under Mao Zedong is well documented. Andrew Nathan, a well-respected China scholar, writes,

> The ideology that bore Mao's name promoted self-denial, defined a person's value in terms of political virtue, and dehumanized the class enemy. A system of work units, class labels, household registrations, and mass movements fixed each citizen in an organizational cage, within which people exercised political terror over themselves and each other. A pervading bureaucracy governed the economy, politics, ideology, culture, people's private lives, and even many of their private thoughts. (Li 1994, xi)

R. J. Rummel (1994, 5) estimated that at least 4.5 million people were killed during Mao's "land reform" (1949–1953) and more than 1.6 million during the "Great Proletarian Cultural Revolution" (1966–1976). However, the most devastating period by far was the "Great Leap Forward Campaign" (1958–1960), during which Chairman Mao created "people's communes" and wishfully sought to transform China into a world economic power—not by embracing markets and trade but by ending any trace of an exchange economy.

During the Great Leap Forward, virtually everyone—from doctors to peasants—had to produce steel in makeshift furnaces, and millions of peasants were shifted from agricultural production to steel production. Labor was completely misallocated, and production targets were vastly overstated. Farmers had no incentive to work hard and save for the future, and the zero price of food at the communal canteens led to overconsumption and waste. In 1958, the wheat harvest was substantial, but much of that harvest rotted in the fields because most able-bodied workers were forced to increase steel production—much of it useless. The ensuing famine in which more than thirty million people perished was the result of failed state-led development, not natural phenomena.[3]

Under severe pressure from Mao to increase agricultural output, local Communist Party leaders submitted false reports of agricultural production. By overstating actual production, the rural areas faced higher taxes, and some places had to deliver most of their produce to the state, leaving less food for the peasants. The perverse incentives led to the situation where, as Mao's personal physician, Dr. Li Zhisui, wrote, "The greater the falsehoods, the more people died of starvation. . . . To minimize their losses and keep enough food to eat, communes were saying that they had been struck by natural disasters" (1994, 283).

China's experience during the Great Leap Forward aptly demonstrates an important principle of development economics—namely, "that advance from subsistence production to wider exchange is indispensable for a society's escape from extreme poverty" (Bauer 2000, 7).

By eliminating opportunities for market production and exchange, Mao ended rational specialization and destroyed wealth. Teachers, farmers, and others were melting down their pots and pans and iron beds to produce useless steel for the state while letting children go uneducated and starve. Famine, according to Bauer (2000, 8), "is not the result simply of unfavorable weather, external causes, or population pressure. It is the result of enforced reversion to subsistence conditions under the impact of the breakdown of public security, suppression of private trade, or forced collectivization. There is a core of truth in the jibe that the weather tends to be bad in centrally controlled economies." Clearly that was the case with China.

The low level of development, high level of human suffering, and chaos under Mao led to the demise of central planning and the rise of China's socialist market system after Deng took power in 1978. No one, however, foresaw the major transformation that was to occur as central planning was dismantled in favor of markets and prices.

2. From Plan to Market

In December 1978, China embarked on economic reform designed to create a "market system with Chinese characteristics." The reform process, however, has been driven more by grassroots efforts than by a blueprint from above. Moreover, the reform process has been evolutionary rather than revolutionary (Lin, Cai, and Li 1996, 128). Experimentation with new economic arrangements, such as the household responsibility system and privatization of small state-owned enterprises, took place at the local level, often spontaneously. After the reforms were successful,

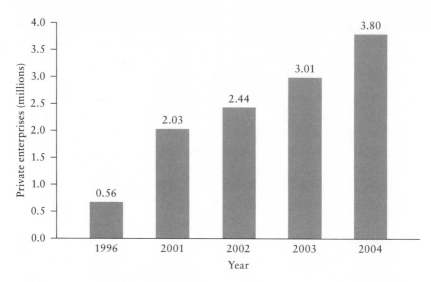

FIGURE **10.3** China's growing private sector
  SOURCES: EAAU (1997, 357); Jiang (2005, 1).

the leadership of the Chinese Communist Party (CCP) took credit and
officially sanctioned them.[4] Jefferson and Rawski (1995) aptly label this
development process "market-leaning institutional change," a key feature
of which is "endogenous or induced privatization." The strategy has been
to grow the nonstate sector rather than to privatize large SOEs. Under it,
the state sector has lost substantial ground, whereas the private sector has
mushroomed (Figure 10.3).

The decollectivization of agriculture after 1978 increased productivity and led to the creation of numerous township and village enterprises.
From 1985 to 1994, TVEs increased from about 850,000 to more than one
million (EAAU 1997, 357). In July 1979, China began to liberalize foreign
trade by establishing special economic zones (SEZs) in the coastal provinces, and in April 1984 fourteen cities were opened to foreign investment.
Economic reform stalled after the 1989 Tiananmen protests but resumed
in early 1992 when Deng Xiaoping took his famous Southern Tour and
visited Guangdong's SEZs in Shenzhen and Zhuhai. Later that year, the
Fourteenth Party Congress adopted the "theory of market socialism," and
in November 1993, at the Third Plenum of the Fourteenth Party Congress
Central Committee, the CCP adopted a fifty-point program for moving

toward a market system.[5] The "Fifty Articles" called for converting some SOEs into joint-stock companies, separating policy banks from commercial banks, making state-owned banks more responsible, and expanding the right to engage in foreign trade (Yabuki and Harner 1999, ch. 5).

Although China has come a long way toward a market economy, the legacy of central planning still exists in the capital markets: interest rates are regulated, the bulk of investment funds are allocated through state-owned banks to SOEs, stock markets are little more than casinos for floating SOE shares, and capital controls strictly limit investment options. In such an environment, it is not surprising that most investment decisions are politicized and inefficient.

The large proportion of nonperforming loans (NPLs) held by state-owned banks is a clear indicator of the misallocation of capital that has occurred under China's socialist market economy (Dorn 2002). What China needs are "free private markets," not regulated socialist markets (Friedman 1990, 5). To strengthen the market, the PRC must continue to remove legal restrictions on private enterprise and—most important— provide an effective legal and constitutional framework to safeguard private property rights (Dorn 2004a, 2004b).

3. Removing Legal Restrictions and Growing the Nonstate Sector

Unlike the former Soviet Union's top-down approach to economic reform, China has taken a bottom-up approach by allowing local officials to remove constraints to market exchange and by permitting private entrepreneurs the space to expand the market process.[6] According to Kate Xiao Zhou (1996, 4), the transition from communal farming to contractual farming—the household responsibility system (*baochan daohu*)— was "a spontaneous, unorganized, leaderless, nonideological, apolitical movement." It was largely the result of the success of local farmers who were willing to challenge the status quo. Their success spurred officials to end the communal system and sanction the new ownership arrangement, which allowed individual households to use land for their own production after satisfying a mandatory quota.

One of the unintended consequences of the rise of household farming was the creation of TVEs—small-scale firms in towns and villages that were not dependent on the state budget and that offered workers an alternative to SOEs. According to Deng Xiaoping (1987, 189),

> Our greatest success—and it is one we had by no means anticipated— has been the emergence of a large number of enterprises run by villages and townships. They were like a new force that just came into being spontaneously. . . . If the Central Committee made any contribution in this respect, it was only by laying down the correct policy of invigo- rating the domestic economy.

Likewise, the creation of the SEZs provided the freedom to experiment with new ownership forms, including FIEs. As legal barriers to foreign trade were removed and nonstate firms sanctioned, economic growth in the coastal areas proceeded rapidly. That success stimulated further insti- tutional change.

In 1978, the central government had tight control over foreign trading rights—that is, the rights to import and export. Only twelve large SOEs were allowed exclusive trading rights. By 2001, thirty-five thousand Chinese firms had the right to engage in foreign trade (Table 10.1). In ad- dition, by 1998, there were more than 150,000 FIEs in China that had the right to import and export, and by 2000, more than 1,000 private firms had full trading rights. Today, virtually all firms enjoy complete freedom to import and export (Lardy 2002, 43, 97).[7]

The gradual relaxation of controls over economic life has increased economic freedom. In 1980, China rated very low on the Fraser Institute's "chain-linked" economic freedom index, achieving only 3.8 out of 10, compared with Hong Kong, which scored 8.6 and was ranked number one in the world.[8] By 2002, China's score had increased to 5.7 (Gwartney and Lawson 2004, 17–18). Using the regular Economic Freedom of the

TABLE 10.1
Growth in foreign trading rights of Chinese domestic firms, 1978–2001

Year	Number of firms
1978	12
1988	>5,000
1998	23,000
2001	35,000

SOURCE: Lardy (2002, 41).

World (EFW) index, rather than the chain-linked index, Gwartney and Lawson (2004, 69) ranked China 93/102 in 1980 and 90/123 in 2002. However, those relatively low rankings ignore the wide variation in economic freedom between the coastal regions and the rest of China.

Fan Gang and his colleagues at the National Economic Research Institute (NERI) in Beijing have devised a "marketization index" for China's provinces that takes into account (1) the size of government, (2) the ownership structure, (3) the extent of trade barriers and price controls, (4) the development of factor markets, and (5) the legal framework. Provinces that rein in government as a share of the economy, grow the non-state sector, promote trade and price liberalization, increase their share of foreign direct investment, improve the allocation of labor and capital, and better protect property rights will achieve a relatively high marketization index score out of ten (Fan, Wang, and Zhang 2001).

Table 10.2 clearly indicates that the coastal provinces are much further ahead on the road to a market economy than are the central and western regions. Indeed, the coastal regions hold nine of the top ten scores. Guangdong, with a score of 8.41, ranks number one and is 166.98 percent further in the marketization process than the western province of Xinjiang.[9]

Provinces with greater economic freedom have grown considerably faster than those with less freedom. For example, Guangdong, Zhejiang, and Fujian—where SOEs account for only a small fraction of output—grew at nearly 20 percent per annum over the period 1990–1995, whereas Heilongjiang, the Ningxia Autonomous Region, and Qinghai—where SOEs are the dominant producers—grew at 7–8 percent per annum (Yabuki and Harner 1999, 99–100). Of course, the 7 to 8 percent growth rates reported for provinces dominated by SOEs are suspect because managers, who are closely connected to the CCP, have an incentive to overstate production, just as they did under Mao, and inventories of state enterprises often have little *market* value (Rawski 2002).

Table 10.3 and Figure 10.4 indicate that provinces in the top quintile of the marketization index have a much higher average per capita income than do provinces with less economic freedom. The six coastal provinces in the top quintile had an average GDP per capita of $2,135 in 2002, compared with $1,262 for the second quintile, $1,159 for the

TABLE 10.2
China's marketization index, 2000

Province	Rank	Score[a]	% of lag[b]	Province	Rank	Score[a]	% of lag[b]
Guangdong (C)	1	8.41		Henan (CR)	16	5.64	49.11
Zhejiang (C)	2	8.32	1.08	Hubei (CR)	17	5.61	49.91
Fujian (C)	3	8.10	3.83	Jilin (CR)	18	5.51	52.63
Jiangsu (C)	4	7.90	6.46	Hunan (CR)	19	5.48	53.47
Shandong (C)	5	7.15	17.62	Jiangxi (CR)	20	5.46	54.03
Shanghai (C)	6	7.04	19.46	Heilongjiang (CR)	21	5.16	62.98
Tianjin (C)	7	6.89	22.06	Yunnan (W)	22	4.89	71.98
Hainan (C)	8	6.41	31.20	Gansu (W)	23	4.86	73.05
Anhui (CR)	9	6.40	31.41	Inner Mongolia (CR)	24	4.76	76.68
Liaoning (C)	10	6.40	31.41	Guizhou (W)	25	4.62	82.03
Hebei (C)	11	6.39	31.61	Shanxi (CR)	26	4.53	85.65
Chongqing (W)	12	6.33	32.86	Shaanxi (W)	27	4.15	102.65
Guangxi (C)	13	5.95	41.34	Ningxia (W)	28	4.02	109.20
Beijing (C)	14	5.74	46.52	Qinghai (W)	29	3.40	147.35
Sichuan (W)	15	5.70	47.54	Xinjiang (W)	30	3.15	166.98

SOURCES: NERI (2001), Zhang (2004, 25).

NOTE: C = coastal region, CR = central region, W = western region.

[a] On scale of 1 to 10.

[b] Percentage by which province lags behind Guangdong; calculated as $[(8.41/x) - 1]100$, where x is the provincial marketization index number.

TABLE 10.3
GDP per capita by province (2002 U.S.$)

Province	GDP per capita	Quintile average
Top Quintile		
Guangdong	1,841	
Zhejiang	2,057	
Fujian	1,657	
Jiangsu	1,760	
Shandong	1,417	
Shanghai	4,080	2,135
Second Quintile		
Tianjin	2,487	
Hainan	925	
Anhui	687	
Liaoning	1,584	
Hebei	1,113	
Chongqing	775	1,262
Third Quintile		
Guangxi	624	
Beijing	2,827	
Sichuan	687	
Henan	786	
Hubei	1,014	
Jilin	1,016	1,159
Fourth Quintile		
Hunan	801	
Jiangxi	713	
Heilongjiang	1,240	
Yunnan	634	
Gansu	549	
Inner Mongolia	888	804
Bottom Quintile		
Guizhou	380	
Shanxi	751	
Shaanxi	677	
Ningxia	712	
Qinghai	794	
Xinjiang	975	715

SOURCES: Table 10.2 and National Bureau of Statistics of China (2003).

third, $804 for the fourth, and $715 for the bottom quintile. Geography obviously matters in determining which regions grow faster, but the degree of marketization appears to matter more than proximity to the coast. China's coastal provinces did not begin to develop fully until Beijing allowed them to open to the outside world and to liberalize.

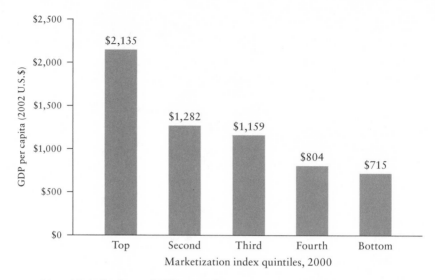

FIGURE **10.4**   Marketization and GDP per capita
s o u r c e s : Table 10.2, Table 10.3, and National Bureau of Statistics of China (2003).

Recent research shows convincingly that the size of the state sector is a drag on development. Kerk Phillips and Shen Kunrong (2005, 1079) "find a robust negative relation between the size of state-owned enterprises and the provincial growth rate." Their estimates for China indicate that a 10-percentage-point decrease in the SOE share of industrial output increases the growth of real per capita GDP by a little more than 1 percent per annum. Reducing the share of the labor force working in SOEs would have an even larger impact on development—a 10-percentage-point decrease in SOE share of employment would increase per capita GDP growth by 3.5 percent per year (Phillips and Shen 2005, 1094).

It is no surprise that the coastal provinces have grown faster. They were the first to have SEZs and have adopted policies favorable to the growth of the private sector and FDI. Guangdong's proximity to Hong Kong no doubt has been an important factor in spreading the "freedom virus." Likewise, Zhejiang began to liberalize at an early stage, and today more than 90 percent of its GDP is produced by the private sector (Zhang 2005). Government intervention, however, remains a serious problem in many provinces. According to the *China Daily*, "The inertia of many governmental departments still impedes the smooth development of the [private] sector" (Jiang 2005, 1).

Fan Gang and others have shown that de facto or "spontaneous privatization" of small SOEs was taking place at local levels long before Beijing formally approved the practice. Cooperative shareholding (CSH) became a popular way by which workers in small SOEs entered the non-state sector. Local officials were glad to rid themselves of parasitic SOEs and to acquire new sources of revenue. The fact that central authorities did not stop spontaneous privatization was a signal to proceed.[10] Nevertheless, the CCP is against privatizing large SOEs, and private property rights are still tenuous. Indeed, the ideological barriers against widespread privatization remain formidable (Fan 1998, 83–84).

Trade liberalization and marketization have led to the decontrol of many prices. Lardy (2002, 24) observes, "By 1999, market prices prevailed in more than nine-tenths of all retail transactions, more than four-fifths of sales of farm products, and almost nine-tenths of all producer goods sales." Interest rates on loans and deposits, however, continue to be regulated. The interest rate on savings deposits is set artificially low to allow state-owned banks to acquire funds cheaply, which they then lend to SOEs at below-market interest rates. In such a system, investment decisions are distorted and capital is wasted.

Steps are being taken to liberalize interest rates, open capital markets, and recapitalize state-owned banks, but progress has been slow. It is no secret why: every step toward capital freedom is a threat to the CCP's monopoly on power; greater economic freedom tends to increase the demand for political freedom, as happened, for example, in Taiwan.

The fact that SOEs account for less than 30 percent of industrial output but absorb nearly 70 percent of state-bank loans implies a highly inefficient use of capital. Studies have found that there is little capital mobility in China because capital is channeled primarily through the government rather than through the market. Genevieve Boyreau-Debray and Shang-Jin Wei (2004, 22–23) find that (1) "investment allocated through government budget and loans made by state-owned financial institutions are (the only) two categories that exhibit a clear negative relationship with marginal productivity of capital"; (2) "it is the allocation of investment by government that is primarily responsible for the peculiar pattern that net capital flows go to less productive regions"; and (3) "the strongest determinant of capital allocation . . . in China appears to be the prominence of SOEs in local economies."

Those results are consistent with the failure of central planning and the futility of traditional models of economic growth that viewed large-scale investment as a key determinant of development. Moreover, they vindicate Bauer, who was nearly alone in 1957 when he wrote:

> It is misleading to think of investment as the only or the principal determinant of development. Other factors and influences, such as institutional and political forces, the qualities and attitudes of the population, and the supply of complementary resources, are often equally important or even more important. . . . It is more meaningful to say that capital is created in the process of development, rather than that development is a function of capital. (Bauer 1957, 119)

Development economists now recognize that the "investment climate," rather than the amount of investment, is the key to growth. What matters are the institutions that shape investment incentives and behavior, not simply the amount of capital per worker. Consequently, in the *World Development Report 2005*, the World Bank (2004, 27) emphasizes that "cross-country studies find little correlation between aggregate investment and growth, particularly if no distinction is made between public and private investment."

Trade liberalization and the strengthening of property rights have improved China's investment climate and led to a surge of private investment, which, in turn, has increased economic growth and reduced poverty. Private investment as a share of GDP doubled over the period 1980–1999, and more than 400 million people were lifted out of absolute poverty by the end of 2001. The higher per capita incomes have been accompanied by an increase in life expectancy and a decrease in infant mortality. By 2002, people expected to live 70.7 years compared with 66.8 years in 1980, and infant mortality decreased from 49 to 32 per 1,000 live births (World Bank 2004, 27, 31).

Even though private investment has increased, private entrepreneurs continue to be discriminated against. They often have to raise capital in informal markets that include trade credit, private brokers, money lenders, credit associations, private money houses, cooperative savings associations, and "Red hat enterprises"—that is, private firms posing as collectives owned by local governments—in order to acquire capital (Tsai 2002, 38). Private entrepreneurs must also rely on FDI to acquire capital and expand, which dilutes domestic ownership and control.

Yasheng Huang, an economist at MIT, argues that China should be less interested in attracting FDI and more interested in "microeconomic and institutional reforms that seek to improve the allocation of resources." He recommends "removing the political, legal/regulatory, and financial constraints on China's truly private firms and tackling the state-owned enterprise (SOE) problem not as a management issue but as an ownership issue" (Huang 2001, 43; see also Huang 2003).

The lack of ownership transparency was evident from the start of the reform movement. Informal ownership reform—"reform from below"—was widely practiced before the legalization of private enterprises in 1988. In Wenzhou, for example, private firms were often classified as "local collective enterprises" or "partnership enterprises" (Liu 1992, 302). Likewise, in Jinjiang, many firms were "collective in name but private in nature" (Chen 1999, 55).[11] To strengthen the private sector, China needs to depoliticize economic life, especially investment decisions. Lasting economic reform will not be possible without political and legal reforms that give better protection to private property rights.

4. Strengthening Property Rights

In October 1987, at the Thirteenth National Congress of the CCP, Zhao Ziyang, who was appointed general secretary, called for "strengthening the socialist legal system" and advocated "new types of institutions . . . to promote the development of a market system." He recognized that trying to graft a market economy onto state planning would lead to corruption. In 1988, he warned that "without reform there will be no way out for China." An important first step, he believed, was to introduce new ownership forms, including converting SOEs into "shareholding" firms (Dorn 1989, 42, 44, 54–55).

Another early proponent of reform, economist Wu Jinglian, recently stated, "Only by matching the rule of law with the market economy can we achieve total success" (Fu 2005, 1). The rule of law is not an actual law but rather a legal doctrine holding that laws should be equally applied and just, in the sense of protecting private property rights (Hayek 1960, ch. 14). China has a long way to go before it complies with the rule of law, but one can see that economic liberalization is pushing China in the right direction.

Since 1978 many national laws have been promulgated that give formal recognition to the informal ownership experiments that were locally sanctioned, and constitutional amendments have given greater recognition to the private sector. It was not until 1988 that private firms with more than seven workers were allowed to operate legally. In the mid-1980s, cooperative and private firms developed under the umbrella of local governments. Those firms were spurred by policies that banned local officials from management positions (Wank 1999, 253). When the Private Enterprise Interim Regulation was enacted in 1988, private firms were legalized, and no limit was placed on the number of employees. Private joint-stock companies were also permitted (Wank 1999, 254). In approving the national regulations, the CCP leaders were influenced by the success of local regulations, such as those in Wenzhou, which allowed the emergence of private firms (Whiting 1999, 176).

In 1993, the Central Committee adopted the Fifty Articles that laid the basis for further legal reform to create a socialist market economy. Greater emphasis was placed on developing the nonstate sector and restructuring SOEs, primarily through "corporatization" but also through outright sales of state assets (Yabuki and Harner 1999, ch. 5; Fan 1999, 81–84). The Central Committee's decision to consider "property rights reforms" in conjunction with restructuring SOEs was an important signal that ownership reforms were now part of the official agenda. In 1997, Beijing formally approved the privatization of small SOEs (Fan 1998, 82, 84).

Converting medium and large SOEs into corporations with limited liability and the right to issue shares will not automatically transform incentives and behavior. Unless those shares can be freely bought and sold so that private parties can acquire full ownership rights, the SOE problem will continue to give the CCP a major headache and threaten long-run growth. NPLs will continue to pile up at state-owned banks, and the private sector will be deprived of the capital needed for development. The solutions to those problems are ultimately political, but continued losses by SOEs and increased foreign competition will likely encourage further liberalization. China's outgoing leader, Jiang Zemin, sounded a positive note at the Sixteenth Communist Party Congress when he said, "We need to respect and protect all work that is good for the people and society and improve the legal system for protecting private property" (McGregor and Kynge 2002, 3).

An important step toward privatization was taken on August 29, 2002, when the Standing Committee of the National People's Congress passed the Rural Land Contracting Law. That law will considerably strengthen farmers' land-tenure rights by prohibiting "administrative re-adjustments" to land-tenure contracts. As a result of the law, China's 210 million farm families will have more secure land-tenure rights. They will have legal protection during the thirty-year land-use contract period, and local officials will not be able to arbitrarily take contracted land and redistribute it, as they have in the past. Markets in land-use rights can now develop more fully, giving individuals the opportunity to increase the value of their land by putting it to more productive uses. Although China does not allow leased land to be mortgaged, and there is no official registration system for land transactions, those institutional changes are sure to be accelerated by the new law (Rural Development Institute 2002).

As individuals have acquired greater economic freedom in China, they have used that freedom to increase their standard of living and to demand greater protection for newly acquired wealth. Minxin Pei (1994, 12) found that "the number of lawsuits filed by citizens against government officials and agencies for infringements of their civil and property rights has risen sharply, and . . . citizens have won about 20 percent of these cases." That positive trend is continuing and will be reinforced by China's recent accession to the WTO.

Eventually, the inconsistencies in China's socialist market system will have to be addressed by constitutional changes that recognize and protect private property rights. Otherwise, markets will be polluted by politics, and corruption will prevail.

5. Toward a Constitutional Order of Freedom

Justin Yifu Lin, one of China's leading economists, has argued, "It is essential for the continuous growth of the Chinese economy to establish a transparent, rule-based, legal system that protects property rights so as to encourage innovations, technological progress, and domestic as well as foreign investments in China" (1998, 71).

China has begun to establish such a system. In 1999, the National People's Congress (NPC) amended Article 11 of the Chinese Constitution to recognize the growing importance of the private sector: "Individual, private and other non-public economies that exist within the limits prescribed by law are *major components* of the socialist market economy" (emphasis added). The CCP, however, does not view private property rights—that is, the right to exclusive use of one's property and the right to transfer it by consent—as fundamental rights. Rather, private property rights are *permitted* to exist and can be taken away at the discretion of the state (Pilon 1998). That uncertainty is clearly detrimental to private investment and long-run growth.

The challenge for China is to create a constitutional order of freedom that reflects the consent of the governed and limits the power of government to the protection of persons and property.[12] Expanding economic freedom is an important first step in that process. China's future will depend on the pace of liberalization, especially financial reform. Freeing capital markets and introducing competition should therefore be a top priority.

Private entrepreneurs were recently invited to join the CCP, a signal of the private sector's growing importance.[13] Many leaders share the sentiment of Zhang Dejiang, secretary of the Zhejiang Provincial Committee of the CCP, who stated, "The contribution of the private sector in pushing forward the rapid economic growth of the province can not be overlooked" (Zhang 2002). Pressure is mounting for greater protection of property rights. In particular, official bodies such as the Chinese People's Political Consultative Conference are being used as "lobbying tools for private interests . . . to advocate revising the constitution to grant private property the same protections as state-owned property" (Pomfret 2002, A25).

In March 2004, the NPC amended the PRC Constitution to give individuals more secure rights to their legally acquired assets and for the first time added the words "human rights" to the document. Three amendments stand out:

- "The state protects the lawful rights and interests of the private sector" (Art. 11, sec. 2).
- "The lawful private property of citizens is inviolable" (Art. 13).
- "The state respects and protects human rights" (Art. 33, sec. 3).

The amendment to Article 13, in particular, signals greater tolerance for the private sector and privately acquired wealth. Prior to the passage of that amendment, Charles Hutzler (2003, A10), a respected China watcher, commented that the "proposed constitutional amendment . . . offers the strongest legal footing for private property in a half-century of communist rule." The lack of an independent judiciary to enforce the new constitutional provisions, however, means they are unlikely to be effective in the short run. Nevertheless, they do indicate a new way of thinking about the role of property rights in China's emerging market system and, therefore, a positive step forward in the march toward a free-market order. In March 2007, the National People's Congress further strengthened private property rights by enacting the long-awaited Property Law.

6. Conclusion

Kathy Chen (1996) has described China's model of development in the post-1978 period as "small government, big society." The nonstate sector is steadily increasing its involvement in providing education, medical care, housing, and charitable services. Civil society is gradually growing along with economic freedom.

China's biggest challenge is to move from a socialist market economy to a full-fledged market system with private property rights protected by a rule of law and, in the process, to embark on political reform. Economic liberalization is a necessary but not sufficient condition for political reform in China. Economic freedom can increase living standards and increase the demand for political reform, but markets cannot magically end single-party rule. Without economic liberalization, China would be less free today. But without *effective* constitutional protections for persons and property, China's economic reform will be trapped by a political and legal system that is closed to competition and justice.

Notes

The author thanks David Jenniches for research assistance and Ben Powell for helpful comments. This article draws on Dorn (2003).

1. See Lin, Cai, and Li (1996, ch. 2) for an excellent description of China's "heavy industry-oriented development strategy."

2. Nutter (1962, 292) notes that "the explanation for the Soviet record lies in the unity of purpose and practice on the part of the rulers—enhancement of state power—and in their selective mobilization of resources—systematic favoring

of industry over other sectors and of investment over consumption, including leisure. The cost has been heavy, in terms of resources expended as well as human suffering."

3. For a discussion of this period, see Chang (1991, ch. 12) and Li (1994, 282–283, 507).

4. In November 1978, Xiaogang Village in Anhui was the first to secretly organize a system of "contracting of production to individual households," well before the central government approved the household responsibility system in 1982 (Zhou 1996, 55–57). Likewise, enterprise reform began as early as October 1978, when officials in Sichuan experimented with greater autonomy for SOEs. In 1992, local governments in Shandong, Guangdong, and Sichuan began privatizing small SOEs. When those efforts proved successful, Beijing sanctioned the policy of "grasping the large [SOEs] and releasing the small" (Qian 2003, 327).

5. See Yabuki and Harner (1999, ch. 3) for a chronology of the reform movement.

6. See Qian (2003) on the general nature of the reform process—especially the "dual-track approach to market liberalization," which allowed market prices to emerge alongside planned prices, and the "fiscal contracting system," which provided local officials with an incentive to allow privatization.

7. The old trading system was one of permission; the new system requires only registration.

8. Use of the chain-linked index ensures that missing components of the economic freedom index for different time periods will not distort comparisons over time. "A country's rating will change across time periods only when there is a change in ratings for components present during both of the over-lapping years" (Gwartney and Lawson 2004, 16).

9. It is important to recognize that the NERI index is not comparable with the EFW index. The marketization index simply indicates a province's movement toward a market economy relative to other provinces. Fan, Wang, and Zhang (2001) note: "The index compares the 'relative distance' between 'marchers' on the road, not the 'absolute distance' between marchers to the destination. The best in the index system, i.e. Guangdong, may be still far away from completion of the reform process, but others are even further."

10. See the case studies in Oi and Walder (1999) for a detailed discussion of spontaneous privatization.

11. According to Chen (1999, 55), "most of these enterprises either adopted the 'leaned-on' (*guakao*) strategy, namely, obtaining a false collective registration for individual or partnership business, or operated as cooperatives (*hezuo jingying*), jointly managed by the collective and peasants."

12. Liu Junning, a former fellow at the Institute of Political Science at the Chinese Academy of Social Sciences in Beijing and now an independent scholar, created an online workshop, "The Constitutional Order of Freedom in China" (www.libertas2000.net/workshop/index2.htm), devoted to classical liberal principles. In mid-2003, during a chill on constitutional debate, the party banned his Web site.

13. On July 1, 2001, President Jiang Zemin announced that private entrepreneurs would be allowed to join the CCP. In fact, "20 percent of China's 1.8 million private entrepreneurs . . . are already party members and have been for years" (Pomfret 2002, A25).

References

Bauer, P. T. 1957. *Economic Analysis and Policy in Underdeveloped Countries*. Durham, NC: Duke University Press.

———. 2000. *From Subsistence to Exchange*. Princeton, NJ: Princeton University Press.

Boyreau-Debray, G., and S.-J. Wei. 2004. "Can China Grow Faster? A Diagnosis of the Fragmentation of Its Domestic Capital Market." IMF Working Paper WP/04/76. Washington, DC: International Monetary Fund.

Chang, J. 1991. *Wild Swans*. London: HarperCollins.

Chen, C.-J. J. 1999. "Local Institutions and the Transformation of Property Rights in Southern Fujian." In *Property Rights and Economic Reform in China*, ed. J. C. Oi and A. G. Walder, ch. 3. Stanford, CA: Stanford University Press.

Chen, K. 1996. "Chinese Are Going to Town as Growth of Cities Takes Off." *Wall Street Journal* (January 4).

Deng, X. P. 1987. *Fundamental Issues in Present-Day China*. Trans. Bureau for the Compilation and Translation of Works of Marx, Engels, Lenin, and Stalin under the Central Committee of the Communist Party of China. Beijing: Foreign Languages Press.

Dorn, J. A. 1989. "Pricing and Property: The Chinese Puzzle." In *Economic Reform in China: Problems and Prospects*, ed. J. A. Dorn and Wang Xi, ch. 3. Chicago: University of Chicago Press.

———. 1997. "The Tao of Adam Smith." *Asian Wall Street Journal* (August 18).

———. 1998. "China's Future: Market Socialism or Market Taoism?" *Cato Journal* 18 (1): 131–146.

———. 2002. "Prepared Statement of James A. Dorn: Testimony on China's Capital Requirements." In *Compilation of Hearings Held before the U.S.–*

China Security Commission: Fiscal Years 2001 and 2002, 743–751. 107th Congress, 1st and 2nd sessions. Washington, DC: U.S. Government Printing Office.

———. 2003. "La sfida cinese: Dal socialismo di mercato al liberalismo di mercato." *Biblioteca della libertà* 169 (May/June): 47–57.

———. 2004a. "How to Build Up and Strengthen the Market Economy: With Special Reference to the Case of China." In *The Changes in Northeast Asian Economic and Political Order and Korea's Preparation for the 21st Century,* ed. Dong-Se Cha and Yoon-Shik Park, 37–58. Seoul, South Korea: Kyung Hee University Press.

———. 2004b. "The Primacy of Property in a Liberal Constitutional Order: Lessons for China." *The Independent Review* 7 (4): 485–501.

EAAU. 1997. *China Embraces the Market: Achievements, Constraints, and Opportunities.* Barton, Australia: Department of Foreign Affairs and Trade, East Asia Analytical Unit.

Fan, G. 1998. "Development of the Nonstate Sector and Reform of State Enterprises in China." In *China in the New Millennium: Market Reforms and Social Development,* ed. J. A. Dorn, 75–85. Washington, DC: Cato Institute.

Fan, G., X. Wang, and L. Zhang. 2001. *Annual Report 2000: Marketization Index for China's Provinces.* Beijing: National Economic Research Institute, China Reform Foundation. Reprinted in *China & World Economy* 5.

Friedman, M. 1990. "Using the Market for Social Development." In *Economic Reform in China: Problems and Prospects,* ed. J. A. Dorn and Wang Xi, 3–15. Chicago: University of Chicago Press.

Fu, J. 2005. "Economists Honoured for Reform Role." *China Daily* (March 25).

Gwartney, J., and R. Lawson. 2004. *Economic Freedom of the World: 2004 Annual Report.* Vancouver, Canada: Fraser Institute.

Hayek, F. A. 1960. *The Constitution of Liberty.* Chicago: University of Chicago Press.

Huang, Y. 2001. "Internal and External Reforms: Experiences and Lessons from China." *Cato Journal* 21 (1): 43–64.

———. 2003. *Selling China: FDI during the Reform Era.* New York: Cambridge University Press.

Hutzler, C. 2003. "China to Protect Private Property in Constitution." *Wall Street Journal* (December 23).

Jefferson, G. H., and T. G. Rawski. 1995. "How Industrial Reform Worked in China: The Role of Innovation, Competition, and Property Rights." In *Proceedings of the World Bank Annual Conference on Development Economics,* 129–170. Washington, DC: World Bank.

Jiang, Z. 2005. "Private Enterprises Expanding Quickly." *China Daily* (February 4).

Lardy, N. R. 2002. *Integrating China into the Global Economy*. Washington, DC: Brookings Institution.

Li, Z. 1994. *The Private Life of Chairman Mao*. Trans. Tai Hung-Chao. New York: Random House.

Lin, J. Y. 1998. "The Current State of China's Economic Reforms." In *China in the New Millennium: Market Reforms and Social Development*, ed. J. A. Dorn, 39–74. Washington, DC: Cato Institute.

Lin, J. Y., F. Cai, and Zhou Li. 1996. *The China Miracle: Development Strategy and Economic Reform*. Hong Kong: Chinese University Press.

Liu, Y. L. 1992. "Reform from Below: The Private Economy and Local Politics in the Rural Industrialization of Wenzhou." *China Quarterly* 130 (June): 293–316.

McGregor, R., and J. Kynge. 2002. "China Leader Says Private Property to Be Protected." *Financial Times* (November 9).

National Bureau of Statistics of China. 2003. *China Statistical Yearbook*. Beijing: China Statistical Press.

National Economic Research Institute (NERI). 2001. *NERI Index of Marketization of China's Provinces*. Beijing: NERI.

Nutter, G. W. 1962. *The Growth of Industrial Production in the Soviet Union*. Princeton, NJ: Princeton University Press for the NBER.

Oi, J. C., and A. G. Walder, eds. 1999. *Property Rights and Economic Reform in China*. Stanford, CA: Stanford University Press.

Pei, M. 1994. "Economic Reform and Civic Freedom in China." *Economic Reform Today* 4:10–15.

Phillips, K. L., and K. Shen. 2005. "What Effect Does the Size of the State-Owned Sector Have on Regional Growth in China?" *Journal of Asian Economics* 15:1079–1102.

Pilon, R. 1998. "A Constitution of Liberty for China." In *China in the New Millennium*, ed. J. A. Dorn, 333–353. Washington, DC: Cato Institute.

Pomfret, J. 2002. "Chinese Capitalists Gain New Legitimacy." *Washington Post* (September 29).

Qian, Y. 2003. "How Reform Worked in China." In *In Search of Prosperity*, ed. D. Rodrik, 297–333. Princeton, NJ: Princeton University Press.

Rawski, T. G. 2002. "Measuring China's Recent GDP Growth: Where Do We Stand?" *China Economic Quarterly* (October): 1–13.

Rummel, R. J. 1994. "Power, Genocide and Mass Murder." *Journal of Peace Research* 31 (1): 1–10.

Rural Development Institute. 2002. "China Adopts Rural Land Contracting

Law: A Breakthrough for Farmers' Land-Tenure Rights." *Monthly News and Notes from Rural Development Institute* (September).

Tsai, K. 2002. *Back-Alley Banking: Private Entrepreneurs in China.* Ithaca, NY: Cornell University Press.

Wank, D. L. 1999. "Producing Property Rights: Strategies, Networks, and Efficiency in China's Nonstate Firms." In *Property Rights and Economic Reform in China*, ed. J. C. Oi and A. G. Walder, ch. 11. Stanford, CA: Stanford University Press.

Whiting, S. H. 1999. "The Regional Evolution of Ownership Forms: Shareholding Cooperatives and Rural Industry in Shanghai and Wenzhou." In *Property Rights and Economic Reform in China*, ed. J. C. Oi and A. G. Walder, ch. 8. Stanford, CA: Stanford University Press.

World Bank. 2004. *World Development Report 2005: A Better Investment Climate for Everyone.* New York: World Bank and Oxford University Press.

Yabuki, S., and S. M. Harner. 1999. *China's New Political Economy*, rev. ed. Boulder, CO: Westview Press.

Zha, J. 1995. *China Pop.* New York: New Press.

Zhang, D. 2002. Quoted in "Chinese Private Economy Seeking Wider Development Space." *People's Daily* (April 7). http://english.peopledaily.com .cn/200204/07/eng20020407_93626.shtml (accessed April 17, 2007).

Zhang, J. 2005. "Nation Now No. 3 Global Trader." *China Daily* (January 12).

Zhang, T. W. 2004. "Measuring China's Drive to Marketization." *Fraser Forum* (May): 25–26.

Zhou, K. X. 1996. *How the Farmers Changed China.* Boulder, CO: Westview Press.

11   India: The Elephant in the Age of Liberation

PARTH J. SHAH AND RENUKA SANE

> When we were young kids growing up in America, we were told to eat
> our vegetables at dinner and not leave them. Mothers said, "think of the
> starving children in India and finish the dinner."
> And now I tell my children: "Finish your math homework. Think of
> the children in India who would make you starve, if you don't."
>
> *Thomas Friedman, 2005*

India has indeed changed. The potential that most people felt India had at the time of its independence in 1947 is finally being realized.
The foreign exchange crisis of 1991 was the watershed event. It was the
second-most defining moment in modern Indian history after independence. The 1991 changes in policy—delicensing of industries, export-
import liberalization—were, of course, changes that policymakers took
deliberately. Some people claim the changes were all the result of the International Monetary Fund (IMF) loan's structural adjustment program. The
truth most likely lies somewhere in between.

However, no one foresaw the magnitude of the impact these hasty,
half-hearted policy changes would have on India's economy and certainly
not on India's society and culture. The momentous changes in the Indian
economy and society after 1991 were completely unpredicted. Through
the reluctant changes in policies, India finally unleashed, albeit partially,
the forces of the market. It allowed, for the first time in more than three
hundred years, its people to be free to create wealth. And luckily such
opportunities were available due to larger geopolitical and technological
changes that realigned the comparative advantage of nations.

Who deserves the credit for the great leap forward? The foreign
exchange crisis! The response to that crisis was largely predetermined by

the changes in the outside world—the collapse of the Soviet Union and the utter failure of central economic planning in India itself. The prime minister in 1991, P. V. Narasimha Rao, later said that the changes went too far and that he should not have allowed such drastic changes in policy, thus declaring that he did not want credit for the full range of reforms.

Then Finance Minister Manmohan Singh is generally considered to be pro-reform, but he has never defended his early 1990s policies publicly. Even during his election campaign for member of Parliament from the South Delhi constituency in 1999, he chose to remain largely silent on economic reforms. The real tragedy is that Dr. Singh, the architect of India's reforms, lost an election in a constituency of middle- and upper-middle-class households that benefited tremendously from his reforms.[1] Overall, the consensus among political pundits in India is that the Congress lost the next general election in 1996 because of those reforms. The foreign exchange crisis deserves the full credit for making it possible for India to begin to realize its "tryst with destiny."

We shall review some of these changes and then end with what we see as the next big challenge for India.

1. The Resurgent India: Demise of the Dirigisme

Rajiv Gandhi became the youngest prime minister in 1984 after the assassination of Indira Gandhi. His government began some reforms in the industrial licensing system. Many observers now believe that those reforms launched a new phase in India's economic development. J. Bradford Delong (2003) and Rodrik and Subramanian (2005) are prominent academics who suggest that the real credit for India's reforms should go to the Nehru dynasty. "The aggregate growth data tells us that the acceleration of economic growth began earlier, in the early or mid-1980s, long before the exchange crisis of 1991 and the shift of the government of Narasimha Rao and Manmohan Singh toward neoliberal economic reforms" (Delong 2003, 186). Rodrik and Subramanian go even further and argue that India's turnaround began in the last term of Indira Gandhi during 1980–1984: "The trigger of Indian economic growth was an attitudinal shift on the part of the national government in 1980 in favor of private business. . . . When Indira Gandhi returned to power in 1980, she re-aligned herself politically with the organized private sector and

<u>dropped her previous [socialist] rhetoric</u>. The national government's attitude towards business went from being outright hostile to supportive."

Does it really matter when India's upsurge began? To most people it does not. But to understand India's transition and to decipher lessons for other countries, it does matter how and when India's trajectory changed. Arvind Panagariya (2005) calls those who say the "growth started in the 1980s group" skeptics and opines that "if those skeptics were right, it would be a major blow to liberal trade and market-friendly policies, not only with respect to India but to developing countries around the world" (p. 1). He offers three arguments to support the thesis that the "real" growth turnaround occurred in the 1990s, not in the 1980s. "First, growth during the 1980s was patchy, with the last three years contributing 7.6 percent annual growth. Without those three years, growth in the 1980s would look, at best, marginally better than that of the previous three decades. Second, the high growth in the last three years of 1980s was, in fact, preceded or accompanied by significant liberalisation under Prime Minister Rajiv Gandhi. . . . Finally, growth was stimulated by expansionary policies that involved accumulation of a large external debt and that ended in an economic crisis. In the end, it was the 1991 market reforms and subsequent liberalizing policy changes that helped sustain growth."

Delong seems to concur: "Would they [1980s reforms] have just produced short-lived flash in the pan—a decade or so of fast growth followed by a slowdown—in the absence of the further reforms of the 1990s? My hunch is that the answer is yes. In the absence of the second wave of reforms in 1990s it is unlikely that the rapid growth of the second half of 1980s could be sustained. But hard evidence to support such a strong counterfactual judgment is lacking" (p. 186).

The attitudinal change from anti-business to pro-business in the 1980s did usher in an era of increasing growth, but it was the more permanent change in the mind-set from being just tolerant of business to becoming openly market friendly that created the sustained boom. The reforms of 1991 have sparked a remarkable growth process. India's ten-year GDP growth rate is 6.3 percent (Kelkar 2004). India is now a part of a globalized production network with very high growth rates of exports, ranging from automobile components and textiles to financial accounting and software. India is earning $40 billion per quarter from the export of goods and services and is attracting about $6 billion per quarter of net capital inflows. The trade-GDP ratio (summing both goods and services) has gone up from 25 percent in 1992–1993 to 35 percent in 2003–2004.

India eliminated quantitative restrictions (quotas) on imports and brought down the peak customs rate on manufactured goods from over 150 percent to a present level of 20 percent. India also has made progress on capital account convertibility, particularly in the last five years. India now has 100 percent convertibility for foreign institutional investors. Indian firms can take up to 100 percent of their net worth out of the country, and Indian citizens can take up to $25,000. India is welcoming larger proportions of foreign investments in many sectors of the economy. The government has transferred ownership and control of several state-run enterprises in telecom, energy, and mining to the private sector. Globalization is no longer a one-way flow: Indian firms have begun investing abroad, with outward FDI from India amounting to $1.4 billion in 2003–2004. Although modest, it is a sign of changing times. Recently, Tata Tea bought Tetley to become world's largest tea supplier and producer.

India has made significant strides in modernizing its ports and has allowed international firms, such as P&O and Maersk, to enter into thirty-year contracts to run container terminals. The turnaround time at ports has dropped by half, from 7.5 days in 1996–1997 to 3.5 days in 2001–2002.

In roads, India has launched massive programs of building four- and six-lane highways with active private-sector participation. The objective is to raise the sustained velocity from thirty kilometers per hour to eighty kilometers per hour, and the results in terms of reduced transactions costs are becoming noticeable. The raw material inventory of nonfinancial firms dropped from seventy-nine days in 1997–1998 to forty-nine days in 2003–2004. Similarly, finished goods inventories dropped from thirty-four days in 1997–1998 to twenty-three days in 2003–2004.

In terms of privatization, the lessons of the Dhabol Power Project are well understood, and the new electricity bill has opened up production, transmission, and distribution to private companies. Quiet progress toward privatizing airports will hopefully translate into reforms of the railways as well (Kelkar 2004).

Poverty reduction has been slower but still impressive, with the poverty rate falling to 26 percent in 2000 from 36 percent in 1993–1994 and nearly 45 percent in 1980. During 1973–1993, the head count of the poor remained at 320 million. This number is said to have dropped by 60 million during 1993–1999. According to some estimates, 100 million people have been removed from poverty (Bhalla 2003).

The infamous "Hindu rate of growth" of about 3.5 percent was the norm during the years of central planning and most certainly a creation of state intervention rather than culture. India's economic growth began to creep upward in response to Rajiv Gandhi's reforms in the 1980s. During the period of the Hindu rate of growth, industry was in the vanguard, whereas the postreform years have been led by services. The reforms forced industrial restructuring, and the new services were largely outside government controls. Software, for example, could be produced and sent to customers without the government even being aware of the activity. The growth of IT and IT-related services was higher before India created a separate ministry to "help" the sector (fuller discussion in a later section).

Before discussing the reforms and their impact on some of the industries in India, let's take a look back, just to emphasize the distance that has been traveled.

A. India's Dirigisme: The License-Permit-Quota Raj

Rates of economic growth and per capita income numbers are generally used to measure the degree of economic change. But in the unfree economy that India was, per capita income numbers (Table 11.1 and Table 11.2) hide more than they reveal. The size of Indian government is not very large; government expenditures in proportion to GDP have

TABLE 11.1
Average growth of real GDP (percent)

	1951/52–1960/61	1961/62–1970/71	1971/72–1980/81	1981/82–1990/91	1992/93–2000/01*
Agriculture	3.1	2.5	1.8	3.6	3.2
Industry	6.3	5.5	4.1	7.1	6.4
Services	4.3	4.8	4.4	6.7	8.1
GDP (factor cost)	3.9	3.7	3.2	5.6	6.3
Per capita GDP	2.0	1.5	0.8	3.4	4.4

SOURCE: Central Statistical Organization, New Delhi.
*Leaving out the reform years of 1991–1992.

TABLE II.2

India on the income scale

Year	National income[a] (billions of Rs.)	Per capita income[a] (Rs.)	Percentage change in national income	Percentage change in per capita income
1951–52	1,366.68	3,744		
1952–53	1,405.27	3,778	2.82	0.91
1953–54	1,493.77	3,941	6.30	4.31
1954–55	1,554.54	4,027	4.07	2.18
1955–56	1,593.03	4,054	2.48	0.67
1956–57	1,681.70	4,194	5.57	3.45
1957–58	1,652.63	4,041	−1.73	−3.65
1958–59	1,779.47	4,257	7.68	5.35
1959–60	1,810.58	4,250	1.75	−0.16
1960–61	1,938.36	4,466	7.06	5.08
1961–62	1,991.65	4,486	2.75	0.45
1962–63	2,025.82	4,462	1.72	−0.53
1963–64	2,127.17	4,584	5.00	2.73
1964–65	2,285.46	4,822	7.44	5.19
1965–66	2,180.79	4,496	−4.58	−6.76
1966–67	2,192.81	4,430	0.55	−1.47
1967–68	2,374.24	4,692	8.27	5.91
1968–69	2,432.92	4,697	2.47	0.11
1969–70	2,595.52	4,906	6.68	4.45
1970–71	2,728.99	5,044	5.14	2.81
1971–72	2,745.78	4,956	0.62	−1.74
1972–73	2,723.79	4,804	−0.80	−3.07
1973–74	2,854.85	4,922	4.81	2.46
1974–75	2,888.69	4,871	1.19	−1.04
1975–76	3,163.16	5,211	9.50	6.98
1976–77	3,190.63	5,146	0.87	−1.25
1977–78	3,436.59	5,420	7.71	5.32
1978–79	3,627.99	5,599	5.57	3.30
1979–80	3,410.33	5,136	−6.00	−8.27
1980–81	3,665.35	5,398	7.48	5.10
1981–82	3,889.62	5,621	6.12	4.13
1982–83	3,971.45	5,609	2.10	−0.21
1983–84	4,264.61	5,898	7.38	5.15
1984–85	4,455.94	6,030	4.49	2.24
1985–86	4,655.74	6,167	4.48	2.27
1986–87	4,824.48	6,257	3.62	1.46
1987–88	4,965.00	6,301	2.91	0.70
1988–89	5,502.81	6,836	10.83	8.49
1989–90	5,861.43	7,131	6.52	4.32
1990–91	6,162.59	7,345	5.14	3.00
1991–92	6,206.58	7,251	0.71	−1.28
1992–93	6,474.08	7,424	4.31	2.39
1993–94	6,859.12	7,724	5.95	4.04
1994–95	7,326.51	8,105	6.81	4.93
1995–96	7,859.90	8,543	7.28	5.40
1996–97	8,475.11	9,055	7.83	5.99
1997–98	8,891.02	9,271	4.91	2.39
1998–99	9,495.25	9,739	6.80	5.05
1999–2000	10,114.74	10,207	6.52	4.81

[a]At constant 1993–94 prices.

been less than 20 percent. The Soviet central planning model that India adopted in the mid-1950s depended as much on regulating private economic activities and creating state monopolies as on outright government spending.

In the late 1960s, my father wanted to buy a scooter. (The personal experience described here is of one of the authors, Parth. For simplicity and directness it is narrated in the first person.) He paid the full price of the scooter in advance to the dealer and then waited. After several years of waiting, he found a way to pay the price of the scooter in dollars, the precious foreign exchange, and pushed himself ahead in the queue. He quickly got his scooter—in just eight years! When my parents decided to settle down in Vadodara in Gujarat, they bought a house and applied for a telephone connection. In India at that time, both were seen as equally important tasks. It took about four years for the telephone to be installed.

The scooter was produced by a private company whose production quota was determined by the government, and the telephone was a state monopoly. It was an all-around scarcity economy.

It was not really much different when I came back to Delhi from the United States in 1997. Like many returnees who feel guilty about hiring domestic help, I also resolved to be as self-sufficient in running my new Indian home as I was at running my American apartment. Cleaning the bathroom and dusting the furniture were indeed more demanding here. However, when I spent more than half a day to pay my first telephone bill and several hours for the electricity bill, my resolve vanished into thin air. I had to wait in a long queue under a blistering sun to *give* my money to the government! I felt utterly helpless; I hired a helper. The dehumanizing effects of government monopoly of businesses were no longer a theoretical speculation in the classroom.

How did I manage, you may ask, to get a house and a telephone in Delhi to begin with? Rent-control and tenancy laws make it nearly impossible to lease any space without close personal contacts. Landlords not only receive (legal) rents below market rates but also are in constant danger of losing the property to their tenants. I was fortunate in finding a well-wisher who had an apartment furnished with telephone and cooking gas (also a state monopoly!).

During my evening walks in the neighborhood, I observed that in the ubiquitous bungalows with two stories and a basement, only the ground floor was generally used. Because of government rules favoring renters, almost half of the residential space was lying unused in the heart of India's capital city! In trying to protect tenants from "arbitrary" expulsion by landlords, the tenancy laws prevented people from becoming tenants.

The realities of this life can hardly be fully captured by per capita income numbers. Prices do not reflect realities. Economic calculations become chaotic. Life becomes unpredictable.

Deepak Lal (1999, 2005) comprehensively documents the results of India's experiment with socialism and the idiocies and idiosyncrasies of India's central economic planning through its unique license-permit-quota raj.[2] Professor B. R. Shenoy was the first to sound the alarm at the statist economic policies (Amin and Shah 2004). He penned a strong note of dissent to the Second Five-Year Plan and challenged the basic premise of the whole exercise.[3] Throughout the 1950s and 1960s he fought a courageous battle against the all-engulfing state.[4] Professor Shenoy received tremendous support and intellectual ammunition from P. T. Bauer (1961).

In 1970, Jagdish Bhagwati and Padma Desai drew attention to the gross failure of the planned goals in their exhaustive empirical study, *India: Planning for Industrialization*. Bhagwati and T. N. Srinivasan (1975) demonstrated serious flaws in India's import-substitution strategy toward international trade. In 1983, after a brief stint in the Planning Commission, Deepak Lal wrote *The Poverty of "Development Economics,"* challenging the orthodox model of development that put more faith in the plan than the market. Despite the long track record of failure and the excellent critiques by these economists, it wasn't until the 1991 crisis that India was able to achieve meaningful sustained reforms.

We have discussed some of the overall changes in India's economic policy architecture. Now we focus on some specific sectors of the economy to understand the nature and degree of this transformation.

2. Sector Reform

A. The Telecom Miracle: A Mobile in Every Hand

One of the biggest success stories of the reforms in India has been the telecom sector. From being a giant government-owned monolith, the sector now has several competing service providers. Slowly and tortuously the telecom policy evolved from the National Telecom Policy in 1994 and opened up all the sectors to private players: basic or fixed-line, cellular, Internet services, national long distance, international long distance, and VSAT services. Instead of service- or circle-specific licenses, the Telecom Regulatory Authority of India, a recently created independent regulatory agency, has proposed a unified licensing regime with uniform rules for all players.[5]

Until 1995, during the more than forty years of government monopoly, there were 9.38 million telephone connections in the country, with one of the lowest teledensities in the world. By 2005, there are 46.19 million fixed-line subscribers and 52.22 million mobile phones (GSM and CDMA). In less than seven years of opening the cellular services to private companies, India has more mobile phones than fixed-line connections (Hussain and Kathuria 2003). It is not uncommon to see street vendors taking orders for home delivery of food or groceries on cell phones. The mobile phone market is now growing at five million a month. Teledensity was predicted to rise to 17 percent by 2006. Unlike in many developed countries, the GSM and CDMA technologies compete in the same market in India. The outsourcing boom would not have occurred without India's telecom sector.

B. IT and BPO: New Kids on the Block

Information technology services and business process outsourcing (BPO) are the sectors that represent the new, vibrant India. They arrived while the government did not know or understand the significance of these sectors. Benign neglect on the part of the government is the biggest reason for their existence and success. As such, they herald the spontaneous order of market processes.

The ITES-BPO industry has grown by about 54 percent, with export earnings of U.S.$3.6 billion during 2003–2004. Output of the Indian electronics and IT industry is estimated to have grown by 18.2 percent to Rs 1,147 billion in 2003. The share of software services in the IT sector rose from 38.7 percent in 1998–1999 to 61.8 percent in 2003–2004. Internet users in the country grew from approximately 6.6 million in 2000 to nearly 32 million in 2003 and to more than 44 million by the end of 2005 (Economic Survey, 2005).

The ITES-BPO segment also proved to be a major opportunity for job seekers, creating employment for around 74,400 additional personnel in India during 2003. The number of Indians working for this sector jumped to 245,500 by March 2004. By the year 2008, the segment is expected to employ more than 1.1 million Indians, according to studies conducted by NASSCOM, a trade association.

Most important, these companies are some of the highest-paying employers in the country. College graduates, who would have never dreamed of living independently from their parents, with a job at a call center could leave town without a second thought. These young, living-alone professionals are defining not only consumption patterns but also the culture.

The IT sector has given India its new icons: N. R. Narayan Murthy of Infosys, Azim Premji of Wipro, and, of course, Bill Gates of Microsoft. Gurcharan Das in his *India Unbound*, a book celebrating the new India, tells the story of "a fourteen-year-old Raju, who hustles between tables [serving tea] during the day and learns computers at night, and has visions of becoming 'Bilgay'" (2002, 347).

This sector has forced the government to mend and repeal many a petty control: working on national holidays; allowing women to work on night shifts; and allowing offices to function twenty-four hours a day all year. India's new economy is run by people who believe more in themselves than in labor unions. Labor has lost its Marxian colors in this industry![6]

C. Birds in the Blue Sky: Private Airlines

Just a few years ago, no one would have dreamed that a great many newlyweds would be flying to their honeymoon destinations. But that is a very common sight at the bustling airports of India. Even so, the aviation policy of the government leaves much to be desired, with its restrictions on foreign investment, partnership with foreign airlines (Indian airlines can have foreign collaborators as long as they are not in the airline business), and access to and tariffs for the use of government airports. The government has allowed only Indian companies to compete with the state monopoly, Indian Airlines. Despite all the hurdles, several companies entered the market, and many of them quickly went bankrupt.

TABLE 11.3
Domestic passenger traffic in India

Year	Air India	Indian Airlines & Alliance Air	Jet Airways	Sahara Airlines	Other private airlines	All private airlines	Total domestic traffic
1990–91	—	747.1	—	—	—	—	747.1
1991–92	31.0	831.2	—	—	—	—	862.1
1992–93	39.3	726.8	—	—	—	—	766.1
1993–94	28.1	723.0	—	—	—	—	751.0
1994–95	37.4	689.8	124.0	—	254.5	378.5	1,105.7
1995–96	53.8	692.7	160.7	7.7	303.9	472.3	1,218.8
1996–97	57.9	719.3	237.0	31.4	124.4	392.8	1,170.0
1997–98	60.7	726.8	312.9	51.0	0.32	367.1	1,154.5
1998–99	68.0	685.5	403.0	45.2	0.08	448.9	1,202.5
1999–00	76.1	652.8	486.8	55.4	—	542.2	1,271.1
2000–01	77.3	632.6	592.5	68.8	—	661.3	1,371.2
2001–02	73.0	569.3	582.0	61.3	—	643.3	1,285.4

SOURCE: www.indiastat.com.

Jet Airways, the largest private carrier, has single-handedly challenged the state monopoly and revolutionized air travel in India (Table 11.3). Following on its success, recently several new "no-frills" airlines have entered the market. The fares of one such airline, Air Deccan, effectively compete with railway prices.

Often the assumptions on which government develops its economic policies become reality, not because the assumptions were accurate but rather because the policies create circumstances that make the assumptions self-fulfilling. Like air travel, cars were considered to be luxury goods by India's first prime minister, and until the 1980s only two companies were allowed to produce them. The companies sold the same model for some forty years, and one could buy it in any color as long as it was white. The government determined the number of cars that could be produced so as to conserve scarce resources for more urgent necessities. And cars remained a luxury good; very few people could afford to buy them until about the 1980s! First the government itself gave up the dogma of the luxury good and partnered with Suzuki of Japan to produce small, affordable cars and later opened up the market to international auto companies. The policies created scarcity—not only of luxuries but also of necessities.

D. Creation of a National Stock Exchange: The Untold Success Story

The role of financial markets in channeling society's savings into productive investments has been well understood. The banking system and equity and debt markets perform the task of financial intermediation. Joseph Schumpeter considered bankers managing the banking system as "ephors" (overseers) of the market economy.

> He [banker] stands between those who wish to form new combinations and the possessors of productive means. He is essentially a phenomenon of development. . . . He makes possible the carrying out of new combinations, authorizes people, in the name of society as it were, to form them. He is the ephor of the exchange economy. (Schumpeter 1954, 74)

Unfortunately, substantial parts of the Indian banking system that were nationalized in 1969 have not yet been deregulated. A few local and international private banks exist, but their role is still marginal in the system. The debt market in India is a similar story. The Reserve Bank of India tightly controls the market, including the entry of brokers, and with the government being the largest issuer of debt, the market is still in a nascent stage. This has left only the equity market to fulfill the function of market-governed financial intermediation.

The Bombay Stock Exchange (BSE) has historically dominated the equity market and the public imagination. There existed twenty other stock exchanges in different parts of the country, albeit with insignificant trading volumes. The BSE was owned and run by its members, that is, the brokers. The BSE was essentially a private club of brokers. Membership in this club required the right friends and contacts. There was no independent regulator because the Securities and Exchange Board of India (SEBI), although created in 1988, achieved legal standing only in 1993. For various reasons, the thinness of the market being one of the important ones, no other competitor came into existence. The BSE therefore operated as an unregulated monopoly.

The BSE operated a phone-based trading floor. This gave rise to several bad practices, with the purchaser being unaware of the exact price at which the security was traded on the floor. The exchange operated an account-period settlement—trades over a certain range of days were netted on a future expiration date, and this was used to generate settlement obligations. However, poor payments systems and lack of any independent monitoring gave rise to an innovation called *badla*. *Badla* allowed obligations to be rolled over from one settlement period to the other, which made trading highly leveraged but without any margins or risk-containment measures. The practice of *badla* was the breeding ground for several payment crises (Shah and Thomas 2000).

These practices and scandals forced several design changes in the securities market. The important landmarks are as follows: 1993, amendment of SEBI Act and establishment of SEBI; 1994, introduction of electronic trading; 1996, establishment of a clearing corporation; 1996, dematerialization of shares through a depository; 2000 and 2001, introduction of derivatives trading; 2001, introduction of rolling settlement on the spot market; 2002, Securitization Act.

The primary change was the creation of a new stock exchange in 1994, the National Stock Exchange of India (NSE). The NSE is owned by a consortium of financial institutions and is structured as a limited liability firm with broker firms as franchisees. Instead of being the owners, the brokers are now franchisees. As it became easy to start a brokerage firm, other corporate entities and foreign brokerage firms have now become members. The NSE also led the creation of a clearing corporation: the National Securities Clearing Corporation (NSCC). The NSCC is the legal counterparty to the net settlement obligations of all brokerage firms. The NSE built an electronic order-matching system by which orders were matched by computers, thereby eliminating any human intervention. This led to fully transparent transactions at the NSE, unlike at the BSE, where a few brokers from South Bombay had a monopoly over market information. The electronic order-matching system also made possible nationwide trading, thereby facilitating order flow and liquidity of the market. The NSE harnessed the availability of information technology to enable nationwide access to trading.

The establishment of the NSCC led to a reduction in transaction costs. With extensive use of information technology, trading platforms were accessible from anywhere in the country. This has had a significant impact on the reach of the market to smaller cities and towns. In 1994–1995, Bombay accounted for 100 percent of the turnover on the NSE. In 2004–2005, this had dropped to 44 percent, with other cities across India accounting for the rest. There are twenty-three operative stock exchanges with 9,413 listed securities. Even though the number of

TABLE 11.4
Tale of two stock markets (billions of Rs)

	MARKET CAPITALIZATION		AVERAGE DAILY TURNOVER	
Year	BSE	NSE	BSE	NSE
1996	5,264.76	4,014.58	2.30	2.73
1997	4,639.15	4,193.67	5.04	11.78
1998	5,603.25	4,815.03	8.49	15.17
1999	5,453.61	4,911.75	12.73	16.56
2000	9,128.42	10,204.26	27.16	32.85
2001	6,255.53	6,578.47	39.67	50.01
2002	6,122.24	6,368.61	12.80	20.44
2003	5,721.97	5,371.33	12.47	24.63
2004	12,012.06	11,209.76	19.68	43.29
2005	16,810.51	16,145.97	20.18	45.06

NOTE: NSE = National Stock Exchange of India; BSE = Bombay Stock Exchange.

firms listed on the NSE is fewer than on the BSE, in terms of average daily turnover the NSE far surpasses the BSE (Table 11.4).

Household participation has been increasing steadily in the securities market. The number of accounts, for example, at the depository grew by 21 percent and 29 percent in 2003 and 2004, respectively, with six million accounts at the end of 2004. India's stock exchanges, the NSE and the BSE, stood at third and fifth place, respectively, among the biggest exchanges in terms of number of transactions in 2003 and 2004. The Nifty index, which trades on the NSE, experienced a sharp growth in the market capitalization from Rs 2.85 billion in 2001 to Rs 9.02 billion in 2004. The average trade size on the NSE and BSE spot markets in 2004 was Rs 27,715 and Rs 23,984, respectively, highlighting the domination of individual investors in price discovery (Economic Survey 2005).

Economic development of a country is largely dependent on the ability of individuals to convert ideas into products. Access to capital is very critical in this process of transformation. Resource mobilization through book-building rose steadily from 25 percent of public equity offerings in 2001 to 53 percent in 2002, 64 percent in 2003, and 99 percent in 2004 (Economic Survey 2005).

The *Indian Venture Capital Association Year Book* states that investments of $881 million were made in eighty companies in 2002 and of $470 million in fifty-six companies in 2003. Services are assuming an increasing share of India's GDP. For its continued growth, it would need a means of mobilizing resources and financing its expansion. Correspondingly, the resources raised by the service industry in the total primary capital issues have shown a significant increase. The service sector raised Rs 278.32 billion through primary issues, which was more than half of the amount raised in 2004 by manufacturing, textiles, chemicals, and machinery.

The formation of the NSE has made many of these achievements possible and has also led to several reforms in the BSE itself. Shareholders of the NSE were users of the securities markets and therefore stood to gain from a modern liquid stock market. This structure also kept the NSE focused on shareholder maximization as opposed to profit maximization of member brokers (Shah and Thomas 2001).

The success of the securities market in initiating and sustaining radical reforms—creation of a new stock exchange—has caused a paradigm shift in how India converts its savings into productive capital. And it has enabled millions of ordinary Indians to share the fruits of a growing, dynamic economy.

3. Liberalization and the Poor: Have They Gained?

Not everyone shares the enthusiasm for the new, resurgent India. Many argue, and our preceding narrative of IT, BPO, airlines, and stock exchanges probably implies, that the reforms have benefited only the middle and upper classes. This has become one of the most contested issues concerning the impact of liberalization in India. It seems, by reading the government data one way, that the poverty ratio and the absolute number of people below the poverty line have declined. But reading the data another way shows a rather weak decline in poverty. This debate on numbers is a nightmare even for statisticians (Bhalla 2003, 2002).

We, however, believe that the poor have not gained as much as they could have in the new India. The reason is simple: the areas in which the middle and upper classes make their living have seen the highest degree of liberalization, whereas the areas in which the poor earn their livelihood have seen the fewest reforms. They still live under the draconian license-permit-quota raj, as the system of extensive government intervention in India was known. Setting up a factory or a call center requires no license. But anyone wanting to run a tea stall or to become a street hawker or a cycle-rickshaw puller or to work as a railway porter requires a license. For entry-level professions that require low skills and little capital, licenses are still required. The number of some of these licenses was fixed thirty to forty years ago and never revised. Because the street entrepreneurs operate illegally, they are open to harassment and extortion by the police and municipal officers.

Consider cycle-rickshaw pullers and street vendors in the cities and towns of India. Delhi has approximately 500,000 cycle-rickshaws, providing an affordable and accessible transportation service to the poor. The Municipal Corporation of Delhi has mandated that rickshaws have to be licensed and that only ninety thousand licenses shall be given out. More than 80 percent of the cycle-rickshaws are illegal. This government-created illegality exposes the pullers to constant harassment and extortion by the police and municipal officers. One study suggests that on average a bribe of Rs 200 per month per cycle-rickshaw is paid. Even the licensed rickshaws have to pay up. The government functionaries extort Rs 10,000,000 a month from the cycle-rickshaw pullers!

Similarly, Delhi's estimated 600,000 street vendors operate without the necessary license and pay up about Rs 12,000,000 per month. This is the burden of the license-permit-quota raj—of economic unfreedom—on the poorest of the poor in Delhi.

During municipal raids, which occur on a weekly or monthly basis, the goods, hand cart, weighing balance, and other equipment of vendors as well as the rickshaws of pullers are impounded. After rickshaws are seized, it takes five to fifteen days and more bribes to get them released. During these days, the pullers lose their means of livelihood. Because of these problems and uncertainties created by the licensing system, the pullers prefer to rent rather than own their rickshaws. If their rickshaws are impounded, then the pullers rent another instead of waiting for the first one to be released; the owner worries about getting the rickshaw back on the road. More than 90 percent of rickshaws in Delhi are rented, not owned. This is despite Delhi's law requiring that the owner and the driver of a rickshaw must be the same person. The law obviously intends to promote ownership and limit exploitation of rickshaw pullers by intermediaries. But the licensing system has created a situation in which hardly anyone desires to own a rickshaw. The law was supposed to outlaw the intermediary, but only intermediaries exist in the rickshaw market. The actual outcome is exactly opposite to what was intended by the law: the law of unintended consequences.

Should we do away with the license raj for rickshaws, give them the freedom to earn an honest living without constant fear? Despite the severe harm caused by the licensing system, many people raise the specter of rickshaws clogging the roads of the city if the license requirements were abolished. They fear rampant growth in the number of rickshaws. But first ask: Why are there .5 million rickshaws in Delhi? And not .4 or .6 million? Because the market demand is for .5 million rickshaws. It is simple supply and demand. The licensed capacity is 90,000, but what impact does that have on the actual number of rickshaws? If the capacity were 70,000 or 1.5 million, how many rickshaws would actually be on the road? About .5 million! Regardless of the number that the government decides to license, the market supplies what the people demand.

The license regime does not really control the number of rickshaws in the city; it does not serve any purpose in traffic or congestion management. It does, however, serve one purpose, probably the only purpose: it makes the rickshaw business illegal and therefore open to extortion and harassment. Shouldn't we abolish this inhumane system? The government restrictions over legitimate economic activities and consequent lack of economic freedom hurt the poor far more than the rich. The same logic applies to street vendors, small shopkeepers—all the entry-level professions to which entry is regulated by government.

This is the story of the urban poor. Graphic details of this gross injustice are documented in *Law, Liberty, and Livelihood: Making a Living on the Street*.[7] Some of the municipal laws speak for themselves (see next page).

The rural poor are dependent on agriculture. And agriculture has been the area of least reform. Much agricultural produce cannot be transported across a district line, let alone across the state or the country. India does not even have a common market for agriculture. A law in the state of Maharastra requires farmers to sell their sugar cane to a specified sugar mill in the district. In Kerala, the law mandates that after a farm is registered as producing one crop, it cannot ever change! Recently, farmers who had planted sugar cane instead of rice saw their crops being uprooted by union workers. Unless agriculture is liberalized, the rural poor have little to look forward to.

The poor are unenthusiastic about current liberalization not because they are becoming poorer, as some claim, but rather because they have not seen much liberalization in their means of livelihoods. We must do for them what we have done for the rich: give them economic freedom.

Delhi Municipal Corporation
Cycle-Rickshaw Bye-Laws, 1960, Section 3
No person shall keep or ply for hire a cycle rickshaw in Delhi unless he himself is the owner thereof and holds a licence granted in that behalf by the Commissioner on payment of the fee that may, from time to time, be fixed under subsection (2) of Section 430. Provided that no person will be granted more than one such licence [Provided further that commissioner may grant more than one licences to a widow or a handicapped subject to the maximum of five licenses.]

Delhi Municipal Corporation
Cycle-Rickshaw Bye-Laws, 1960, Section 17A
Any cycle rickshaw found plying for hire without a licence or found driven by a person not having proper licence as provided under bye-law 3(1) and (2) shall be liable to be seized by the Commissioner or a person duly authorised by him in his behalf. The cycle rickshaw, so seized shall be disposed off by public auction after dismantling, deformation of such process including smashing it into a scrap after a reasonable time as may be decided by the Commissioner from time to time.

Delhi Municipal Corporation Act, 1957, Section 420
Street Hawkers: Technical Conditions Refrigerated Water Trolleys (Rule 5)
It has been decided by the Commissioner that distance of 50 metres between 2 water trolleys in congested areas of City, Sadr Pahar Ganj, Civil Line and K.B. Zones and 100 metres in less congested areas of Shahdra, New Delhi, South, West and Rural Zones be observed. However, this shall not hold good in case of parking of water trolleys near cinemas, markets and other places of recreation etc. Even at such places a distance of about 10 metres shall have to be maintained

Delhi Municipal Corporation Act, 1957
Guidelines for grant of Tehbazari [license] Rule (iv)
No tehbazari will be allowed on roads which are visited by VIPs, like Bahadur Shah Zafar Marg, Subhash Marg, Indraprastha Marg, etc.

4. Economic Freedom in India: Understanding the New Success and the Continuing Failure

A focus on economic freedom helps explain both India's economic success and its failure. As Figure 11.1 shows, India's economic freedom score has improved in some areas but has stagnated in others.[8]

The shift in India's economic policy in 1991 is captured by the increase in the economic freedom rating from 4.8 in 1990 to 6.4 in 2002. But, in relative terms this improvement has barely kept pace with the liberalization of the rest of the world. India's rank improved only from 93rd (out of 115) to 86th (out of 123) in the 1990s.

The largest increase in freedom came from reductions in the size of the government. Freedom to trade internationally improved substantially. This explains the success of the new economy sectors—IT, software, BPO—all internationally traded services.

The almost stagnant score on regulation indicates the big failure of India in regulatory reforms—the strict controls and license regime on street entrepreneurs and small businesses. A World Bank study (Tables 11.5

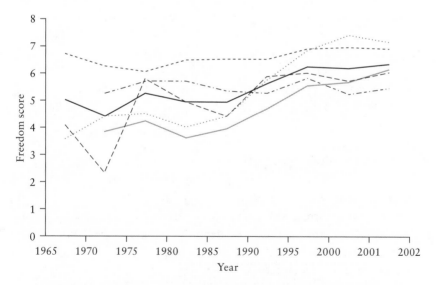

····· Size of Government   − − Legal System & Property Rights   - - - Sound Money
—— Freedom to Trade Internationally   − · · · Regulations   —— Summary Index

FIGURE **11.1** India's freedom score, 1970–2002

TABLE 11.5

Starting a business in India

Procedure	Duration (days)	Cost (U.S.$)
1. Obtain preapproval of name, have documents vetted	7	10.41
2. Stamp the Memorandum and Articles of Association	2	25.40
3. File for registration	9	193.60
4. Make a seal	7	10.41
5. Obtain permanent account number	60	1.35
6. Obtain tax account number	45*	0
7. File for sales tax	15*	2.60
8. Register for profession tax	2*	0
9. Register with Mumbai Shops and Establishment Act	2*	20.82
10. File for Employee Provident Fund	2*	0
11. File for Employees State Insurance Corporation	1*	0
TOTAL:	89	264.59

SOURCE: http://rru.worldbank.org/DoingBusiness/ExploreEconomies/BusinessClimateSnapshot
.aspx?economyid=89.

*This procedure runs simultaneously with previous procedures.

TABLE 11.6

Country comparisons of starting a business

Country	Number of procedures	Duration (days)	Cost[a]
India	11	89	49.5
Sri Lanka	8	50	10.7
Pakistan	11	24	36.0
Nepal	7	21	74.1
Bangladesh	8	35	91.0
Hong Kong	5	11	3.4
Singapore	7	8	1.2
Australia	2	2	2.1

SOURCE: http://rru.worldbank.org/DoingBusiness/ExploreEconomies/Economy
Characteristics.aspx.

[a]Cost is given as percentage of gross national income per capita.

and 11.6) demonstrates the distance that India has to travel on the path of regulatory reforms. Although licenses have been abolished for the industrial sector, labor and environmental laws have helped continue the inspector raj and extortion by government inspectors. The old economy— agriculture and manufacturing—has experienced little deregulation.

The improvement in the legal structure and property rights reflects the increasing independence of the judiciary and of the agencies that supervise the government, such as the Central Vigilance Commission, Comptroller and Auditor General, and the Election Commission.

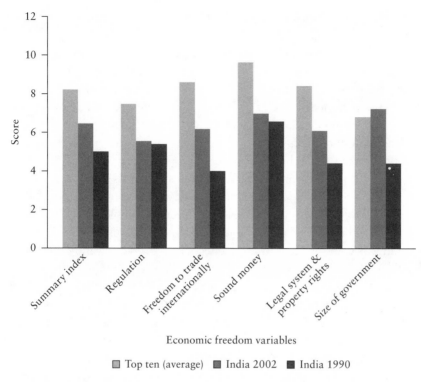

Economic freedom variables

☐ Top ten (average)   ▩ India 2002   ■ India 1990

FIGURE **11.2**   Comparison of India in 1990 and 2002 with top ten freest nations

Figure 11.2 compares India of 1990 and 2002 with the average score of the top ten countries in the Economic Freedom of the World index. It points out the areas as well as the extent of reforms where they have occurred. It also clearly identifies the areas where India lags behind the top ten—the second-generation reforms necessary to rise to a growth rate of higher than 8 percent.

5. The Way Forward: Second-Generation Reforms

Discussions about the future of reforms center on two main components: economic and social infrastructure. Many experts have given an exhaustive list of economic reforms; there is little new to add: contractual freedom in labor markets, common market for agricultural products, de-reservation of items for small-scale industries, removal of redundant departments and ministries, corporatization and privatization of the banking and insurance sectors, disinvestment of public sector companies, rationalization of bankruptcy laws, continuing reductions in tariffs (for example, Jalan 2005; Debroy 2004). The exact articulation and degree of radicalism would vary among policy wonks, but a general agreement does exist on the overall nature of changes necessary for the next big leap forward.

The consensus seems to be that government should remove itself from the economic arena. However, the expert prescription for social infrastructure requires massive involvement of government. It is difficult to understand this schizophrenia of experts between economic and social goods. If government interventions and controls play havoc in the production of simple economic goods, how could they be expected to offer opposite results in the production of rather complex social goods? If government is inefficient in producing food—cultivating land—then how could it become efficient in producing education—cultivating the mind? Tilling land is certainly a far simpler task than training the young.

Moreover, India's reform experience provides a telling example of how people find ways to meet both their economic and educational needs, if only they are left free to do so. At the launch of reforms in 1991, the rate of literacy was about 50 percent. After they were given the freedom from industrial licensing and trade restrictions, these half-literate people produced the highest rates of economic growth the country has ever seen—6, 7, 8, 9, and, for a quarter, 10 percent! This was more than double the "Hindu rate of growth" that could be muscled up by all the wise men of India's Planning Commission in the previous forty-odd years.[9]

During these years, more people became literate. The literacy rate rose from 50 to about 65 percent—the highest increase in the rate compared with any other decade in India's modern history. The government gave more economic freedom, and the people of India produced not only the highest rate of economic growth but also the largest increase in the rate of literacy. They created wealth and invested a part of it in the future. Is there any better demonstration of the fact that economic freedom trumps even literacy? What the people of India needed was not necessarily more government spending on education but rather the freedom to produce and trade.

Private schools for the poor that charge Rs 25–200 a month are one of the fastest-growing industries in the country—in urban as well as in rural India (Tooley 2005). The media research firm TAM found that educational institutions were the single largest advertisers in the print media in 2004, up from the sixth position in 2003 (*Business Standard,* April 20, 2005). A recent National Sample Survey by the government shows the sharp increase in household expenditures on education. Education comprised 1.2 percent of the per capita consumption expenditure in 1983, rose to 2.4 percent in 1993, 2.8 percent in 1999, and 4.4 percent in 2003. In urban areas, the private educational expenditure has increased even faster. It went from 2.1 percent in 1983 to 6.3 percent in 2003.

Lack of economic freedom affects not only economic achievements but also fulfillment of social objectives, for example, of universal education. The Delhi Education Act of 1973 requires an "Essential Certificate," a license, from education authorities for opening a new school or even for expanding an existing one. The authorities are required to assess "any adverse impact" of the opening of a new school on existing schools in the area. The license-permit-quota raj that ruled the industry in India until 1991 still operates in the field of education. Severe scarcity of schools and poor quality of education are the predictable results of the license-permit-quota raj in education. Economic freedom is as much a solution in education as it is in industry.

India of the reform years is a classic example of how expansion of economic freedom leads not only to higher economic growth but also to enhanced literacy and education. Economic freedom is still the best benchmark for India's second-generation reforms.

6. Governance: The Next Challenge

The real challenge in India is of governance and of the mind-set of the people in the government. Ultimately the institutions of government—legislative, executive, and judicial branches—would design and implement policy changes. Without significant improvement in the quality of governance, the more difficult and contentious policy changes will become extremely tortuous, slow, and often misguided.

Let us first illustrate the issue of the mind-set with examples of import barriers and foreign direct investment (FDI) policies. Table 11.7 shows different types of nontariff barriers and the number of items covered under these barriers. The overall trend across all the types of barriers is significantly downward. Notice that the government enumerates each

TABLE 11.7
Types of nontariff barriers on India's imports (number of items)

Type of NTB	YEAR							
	1996	1997	1998	1999	2000	2001	2002	2003
Prohibited	59	59	59	59	59	59	52	52
Restricted	2,984	2,322	2,314	1,183	968	479	554	484
Canalized/STE	127	129	129	37	34	29	33	32
SIL	765	1,043	919	886	226	—	—	—
Total	3,935	3,553	3,421	2,165	1,287	567	639	568
Free	6,161	6,649	6,781	8,055	8,854	9,582	11,032*	11,103

SOURCE: Reserve Bank of India, *Report on Currency and Finance* (2002–2003).
NOTE: NTB = nontariff barrier, SIL = special import license, STE = state trading enterprises.
*This includes 148 items with conditions.

item that is prohibited, restricted, canalized (allowed to be imported only by government enterprises), or that requires a special import license. The number of controlled items has declined from 3,935 in 1996 to 568 in 2003. But it does not stop there: it also lists items that are allowed to be freely imported. Their number has increased from 6,161 in 1996 to 11,103 in 2003. The mind-set is still that everything is prohibited except what is specifically allowed.

There is a similar story for foreign direct investments. For increased inflow of FDI, the government established Fast Track Committees in about thirty departments and ministries, created the Foreign

TABLE 11.8
*Foreign direct investments in India
(millions of U.S.$)*

Year	Approvals	Inflows
1991	527	165
1992	1,976	393
1993	2,428	654
1994	3,178	1,374
1995	11,439	2,141
1996	11,484	2,270
1997	10,984	3,682
1998	7,532	3,083
1999	4,266	2,439
2000	5,754	2,908
2001	3,160	4,222
2002	1,654	3,134
2003	1,353	2,776
2004	1,475	2,549
TOTAL	67,210	32,290

Investment Promotion Board for single-window clearance, and set up several high-level cabinet committees to review FDI proposals quickly. Because of a mind-set that is suspicious of everything foreign and equates multinational corporations (MNCs) with the East India Company, the actual FDI is less than half of what has been approved by the government (Table 11.8). One arm of the government approves the investment, but all the other arms work to check it. The mind-set that sees globalization as neoimperialism still dominates the government machinery.

A. Thought at the Speed of Government

Bureaucracy still runs rampant in India. Arun Shourie, who served in many departments and ministries of the central government under Prime Minister A. B. Vajpayee, wrote a book about his experiences, *Governance and the Sclerosis That Has Set In*, in which he narrates the following story.

Two officers in the Ministry of Steel some time in early 1999 made notings on some files in red and green ink. This led the superiors to raise the question, "Can officers use inks other than blue and black?" The ministry sought guidance from the Department of Administrative Reforms. "Research began. Consultations commenced. Ultimately it was decided that, as the matter concerned ink," the Directorate of Printing should be consulted (Shourie 2004, 3). After three weeks of deliberations, the directorate replied that there are no "orders/ instructions/ guidelines in respect of use of different colours of ink" and suggested that the Department of Personnel and Training, Ministry of Home Affairs be consulted. After about three weeks of deliberations on this suggestion, the Department of Administrative Reforms sent the letter of inquiry.

Now the Department of Personnel and Training held meetings and consultations. Again, after about three weeks, it replied that the question pertains essentially to the *Manual of Office Procedure*, which is regulated by the Department of Administrative Reforms (DAF), so the department itself may take a view. After some meetings, DAF decided that the criterion for adjudging the issue should be the longevity of the ink—the files in categories A and B are kept permanently, so the ink used on those files should be long-lasting. This proposal was taken up at the Senior Officers Meeting of DAF, and the officers noted that the longevity of the ink might be affected not only by what color it was but also by the quality of ink and the type of pen used, ballpoint or fountain pen. So these factors must also be taken into account in making the final decision. The custodian of government records, the National Archives of India, must be consulted about the longevity of inks. The director general guided them to the standards set by the Bureau of Indian Standards for various colors of ink and noted that for fountain pen ink the permanent colors are blue and black and for ballpoint ink, blue, black, red, and green.

This meant that if the officers used a ballpoint pen, it could be of any of the four colors, but if they used a fountain pen, then only blue and black could be used. "Longevity clearly was not a sufficient criterion to clinch the question" (p. 5). They decided to consult the armed forces, particularly the Army. The Ministry of Defense replied that red ink is used by the chiefs of staff, green by principal staff officers, and blue and black by all the other officers. The color is decided not by longevity but rather by hierarchy.

The Department of Administrative Reforms proposed an amendment to the relevant paragraphs of the *Manual of Office Procedure* "in regard to the use of different colored inks in the activity of noting/ drafting/ correspondence." The Ministry of Steel, which raised the query in early 1999, finally received a reply on April 27, 2000.

In another chapter, Shourie describes the evolution of the national telecom policy from 1994, when the government began to invite private players in landline and cellular services and to end the monopoly of the Department of Telecom. With some of the smartest people working in the government (the Indian Administrative Service recruits through a very tough competitive process), the convoluted path the telecom policy walked to finally arrive at the Universal Access License is simply unbelievable. By 1994, several countries had evolved mechanisms to license the telecom spectrum to private companies. India could have easily learned from them without having to repeat or create more problems and complications. But the government seems to have decided that it must learn only by its own mistakes.

"The licenses were service-specific, they were user-specific, they were technology-specific, they were area-specific, they were vintage-specific" (p. 254). After reading the chapter, one wonders how the telecom miracle came about. But the achievements of the telecom sector are a testament to the entrepreneurship and drive of the new economy entrepreneurs who are laboring against all odds to put a cell phone in every hand.

These stories and examples illustrate the quality of governance and the government mind-set in reforming India. Unless these problems are effectively dealt with, the second generation of economic reforms would become more and more difficult, and if undertaken, they would more easily fall prey to the law of unintended consequences. The real challenge of India is to address the crisis of governance.

B. Governance Reforms

The following specific reforms would help improve governance in India.

The Legislative Branch[10]

- Fixed five-year tenure of the Parliament: after it is elected, the government must serve the full tenure. Nonconfidence motion is not allowed. The ministers and even the prime minister may change, but the government should remain in power for five years.
- Proportional representation: move away from the first-past-the-post electoral system to a proportional representation system with a party list.
- Direct election of state governors: this seems to be an effective way to improve governance at the state level. Instead of a chief minister, have a directly elected governor for the state.
- Reduce executive functions: the legislature should only legislate and have little involvement with the day-to-day running of the government.

The Executive Branch

- Political appointees to head departments and agencies: the current system of career bureaucrats to head government departments, intended to keep politics out of governance, has not worked and cannot work. Each new government would— and rightly so—want to put its own people in charge, not just to satisfy patronage but also to carry out the program it promised to the people during the election. It is time to recognize that simple fact.

The Judicial Branch

- The unbearable heaviness of the judiciary: the number of cases pending in the courts of India is just unimaginable (Table 11.9). Some people estimate that at the current rate it would take more than three hundred years to clear the backlog, assuming no new cases are filed. Even in the Supreme Court, 29,315 cases were pending as of July 2004. Without an efficient judicial system, the economy would be severely hampered.
- Establish separate full-fee courts: let those people who can afford to pay for quick justice pay what it costs to get it. Private companies can set up the full infrastructure and charge fees from the users, as for a toll road. Judges would be appointed and paid by the government, as with the regular judicial system.
- Encourage alternative systems of arbitration: this is another effective way to reduce the load on the regular judicial system. Law schools and bar associations should take the lead in creating diverse systems of redressal.

TABLE 11.9

High court cases pending for more than five years

High courts	Civil cases	Criminal cases	Total	As of
Allahabad	466,851	88,568	555,419	June 30, 2004
Andhra Pradesh	36,803	1,017	37,820	June 30, 2004
Bombay	119,690	12,296	131,986	June 30, 2004
Calcutta	115,969	29,809	145,778	June 30, 2003
Delhi	36,288	3,270	39,558	December 31, 2003
Gujarat	54,938	11,191	66,129	March 31, 2004
Gauhati	3,439	516	3,955	December 31, 2002
Himachal Pradesh	2,192	428	2,620	June 30, 2004
Jammu & Kashmir	3,630	217	3,847	June 30, 2004
Karnataka	4,813	589	5,402	September 31, 2004
Kerala	19,113	3,212	22,325	March 31, 2004
Madras	37,022	2,165	39,187	June 30, 2004
Madhya Pradesh	23,882	19,721	43,603	June 30, 2004
Orissa	49,524	4,004	53,528	June 30, 2004
Patna	11,066	1,831	12,897	March 31, 2004
Punjab & Haryana	94,899	11,367	106,266	June 30, 2004
Rajasthan	45,428	13,148	58,576	June 30, 2004
Uttaranchal	12,004	1,884	13,888	NA
TOTAL	1,137,551	205,233	1,342,784	

- Allocate more funds and the freedom to use them: one of the primary functions of the state is to protect people against violence and to enforce contracts and property rights through objective dispute-settlement mechanisms. The judiciary should receive the top priority in government's decisions for allocation of tax revenue.

7. Conclusion

We are very optimistic about the future of India, if for no other reason than demographics: more than 50 percent of the population is under the age of twenty-five and about 75 percent under the age of thirty-five. The majority of these people have a rather faint memory of and experience with India's socialist past. They are the product of one hundred television channels, even more print media, and, of course, the Internet. They have tasted the fruits of economic freedom, so there is almost certainly no turning back. This is true not only of the mind-set and expectations but also of actual policies of the government. The socialists and the Marxists can only delay the inevitable; they cannot reverse the reforms.

All this does not mean that we can do without reformers. But they need to think big and not just tinker at the edges, as in improving the focus and efficiency of the Planning Commission instead of abolishing it. It should be remembered that institutions, like individuals, have a nature that cannot be just wished away. The biggest failure of reformers in India is their failure to use the powerful public platform to articulate and argue for continuation and, in some cases, initiation of reforms. The current prime minister and the finance minister, two of the best-known faces of India's reforms, have not used the power of their office to create and lead public discourse on economic and social reforms. They must use their bully pulpit effectively.

Unlike most of the economically developed democracies, India has a very small welfare state. The family and community bonds are still very strong. And these two facts together present an extraordinary opportunity to shape a genuinely liberal society in India. Before the state takes over the welfare functions, civil society institutions must be developed—or created, if necessary—to perform those functions with greater care, affection, and effectiveness.

We conclude with a longer quote from Gurcharan Das that we have taken the liberty of synthesizing from three pages of his book, *India Unbound*.

> The new India is increasingly one of competition and decentralization. We have good reasons to expect that the lives of the majority of Indians in the twenty-first century will be freer and more prosperous than their parents' and grandparents' lives. Never before in recorded history have so many people been in a position to rise so quickly. India offers a spiritual guide to the art of living. In the past fifty years more and more spiritual movements from India have been exported to the West. This explains the persistent hold of India as a destination for young people in the West (and increasingly the East) seeking an alternative way to live their lives. This "Indian way of life" presents an appealing alternative to a developed postindustrial liberal society. . . . (pp. 355–357)

Notes

Renuka Sane benefited from discussions with Ajay Shah, S. Narayan, and Susan Thomas. Debanjana Chatterjee helped in gathering much of the data, Bhupinder Singh converted the data into a usable format, and Christopher Lingle improved the readability of the text.

1. After the 2004 general elections, Dr. Singh became the prime minister. P. Chidambaram, who had earlier played an important role in continuing the reform process, is now the finance minister. Two of the best political economists of India occupy the two most powerful positions in the government. They are obviously constrained by the left parties, partners of the ruling coalition. Nonetheless, both of them have been rather reluctant to use even the bully pulpit to make a case for further reforms openly.

2. Kamath (1994) provides an unique analysis of India's brush with central planning within the framework of Thomas Sowell's conception of "constrained" and "unconstrained" visions.

3. Milton Friedman came to India as an adviser to the government in 1955 and wrote his own critique of the proposed centralization of economic decisions. His *Memorandum to the Government of India 1955* was never published by the government. The *Memorandum*, along with an unpublished 1963 article, "Indian Economic Planning," are reprinted in Shah (2000). In the 1963 article, Friedman presciently stated that India's biggest resource is its people and that the government would have done all it can if it invested in developing that human capital.

4. There were only a handful of individuals at that time who saw the fallacies of central planning. When Prime Minister Jawaharlal Nehru began to hint at some form of collectivization of agriculture, these individuals came together to form a political party, the Swatantra (Freedom) Party, India's first free-market party. The lives of some of these individuals, including B. R. Shenoy, are narrated in Shah (2001).

5. Overall, the telecom-sector reforms have been successful, but the ten-year-long process of small-step-by-small-step reforms that finally arrived at a unified licensing system has been very expensive. We will discuss later the costs of this learning-by-doing approach of the government in designing the regulatory framework for the telecom spectrum.

6. The Marxist government of the state of West Bengal has declared IT an "essential service" that bans labor strikes.

7. The book, co-edited with Naveen Mandava, recommends the Livelihood Freedom Test: test all existing and new rules and regulations for their impact on the freedom to earn an honest living. Does any law restrict opportunities for any person to earn a living, particularly in a profession that requires little capital or skills? If so, then review, revise, or remove. Instead of massive employment-generation schemes and poverty-alleviation programs, the Livelihood Freedom Test should be the priority of the government.

8. The scores are from the Fraser Institute's Economic Freedom of the World index at www.freetheworld.com (accessed April 17, 2007).

9. Although the pre-1980 rate of growth is commonly referred to as the "Hindu rate of growth," it would be more accurate to call it the "PC rate of growth," the "Planning Commission rate of growth," or the "P. C. Mahalanobis rate of growth," P. C. Mahalanobis being the grandfather of India's central planning. Instead of castigating a religion, it is better to assign credit where it is due.

10. These reforms have been discussed and cogently argued by Jayprakash Narayan. See www.loksatta.org (accessed April 17, 2007).

References

Amin, R. K., and Parth J. Shah. 2004. *B R Shenoy: Economic Prophecies*. New Delhi: Centre for Civil Society.

Bauer, P. T. 1961. *Indian Economic Policy and Development*. Bombay: Popular Prakashan.

Bhagwati, Jagdish, and Padma Desai. 1970. *India: Planning for Industrialization*. London: Oxford University Press.

Bhagwati, Jagdish, and T. N. Srinivasan. 1975. *Foreign Trade Regimes and Economic Development: India*. New York: Columbia University Press.

Bhalla, S. S. 2002. *Imagine There's No Country: Poverty, Inequality, and Growth in the Era of Globalization.* Washington, DC: Institute for International Economics.

———. 2003. "Not as Poor, Not as Unequal as You Think: Poverty, Inequality and Growth in India, 1950–2000." Final report of a project undertaken for the Planning Commission, Government of India.

Das, Gurcharan. 2002. *India Unbound.* London: Profile Book.

Debroy, Bibek. 2004. *India: Redeeming the Economic Pledge.* New Delhi: Academic Foundation.

Delong, Bradford J. 2003. "India since Independence: An Analytic Growth Narrative." In *In Search of Prosperity: Analytic Narratives on Economic Growth,* ed. Dani Rodrik. Princeton, NJ: Princeton University Press.

Friedman, Thomas. 2005. *The World Is Flat.* New York: Farrar, Straus and Giroux.

Government of India. 2005. *Economic Survey, 2004–05.* New Delhi: Government Press.

Jalan, Bimal. 2005. *The Future of India.* New Delhi: Penguin Books.

Kamath, Shyam. 1994. "The Failure of Development Planning in India." In *The Collapse of Development Planning,* ed. Peter J. Boettke. New York: New York University Press.

Kelkar, V. 2004. "India: On the Growth Turnpike." 2004 Narayan lecture delivered at Australian National University, Canberra.

Lal, Deepak. 1983. *The Poverty of "Development Economics."* London: Institute for Economic Affairs.

———. 1999. *Unfinished Bussiness: India in the World Economy,* 1st ed. New York: Oxford University Press.

———. 2005. *Hindu Equilibrium,* rev. ed. London: Oxford University Press.

Panagariya, Arvind. 2005. "The Triumph of India's Market Reforms: The Record of the 1980s and 1990s." Policy Analysis no. 554. Washington, DC: Cato Institute.

Rodrik, Dani, and Arvind Subramanian. 2005. "From 'Hindu Growth' to Productivity Surge: The Mystery of the Indian Growth Transition." *IMF Staff Papers* (52) 2.

Schumpeter, Joseph. 1954. *The History of Economic Thought.* New York: Oxford University Press.

Shah, Ajay, and Susan Thomas. 2000. "David and Goliath: Displacing a Primary Market." *Global Financial Markets* (Spring): 14–23.

———. 2001. *The Evolution of the Securities Markets in India in the 1990s.* Technical report. Bombay: IGIDR.

Shah, Parth J., ed. 2001. *Friedman on India.* New Delhi: Centre for Civil Society.

———, ed. 2004. *Profiles in Courage: Dissent on Indian Socialism.* New Delhi: Centre for Civil Society.

Shah, Parth J., and Naveen Mandava, eds. 2005. *Law: Liberty and Livelihood: Making a Living on the Street.* New Delhi: Centre for Civil Society and Academic Foundation.

Shourie, Arun. 2004. *Governance and the Sclerosis That Has Set In.* New Delhi: ASA Publications.

Tooley, James. 2005. "Is Private Education Good for the Poor?" Working paper. E. G. West Centre, University of Newcastle, Newcastle, UK.

12   Economic Freedom and Growth: The Case of the Celtic Tiger

BENJAMIN POWELL

Ireland was one of Europe's poorest countries for more than two centuries. Ireland achieved a remarkable rate of economic growth during the 1990s. By the end of the decade, its GDP per capita stood at 25,500 (U.S.$ ppp), higher than that of both the United Kingdom at 22,300 and Germany at 23,500 (Economist Intelligence Unit 2000, 25). Almost all of the catching up occurred in slightly more than a decade (see Figure 12.1). In 1987, Ireland's GDP per capita was only 63 percent of the United Kingdom's (*Economist* 1997). From 1990 through 1995, Ireland's GDP increased at an average rate of 5.14 percent per year (International Monetary Fund 2001). From 1996 through 2000, GDP increased even more rapidly at an average rate of 9.66 percent (International Monetary Fund 2001).

Most theories of economic growth can be dismissed as an explanation for the rapid growth of the Irish economy. The thesis of this essay is that no one particular policy is responsible for the dramatic economic growth of Ireland but rather that a general tendency of many policies to increase economic freedom has caused Ireland's economy to grow rapidly.

The first section of this essay looks at general policies and economic growth in Ireland from 1950 to 1973. The second section examines Ireland's experience with Keynesian policies and a fiscal crisis in the period between 1973 and 1987. We then look at the policies to correct

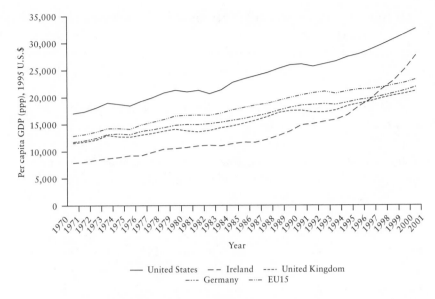

FIGURE **12.1**   Ireland's per capita GDP convergence
s o u r c e : Organisation for Economic Co-operation and Development (2002).

the fiscal crisis and to achieve the dynamic growth that occurred from
1987 through 2000. The policies in the preceding periods are explained
more broadly in the context of economic freedom and its relationship to
economic growth in the fourth section. Then other possible explanations
of Irish economic growth are briefly explored. The essay ends with conclusions that can be drawn from Ireland's experience.

1. 1950–1973: Early Prospects for Growth

The Irish Republic had a dismal record of economic growth before
1960. At the turn of the twentieth century, Ireland had a relatively high
GDP per capita, but it declined markedly vis-à-vis the rest of northwest-
ern Europe until 1960. During the 1950s, the policy stance of successive
governments was that of protectionism. Exports as a proportion of GDP
were only 32 percent, with more than 75 percent of these exports going to
the United Kingdom (Considine and O'Leary 1999, 117). The high level
of government interference in trade and the other parts of the economy
caused dismal economic performance during the 1950s. Average growth

rates during the 1950s were only 2 percent—far below the postwar European average (Economist Intelligence Unit 2000, 5). The poor economic performance of the 1950s was reflected in the massive emigration, which over the course of the 1950s subtracted one-seventh of Ireland's total population (Jacobsen 1994, 68).

During the 1960s, the policy stance of the Irish government shifted away from highly protectionist policies. That is not to say that Ireland embraced the full principles of laissez-faire. Jacobsen notes, "In the 1960s, Irish administrators squeamishly made way—minimal way—for a planning system designed to operate 'only to the degree that it is compatible with the market'" (Jacobsen 1994, 70). Mostly what they made way for was a strategy of export-led growth (Considine and O'Leary 1999, 117). Unilateral tariff cuts in 1964 and again in 1965, as well as the Anglo-Irish Trade Agreement in 1965, which swapped duty-free access of Irish manufactures to Britain for progressive annual 10 percent reductions in Irish tariffs, were particularly beneficial policies. These and other free-trade policies helped to make Ireland more attractive to foreign investors (Jacobsen 1994, 81).

The freer trade policies in Ireland during the 1960s helped it to achieve higher levels of economic growth. During the 1960s, Ireland had an average output expansion of 4.2 percent, just about double that achieved in the 1950s (Economist Intelligence Unit 2000, 5). Still, there was a great deal of state intervention in the economy during this time, and although the growth was much higher than in the 1950s, it was not nearly as remarkable as the growth Ireland has experienced since 1990. During the decade of the 1960s, the rest of Europe was also experiencing about 4 percent GDP growth. Ireland's relative opening of its economy merely allowed it to cash in on the generally good growth rates the rest of Europe was experiencing. Ireland made no progress converging to the rest of Europe's standard of living during the 1960s; in fact, it actually fell slightly, from 66 percent of the EU 12 average in 1960 to 64 percent in 1973 (Considine and O'Leary 1999, 117).

2. 1973–1986: Keynesian Policies and Fiscal Mismanagement

In the early 1970s, Ireland made further advances in trade liberalization, such as joining the European Economic Community in 1973. For the most part, however, the period from 1973 to 1986 was characterized by Keynesian macroeconomic policies that led to a fiscal crisis. After the first oil shock in 1973 and continuing through the second oil shock in 1979, Ireland tried to boost aggregate demand through increased government expenditures. This policy did not help to revive the Irish economy.

The expansionary fiscal policies had the effect of putting the government in poor fiscal condition. The government had run substantial deficits associated with the first oil shock, mostly for the purpose of financing capital accumulation until 1977, which caused a ballooning current deficit (Honohan 1999, 76). After 1977, the government engaged in an even more unsustainable fiscal expansion, causing public sector borrowing to rise from 10 to 17 percent of GNP despite increased taxation (Honohan 1999, 76). All categories of government spending were increased between 1977 and 1981. Wages and salaries increased due to national pay agreements, public bodies took on more staff to try to reduce unemployment, transfer payments increased, and an ambitious program of public infrastructure expansion caused capital spending to increase (Honohan 1999, 76). The government's interest payments also increased during this time. International interest rates were at an all-time high, and in addition, because of Ireland's accumulated debt, lenders required a high risk premium on Irish debt. This resulted in interest rates in Ireland that were 15 percent higher than those in Germany (Considine and O'Leary 1999, 118). Also during this time, Ireland did not even stay within its high budgeted amounts. In 1981, expenditures were 7 percent higher than their budgeted amounts (Honohan 1999, 77).

The government introduced tax increases to try to solve its budget problems in the early 1980s. Through these increased tax rates on labor and consumption, the Irish government was able to cut the primary deficit in half. However, with high real interest rates and slow growth, the debt-to-GDP ratio continued to climb, and by 1984 further tax increases were not seen as a viable solution to Ireland's fiscal situation (Lane 2000). The level of accumulated debt was 116 percent of GDP by 1986 (Considine and O'Leary 1999, 119). These high levels of government debt, interest payments, and expenditures put the Irish government in a poor fiscal position.

Ireland's economic growth during this period was as dismal as its fiscal condition. Ireland averaged 1.9 percent expansion of GDP per year between 1973 and 1986 (Considine and O'Leary 1999, 111). Although this was the same low level of growth from the 1950s, the difference during this period is that the rest of Europe also grew slowly, resulting in Ireland remaining at about two-thirds the level of GDP per capita of the EU 12. There was one sector of the Irish economy that did do relatively well during this period. Because of Ireland's increasing openness to trade, the foreign-owned firms continued to expand, increasing their employment by 25 percent (Considine and O'Leary 1999, 119).

3. 1987–2000: Unleashing the Tiger

A radical policy shift was needed because of Ireland's fiscal crises. The newly elected prime minister, Charles Haughey, had not followed a policy of limited government while previously in office from 1979 to 1982. In fact, his big spending policies played a part in creating the crisis (*Economist* 1988). Prior to the 1987 reforms, Haughey and the incoming Fianna Fail government had campaigned on a populist platform against cutting public spending. It was the urgency of the fiscal crisis, not an ideological shift, that caused policy to change in Ireland. As Lane (2000, 317) notes, "The fiscal adjustment program was broadly based and non-ideological. Rather, there was a wide consensus that drastic action was the only option, with the alternative being a full-scale debt crisis requiring external intervention from the IMF or EU." Haughey himself said, "The policies which we have adopted are dictated entirely by the fiscal and economic realities, I wish to state categorically that they are not being undertaken for any ideological reason or political motives" but rather that they are "dictated by the sheer necessity of economic survival" (Jacobsen 1994, 177). Even the main opposition party supported Haughey's reforms (Lane 2000).

Because Ireland was a member of the European Monetary System (EMS) and had just successfully cut back its rate of inflation from 19.6 percent in 1981 to 4.6 percent in 1986, monetizing the debt through inflation was not a viable option (Lane 2000). Tax increases had already failed to resolve the crisis in the early 1980s. With both inflation and tax increases ruled out, reducing government expenditures was Ireland's only option to resolve its fiscal crises.

In order to bring Ireland's budget under control, a variety of areas received budget cuts. Health expenditures were cut 6 percent, education was cut 7 percent, agricultural spending fell 18 percent, roads and housing were down 11 percent, and allocations to the IDA, Marketing Board, and Tourist Board were also reduced. The military budget was also cut 7 percent. Foras Forbatha, an environmental watchdog, was abolished, as were the National Social Services Board, the Health Education Bureau, and the Regional Development Organizations. Through early retirement and other incentives, public sector employment was voluntarily cut by eight thousand to ten thousand jobs (all statistics in this paragraph are from Jacobsen 1994, 177–178).

After cutting government spending in 1987, a budget was set for 1988 that had the biggest cuts in spending Ireland had seen in thirty years. "In cash terms, current spending in 1988 will be 3 percent down on 1987 and capital spending 16 percent" (*Economist* 1988). The reductions in government spending got Ireland out of its fiscal crisis. The primary deficit was eliminated in 1987, and the debt-to-GDP ratio started falling sharply from its 1986 peak. By the end of 1990, government debt was less than 100 percent of GDP (Honohan 1999, 81).

Although the reductions in government spending were made to solve the fiscal crisis and not to achieve a more economically liberal state, over the course of a few years they did have the effect of reducing the size of the government's role in the economy. Government noninterest spending declined from a high of about 55 percent of GNP in 1985 to about 41 percent of GNP by 1990 (Honohan 1999, 80).

With the reduced size of government in the economy, the stabilized macroeconomic environment, and the free-trade policies that had existed for decades, Ireland's economy began growing. GDP was growing at a rate of 4 percent by 1989 (Jacobsen 1994, 181). This level of growth was impressive compared with the 1.9 percent growth that Ireland had averaged between 1973 and 1986, when the government had been pursuing activist fiscal policies. However, the 4 percent growth is not nearly as remarkable as the "tiger" growth experienced in the late 1990s. The government made further policy changes in the period from 1990 to 1995 that helped to bring about the higher rate of growth.

After Ireland resolved its fiscal problems, there was the possibility that it could begin engaging in reckless expansionary fiscal policies again. The signing of the Maastricht Treaty in 1992 helped to make Ireland's commitment to sound fiscal policies more credible and permanent. The treaty required members to maintain fiscal deficits below 3 percent of

GDP and to set a target of a 60 percent debt-to-GDP ratio by the start of the EMU in 1999. This constrained Ireland's ability to issue debt in order to expand government spending. It is an imperfect constraint because Ireland could always pull out of the EU; however, it does lend some additional credibility that Ireland would not engage in reckless debt issue again.

Inflation is another option to finance an expansion of government spending. Ireland has been a member of the European Monetary System from the outset in March of 1979. This has fixed the exchange rate between the Irish currency and that of the other EMS members, limiting Ireland's ability to pursue an expansionary monetary policy. Although there have been several changes in the fixed rates, during most of the period since 1979 Ireland has pursued low rates of monetary growth. This has resulted in low levels of price inflation. With the exception of an early bout of high inflation through 1984, Ireland's annual rate of change in the CPI has been under 5 percent in all but two years (CSO Ireland) and had an average annual inflation rate of only 1.9 percent from 1995 to 1999 (Economist Intelligence Unit 2000, 35).

With commitments limiting the government's ability to fund increased spending through inflation or debt issue, increased taxation is the only other available method. Traditionally, it has been harder to increase government spending through taxation because it is a more obvious burden to voters. This has helped to assure investors that the government is not likely to engage in another dramatic increase in spending.

High levels of taxation were already in place in Ireland before either monetary or debt policy was constrained. Ireland had top marginal tax rates as high as 80 percent in 1975 and 65 percent in 1985. During the 1990s, both personal and corporate tax rates decreased dramatically, and tariff rates continued to decline. In 1989, the standard income tax rate was lowered from 35 percent to 32 percent, and the top marginal rate was lowered from 58 percent to 56 percent (Jacobsen 1994, 182). The standard rate was down to 24 percent and the top rate down to 46 percent by 2000. These were further reduced for 2001 to 22 percent and 44 percent, respectively (Economist Intelligence Unit 2000, 28).[1]

Although Ireland has had relatively free trade for a long time, the mean tariff rate continued to decline from 1985 to present. It has fallen from 7.5 percent in 1985 to 6.9 percent in 1999.

The standard corporate tax rate fell from 40 percent in 1996 to 24 percent by 2000 (Economist Intelligence Unit 2000, 29). There is also a special 10 percent corporate taxation rate for manufacturing companies and companies involved in internationally traded services or located in Dublin's International Financial Services Centre or in the Shannon duty-free zone (Economist Intelligence Unit 2000, 29). Ireland came under pressure from the European Commission to eliminate the special 10 percent corporate tax. In an agreement with the EC, Ireland eliminated the special 10 percent rate; however, it also lowered the standard rate. In 2003, the standard rate was lowered to 12.5 percent, and the 10 percent rate was no longer offered to new firms. Some firms that already were receiving the 10 percent rate will keep it until 2005 or 2010. Overall, this should be beneficial to Ireland's economy because it will cut the standard corporate tax rate almost in half, and it will eliminate the bias toward particular industries and areas that the special 10 percent rate created.

Because of the many decreases in tax rates and the growth of the Irish economy, Ireland now enjoys a lower tax burden than any other EU country except Luxembourg. Ireland's total tax revenue in 1999 (including social security receipts) was 31 percent of GDP, much lower than the EU average of 46 percent (Economist Intelligence Unit 2000, 28).

During the period from 1987 through 2000, Ireland closed and surpassed the living-standard differential with the rest of Europe. There was strong growth in the early part of the 1990s and remarkable "tiger" growth in the late 1990s when GDP growth averaged 9.9 percent from 1996 through 2000. The policies undertaken in this time were not the sole cause of the growth that has taken place but rather are better viewed as the final missing piece, which when finally put into place allowed the broader cause of economic growth to take hold.

4. Economic Freedom and Growth in Ireland

Government actions that hinder people's ability to engage in mutually beneficial exchanges limit the standard of living that people are able to achieve. Restrictions on international trade and domestic regulations interfere with some mutually beneficial trades. Taxes and inflation take away from citizens wealth that could have been used to make trades to increase their well-being. Legal security and the rule of law give people the confidence that when they undertake long-term projects for mutual benefit, the government or other citizens will not be able to arbitrarily seize their increased wealth. Although an imperfect measure, per capita GDP roughly reflects individuals' standard of living. As the Irish government interfered less with the economic freedom of its citizens, their per capita GDP increased.

Holcombe (1998) provides a theory of the Kirznerian entrepreneur (Kirzner 1973) as the endogenous engine of economic growth.[2] According to Holcombe's theory, when entrepreneurs take advantage of profit opportunities, they create new entrepreneurial opportunities that others can act upon. In this way, entrepreneurship creates an environment that makes more entrepreneurship possible. Because the Kirznerian entrepreneur is alert to profit opportunities (that satisfy consumer desires), the more entrepreneurship there is, the more consumer desires are satisfied, and the more growth will result. Because the Kirznerian entrepreneur is omnipresent, the institutional environment in which he or she operates must be considered to explain differences in economic growth. Holcombe wrote:

> When entrepreneurship is seen as the engine of growth, the emphasis shifts toward the creation of an environment within which opportunities for entrepreneurial activity are created, and successful entrepreneurship is rewarded. Human and physical capital remain inputs into the production process, to be sure, but by themselves they do not create economic growth. Rather, an institutional environment that encourages entrepreneurship attracts human and physical capital, which is why investment and growth are correlated. When the key role of entrepreneurship is taken into account, it is apparent that emphasis should be placed on market institutions rather than production function inputs. (1998, 58–59)

Harper (1998) examines the institutional conditions for entrepreneurship. His central thesis is that the more freedom people have, the more likely they are to hold internal locus of control beliefs, and the more acute will be their alertness to profit opportunities. This increased alertness leads to more entrepreneurial activity.

Combining Holcombe (1998) and Harper (1998), we have a theoretical argument for why increases in economic freedom provide an institutional environment that promotes more entrepreneurship and for how more entrepreneurship functions as an endogenous source of growth. This argument is consistent with empirical investigations into the relationship between economic freedom and growth.

There is a vast amount of literature linking economic freedom to growth and measures of well-being. Studies by Scully (1988 and 1992), Barro (1991), Barro and Sala-I-Martin (1995), Knack and Keefer (1995), Knack (1996), and Keefer and Knack (1997) all show that measures of well-defined property rights, public policies that do not attenuate property rights, and the rule of law tend to generate economic growth. Gwartney, Holcombe, and Lawson (1998) found a strong and persistent negative relationship between government expenditures and growth of GDP for both Organisation for Economic Co-operation and Development (OECD) countries and a larger set of sixty nations around the world. They estimate that a 10 percent increase in government expenditures as a share of GDP results in approximately a 1 percentage point reduction in GDP growth. Using the Fraser and Heritage indexes of economic freedom, Norton (1998) found that strong property rights tend to reduce deprivation of the world's poorest people, while weak property rights tend to amplify deprivation of the world's poorest people. Grubel (1998) also used the Fraser Institute's index of economic freedom to find that economic freedom is associated with superior performance in income levels, income growth, unemployment rates, and human development. All of these findings are consistent with Holcombe's entrepreneurial theory of endogenous growth and Harper's theory of institutional conditions conducive to entrepreneurship. This theoretical structure and these empirical regularities are also consistent with Ireland's economic freedom and growth.

Some aspects of economic freedom have been present in Ireland for a long time. During times when gains in economic freedom occurred, growth improved. The rapid growth of the "Celtic Tiger" occurred only after all aspects of economic freedom were largely respected at the same time.

After the protectionist decade of the 1950s, when economic growth averaged only 2 percent a year, the 1960s saw the liberalization of trade policy, which increased economic freedom, and growth improved, averaging 4.2 percent over the course of the decade. The 1970s saw further advances in the liberalization of international trade, but at the same time the government was engaging in Keynesian interventionist fiscal policies that interfered with citizens' economic freedom. Growth stagnated in Ireland as well as in the rest of Europe. During the early 1980s, high inflation, fiscal instability, a high level of government spending, and high taxation all limited economic freedom, resulting in an average growth rate of only 1.9 percent from 1973 to 1986. The contraction in the level of government spending in response to the fiscal crises increased economic freedom, and growth resumed. During the 1990s, further tax reductions and credible commitments not to engage in a reckless expansion of government spending continued to increase economic freedom. Never before had all of the components of economic freedom been present simultaneously in Ireland. When all aspects of economic freedom were respected simultaneously in Ireland, the synergy between the components allowed the dynamic growth that occurred in the late 1990s.

The preceding description of economic policies that increased and decreased economic freedom is broadly reflected in the Fraser Institute's

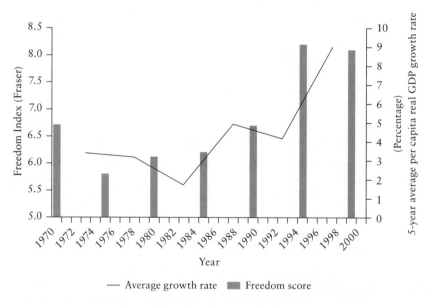

FIGURE **12.2**   Ireland's freedom index score and five-year average growth rate
SOURCES: Gwartney and Lawson (2002); Organisation for Economic Co-operation and Development (2002).
NOTE: The growth rate plotted in 1973 is the average growth rate for the years 1971–1975; the point at 1978 is for 1976–1980.

2002 Index of Economic Freedom. Ireland was the thirteenth-freest country in the world in 1970 and had an overall summary rating of 6.7. The rating had fallen to 5.8 in 1975, and by 1985 it had increased to 6.2. By 1990, when Ireland's economic growth began to pick up, Ireland's score had increased to 6.7. When Ireland was experiencing its rapid "tiger" growth, in 1995 it was the world's fifth-freest economy, and in 2000 it was the seventh-freest economy, achieving scores of 8.2 and 8.1, respectively. Ireland improved its score in all five of the freedom index's broad categories from 1985 to 2000.

Figure 12.2 plots Ireland's average growth rates over five-year time periods and Ireland's Fraser Institute overall freedom scores in five-year increments. The figure shows that Ireland's growth was strongest when its freedom scores had their most dramatic improvements.

5. Other Possible Explanations of Ireland's Growth Considered

There are a number of other possible explanations for Ireland's dramatic economic growth. One explanation is that the neoclassical growth model predicts convergence, so Ireland's economic growth should be expected. Another explanation is that transfer payments from the EU have caused economic growth in Ireland. Other explanations focus on foreign direct investment (FDI) or economies of agglomeration as the source of Ireland's growth. Finally, some have even suggested that the dramatic growth is only an illusion in the GDP account. All of these explanations are either incorrect or incomplete. Each will be considered in turn.

One alternative explanation is that there has not been a "Celtic Tiger." As recently as 1997, the *Economist* reported, "Is it too good to be true? Yes a few critics say: it was all done with smoke mirrors and money from Brussels" (May 17, 1997, 21). One fact pointed out is that GDP is much higher than GNP because of the amount of profits that foreign-owned companies send back to their owners overseas. It is argued that the high GDP numbers do not necessarily translate into wealth for the Irish citizens. In 1998, GNP was 13 percent lower than GDP (Economist Intelligence Unit 2000, 24). This is not new for Ireland, though, and the same article in the *Economist* notes that "Ireland's GNP has been growing nearly as quickly as its GDP" (May 17, 1997, 21). The dramatic economic growth in the 1990s is evident not only in the increases in both

GDP and GNP but also in other statistics. For example, by 1995 life expectancy at birth was 78.6 years for women and 73 years for men, up from 75.6 and 70.1, respectively, in 1980–1982 (Economist Intelligence Unit 2000, 17). The economic growth is also translating into more material goods for the Irish population. For example, between 1992 and 1999 the number of cars registered in Ireland increased by 40 percent (Economist Intelligence Unit 2000, 19). Perhaps the strongest indication that economic growth really exists in Ireland is immigration statistics. Ireland has typically experienced emigration; however, the trend reversed itself in the 1990s. Between 1996 and 1999 there was an average annual increase in the population of 1.1 percent—higher than the population growth rate of any other EU country during that time. In the twelve months leading up to April 1998, Ireland received 47,500 immigrants, the most immigrants Ireland had recorded up to that time (Economist Intelligence Unit 2000, 15). Regardless of any difficulties with measurement of GDP or GNP, all statistics point to a dramatic improvement in the Irish economy over the 1990s.

Both theoretical evidence and empirical evidence show that EU subsidies have not been a major cause of Ireland's economic growth. The difficulties of economic calculation and public choice problems present theoretical reasons why transfers to the Irish government cannot be a major cause of growth.

The government needs some method to calculate which projects have the most potential if a transfer to the Irish government is going to be used to create the greatest possible growth. When businessmen face this problem, they look at expected profits and then use profit-and-loss accounting to evaluate their decisions ex post to make corrections. The government does not have this method of calculation available to it (Mises 1949). The objectives of public administration are not bought and sold on the market, so they do not have money prices, and there is no method of economic calculation available to the government (Mises 1944). The receiving and spending of money by the government on a project obviously raise measured GDP by the very act of spending money. However, the government has no way to evaluate whether the project was the citizens' highest-valued use of the EU transfer or if the project was valued at all. The GDP that is created is not necessarily wealth enhancing. It may actually retard growth by directing scarce resources to government projects that could have been better used by private entrepreneurs if the government had not bid the resources away.

Agricultural subsidies are one component of EU transfers and are an example of how well-meaning transfers can get in the way of economic development. McMahon (2000, 89–90) notes that "these [subsidies] boost rural incomes but have little impact on investment and may retard economic adjustment by keeping rural populations artificially high." The subsidies change the marginal incentives for farmers, making them more likely to stay on their farms instead of migrating to the cities. In this way, the subsidies hinder the process of moving resources to their most highly valued use. As long as people are subsidized to stay in particular professions, Ireland will not fully exploit its comparative advantage in the international division of labor. This depresses incomes and slows growth.

Public choice arguments present another theoretical problem with the argument that EU transfers have caused massive growth. Why would government officials ever allocate the resources to the most growth-enhancing project even if they were able to calculate its value? Entrepreneurs direct resources to the highest-valued projects because they have a property right in the profits from the investment. Government officials have no such residual claim. They can benefit more by giving the transfers to projects that benefit their political supporters than by directing them to the most growth-enhancing projects. This would impose a dispersed opportunity cost on the rest of society while creating a concentrated benefit for their political supporters (Olson 1965). Unless the political election process perfectly disciplines elected officials and bureaucrats for not allocating EU transfers to the most growth-enhancing projects, they will not have incentives to do so. Because voters have incentives to remain rationally ignorant, there is little reason to believe they do perfectly discipline public officials.

The presence of EU funds retards growth in another way as well. Baumol (1990) argues that although the total supply of entrepreneurs varies among societies, the productive contribution of a society's entrepreneurial activities varies much more because of their allocation between productive activities, such as innovation, and unproductive activities, such as rent seeking. The presence of EU funds creates a rent for Irish entrepreneurs to seek. This will cause some entrepreneurs, who were previously engaging in productive and innovative activity, to engage in rent seeking instead. This rent seeking wastes both physical and human resources that could have been used to satisfy consumer demands and increase economic growth.

There is no theoretical case for EU structural funds being the cause of Ireland's economic growth. The government has no method to calculate what the most growth-enhancing projects are, and even if it did, it has little incentive to undertake them.

Empirically, if EU transfers were a major cause of Ireland's growth, we would expect Ireland's growth to be highest when it was receiving the greatest transfers. We would also expect other countries receiving similar EU transfers to grow rapidly. Ireland began receiving subsidies after joining the European Community in 1973. Net receipts from the EU averaged 3.03 percent of GDP during the period of rapid growth from 1995 to 2000, but during the low-growth period, from 1973 through 1986, they averaged 3.99 percent of GDP (statistics in this paragraph are from the Department of Finance, Ireland). In absolute terms, net receipts were at about the same level in 2001 as they were in 1985. In 1985, Ireland's net receipts were €1,162.3 million, and in 2001 they were €1,268.8 million. Throughout the 1990s, Ireland's payments to the EU budget steadily increased from €359.2 million in 1990 to €1,527.1 million in 2000. Yet in 2000, the receipts from the EU were €2,488.8 million, less than the 1991 level of €2,798 million. Ireland's growth rates have increased, whereas net funds from the EU have remained relatively constant and have shrunk in proportion to Ireland's economy (see Figure 12.3).

If the subsidies were really the cause of Ireland's growth, we would expect other poor countries in the EU that receive subsidies to also have a high rate of economic growth. EU Structural and Cohesion Funds represented 4 percent of Greek, 2.3 percent of Spanish, and 3.8 percent of Portuguese GDP (Paliginis 2000). None of these countries achieved anywhere near the rate of growth that the Irish economy achieved. Greece averaged 2.2 percent GDP growth, Spain averaged 2.5 percent GDP growth, and Portugal averaged 2.6 percent GDP growth from 1990 to 2000 (Clarke and Capponi 2001, 14–15).

Ireland's growth also cannot be explained by the neoclassical convergence that a Solow growth model would predict. This model predicted Irish convergence incorrectly for more than one hundred years. Even during the 1960s, when Ireland's economy had a high rate of growth,

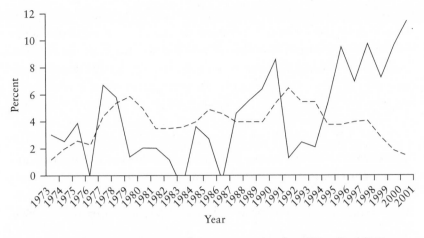

— Real per capita GDP growth   – – Net receipts from EU as % of GDP

FIGURE **12.3**   Net EU receipts and growth rates
SOURCE: Ireland Department of Finance (2002).

it still was not converging on the standard of living of other European nations. It was actually losing ground. All of Ireland's convergence occurred in a thirteen-year period from 1987 through 2000. The *Economist* is wrong when it reports that "there is more to it than the surge since 1987. Ireland has been catching up for decades." And it further states, "In many ways the dreadful years between 1980 and 1987 were more unusual than the supposedly miraculous ones since 1990" (May 17, 1997, 22). Ireland had not done any catching up before 1987. In 1960, the Irish Republic had a GDP per capita that was 66 percent of the EU 12 average, and in 1986 it had actually decreased to 65 percent of the average (Considine and O'Leary 1999). There had been some growth during that time, but it was less than the EU 12 experienced. The model needs to explain why Ireland converged only after 1987 and why it converged so rapidly.

Knack (1996) found empirical evidence of strong convergence in per capita incomes among nations with institutions (namely, secure private property rights) conducive to saving, investing, and producing. This form of conditional convergence, with free-market institutions introduced, is much more plausible in Ireland's case than just general neoclassical convergence. Ireland did experience increases in economic freedom just prior to and during its remarkable growth. The extent to which it was conditional convergence that drove growth, as opposed to just adoption of the appropriate institutions, is not clear. The fact that the Irish economy has not slowed since achieving convergence casts doubt on the importance of even conditional convergence and instead points to the adoption of appropriate institutions as the source of growth. After Ireland had converged with the EU and the United Kingdom's standard of living, it achieved record growth of 11.5 percent during 2000 (Economist Intelligence Unit 2001, 11). Although convergence conditional on an institutional environment of secure private property rights is more consistent with Ireland's experience than is general neoclassical convergence, both fail to explain Ireland's rapid growth in the last few years of the 1990s and in 2000.

Foreign direct investment and economies of agglomeration are two explanations of Ireland's growth that do have some merit but that are incomplete by themselves. FDI has certainly played a role in Ireland's growth. The United States alone had $10 billion ($3,000 per capita) invested in Ireland by 1994, and by 1997 foreign-owned firms were said to account for 30 percent of the economy and nearly 40 percent of exports (*Economist* 1997). Economies of agglomeration, in which like firms try to locate near each other to take advantage of positive externalities, have also helped. Ireland has had particular success in attracting industrial developments with large numbers of high-tech and manufacturing companies that benefit from being near each other. The relevant question is: Why didn't massive FDI, which has spurred economies of agglomeration, occur sooner? What changed in Ireland were the institutional conditions that attracted FDI. FDI and economies of agglomeration are an indication of institutional factors favorable to economic growth, not the cause of the growth.

Some of the preceding explanations for Irish growth are simply wrong. The last two, FDI and economies of agglomeration, both have some positive feedback loops for economic growth but fail to explain why they occur in the first place. The interesting question to ask is: What gives rise to favorable conditions that allow growth to occur? This essay has maintained that it is the institutional framework that hinders or helps the market achieve economic growth. The key institutional factor is the degree of economic freedom enjoyed by the people.

6. Conclusion

In 1997, an article in the *Economist* said, "How much longer the Irish formula will deliver such striking success is difficult to say." It continued to say that beyond the short term, simple forces are likely to prevail. "Ireland grew quickly for more than thirty years because it had a lot of catching up to do, and because policy and circumstances conspired to let it happen. Success of that kind, impressive and unusual though it may be, contains the seeds of its own demise." The article concluded by saying, "If Ireland has another decade as successful as the last one, it will be a miracle economy indeed" (May 17, 1997, 24).

The fact is that Ireland had not been catching up for thirty years. It did all of its catching up in thirteen years. Rapid "tiger" rates of growth continued to be recorded through 2000, even though Ireland had already converged with Europe's standard of living. The neoclassical convergence growth model is not what drove Ireland's dramatic economic growth. Ireland's rapid growth has been driven by its increases in economic freedom. Ireland continued to lower taxes and to promote economic freedom after the *Economist* published its article in 1997, and it continued to grow rapidly. Increases in economic freedom are what have continued to drive increased rates of economic growth, not the slower rates of growth that the neoclassical model would have predicted.

Since 2000, Ireland, although remaining very high in the economic freedom rankings, has not continued to improve its institutional environment. According to the 2005 *Economic Freedom of the World Annual Report*, Ireland achieved its highest economic freedom score of 8.2 in 1995 while ranking as the fifth-freest economy in the world. That was largely maintained through 2000, when Ireland scored 8.1. Since 2000, Ireland has not continued to improve its institutional environment. By 2003, Ireland experienced some minor backsliding, ranking as the eighth-freest economy in the world with a score of 7.9. The index subcomponents indicate that government consumption and transfers as well as regulation in labor markets had increased.

Ireland's rapid growth ended precisely as improvements in its institutional environment stalled. Per capita GDP growth fell from the nearly 10 percent rate averaged in the late 1990s to 4.8 percent in 2001, 5.1 percent in 2002, and 2 percent in 2003 (World Bank 2005). Similarly, unemployment was up from its low of 3.6 percent in 2001 to 4.4 percent in 2004 (Central Statistics Office, Ireland 2005). Some of the slowdown is surely attributable to the recession in the U.S. economy, but as the United States has recovered, Ireland has not regained its former rapid rates of economic growth, nor is it forecast to do so in the near future. The rapid rates of economic growth in Ireland were caused by equally dramatic improvements in Ireland's institutional environment. If Ireland continues to maintain its current level of economic freedom, it will likely continue to grow steadily but will not achieve the dramatic growth that it experienced in the 1990s reform period. For another period of rapid growth, Ireland will have to embark on another series of reforms that promote economic freedom. Unfortunately, this seems unlikely because the prior period of reform was brought on by a fiscal crisis that was not accompanied by any major ideological change. Now that Ireland is out of crisis mode, and reforms have stalled, it will take another shock, from either outside forces, ideological change among the populace, or a charismatic pro-economic-freedom reform leader, to get Ireland on a rapid development path again.

Notes

This chapter is reprinted from the *Cato Journal* 22 (3) (Winter 2003). The conclusion has been rewritten from the original version to take account of developments in Ireland since 2001, when the original article was written. I would like to thank Peter Boettke, Christopher Coyne, Todd Zywicki, the participants at the Association of Private Enterprise Education conference in Cancun in 2002, the participants at the Mercatus Center "brown bag" series, and an anonymous referee for helpful suggestions in earlier drafts. I would also like to thank the Mercatus Center and the American Institute for Economic Research for financial support in writing the original journal article. Any remaining errors are my responsibility.

1. The social partnership agreement between government, employer federations, and labor unions has played a role in the continued tax reductions and low inflation. The agreements began in 1987 and have been continually renewed with minor revisions since. These agreements have effectively turned unions into a force lobbying for reductions in taxes and inflation. Lane (2000) notes that the unions promised wage moderation, partly compensated by a reduction in labor taxes and with the implicit promise that the government would maintain price stability. McMahon (2000) argues that holding down wage rates by these

agreements was important for making Ireland more competitive in attracting companies, which resulted in growth. It is important to remember, though, that the wage constraint on the part of the unions was not so much a sacrifice by workers to attract business as it was the unions forcing a reduction in taxes to compensate the workers, so their real after-tax wage could still increase while attracting more businesses and creating more jobs.

2. For a survey of the endogenous growth literature that Holcombe is incorporating his theory into and contrasting his theory with, see Paul Romer (1994), "The Origins of Endogenous Growth," *Journal of Economic Perspectives.*

References

Barro, R. 1991. "Economic Growth in a Cross-Section of Countries." *Quarterly Journal of Economics* 106:407–443.

Barro, R., and X. Sala-i-Martin. 1995. *Economic Growth.* New York: McGraw-Hill.

Barry, F. 1999. "Irish Growth in Historical and Theoretical Perspective." In *Understanding Ireland's Economic Growth,* ed. F. Barry. New York: St. Martin's Press.

Baumol, W. 1990. "Entrepreneurship: Productive, Unproductive, and Destructive." *Journal of Political Economy* 98 (5): 893–921.

Central Statistics Office, Ireland. 2001. *Principle Statistics, Prices and Sales.* www.cso.ie/ (accessed May 30, 2007).

———. 2005. *Measuring Ireland's Progress, 2004.* www.cso.ie/releasespublica tions/documents/other_releases/2004/progress/measuringirelandsprogress .pdf (accessed April 18, 2007).

Clarke, R., and E. Capponi. 2001. *OECD in Figures.* Paris: OECD Publications.

Considine, J., and E. O'Leary. 1999. "The Growth Performance of Northern Ireland and the Republic of Ireland 1960 to 1995." In *Political Issues in Ireland Today,* ed. N. Collins. New York: Manchester University Press.

Department of Finance, Ireland. 2002. *Budgetary and Economic Statistics March 2002.* www.finance.gov.ie (accessed May 30, 2007).

Economist. 1988. "Survey Republic of Ireland." (January 16).

———. 1997. "Europe's Tiger Economy." (May 17).

———. 2000. "Hot and Sticky in Ireland." (June 29).

Economist Intelligence Unit. 2000. *Country Profile 2000 Ireland.* London: Economist Intelligence Unit.

———. 2001. *Country Report Ireland.* London: Economist Intelligence Unit.

Grubel, H. 1998. "Economic Freedom and Human Welfare: Some Empirical Findings." *Cato Journal* 18 (2): 287–304.

Gwartney, J., R. Holcombe, and R. Lawson. 1998. "The Scope of Government and the Wealth of Nations." *Cato Journal* 18 (2): 163–190.

Gwartney, J., and R. Lawson. 2002. *Economic Freedom of the World: 2002 Annual Report.* Vancouver, Canada: Fraser Institute.

———. 2005. *Economic Freedom of the World: 2005 Annual Report.* Vancouver, Canada: Fraser Institute.

Harper, D. 1998. "Institutional Conditions for Entrepreneurship." *Advances in Austrian Economics* 5:241–275.

Holcombe, R. 1998. "Entrepreneurship and Economic Growth." *Quarterly Journal of Austrian Economics* 1 (2): 45–62

Honohan, P. 1999. "Fiscal Adjustment and Disinflation in Ireland: Setting the Macro Basis of Economic Recovery and Expansion." In *Understanding Ireland's Economic Growth*, ed. F. Barry. New York: St. Martin's Press.

International Monetary Fund. 2001. *International Financial Statistics Year Book.* Washington, DC: International Monetary Fund.

Jacobsen, J. 1994. *Chasing Progress in the Irish Republic.* New York: Cambridge University Press.

Keefer, P., and S. Knack. 1997. "Why Don't Poor Countries Catch-Up? A Cross-National Test of Institutional Explanations." *Economic Inquiry* 35:590–602.

Kirzner, I. 1973. *Competition and Entrepreneurship.* Chicago: University of Chicago Press.

Knack, S. 1996. "Institutions and the Convergence Hypothesis: The Cross-National Evidence." *Public Choice* 87:207–228.

Knack, S., and P. Keffer. 1995. "Institutions and Economic Performance: Cross-Country Tests Using Alternative Institutional Measures." *Economics and Politics* 7:207–227.

Lane, P. 2000. "Disinflation, Switching Nominal Anchors and Twin Crises: The Irish Experience." *Journal of Policy Reform* 3:301–326.

McMahon, F. 2000. *Road to Growth: How Lagging Economies Become Prosperous.* Halifax, Canada: Atlantic Institute for Market Studies.

Mises, L. 1944/1996. *Bureaucracy.* Grove City, PA: Libertarian Press.

———. 1949/1998. *Human Action.* Auburn, AL: Ludwig Von Mises Institute.

Norton, S. 1998. "Poverty, Property Rights, and Human Well-Being: A Cross-National Study." *Cato Journal* 18 (2): 233–245.

Olson, M. 1965/1971. *The Logic of Collective Action.* Cambridge, MA: Harvard University Press.

Organisation for Economic Co-operation and Development. 2002. *Annual National Accounts—Comparative Tables.* http://www.oecd.org/document/

39/0,2340,en_2649_34245_1914151_1_1_1_1,00.html (accessed May 30, 2007).

Paliginis, E. 2000. "Institutions and Development in the EU Periphery." *Zagreb International Review of Economics & Business* 3 (2): 81–92.

Romer, P. 1994. "The Origins of Endogenous Growth." *Journal of Economic Perspectives* 8 (1): 3–22.

Scully, G. 1988. "The Institutional Framework and Economic Development." *Journal of Political Economy* 96:652–662.

———. 1992. *Constitutional Environments and Economic Growth*. Princeton, NJ: Princeton University Press.

World Bank. 2005. *World Development Indicators Online*. http://web .worldbank.org/WBSITE/EXTERNAL/DATASTATISTICS/0,,content MDK:20523710~hlPK:1365919~menuPK:64133159~pagePK:64133150~ piPK:64133175~theSitePK:239419,00.html (accessed April 18, 2007).

13 Why Have Kiwis Not Become Tigers? Reforms, Entrepreneurship, and Economic Performance in New Zealand

FREDERIC SAUTET

The New Zealand economy is now famous in policy circles for its turnaround during the 1980s and 1990s. Starting from a state of semiautarky in the early 1980s, New Zealand now has one of the most vibrant economies in the world. In fifteen years, successive governments reformed the country's institutional environment by injecting high doses of deregulation and opening the economy.

After these changes, the New Zealand economy climbed the ladder of the Index of Economic Freedom of the World: New Zealand's score increased from 5.9 in 1985 to 8.2 in 2002 (Gwartney and Lawson 2004). Yet its average growth rate in the past decade does not compare with that of the Asian tigers, Singapore and Hong Kong, or that of Ireland, Estonia, and Luxembourg, countries that share some of the best ranks in the index.

In addition to the modest growth in the past decade, the relatively poor growth prospects for the years ahead have fueled the debate about the success of the New Zealand reforms. Some economists think that New Zealand's less-than-stellar economic performance results from the failure to complete the reform process. Others believe that New Zealand's current situation is the result of too much reform: New Zealand has been a "laboratory" for free-market policies, and it went too far. Some maintain that it is now time to go back to more middle-of-the-road policies, taking into account not only economic efficiency but also income distribution, the environment, and many other issues left out by the reform process. In this view, better "management" of the economy should help to improve growth prospects. The Labour government espoused this opinion when it was elected in 1999 (Kay 2000). Still others think that owing to New Zealand's cultural heritage, its inhabitants are relatively uninterested in high levels of economic growth.[1] New Zealanders, it is said, do not need much money to be happy because they hold dear some egalitarian ideas that go back to the nineteenth century, reflected today in the romantic search for a peaceful and green New Zealand and perhaps also in the revival of Maori *tikanga*.[2] It is now becoming clearer that in spite of the modest achievements and low productivity growth, the reforms have been hugely beneficial to the economy.[3] In opposition to its earlier views, the Labour government now recognizes the importance of the reforms, as a 2005 Budget Policy Statement shows: "NZ's recent growth performance can be attributed to past structural reforms that began in the mid-1980s, which have resulted in a trend increase in NZ's growth rate since the early 1990s . . . a more flexible economy better able to absorb adverse shocks and take advantage of favourable shocks, and sound macroeconomic policy settings" (as quoted in Kerr 2005c, 1). This support is not wholehearted; the phrase "failed policies of the past" has been used at times to characterize what was done during the reforms of the 1980s and 1990s. However, a consensus is now emerging in regard to what has made the economy more vibrant and prosperous. The reforms have had a very positive impact on the entrepreneurial environment; unemployment is low; and growth is reasonably rapid. Most commentators today recognize this situation.

In the long run, what matters is the quality of the entrepreneurial environment. When the institutional and cultural environment enables individuals to discover and seize profit opportunities, growth occurs (Boettke and Coyne 2003; Sautet 2005). Taking this factor into account, I argue here that

- The reforms have vastly improved the entrepreneurial environment, and, as a result, given the starting point, they have greatly enhanced New Zealand's economic performance.
- To go beyond current levels of economic performance, New Zealanders need to improve the entrepreneurial environment further. New Zealand failed to become a growth miracle

because the reforms that were implemented, although good, were not exceptional.

I first describe briefly the context in which New Zealand's reforms took place and then consider the five main reforms that changed the New Zealand economy positively. In the third section, I examine the reasons why the New Zealand economy is failing to perform like that of an Asian tiger. Before concluding, I offer some policy implications.

1. Background of New Zealand's Reforms

Much has been said about New Zealand's reforms of the 1984–1996 period. In the words of David Henderson of the Organisation for Economic Co-operation and Development (OECD), the reform period in New Zealand was "one of the most notable episodes of liberalization that history has to offer" (as quoted in Evans et al. 1996, 1856). Let us consider the context in which these reforms took place (for more on the context, see especially Evans et al. 1996).

A. A Long Time Ago in a Country Far Away

To understand the context of the 1980s, one must go back one hundred years. At the end of the nineteenth century, New Zealand was, along with Germany, one of the first countries in the world to implement comprehensive social legislation. Even before the ravages of World War I created a demand for social assistance in Western countries, New Zealand stood at the forefront of social policies. For example, women obtained the right to vote in 1893. Labor-market reforms were introduced in 1894 in the form of a compulsory arbitration system, and a pension scheme was set in place for the "deserving poor" in 1898. The expectation slowly developed that the state should provide "cradle to grave" protection against life's hazards.[4] From the late nineteenth century to 1920s, the country was one of the five richest countries in the world as measured by gross domestic product (GDP) per capita. This wealth came from exports of farm produce to England (thanks to the advent of refrigeration) and from a high productivity in agriculture, which reflected a small population and an abundance of fertile land.

In New Zealand during the 1930s, as in many other countries, a rise of protectionist policies (for example, import licensing in 1938), along with a surge in the welfare state, had a negative impact on economic performance. During World War II, many controls were introduced, and the economic decline so prominent in the 1930s continued. In the post–World War II period, New Zealand's international ranking deteriorated further because the wartime controls were kept in place.

As Evans and his co-authors explain, New Zealand's gross national product (GNP) per capita in 1938 was 92 percent of that in the United States. By 1950, the ratio was 70 percent, and by the 1980s it was 50 percent (1996, 1860). In other words, over a period of almost fifty years, New Zealanders experienced constant relative decline in their standard of living. Whereas Australia's relative income per capita leveled off in the 1970s, and the United Kingdom bounced back in the 1980s, New Zealand continued to sink—to around the twentieth rank by the time the reforms started in 1984.

By the 1970s, New Zealand had the most regulated economy in the OECD. Until 1973, when the United Kingdom joined the European Community, it represented the main export market for New Zealand products. Afterward, however, that export market disappeared, and the consequences of the policies of the postwar period surfaced. In the 1970s, New Zealand emerged as a semiautarkic economy, the so-called Fortress New Zealand. By the end of that decade, more and more young people were leaving the country to gain work experience abroad. For the first time, a generation of New Zealanders found overseas experience not only necessary but also preferable to the opportunities offered at home.

Besides imposing high tariffs and employing import licenses to control the balance of payments, the New Zealand government adopted many other harmful policies. Revenues from high taxes were used to provide subsidies to many major industries. Agriculture, for example, enjoyed large subsidies and had many producer boards protected by law. The government used the public-employment model of welfare to maintain high wages and employment among the masses by employing people in government-owned enterprises, thus keeping the unemployment rate artificially low. As in many Western countries at the time, inflation was rampant (between early 1970 and late 1984, it averaged almost 12 percent per year), and wage and price controls were (unsuccessfully) employed to limit its effects. The labor market was highly regulated. The exchange rate was fixed and set at levels that eventually were no longer credible, given the loose monetary policy and the weak terms of trade.

As a result of such policies, government spending rose from approximately 22 percent of GDP in 1970 to more than 35 percent by 1983, and government debt rose from approximately 5 percent to more than 30 percent of GDP; it continued to grow to 51 percent by 1992. Although these trends were not exceptional—indeed, they were common to most countries in the Western world—their effects, combined with extensive market regulations in a semiautarkic economy, stifled growth and led to the relative impoverishment of New Zealand's people. Unemployment, negligible in the 1960s, was pushing higher than 4 percent of the labor force by the late 1970s.

B. "There's Got to Be a Better Way!"

The first attempts to reform the economy were made in the early 1980s. Roger Douglas, an opposition politician who would later become the architect of the first wave of reforms, proposed important economic changes in 1980.[5] The Treasury had been giving advice for a few years on regulatory and tax reforms without much success before Prime Minister Robert Muldoon implemented the first serious change, signing the Closer Economic Relations Treaty with Australia. Moves toward freer trade were in the air, but not until 1984, with the change of government, did deeper and more comprehensive reforms become part of the agenda.

In 1984, New Zealand faced a severe crisis. As the elections neared, market participants lost their trust in the Reserve Bank's capacity to maintain the fixed exchange rate. As a result, money poured out of the system, and a currency crisis followed. The Reserve Bank lost almost all its foreign reserves and had to close its currency-trading window before markets reopened on the Monday after the elections. This event caused a governmental crisis, with the outgoing prime minister refusing to implement the instructions of the newly elected Labour government during the interregnum.

Once in place, the new Labour government, led by Prime Minister David Lange and Finance Minister Roger Douglas, devalued the dollar and started implementing changes in the institutional landscape. Many reforms took place in the 1980s under Douglas's leadership and later in the early 1990s when Ruth Richardson became finance minister with the election of the National government in 1990. These far-ranging reforms dealt with taxation, government spending and other fiscal issues, financial markets, market regulations (especially industrial policy and labor markets), public-sector structure, and social assistance, among other things. Although not all sectors enjoyed successful reforms (the health sector was extensively but unsuccessfully reformed during the 1990s, for example), some of the reforms became models for the rest of the world.

2. Five Reforms That Changed the Economy

It is often said that there is no silver bullet for reforming an economy; economic reforms must be undertaken as a package, and rarely is a single policy responsible for an economy's success. These observations certainly apply to New Zealand, where an ensemble of policies brought about the economy's resurrection. Among these policy changes, however, five areas of policy may have done 80 percent of the job: tax reforms, labor-market reforms, trade reforms, monetary-policy reforms (including the establishment of Reserve Bank independence), and fiscal reforms.[6] In this section, I briefly examine the impact of these reforms on the economic (especially entrepreneurial) environment. They ushered in a better tax system, a fluid labor market, more extended markets, a stable money supply, budget surpluses, and a reduced public debt.

A. The Tax System

In its *Statement of Government Expenditure Reform* in August 1985, the government announced the reduction of the top marginal income tax rate and the implementation of a new value-added tax (goods and services tax [GST]) to replace a multitude of indirect taxes. The idea behind the changes was to broaden the tax base—that is, to tax hitherto-untaxed income and to reduce marginal tax rates. The reduction in the marginal tax rate would improve efficiency by reducing the deadweight loss of taxation, and the broadening of the base would reduce the incentives to pursue certain activities simply to avoid taxation. The top marginal income tax rate was halved, dropping from 66 percent to 33 percent between 1985 and February 1988. The GST covered almost all sales transactions, excluding exports, at a flat rate originally set at 10 percent but later increased to 12.5 percent in 1989. Corporate and personal income taxes were integrated by the introduction of an imputation system, which removed the double taxation of income by giving shareholders a tax credit for any tax paid at the corporate level. The system was extended in 2003 to New Zealand shareholders owning shares in Australian companies via a trans-Tasman imputation system.

The tax reforms in New Zealand were characterized by an emphasis on compliance costs—a direct influence of the transaction-costs approach that prevailed in the New Zealand Treasury in the 1980s. The tax system was designed to be a coherent structure that would minimize the deadweight losses and reduce the compliance costs. One of the most conspicuous results of the focus on compliance costs was that most taxpayers no longer filed a tax return. The tax changes improved the business environment. Investment choices became less influenced by tax considerations, and the tax system did not lend itself to lobbying as much as it had in the past.

In 2000, the first Labour government increased the top marginal income tax rate from 33 percent to 39 percent for incomes above NZ$60,000. Doing so disrupted the alignment between the company, trust, and top marginal income tax rates and made taxation a more important variable in people's choices: whereas previously the top personal income tax rate of 33 percent had been aligned with the corporate tax rate and applied also to income from trust, the income tax change broke the alignment and reintroduced the potential for tax arbitrages. Even though a top marginal tax rate of 39 percent is still not very high by international standards, increasing the marginal rate did not improve the tax system, especially in an era of fiscal surplus. According to Davidson, the threshold of the top income tax bracket as a proportion of GDP per capita is 1.21 for New Zealand. It is only 0.50 for Hong Kong, but that jurisdiction has a marginal tax rate of just 17 percent. In Singapore, the threshold income to GDP per capita is 9.53, and the marginal tax rate is 22 percent (all foregoing figures from Davidson 2005).

The tax system creates some problems, especially with regard to the capital-labor boundary and the interface between the welfare system and the income tax schedule. For example, tax credits and the other welfare benefits tied to income that a recipient may receive are abated as income rises. This abatement creates very high effective marginal tax rates, which increase the opportunity cost of improving one's own income situation. In other words, welfare benefits and low-income tax credits inevitably contribute to the creation of poverty traps. Also, the amount of posttax profits that entrepreneurs can capture affects entrepreneurial activity. The higher the posttax profits, the more likely that hitherto-unknown possibilities to trade will be discovered. The tax system therefore affects entrepreneurial discovery because it influences the pure monetary profit that emerges through exchange (Kirzner 1985a).

B. Labor-Market Liberalization

Labor markets have long been regulated in New Zealand. Early landmarks include the adoption of compulsory arbitration in 1894 and compulsory union membership in 1936 (see Baird 1996; Evans et al. 1996; Kerr 1999, 2005a; Carroll et al. 2002; Mills and Timmins 2004). The Employment Contract Act of 1991 was, in Charles Baird's words, "a bold, giant step toward the worthy goal of restoring freedom of contract to New Zealand labor markets" (1996, 1). The act replaced centralized bargaining with decentralized enterprise (or individual) bargaining. It gave employees and employers a choice of individual employment contracts or collective ones, and under it, no special agent needed to represent the parties to the labor contract. In most cases, individuals chose to represent themselves.

The Employment Contract Act, alongside other reforms, had an enormous impact. The unemployment rate fell from 11 percent to less than 4 percent between 1991 and 2004. During this period, the nature of contracts changed dramatically: multiemployer contracts virtually disappeared, and direct contracts between employer and employee became the norm. The labor market became much more fluid.

Labor laws constitute one of the major elements determining the quality of the entrepreneurial environment. To some extent, a business firm is a locus of planning, where entrepreneurs hire the services of factors in order to exploit discovered opportunities.[7] Labor is the primary factor in almost all business organizations. Therefore, the nature of labor laws clearly influences the way entrepreneurs can contract with the owners of resources that are crucial to the capture of profit opportunities. When profit opportunities are discovered, entrepreneurs need to bid away resources already at work in the economy. The process of "efficient allocation" of resources at the heart of neoclassical economic analysis begins with and can exist only within the entrepreneurial discovery process. This process requires the ability to contract as freely as possible for the use of the resources needed to capture the gains that entrepreneurs discover. When labor laws restrict contractual possibilities, they adversely affect entrepreneurial activity by shrinking the population pool entrepreneurs can use.

C. Trade Liberalization

In the 1970s and the first part of the 1980s, New Zealand had one of the least open economies among the OECD countries. As Evans and his colleagues put it, "For most categories of goods there was little variety" (1996, 1883). Many import restrictions set in place during World War II lasted until the mid-1980s. Many goods produced or assembled in New Zealand in the 1970s would have been produced elsewhere had free trade been possible. Entrepreneurs were limited in their capacity to differentiate their goods; trade restrictions stifled the exploitation of comparative advantage.

In some ways, the reforms to improve trade conditions started in 1984, when the first Labour government devalued the New Zealand dollar. Capital flows were also partially liberalized during the same year, which increased foreign ownership of New Zealand assets. In 1990, complete free trade of goods with Australia was implemented, and tariffs on goods from all other countries were gradually reduced. In September 1998, the government announced plans to remove most tariffs by July 2001 and all tariffs by 2006 — that is, to adopt unilaterally complete free trade with all countries.

Trade liberalization reforms dramatically increased the range of goods and services available in New Zealand, and the impact on consumer welfare was enormous. For example, between 1983 and 1993 the ratio of imports plus exports to GDP rose by 42 percent, dramatically increasing the diversity of goods available to New Zealanders (Evans et al. 1996, 1883). Trade liberalization also increased entrepreneurial activity by extending the market available to entrepreneurs, creating an effect similar to an increase in population size.

D. Monetary Policy and the Reserve Bank

The Reserve Bank Act of 1989 was another stepping-stone in the reform process. It replaced the 1964 Reserve Bank Act, which had given politicians the freedom to use monetary policy to deal with whatever problems the government thought it had. Monetary policy was one of the most inconsistently used instruments of macroeconomic policy, with multiple targets and lack of accountability (Evans et al. 1996). The Labour government in 1984 took a different approach: monetary policy would no longer be a short-term instrument in the government's hands; it had to become a long-term instrument aimed at creating a stable environment by containing inflation. Not only was inflation high in the early 1980s, but also inflation expectations were not in line with inflation outcomes: expectations were higher than actual inflation because the Reserve Bank's credibility was low. Monetary policy under previous governments had not achieved the desired results. Reducing inflation and making monetary policy more credible were the main reasons for the enactment of a new Reserve Bank Act. Moreover, inflation was not to be used any longer to finance the fiscal deficit. Deficits would be financed by the issuance of debt, then eventually reduced and turned into surpluses.

The key elements of the Reserve Bank Act of 1989 were a clear, single target; transparent objective setting; and operational independence and accountability of the Reserve Bank. The inflation target in the first policy target agreement, reached in 1990, was 0–2 percent inflation (measured in terms of the annual change in the consumer's price index). Subsequent policy target agreements were signed in 1992, 1996, 1997, 1999, and 2002. In 1996, the twelve-month increase in the consumer's price index consistent with price stability was enlarged from 0–2 percent to 0–3 percent. When Governor Alan Bollard took office at the Reserve Bank in 2002, the new target agreement raised the bottom of the inflation target to 1 percent while retaining the 3 percent upper limit.

Although in 1989 the Reserve Bank's function was identified exclusively as the maintenance of price stability, the bank's objectives have changed slightly over the years. The intent of the 1989 Reserve Bank Act remains, but broader economic goals are now also part of the mission. As Bollard has recently declared,

> Price stability is the Reserve Bank's "primary function," but we also seek to avoid "unnecessary instability in output, interest rates and the exchange rate." The shift to an inflation target "on average over the medium term" allows us to better achieve this. This helps economic growth, which, we all agree, New Zealand needs, by enhancing predict-ability and confidence and, by that, savings and productive investment. The raising of the bottom of the band brings the overall target more in line with New Zealand's inflation outcomes in recent years and those in other countries. (Reserve Bank of New Zealand 2002)

Since June 1991, inflation as measured by the consumer's price index has averaged 2.1 percent, which is within the target band (Reserve Bank of New Zealand 2005)—a substantial achievement, considering the history of monetary policy in New Zealand and its outcomes before the 1989 act. However, the recent changes to the policy target agreement have given monetary policy broader goals (for example, avoiding unnec-essary instability in output), which will not be achieved through mon-etary policy and which will contribute to the deterioration of the quality of the entrepreneurial environment.[8]

A stable monetary environment is important to entrepreneurship. Monetary prices convey information about market demands and supplies that is crucial to the discovery of profit opportunities. Monetary calcu-lation can be carried out best if money plays its role well by providing a medium of exchange with reasonably stable purchasing power.[9] The presence of price inflation (induced by bad monetary policy) reduces the effectiveness of money to convey accurate information and thereby wors-ens the entrepreneurial environment.

E. Fiscal Policy and Balanced Budgets

Public debt in New Zealand rose from less than 10 percent of GDP in the 1970s to more than 50 percent in 1993. As the Labour government took office in 1984, the fiscal position was becoming more difficult to sustain. In spite of immediate measures, ongoing deficits and large bor-rowing costs continued to climb into the early 1990s. Part of this debt spiral was the cost of the reforms, but it was also the result of years of bad

Keynesian policies. As a consequence of the debt situation, Standard and Poor's and Moody's Investor Services downgraded New Zealand's credit rating for sovereign currency debt: the country lost its "triple A" rating in 1983 and did not recover it until nineteen years later, in 2002.

In 1984, a program of fiscal stabilization was started. In 1989, Parliament adopted the Public Finance Act, and in 1994, Finance Minister Ruth Richardson introduced the Fiscal Responsibility Act. The Public Finance Act replaced an input-focused system for controlling government base spending with an output-focused one. Although this change was controversial at the time, government departments have adapted well to it since then. By further rationalizing government spending decisions, the Public Finance Act helped departments be more responsible with taxpayers' money. For example, whereas under the old system all spending increases were indexed, departments now must prove that nominal spending should be increased because cost increases outweigh productivity gains (nevertheless, many programs remain indexed). At least until the mid-1990s, this act had a positive impact on controlling government spending by constraining increases in nonindexed government spending and thus helped to reduce budget deficits and public debt.

Whereas the Public Finance Act focuses on how departments spend money, the Fiscal Responsibility Act provides rules for the conduct of fiscal policy. Its goal is to improve that policy by establishing five principles of fiscal management and by strengthening reporting requirements. The five principles laid down are:[10]

1. increase the transparency of policy intentions and the economic and fiscal consequences of policy;
2. bring a long-term (as well as an annual) focus to budgeting;
3. disclose the aggregate impact of a budget in advance of the detailed annual budget allocations;
4. ensure independent assessment and reporting of fiscal policy; and
5. facilitate parliamentary and public scrutiny of economic and fiscal information and plans.

The Fiscal Responsibility Act contributed to the fiscal stabilization of the 1990s. The increased transparency of the government's short-term and long-term fiscal intentions and the high standards of financial disclosure improved government incentives. However, the change in the electoral system in 1993 and the election of the first coalition government in 1996 led to higher spending per capita.

The New Zealand government ran its first operating surplus (more than $900 million) in the 1993–1994 fiscal year. It was the first budget surplus in seventeen years and was dedicated to debt repayment. Since then, the government has run only budget surpluses. Moreover, net public debt in 2004 was down to approximately 10 percent of GDP and was forecast to decline further in the years to come (New Zealand Treasury 2005c).

Although fiscal discipline is now a reality in New Zealand, it is difficult to establish the extent to which the improvement is the result of the Fiscal Responsibility Act because the fiscal position also improved with the betterment of the economy.[11] Although the fiscal situation would have been worse without it, the act has little power over the growth and quality of government spending. In Bryce Wilkinson's words, the "biggest concern . . . is [the act's] failure to do more to impose value-for-money disciplines on new and existing government spending" (2004, 13).

3. The Missing Link Between Kiwis and Tigers

The Irish economy grew by 8 percent annually between 1995 and 2000 (Lynch 2005). This sterling performance surprised many commentators, including some policymakers who participated in the Irish reform process. According to economist Colin Lynch, no magic recipe explains Ireland's economic success. Rather, it springs from a series of reforms that, taken together, changed the business environment in a very favorable way. As Benjamin Powell (2003) explains, the massive increase in economic freedom in the past twenty years is the best overall explanation of the Irish miracle.

As Figure 13.1 shows, New Zealand's GDP per capita in 1960 was approximately the same as that of Great Britain and was considerably greater than that of Australia or Ireland (although less than that of the United States). By 2003, New Zealand was last in this group, well behind Great Britain, Australia, Ireland, and the United States. In other words, the reforms have not helped the economy climb back up the OECD rank-

FIGURE **13.1**   Per capita GDP for New Zealand and four other countries, 1960–2003
SOURCE: World Bank (2005).

ings of income per capita to the same extent that Ireland's reforms have propelled its economy upward.

Although the reforms have improved New Zealand's rankings in the Index of Economic Freedom, they have stopped the economy from deteriorating further only relative to other OECD countries. The five policy changes discussed earlier have dramatically changed the entrepreneurial environment, and New Zealand has become a reasonably deregulated and competitive market economy, but it has not become a growth dynamo (Wolf 2004).

In contrast to New Zealand's economy, Ireland's economy has experienced a phenomenal recovery (see Figure 13.1). In 1960, Ireland was the poorest country in the group by a big margin (the Irish GDP per capita was less than half that of New Zealand). By 1996, however, after two decades of reforms, Ireland's GDP per capita was higher than that of New Zealand; in 1997, it was higher than that of Australia; and by 2000, it was higher than that of Great Britain. No single factor lies at the root of New Zealand's relatively slow growth, but rather a series of factors that, taken together, have limited the incentives for entrepreneurs. In the remainder of this section, I examine why the New Zealand economy has not yet become the "tiger of the South Pacific."

A. The Size of Government

Many commentators on the New Zealand economy do not see the size of government as an explanation of relatively poor economic performance. The New Zealand Treasury (2004) and the Ministry of Economic Development (2005) see the source of sluggish growth in the low investment ratio, not in government spending.

The level of central government spending in New Zealand has not changed much since the early 1980s. What have changed are the efficiency of tax collection and the ways tax revenue is being spent. This fact shows that not only the amount of government spending but also its structure matters. The enormous restructuring of New Zealand's public sector and the resulting improved quality of its decision-making processes have reduced the government's burden on the economy.

Nevertheless, the proposition that countries with big government do not grow fast has been corroborated empirically.[12] It is true that many OECD countries have big governments, but none of them has grown fast for long periods in this condition.[13]

One reason for this relationship is that large government spending causes more entrepreneurs to respond to government-created price signals, setting in motion what Israel Kirzner calls the "superfluous discovery process." The discoveries are superfluous because they are based on false profit signals created by government activity, which do not reflect individuals' preferences and, as a result, change the economy's patterns of saving and consumption. False profit signals (that is, those profit opportunities created or induced by government activity) lead to unproductive entrepreneurship and poorer economic performance (Kirzner 1986; Sautet 2002, 2005).

Another reason for the relationship is that even with improved government structures, governments are not capable of acting entrepreneurially. Much government activity involves transferring resources through taxation, not creating value. When cost-benefit analysis is used by governments, it is often, although not always, guesswork.[14] Core government spending and government transfers of all kinds do not and cannot rely on the profit-and-loss guide that entrepreneurs use in the discovery process. Because government decision making is not guided by profit and loss, government bureaucrats are not entrepreneurs.

It is true that the New Zealand government owns commercial entities (state-owned enterprises). However, it is not clear what would happen if one of them were to experience losses. The government might bail out the enterprises it owns more readily than it bails out private companies experiencing losses.

Most government spending weakens the general entrepreneurial discovery process because such spending consumes resources that entrepreneurs would have used to create value. It is impossible to elicit high levels of productive entrepreneurship and at the same time to have the government use up a large amount of the economy's resources.

The burden of New Zealand's current levels of government expenditures could be diminished by freezing those expenditures. If held at 2004 levels, government spending would be down to 26.7 percent of GDP by the year 2008–2009 (Wilkinson 2005). Adoption of constitutional constraints on government spending might help achieve such a result.[15] Freezing government spending would force harder choices to be made by revealing the trade-offs associated with the status quo. This revelation might lead, for example, to a reduction in welfare expenditures. Total expenditure on social welfare as a proportion of national income has increased since the beginning of the reform process.[16] The incentives are now great for low-income individuals to receive welfare income instead of working. Government transfers constitute one of the biggest items in the budget. Freezing government expenditures would also force the government to finish privatizing some of its assets (for example, state-owned enterprises). Finally, it would limit public choice problems: with less money being spent, interest groups have less incentive to dedicate resources to rent seeking.[17]

The 2005 budget included significant additional spending to promote increased opportunities, particularly through education; to enhance security through health spending, additional police staff, a long-term defense-spending plan, and funding for Working for Families and the Rates Rebates scheme; and to support economic growth (New Zealand Treasury 2005a). These large increases in spending help to explain the deteriorating growth forecast for the years up to 2009. Instead of freezing expenditures, the Labour government has chosen to increase them, which will only cause further damage to the entrepreneurial environment.

B. Taxation

The design principle of the New Zealand tax system—broad-base, low-rate taxation—is desirable insofar as low rates compensate for the broader base. If rates are not lowered enough and the base is expanded, average tax rates remain high. Although the incentive to engage in market activities (vis-à-vis nonmarket activities) has increased because marginal rates have fallen, the base has been broadened, which reduces the scope for untaxed activity. As Davidson puts it, "Unlike the situation in many countries, New Zealand's income tax base is relatively broad and provides limited scope for taxpayers to avoid the top tax rate" (2005, 3). (Individuals can use trusts to shelter income at a lower marginal rate: trusts are taxed at 33 percent, whereas the top rate on individual income is now 39 percent.)

The broadening of the tax base can be illusory. It is not true that consumption can be taxed independently from income. At the end of the day, there is only one tax base: the income realized through exchange. Simultaneous taxation of any other base is double taxation. This fact has been recognized to some extent in New Zealand—for example, by the abolition of death duties. However, the income tax, the GST, and excises all deduct from the same base, even if they offer different opportunities for avoidance.

Designing the tax base opens the door to many problems, such as whether capital gains and imputed rental income in owner-occupied housing should be taxed. Other considerations—such as compliance costs, political feasibility (that is, income distribution), and fluctuations of tax revenues—are often taken into account in the design. Although using monetary income and consumption as the tax base may make sense, doing so creates multiple layers of taxation and therefore increases the tax burden.

The overall impact of the New Zealand tax reforms on the entrepreneurial environment has been positive. Average and marginal tax rates, however, are still high, and this condition affects the entrepreneurial discovery process.[18] Between 1985 and 2002, the total burden of taxation relative to GDP per capita increased by 3.6 percentage points, rising from 31.3 to 34.9 percent. In comparison, the burden of taxation in Ireland declined from 35 percent to 28.4 percent.[19]

The complexity of the effects of taxation in practice can be seen by examining corporate taxation in Ireland. In 1980, the Finance Act introduced manufacturing relief, which established an effective rate of corporate tax of 10 percent. The category "Manufacture" was extended in 1987 to include financial services, shipping, films, and other sectors. The regular corporate tax rate in Ireland was 45 percent in 1980 and was increased to 50 percent in 1982. From 1988 onward, it was reduced, finally reaching 12.5 percent in 2003 (Martyn and Reck 2004, 50). In practice, the extent of the manufacturing sector was not always clearly defined. Given the difference between the regular corporate tax rate and the manufacturing corporate tax rate, a large number of tax-arbitrage structures were set in place to reduce the effective tax rates of corporations.

Small open economies depend to a greater extent than do big countries on foreign direct investment. The tax treatment of those foreign investments, in conjunction with other factors, is important to capital markets. Although foreign investment did not increase in Ireland for years, the broader changes in the institutional environment created the momentum for it to grow by taking advantage of the 10 percent tax rate offered to foreign corporations.

The New Zealand government's 2005 budget included a few changes to taxation—in particular, small tax cuts to encourage investment and savings and to assist small businesses. These cuts may be paid for in part by a new carbon charge in the future. Tax thresholds will increase to catch up with inflation. A new work-based savings scheme, KiwiSaver, will also be created. These tax changes will not reduce the overall burden of taxation, however, and therefore are likely to have very little positive impact on entrepreneurial activity.

C. The Openness of the Economy

Only in the past twenty years has the New Zealand economy begun to open its borders fully to trade. The effects of more-open borders take time to surface because entrepreneurs often rely on their knowledge of local market conditions. As the economy opens up, trade with more-distant lands becomes possible, but the accumulation of knowledge about foreign-market conditions requires time. Modern information technology reduces that lag time but does not eliminate it.

Time is also needed for foreign-market participants to realize the extent of the changes in a country and the effects of those changes on the quality of the country's products. In the 1950s, Japan and Taiwan were considered places that made cheap, low-quality products. Thirty years later, opinions of their goods had improved because the two countries had become a source of high-quality and high-tech products. Likewise, New Zealand's image as little more than an exporter of lamb and mutton has dramatically changed since the early 1990s. This change will probably continue and accelerate over the next decade or two.

This factor also relates to the issue of size. Although openness can compensate for the small size of New Zealand's economy, New Zealand does not have access to a common market of 300 million people as Ireland does. Foreign tariffs erected against New Zealand products hurt the New Zealand economy, reducing the size of the market available to its producers and damaging the entrepreneurial environment. For example, the United States taxes New Zealand lamb and cheese heavily. Because of the barriers to trade posed by foreign tariffs, New Zealand is not in a situation similar to that of Ireland with regard to market size. In this respect, New Zealand would benefit from joining the free-trade agreement between the United States and Australia, provided the agreement allowed for free trade in agricultural goods. Doing so would open the door to the North American trade zone, which comprises more than 300 million people.

In the 1950s, some forty thousand people emigrated every year from Ireland.[20] In 2004, the flow was the reverse: more than thirty thousand individuals immigrated to Ireland (Ireland Central Statistics Office 2004). This recent influx is both a consequence and a cause of the economic change. Individuals also decide to stay in the country because they see the better quality of life that can be obtained in Ireland. The net population inflow creates a cumulative process in which more people entering the country expand internal markets and the community of entrepreneurs, thereby enhancing the division of labor and knowledge necessary for effective capital accumulation.

The same process is occurring in New Zealand, where the "brain drain" has stopped: net permanent long-term migration has been positive since the 1990s (except in 1999) and is increasing, although it remains volatile.[21] New Zealand is becoming a better place to live, and net positive long-term migration is one result of that improvement. The virtuous cycle of immigration will help to improve New Zealand's economy by expanding internal markets and the community of entrepreneurs. It has been said that Ireland has benefited from its links to the United States forged by the Irish diaspora. Although New Zealand may not be in a similar situation, New Zealanders have more international connections today than they had twenty years ago. The world in effect has become a smaller place, and people have better knowledge of foreign markets, which helps entrepreneurs to build the bridges they need to distant markets and slowly increases New Zealand's integration with the rest of the world.

Free trade in goods is a substitute for free migration. For a long time, New Zealand allowed people to migrate—free migration with Australia has always been enforced, and many New Zealanders have British passports—but goods could not pass freely. The economic reforms dramatically changed this situation, and today New Zealand embraces free trade more completely than do most OECD countries. In September 2003, the government announced its tariff policy for post-2005. The highest tariff rates, between 17 to 19 percent, will be reduced to 10 percent by July 1, 2009. Tariff rates on all other goods will be reduced to 5 percent by July 2008. Alternative specific tariffs reverted to the apparel ad valorem tariffs on July 1, 2005. It is difficult to know what the overall effect of such measures will be on the entrepreneurial environment, although they should be positive. For now, however, the path to complete free trade remains obstructed (especially by foreign tariffs imposed on New Zealand products), which greatly reduces entrepreneurial activity, job creation, and economic performance.

D. The Regulatory Framework

The overall regulatory environment in New Zealand is of very good quality and has dramatically improved since the mid-1980s. The World Bank Doing Business Indicator (World Bank 2005) ranked New Zealand number one in 2005. The enforcement of property rights is excellent, the level of corruption is negligible, and the major costs associated with the conduct of business affairs are relatively small.[22] Although the overall regulatory environment and the general institutional framework are solid, some issues still need to be considered.

First, although the labor market has become much more fluid after enactment of the Employment Contract Act in 1991, the act contained some restrictions on contractual arrangements, which have worsened over time. The limits to freedom of contract are:

- No contract that requires any person to be a member, not to be a member, or to leave a union is permitted.
- No one can contract out of a provision of the act.

The act's mandatory personal-grievances provisions are especially rigid in the case of unjustifiable dismissals: employment at will was abolished in New Zealand in 1991, although it accounted for a significant portion of all labor contracts until then.[23]

Disputes with regard to employment contracts must be settled in the Employment Court, a special court for labor issues. Over the years, this court has partially undermined the intentions of the framers of the act by emphasizing procedural correctness and "fairness" in dismissals. The Labour government elected in 1999 repealed the Employment Contract Act and replaced it with the Employment Relations Act, which came into effect in October 2000. The Employment Relations Act introduced or reintroduced "good faith" bargaining, the promotion of mediation over litigation, and union monopoly on collective bargaining. By and large, it promotes collective bargaining by various means, such as the requirement that employers give union representatives information and workplace access. Yet it retains the idea of freedom of contract.

The Labour government in its second term made more changes in the Employment Relations Act that came into effect in December 2004. Taken together, these modifications further restrict the possibility for entrepreneurs to contract out for labor services. They offer special privileges to employees by facilitating collective bargaining, unionization, and multiemployer collective agreements.[24]

So far these changes have not had negative impacts on employment. Unemployment in New Zealand stood at 3.6 percent in December 2004, and labor-market participation was more than 75 percent. New Zealand has a rate of job creation and destruction twice as high as that of most European countries. By and large, the labor market is fluid and working well.

However, labor laws have become more rigid since the new Labour government took office in 1999. The implementation of the Employment Relations Act in 2000 and its changes in 2004 have worsened the entrepreneurial environment, as reflected in the Economic Freedom of the World Index, in which in 2004 New Zealand received a score of only 5.9 for labor regulation, relative to 10, the best possible score (Gwartney and Lawson 2004).

New Zealand's regulation of utilities, especially gas and electricity, is ill conceived and excessive. The government is now going back to a more regulated environment, adopting forms of utility regulation that other OECD countries have used, such as establishing dedicated policy watchdogs, a role the Commerce Commission is now undertaking. The utilities reform of the 1990s was based on the idea that utilities were similar to any other commodity producers and thus could be left to operate in the market. However, the dominant views about monopoly and market power have influenced the reform process in ways that never permitted the market to operate fully. Privatization and deregulation of utilities in New Zealand are incomplete and are now going backward, with the Labour government reintroducing the visible hand of regulation.

The government has resumed ownership of commercial enterprises, such as Kiwibank, Air New Zealand, and the railway system. Although these enterprises face commercial incentives, their cost of capital is artificially reduced, which may weaken their performance. Taxpayers' money would be better invested by the taxpayers themselves. Instead, state-owned enterprises that should be privatized immediately still await privatization.

Other smaller but still important regulations have changed in a way that is unfriendly to the entrepreneurial environment. Examples include takeover regulations, the Commerce Act, industrial policy (for example, the government's Growth and Innovation Framework), and the Kyoto Accords.

The devil is in the details. Although the major costs of doing business are still relatively small, the trend is now toward more regulation.[25] New Zealand should strive to keep its regulation light-handed in accordance with the mantra of the 1980s reforms. Any other approach contributes to the growth of government and thus is detrimental to the entrepreneurial environment.[26]

4. Unfinished Business

A recent survey shows New Zealanders' attitudes toward business and the economy to be reasonably good.[27] New Zealanders are interested in a good quality of life, have ambition and motivation in their personal lives, and favor business and economic growth. Like many other people, they are interested in bettering their lives. After years of reform, they also understand that to create wealth one needs to work and have a cultural attitude that by and large favors the market system over government dirigisme. This cultural attitude is important to the future of the economy because it may help people to resist the temptation of more intervention if economic conditions deteriorate.

Nevertheless, the reform process has stalled in the past ten years, and to a large extent New Zealand has lost its bearings: the consistent reform of the 1984–1995 period has given way to a stop-start, zigzag reform effort (Kasper 2002). Among other things, the Labour government sees more-active policies as a way to improve economic performance (Clark 2002). The founding of the economic development agency New Zealand Trade and Enterprise manifests this view. Some in power still see picking winners and conducting an active industrial policy, such as clustering and awarding grants to businesses, as a route to prosperity.

Governments around the world have used such policies with little success. The example of Ireland is often cited as a case in which grants from European Union (EU) structural funds have made a difference. In reality, however, Ireland's economic growth occurred in spite of EU transfers. Net EU receipts and Irish growth rates have moved in opposite directions, and the high growth of the late 1990s occurred as EU transfers were phased out.[28] EU transfers have not contributed to improvement of the entrepreneurial environment in Ireland, which is what ultimately matters. Similarly, New Zealand's recent active industrial policy has not contributed to improvement of the entrepreneurial environment. Quite the opposite: it has contributed to the deterioration of that environment by creating rents that entrepreneurs seek and by disturbing market signals.

Another issue emerging since the mid-1990s is the impact of the electoral system. The Electoral Act of 1993 introduced proportionality—called "mixed-member proportionality" (MMP)—in the New Zealand electoral system, replacing the first-past-the-post (FPP) system.[29] The first election under MMP was held in October 1996. Since then, every government has been formed as a coalition of various parties. No electoral system is perfect, to be sure, yet MMP, by fostering coalition governments, can stifle the capacity for reform and can thus increase public spending. The reforms of the 1984–1995 period were possible in part because of the FPP system and the unicameral parliamentary system. Moreover, various studies have shown that public spending is higher under proportional representation than under the FPP system.[30] The existence of coalition governments helps to explain the modest growth New Zealand has experienced since 1996, and it is likely to stifle more reforms in the future.

The Labour government has made growth a top priority, but this commitment has not contributed to improved economic performance. Governments cannot engineer growth; they can only create the context in which entrepreneurial activity takes place. By improving the institutional context, government indirectly steers entrepreneurship toward productive and socially beneficial activities (Boettke and Coyne 2003; Sautet 2005).

The New Zealand government should now focus on four major policies to improve entrepreneurial incentives.

1. Reduce the size of government by freezing its spending. Although the structure and quality of government spending have improved, the magnitude of that spending relative to GDP has remained almost unchanged since the period preceding the reforms.[31]
2. Reduce the overall burden of taxation, especially marginal tax rates. Taxation affects entrepreneurial incentives by reducing the size of profit opportunities.
3. Continue opening the economy because entrepreneurship, leading to the division of labor and specialization, is enhanced by expanding markets.
4. Continue improving the regulatory environment because in some cases it is becoming worse.

These four types of measures would further improve the entrepreneurial environment, and over time such improvement will raise the prospects for economic growth.

5. Conclusion

Modest growth in New Zealand is not the result of an overdose of reforms or bad cultural attitudes. Much progress has been made since the 1980s, but more remains to be done if Kiwis are to become tigers. In short, the reform process has not been completed, and more reforms need to be implemented. As Martin Wolf put it in the *Financial Times* in November 2004, "It is simply wrong to describe [the] reforms as delivering a *laissez-faire* paradise. The end point is, rather, a reasonably deregulated, competitive market economy, with prudent fiscal and monetary policies and a better-run government." A "reasonably deregulated, competitive market economy," however, is not enough to generate a high rate of growth in income per capita. The way to better economic performance is only through creating a better entrepreneurial environment. Only by guaranteeing the free emergence, discovery, and exploitation of profit opportunities can countries improve their growth prospects over time.

The reforms have delivered substantial results, considering the point of departure, but New Zealand has not become a growth dynamo like Ireland because the reforms implemented did not go beyond OECD standard practice. To become tigers, Kiwis must adopt more-radical reforms. Unfortunately, the Labour government in its 2005 budget (and in its new incarnation after the September 2005 election) shows little inclination toward improving the institutional context in which entrepreneurial activity takes place. Rather, it prefers to continue to increase the size of government spending, tinkering at the margin with the rules of the game.

Notes

This article originally appeared in the *Independent Review* 10 (4) (Spring 2006).

1. Tyler Cowen entertained this idea on his Web log. Aidan Walsh told me that the same was said about Irish people before the 1990s.

2. Maori *tikanga* is the culture of the Maori people, who are the indigenous people of New Zealand.

3. A recent instance of this debate is John McMillan's 2004 observation that "markets are doing their job" and the lack of high growth must be found elsewhere (in geography, lags in adjustment, and so forth). Kerr (2005c) notes that growth since 1999, although reasonably fast, has not been faster than the average of the 1990s, which shows that the new Labour government policies have not had, as of yet, the impact their supporters claimed they would have.

4. For a general history of New Zealand at the turn of the twentieth century, see King (2003), especially chapter 18. Before the enactment of social legislation, the government had an active role in land acquisition and infrastructure development.

5. This proposal was published under the title *There's Got to Be a Better Way!* (Douglas 1980).

6. Many other reforms also played an important role. For example, competition law was overhauled and simplified: the new drafted Commerce Act of 1986 entirely replaced the Commerce Act of 1975.

7. See Sautet (2000), especially chapter 2 on the notion of the "simple firm."

8. As history showed in the 1970s, central-bank policies designed to achieve macroeconomic results are generally not successful. Looser monetary policy achieves only greater inflation and poorer economic performance in the long run.

9. Money's purchasing power can never be completely stable. Still, the price inflation that results from increases in the money supply diminishes the purchasing power of money more than it would diminish because of other changes in the market.

10. See New Zealand Treasury (2005b). The 1994 Fiscal Responsibility Act was replaced by the Public Finance (State Sector Management) Bill in 2003. In this new legislation, "fiscal management" replaces the "fiscal provisions" approach. However, the intent of the bill remains the same, which shows how even with multiple changes of government, the idea of fiscal discipline is now well accepted in New Zealand.

11. See Wilkinson (2004) for an analysis of the impact of the Fiscal Responsibility Act during the 1994–2004 period.

12. See Gwartney, Holcombe, and Lawson (1998); Bates (2001); Kerr (2002); and Wilkinson (2004, sec. 3.4). See also Grimes (2003) for the opposite view when applied to the New Zealand case, and see Wilkinson (2004, 35) for a rebuttal of Grimes's view.

13. The proposition is that no OECD country has achieved sustained growth of GDP per capita of 4 percent or more annually with total government outlays at 40 percent of GDP (Wilkinson 2004). New Zealand's total government

outlay was 34.1 percent in 2004, Ireland's was 34.3 percent, and Australia's was 35.5 percent (OECD 2005).

14. The use of cost-benefit analysis signals progress in the management of governments. However, in most cases, it does not rely on market prices and is therefore more akin to guesswork than to economic calculation.

15. See sections 4 and 5 of Wilkinson (2004) for a discussion of mechanisms to limit government spending; see also section 3.5 for a discussion of the nature of core government spending. Wilkinson concludes that 20 percent of GDP would be enough to finance the core government roles and a safety net.

16. See Kasper (2002) and Brash (2001). Don Brash regards transfer payments as a major burden on the New Zealand economy.

17. A good indicator is the number of government employees (government administration and defense), which decreased from 58,000 in 1990 to 42,000 in 2000. It increased again after that and in 2005 stood at 52,000 (Statistics New Zealand 2005).

18. This fact is reflected in the Heritage Foundation 2005 Index of Economic Freedom: New Zealand scores four out of five (best being one) in the "Fiscal Burden of Government" category (Miles, Feulner, and O'Grady 2005).

19. See OECD Revenue Statistics 1965–2003 (OECD 2004). However, comparing figures for taxes as a percent of GDP across countries is difficult. Differences in tax systems may not be accounted for in tax revenue figures; for example, social security contributions come from general taxation in New Zealand, but in some other countries they do not. Also, GDP growth can get ahead of the political economy of taxation.

20. Net annual emigration from Ireland averaged 39,000 per year from 1951 to 1956 and 42,000 per year from 1956 to 1961 (Redmond 2000, 14).

21. See Statistics New Zealand (2005) for key demographic indicators as well as Glass (2004).

22. World Bank Doing Business Indicator (World Bank 2005), the Corruption Perceptions Index (Transparency International 2004), and KPMG (2003); see also Djankov et al. (2002).

23. Employment at will is the employer's ability to hire and to dismiss without showing a cause, along with the employee's ability to quit without justifying his action (unless otherwise stipulated in the contract).

24. Many other regulations affect labor contracts, touching on health and safety requirements, discrimination (regulated by the Human Rights Act), minimum wage, legally mandated holidays, the state monopoly in accident insurance (opened to competition in 1998, then renationalized in 2000), and taxpayer-funded paid parental leave.

25. See Tyler Cowen's Web log of July 8, 2004: "Is New Zealand Backsliding?"

26. See Wilkinson (2001), especially chapter 8, on the ways to constrain government regulation.

27. See New Zealand Growth and Innovation Advisory Board (2004), a government-sponsored report, as well as Kerr (2005b).

28. See Powell (2003). See also Powell (2004) for an analysis of the role of industrial policy among the East Asian tigers and Desrochers and Sautet (2004) for an analysis of clustering policies.

29. Under the FPP system, members of Parliament are elected because they gain more votes than any other single candidate in their particular electorate. This system was replaced because it tends to foster a two-party system and delivers majority governments, thus ignoring third parties even when they achieve a significant level of support.

30. On the impact of electoral rules on fiscal policy, see Persson and Tabellini (2004).

31. Moreover, the quality of many policies, especially in health and education, has stagnated in the past ten years. A great deal of money has been spent to little effect.

References

Baird, Charles. 1996. "Deregulation of the New Zealand Labour Market: Things Done and Left Undone." "Moving Forward" Conference on the Employment Contract Act 1991. http://www.nzbr.org.nz/documents/speeches/speeches-95-96/baird-eca.doc.htm (accessed April 19, 2007).

Bates, Winton. 2001. *How Much Government? The Effects of High Government Spending on Economic Performance.* Wellington: New Zealand Business Roundtable. http://www.nzbr.org.nz/documents/publications/publications-2001/how_much_govt.pdf (accessed April 19, 2007).

Boettke, Peter, and Christopher Coyne. 2003. "Entrepreneurship and Development: Cause or Consequence?" *Advances in Austrian Economics* 6: 67–87.

Brash, Don. 2001. "Faster Growth? If New Zealanders Want It." *Policy* 17 (3): 12–17. http://www.cis.org.au/policy/Spring01/polspr01-3.pdf (accessed April 19, 2007).

Carroll, Nick, Dean Hyslop, David Mare, Jason Timmins, and Julian Wood. 2002. "The Turbulent Labour Market." NZ Association of Economists Conference, June. http://www.nzae.org.nz/conferences/2002/2002-Conference-Paper-16(2)-CARROLL-TEXT.PDF (accessed April 19, 2007).

Central Statistics Office. 2004. *Population and Migration Estimates.* Dublin, Ireland: Central Statistics Office. http://www.cso.ie/releasespublications/documents/population/current/popmig.pdf (accessed April 19, 2007).

Clark, Helen. 2002. "Moving On with the Growth and Innovation Agenda."
    Media statement. http://www.giab.govt.nz/uploadedfiles/Documents/
    Reports/press_growth.pdf.

Cowen, Tyler. 2004. Web log. http://www.marginalrevolution.com/ (accessed
    April 19, 2007).

Davidson, Sinclair. 2005. *Personal Income Tax in New Zealand: Who Pays
    and Is Progressive Taxation Justified?* Wellington: New Zealand Business
    Roundtable. http://www.nzbr.org.nz/documents/publications/publications-
    2005/120405tax.pdf (accessed April 19, 2007).

Djankov, Simeon, Rafael La Porta, Florencio Lopez-de-Silvanes, and Andrei
    Schleifer. 2002. "The Regulation of Entry." *Quarterly Journal of Economics*
    117:1–37.

Douglas, Roger. 1980. *There's Got to Be a Better Way!* Wellington, New
    Zealand: Fourth Estate Books.

Evans, Lewis, Arthur Grimes, Bryce Wilkinson, and David Teece. 1996. "Eco-
    nomic Reform in New Zealand 1984–95: The Pursuit of Efficiency." *Jour-
    nal of Economic Literature* 34:1856–1902.

Glass, Hayden. 2004. "Immigration Policy." Policy Backgrounder no. 2. Wel-
    lington: New Zealand Business Roundtable. http://www.nzbr.org.nz/
    documents/policy/policy-2004/PB_No2.pdf (accessed April 19, 2007).

Grimes, Arthur. 2003. "Economic Growth and the Size and Structure of Gov-
    ernment: Implications for New Zealand." Motu Working Paper no. 03-10.
    http://ideas.repec.org/p/mtu/wpaper/03_10.html (accessed May 30, 2007).

Growth and Innovation Advisory Board. 2004. "Research on Growth and Inno-
    vation." http://www.giab.govt.nz/ (accessed April 19, 2007).

Gwartney, James, Randall Holcombe, and Robert Lawson. 1998. "The Scope
    of Government and the Wealth of Nations." *Cato Journal* 18 (2): 163–190.
    http://www.cato.org/pubs/journal/cj18n2/cj18n2-1.pdf (accessed April 19,
    2007).

Gwartney, James, and Robert Lawson. 2004. *Economic Freedom of the World:
    2004 Annual Report.* Fraser, Canada: Fraser Institute. http://www.freethe
    world.com/2004/efw2004complete.pdf (accessed April 19, 2007).

Kasper, Wolfgang. 2002. *Losing Sight of the Lodestar of Economic Freedom.*
    Wellington: New Zealand Business Roundtable. http://www.nzbr.org.nz/
    documents/publications/publications-2002/losing_sight.pdf (accessed
    April 19, 2007).

Kay, John. 2000. "The Downfall of an Economic Experiment." *Financial Times*
    (August).

Kerr, Roger. 1999. "Successes and Failures of Labour Market Reform in New
    Zealand." Dublin Economic Workshop, October. New Zealand Business

Roundtable. http://www.nzbr.org.nz/documents/speeches/speeches-99/ successes_and_failures_dublin.doc.htm (accessed April 19, 2007).

———. 2001. "Economic Success: Lessons from the World." Chamber of Commerce of Tauranga, May. New Zealand Business Roundtable. http://www .nzbr.org.nz/documents/speeches/speeches-2001/economic_success.doc.htm (accessed April 19, 2007).

———. 2002. "Memo to Dr Cullen: Big Government Harms Growth." New Zealand Business Roundtable, September 25. http://www.nzbr.org.nz/ documents/speeches/speeches-2002/memo_to_dr_cullen.pdf (accessed April 19, 2007).

———. 2005a. "Lessons from Labour Market Reform in New Zealand." H R Nicholls Society's XXVI Conference, Melbourne, Australia, March. New Zealand Business Roundtable. http://www.nzbr.org.nz/documents/speeches/ speeches-2005/180305rk_labour_markets.pdf (accessed April 19, 2007).

———. 2005b. "We Set Up the Economic Conditions after 2010 Today." Speech given at the Shepherds' Club, March. New Zealand Business Roundtable. http://www.nzbr.org.nz/documents/speeches/speeches-2005/ economic_conditions_140305.pdf (accessed April 19, 2007).

———. 2005c. "Let's Stop Beating Up on Ourselves." Speech given at the Plimmerton Rotary Club, Wellington, New Zealand, July.

King, Michael. 2003. *The Penguin History of New Zealand*. Auckland, New Zealand: Penguin Books.

Kirzner, Israel. 1979/1985. "The Perils of Regulation: A Market-Process Approach." In *Discovery and the Capitalist Process*. Chicago: University of Chicago Press.

———. 1985. "Taxes and Discovery: An Entrepreneurial Perspective." In *Taxation and Capital Markets*, ed. Dwight R. Lee. San Francisco: Pacific Institute for Public Policy Research.

KPMG. 2003. "The Business New Zealand–KPMG Compliance Cost Survey." http://www.businessnz.org.nz/file/556/BusinessNZ_KPMG_Compliance CostSurveyReport.pdf (accessed April 19, 2007).

Lynch, Colin. 2005. "Can We Learn from Ireland's Experience? An Irishman's Perspective." Policy Backgrounder no. 6. Wellington: New Zealand Business Roundtable. http://www.nzbr.org.nz/policy.asp?DocType=PolicyBackgroun ders (accessed April 19, 2007).

Martyn, Joe, and Paul Reck. 2004. *Taxation Summary*, 28th ed. Dublin: Irish Taxation Institute.

McMillan, John. 2004. "Quantifying Creative Destruction: Entrepreneurship and Productivity in New Zealand." Working paper, Graduate School of Business, Stanford University, Stanford, CA. http://faculty-gsb.stanford.edu/

mcmillan/personal_page/documents/NZ%20Treasury%20McMillan%20
Dec%202004.pdf (accessed April 19, 2007).

Miles, Marc, Edwin J. Feulner, and Mary Anastasia O'Grady. 2005. "The 2005
Index of Economic Freedom." Heritage Foundation and *Wall Street Journal*.
http://www.heritage.org/research/features/index/ (accessed April 19, 2007).

Mills, Duncan, and Jason Timmins. 2004. "Firms Dynamics in New Zealand."
NZ Association of Economists conference, July.

Ministry of Economic Development and New Zealand Treasury. 2005. "Economic Development Indicators 2005: Growth through Innovation." http://
gif.med.govt.nz/aboutgif/indicators-2005/report/report.pdf (accessed
April 19, 2007).

New Zealand Treasury. 2004. "New Zealand Economic Growth: An Analysis
of Performance and Policy." http://www.treasury.govt.nz/release/economic-
growth/ (accessed April 19, 2007).

———. 2005. "Budget 2005." http://www.treasury.govt.nz/budget2005/ (accessed April 19, 2007).

OECD. 2004. *Revenue Statistics 1965–2003*. Paris: OECD. http://www.oecd
.org/document/54/0,2340,en_2649_34533_34358774_1_1_1_1,00.html
(accessed April 19, 2007).

———. 2005. *Economic Outlook No. 77, Annex Tables*. Paris: OECD. http://
www.oecd.org/document/61/0,2340,en_2649_34109_2483901_1_1_1_
1,00.html (accessed April 19, 2007).

Powell, Benjamin. 2003. "Economic Freedom and Growth: The Case of the
Celtic Tiger." *Cato Journal* 22 (3): 431–448. http://www.cato.org/pubs/
journal/cj22n3/cj22n3-3.pdf (accessed April 19, 2007).

———. 2004. "State Development Planning: Did It Create an East Asian Miracle?" Working Paper no. 54. Independent Institute. http://www.independent
.org/publications/working_papers/article.asp?id=1370 (accessed April 19,
2007).

Redmond, Adrian, ed. 2000. *That Was Then, This Is Now: Change in Ireland
1949 to 1999*. Dublin, Ireland: Central Statistics Office, Stationery Office.

Reserve Bank of New Zealand. 2002. "Joint Press Statement by Finance Minister Michael Cullen and Incoming Reserve Bank Governor Alan Bollard."
http://www.rbnz.govt.nz/news/2002/0124629.html (accessed April 19,
2007).

———. 2005. "Time Series." http://www.rbnz.govt.nz/statistics/econind/a3/
download.html (accessed April 19, 2007).

Sautet, Frederic. 2000. *An Entrepreneurial Theory of the Firm*. London:
Routledge.

———. 2002. "Kirznerian Economics: Some Policy Implications and Issues." *Journal des Economistes et des Etudes Humaines* 12 (1): 131–152.

———. 2005. "The Role of Institutions in Entrepreneurship: Implications for Development Policy." Mercatus Policy Series. Arlington, VA: Mercatus Center at George Mason University. http://www.mercatus.org/pdf/materials/1053.pdf (accessed April 19, 2007).

"Statistics New Zealand." n.d. www.stats.govt.nz/ (accessed April 19, 2007).

Transparency International. 2004. "The Corruption Perceptions Index." http://www.transparency.org/ (accessed May 30, 2007).

Wilkinson, Bryce. 2001. *Constraining Government Regulation.* Wellington: New Zealand Business Roundtable. http://www.nzbr.org.nz/documents/publications/publications-2001/constraining_govt.pdf (accessed April 19, 2007).

———. 2004. *Restraining Leviathan: A Review of the Fiscal Responsibility Act 1994.* Wellington: New Zealand Business Roundtable. http://www.nzbr.org.nz/documents/publications/publications-2004/restraining_leviathan.pdf (accessed April 19, 2007).

———. 2005. "New Zealand's Economic Freedom, Growth & Fiscal Rules." Presentation to the Politics, Philosophy and Economics Workshop, George Mason University, Department of Economics, May 9.

Wolf, Martin. 2004. "False Rumours of a Death in the South." *Financial Times* (November 16).

World Bank. 2004. "Doing Business Indicator." http://rru.worldbank.org/DoingBusiness/ (accessed April 19, 2007).

———. 2005. *World Development Indicators.* http://publications.worldbank.org/WDI/ (accessed April 19, 2007) (subscribers only).

14   **Look, Botswana: No Hands!**
      Why Botswana's Government Should
      Let the Economy Steer Itself

SCOTT A. BEAULIER

This essay is a study of how the institutional levers of government affect economic activity. The underlying logic is that changes in the "rules of the game" can affect economic outcomes. When changes in the rules of the game leave property rights more well-defined, the production possibilities curve shifts outward; if we move toward the collectivization of property rights, the production possibilities curve shifts inward.

Unfortunately, most revisions of property rights laws in the developing world have involved inward shifts of the production possibilities curve (PPC). In sub-Saharan Africa, poor government decision making has left many countries no better off today than they were at the end of colonialism. When communism collapsed in eastern Europe and the former Soviet Union, we were able to observe just how costly the command-and-control approach of communism can be to individual well-being. Yet many parts of the world have yet to learn from past mistakes.

There remains a deep desire, in the individuals in power, to control economic systems and the people living within particular regions. Only time will tell how far the PPC shifts inward in places such as North Korea, Zimbabwe, and Rwanda.[1]

Despite their best efforts, governments rarely reform in a way that reduces their size and scope. In fact, one would be hard-pressed to find more than a handful of cases in which underdeveloped countries have been successful in making the jump to middle-income or high-income economies. Even though there are a few exceptions worthy of detailed examination, we do not have a useful model for how a government can go about reforming an underdeveloped economy.

This essay explores one of these exceptions. Since independence, most African countries have endured an "African growth tragedy" (Easterly and Levine 1997). In many of them, the overall level of development today is no higher than it was at the end of colonialism. Like most African countries emerging from colonialism, Botswana was an extremely poor nation at the time of independence. Unlike most other African countries, Botswana managed to escape Africa's poverty trap. Without much foreign aid, and in the absence of a large state, Botswana went from being the third-poorest nation in the world in 1965 to an upper-middle-income nation today. Between 1966 and 1996, it was the fastest-growing nation in the world, with an average annual growth rate of 7.7 percent during this time frame. Whereas so many newly independent African nations chose anticapitalist, statist routes as they emerged from the devastating experience of colonialism, Botswana's leaders chose the path less traveled.

Why did Botswana's leaders and citizens choose to approach development differently than most other African countries? More important, how did their decisions affect economic development? Botswana grew because it made steady strides to secure property rights and to limit the government's role in the economy. To return to our PPC discussion, Botswana's leaders actually followed basic microeconomics. They sought to expand the production possibilities curve by changing the rules of the game for the better. Botswana's economic success was really quite simple; by choosing to respect the rule of law, protect property rights, and limit the government's scale and scope, Botswana was able to enjoy steady economic growth.

I should make one final note regarding my research methodology. Because sub-Saharan African data are often inaccurate, dirty, or completely lacking, I use original, on-the-ground fieldwork and conventional data sources to support the claims being made throughout this essay. The research approach readers will find in this essay could be described as an ethnographic approach.[2] My research is based on seven weeks of fieldwork, a lengthy review of historical examinations of Botswana, and an extensive survey of the University of Botswana's historical archives. In all, my team of researchers conducted thirty-five interviews with businessmen, government officials, expatriates, and local citizens during the summer of 2004 in Botswana. By being on the ground in Botswana, we were able to get a better feel for the policies that are promoting and hampering growth. One final note: dates and locations of all interviews are provided, but several of the respondents preferred to remain anonymous.

1. Botswana's Experiment with Limited Government

Botswana's experiment with limited government and fairly open markets began immediately after it gained independence from Great Britain in 1965. Immediately after independence, Sir Seretse Khama became prime minister of Botswana. The next year, Khama became the first elected president of Botswana.

Khama had been trained in the United Kingdom and had married a white Englishwoman, Ruth Williams, in 1948. Together, he and Ruth had to fight apartheid sentiments. Because of their interracial marriage, they were prohibited from returning to Botswana. By the mid-1950s, the ban on Khama's return had escalated into an international news story. Human rights groups were outraged, and the British government was criticized for actively encouraging and upholding a racist protectorate. Although the crisis was undoubtedly difficult for Khama, it did make him the most popular and charismatic political figure in Botswana by the time he was allowed to return to his homeland in 1956.

At the beginning of Botswana's independence, President Khama faced some huge obstacles. Botswana was thought to be Africa's poorest nation. According to the British government's Economic Survey Mission (1960), Botswana was "close to the poorest" country in the world and had "dismal economic prospects [that were] based on vague hopes of agriculture, salt, and coal." A newly independent, landlocked country in sub-Saharan Africa, it was desolate and sparsely populated. It was beset by the typical problems of poor African countries—famine, illiteracy, lack of adequate potable water, minimal health facilities, and a lack of other social amenities—and had virtually no infrastructure. More than 80 percent of the population was dependent on subsistence farming, and the government did not have enough tax revenue to balance its budget.

In many ways, the British government was thrilled to be getting rid of this costly protectorate. Experts were providing gloomy predictions for Botswana's future: Botswana would become heavily indebted to the British Empire; it would never be able to become independent of South Africa; and the new nation would most certainly struggle to develop. But the experts ended up being wrong about Botswana's prospects because Botswana broke most economic ties with the British Empire in its first decade of independence and grew faster than any nation in the world between 1966 and 1996.

The formula responsible for Botswana's success was a rather simple one. Botswana did not grow because some kind of unique factor emerged to help it escape its postcolonial poverty. Nor did Botswana grow because it was blessed with nice land and beautiful coasts; Botswana is an arid, landlocked country in sub-Saharan Africa. Botswana grew because its ruling elite made deliberate choices to increase economic freedom, and they avoided engaging in predatory practices. Botswana's leaders were not interested in lining their own pockets at the expense of Batswana (the proper term for people of Botswana).[3]

In the early years, guided by the leadership of Khama, Botswana took a no-nonsense approach to development. The new government tried to constrain spending by developing National Development Plans (NDPs). The NDPs allocated government spending and established developmental goals for a five-year period; for example, the first plan focused on macro-economic stability and fiscal balance. Projects were approved only if they passed an economic feasibility test or a social rate-of-return test or both.[4] Unlike many organizations using cost-benefit estimates, Botswana's government was quite conservative in estimating the economic and social benefits of different programs. Even Seretse Khama was constrained by the NDPs. According to Derek Hudson, a former expatriate and important reformer in Botswana's earlier years:

> They did a lot of good things, at the beginning. One of the most famous stories is that to build the roads, from dirt to hardtop, roads were ranked according to economic return. One of the roads passed by the house of the first president [Seretse Khama]. The planners offered to build his road first, even though it did not pass the rate of return tests, but he refused and said, "I'll wait my turn," and he did.[5]

Today, Botswana is beginning its eighth National Development Plan. The NDPs have served as an effective constraint on government.

They cannot be amended without the unanimous approval of the legislature. Any individual legislator looking to increase spending on some particular pet project can count on resistance from some group. Thus the only spending programs that gain approval are ones that all parties view as essential.[6]

Khama's claim was that his reforms were not based on any one ideology but were instead grounded in "certain fundamental values" that are considered "universal" (Carter and Morgan 1980, 294). However, if one were to try to put a label on Khama's overall reform approach, the most appropriate label would be "pragmatic classical liberal" or "classical liberal realist." Although he did depart from a pure laissez-faire approach by intervening from time to time and by supporting state aid to the poor during a severe drought in the mid-1960s, his policy stances were far more free market and libertarian than those of any other leader in sub-Saharan Africa.

As early as 1968, Khama was making statements such as the following: ". . . our main concern for this country is to lessen its dependence on external aid, and ultimately to make it economically viable" (Carter and Morgan 1980, 295). He was less outspoken about domestic policies, but the overall results of his reforms suggest that he was committed to low taxes, low government spending, balanced budgets, and free commerce.

Botswana's new ruling party also chose to adopt many of the common law rules that the British had introduced during the colonial period. Unlike most other African countries, Botswana did not call into question every aspect of the British common law system after it gained independence; compared with other sub-Saharan African nations, Botswana bucked the trend by keeping some of the British institutions in place. In places such as the former Belgian Congo, Ghana, and Togo, newly independent African leaders went about trying to re-create entire legal and economic systems in response to the scars left by colonialism; rather than admit that some colonial institutions added value, leaders tried to get rid of anything connected to the colonial period. As Ayittey notes:

> The African leaders' rejection of colonialism and Western institutions was an understandable reaction. But in their overzealousness to eradicate all vestiges of Western colonialism, virtually all sense of purpose and cultural direction was lost. After independence, many African leaders, proclaiming themselves "free and independent under black rule,"

hauled down the statues of European monarchs and erected, not those of Martin Luther King, Jr. or Kankan Musa, but of another set of white aliens—Marx and Lenin. (Ayittey 1992, 10)

There were no statues of Marx or Lenin in Botswana. Rather than run from institutions left behind by colonialism, leaders embraced some of them and erased only the parts of colonialism that seemed inefficient or deplorable. As we try to explain Botswana, then, it is important that we make note of how its commitment to many English laws was fairly unique in postcolonial Africa.[7]

In the early period, the government's overall size was also kept in check. If we believe the conventional measures, Botswana's government spending as a fraction of gross domestic product in 1965 was 23 percent of GDP. There is reason to believe that the size of Botswana's government was actually much smaller than its reported size. In the immediate postcolonial period, Botswana's economy was far more informal than it is now, but informal activity was not accounted for in GDP estimates of Botswana. Therefore, Botswana's GDP was underestimated. As Botswana grew and the government stabilized, production shifted from the informal economy to the formal economy. With this shift in economic activity, a more accurate accounting of Botswana's growth level and government size resulted.[8]

Between 1965 and 1972, Botswana experienced a steady decline in the size of government. Khama and his postcolonial leaders were actively promoting reforms that resulted in rapid growth and tremendous improvements in individual well-being. As Tanzania's former president, Julius Nyerere, put it, "[Khama] devoted his energies to considering how—not whether—to maximize the people's freedom" (Carter and Morgan 1980, x). Throughout Botswana's early years, Khama's platform emphasized self-reliance, economic freedom, antiapartheid governance, "good neighborliness" with South Africa (while still condemning its racist rule), and openness to foreigners and trade.

Batswana in general—expatriates and natives alike—deserve a great deal of credit as well. Khama alone would not have been able to enact his policies if Batswana were lacking trust in Khama or skeptical of arguments for minimal government. The Batswana showed a great deal of patience and tremendous ingenuity in developing their new nation. Citizens were quite active in helping the Botswana Democratic Party (BDP) develop its 1965 manifesto by giving the BDP feedback on early drafts and attending political meetings. Some of the key features of the BDP's original platform included promises to

1. Safeguard the liberty of the individual by the maintenance of law and order and to guarantee every individual citizen the rights of man as defined in the Constitution.
2. Not allow any form of discrimination, whether political, social, or economic, against any minority racial group in the country. . . . Neither shall the laws of the country recognize any preferential considerations of a political, economic, or social nature for any tribal or racial group.
3. Keep the judiciary independent of the executive.
4. Not destroy any communal associations or bonds based on such common interests as religion, language, culture, and so forth.
5. Treat all men as equal before the law.

The fact that the Botswana Democratic Party offered such a liberal (in the classical sense) platform immediately after colonialism and the fact that 80 percent of voters supported the BDP tell us something about the general mind-set of citizens in Botswana. The hearts and minds of the Batswana were committed to liberty and constitutional restraints to a much greater extent than those of citizens in other countries where concerns about social justice and race dominated the postcolonial debate.

The Batswana did more than lay out some general principles that look good on paper. They engaged in a number of actions that reflected a genuine commitment to the principles of equal opportunity, nonracism, and tolerance. For example, a number of civil society organizations, such as the Village Development Committees, school committees, and leisure clubs, emerged around the time of independence. Many of the new clubs provided crucial social capital; others actually allowed for the open debating and criticism of current political issues. Quite often Khama and other legislators would join local citizens at meetings to take criticism and discuss current issues. As one former Bank of Botswana governor and long-time citizen of Botswana put it in a personal interview:

> In the early days, we often got together right around the corner from here [Grand Palm Hotel and Casino]. Sometimes we would talk about ways to help the youth out through tennis programs and recreational

clubs. Often we would talk about the more pressing needs of the nation. Khama frequently attended these meetings, and he sat there with us like an equal who was genuinely interested in results rather than ideology.[9]

When it came to foreign policy, the Batswana welcomed foreigners and dissidents with open arms. The increase in immigrants was not only humane but also undoubtedly improved Botswana's workforce and productivity. In a number of speeches between 1965 and 1975, Khama explicitly told refugees that they were welcome in Botswana. Even though the welcoming of refugees led to greater tensions with hostile neighbors, Khama argued that welcoming refugees was consistent with the higher "principle of universal self-determination." As Khama put it,

> Whilst we respect the principles of non-interference in the affairs of other sovereign states, we are as a non-racial democracy bound to raise our voice in international forums in support of the principle of universal self-determination. The same sense of duty and our geographical position means that we must continue to provide a refuge for those who have found themselves unable for one reason or another to continue to live in neighbouring minority-ruled territories. (Carter and Morgan 1980, 83–84)

Refugees were not treated as second-class citizens in Botswana. Quoting Khama once more,

> We have granted refugees recognition of their status and done all within our power to settle them and assist them in beginning a new life in Botswana. All we ask in return is that refugees should respect our laws and our national principles, and refrain from activities which are prejudicial to our security . . . (Carter and Morgan 1980, 84)

Khama's commitment to refugees was not just rhetoric as Botswana attracted thousands of refugees during Khama's rule.

Taken as a whole, the policies of openness, toleration toward others, and a respect for the rule of law allowed for entrepreneurship, economic development, and social development. This period of limited government and economic freedom led to one of the most rapid national growth explosions we have ever seen. Between 1965 and 1975, Botswana's average annual rate of growth was 10.74 percent. To put that number in perspective, Botswana's per capita income went from $372 in 1965 to $1,032 in 1975; if the United States were to grow at this rate for a ten-year period beginning in 2003, the average annual income in the U.S. in 2013 would be $90,200.

2. The Growth of Government in Botswana

Botswana's experiment with limited government ended sometime around 1975. The period from the mid-1970s to the present is a difficult period to understand. On the one hand, Botswana was able to continue to grow at a rapid rate. From 1975 to 2003, Botswana's growth rate averaged a strong 5.1 percent per year. Cattle ranching became a less significant source of income, and the service sector became more significant. Tourism also became an important source of revenue as visitors from South Africa, western Europe, and the United States began to learn of the beautiful wildlife in the Okavango Delta and Chobe National Park. According to Botswana's Ministry of Trade, Industry, Wildlife, and Tourism, export revenue from Botswana's tourism business is second only to that of the diamond industry.[10] Botswana's network of paved roads and its air travel expanded at rapid rates.[11] The quality and quantity of education increased steadily during this period.[12]

On the other hand, the steady growth in income and the discovery of diamonds in 1972 led to massive increases in government spending and taxation: between the mid-1970s and 2003, the size of Botswana's government (as a percentage of GDP) went from approximately 15 percent to 30 percent.[13] Some of the legal and constitutional constraints placed on legislators were relaxed after 1975. Khama's administration became more concerned with income inequality, so in 1974 it established an Agricultural Board that was responsible for setting price floors on grain. In the early 1970s, a number of new textile industries were subsidized by the government to help create jobs in underdeveloped communities. Rather than cut its losses on a struggling copper-nickel mine in the mining town of Selebi-Phikwe, Botswana's government continued to pour money into upgrades of the mine under Khama's watch.[14]

Around the same time, the government decided to end its monetary connection with South Africa by abandoning the rand and creating its own currency, the pula. Khama argued that Botswana was "trying to extricate [itself] from a situation in which [its] economic life and future [were] decided . . . by others in foreign capitals." To make this break from South Africa, the government created a central bank responsible for monetary policy. Although cutting ties with South Africa's monetary regime undoubtedly gave Botswana a greater sense of autonomy and control over its monetary policy, with this autonomy came greater risks of monetary mismanagement.[15]

When one tries to make sense of Botswana, it is clear that the governmental apparatus established in postcolonial Botswana in 1965 was much more limited in its scale and scope than the government of modern-day Botswana. As Figure 14.1 indicates, the government's size has been steadily increasing since 1972. Today, the size of government in Botswana is alarmingly large. According to *World Development Indicators 2004*, government spending as a percentage of gross domestic product accounted for one-third of all economic activity in 2003. Moreover, the trend throughout the 1990s and early 2000s has been one in which government spending in Botswana has been increasing quite rapidly; between 1995 and 2003, Botswana's government spending increased at an average annual rate of 8.3 percent per year. Over that same period of time, Botswana's average annual rate of growth was only 4.4 percent per year. Although Botswana has continued to grow, despite the increases in government spending, this overall growth in government should be cause for concern because government spending is increasing at nearly twice the rate of the overall economy.

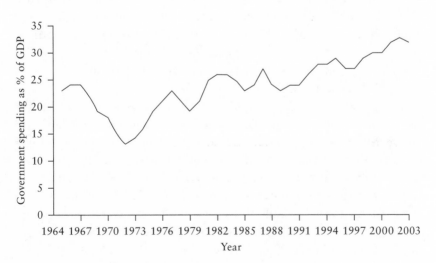

FIGURE **14.1**   Growth of government in Botswana, 1965–2003
SOURCE: World Bank (2004).

One of the biggest changes in Botswana, occurring in the mid-1970s, involved spending on national defense. Until 1976, there was no conventional military establishment in Botswana. There was a small paramilitary unit, the Police Mobile Unit, attached to the police force. This unit was in charge of handling strikes, protests, and other disputes that could not be handled by the traditional police force.

The lack of an army in the early years was the result of deliberate government action based on two different arguments. First, the government thought the best defense was no defense. In other words, if Botswana had strong international ties and complete vulnerability, another nation (such as Great Britain or the United States) would step in to handle any invasions. Second, the government chose not to have a national military in the early years because of concerns that developing a military would provoke the hostile apartheid governments of South Africa or Ian Smith's corrupt regime in Rhodesia.

Botswana's government decided to begin developing a national defense as its income increased, as it felt more concerned about protecting diamond interests, and, perhaps most important, when it felt threatened by South Africa due to a number of violent raids by South Africans who crossed the border into Botswana. By the mid-1970s, Botswana had become an asylum for refugees from a number of southern African countries and had allocated land on which international organizations such as the Red Cross, Amnesty International, and the United Nations could establish refugee camps. This tolerant stance incensed the South African government, and it launched a number of raids into Botswana. The raids were usually aimed at refugees, but a number of innocent Batswana were also killed between the mid-1970s and 1987.

Rhodesia was also enraged by Botswana's openness. A Rhodesian organization known as the Selous Scouts raided a number of villages just inside the Botswana–Rhodesia border. The organization attacked villages to discourage "freedom fighters" from welcoming refugees.

The frequent and brutal raids created a problem for Botswana's government. In all, the raids had resulted in hundreds of civilian deaths (in addition to the refugee deaths). By the late 1970s, the affected groups, and many citizens who were not directly affected, were lobbying hard for national defense; Khama ultimately gave in to their demands. Shortly thereafter, the Police Mobile Unit was converted into the Botswana Defence

Force (BDF). Since its establishment, the BDF has expanded enormously, and it now takes up nearly 15 percent of total government spending.[16]

The shift from the Police Mobile Unit to the Botswana Defence Force might have been an understandable and acceptable increase in government. The public attitude regarding the establishment of a national defense in Botswana was based on this kind of sentiment:

> It was a very uncertain and scary period. I think most people bought into the idea that every democratically elected government is responsible for the security of its people. Therefore, the decision was taken to establish an army.[17]

Fear of attacks also led to a shift in the way Batswana viewed immigrants. With the raids came a concern that openness was provoking violent responses from other countries. By the late 1970s, Botswana's government was beginning to take measures to restrict foreign access by inspecting vehicles crossing the borders and by allowing random searches of vehicles within Botswana's borders. Even when the raids ended around 1987, the xenophobic policies persisted; Batswana simply shifted their fear from a fear of raids to a fear of foreigners (particularly Zimbabweans) entering the country and taking good jobs. Police have been granted free rein to search vehicles and to inquire where travelers are going (much like U.S. Customs, but Botswana allows these actions both at the borders and throughout the country).[18]

Even if a case can be made for developing a national defense and being afraid of foreigners because of the increased uncertainty of raids, there were a number of other areas in which the government's scale and scope increased rapidly around this same time period. As mentioned earlier, the government took on a larger role in agriculture and industry. In addition, there were new spending programs, such as the Citizen Entrepreneurship Development Agency (CEDA) to support the diversification of industry; environmental awareness projects created by the Atmospheric Pollution Act of 1971 and the Agricultural Resources (Conservation) Act of 1973; and legislation pushed by the labor rights movements, such as the Mines, Quarries, Works and Machinery Act of 1978.

In the early 1970s, human-capital investments in secondary education became the new growth panacea. Botswana followed the rest of the world by rapidly increasing education spending. Between 1975 and 1999,

TABLE 14.1

Rate of change in public education spending, 1970–1999

Year	Level (current U.S.$)	Rate of change*
1970	4,108,424	N/A
1980	63,655,440	31.5%
1990	185,028,060	11.3%
1999	452,168,730	10.4%

SOURCE: World Bank (2004).

*Average annual rate of change during the preceding decade.

education spending (as a percentage of GDP) increased from 6 percent of GDP to 9 percent. Although the fraction of GDP being spent on public education might not seem too high, GDP was also growing at a rapid rate over this time period. In other words, the overall share of the pie going to education did not change much between 1975 and 1999, but the size of the slice grew tremendously.

When we look at the annual rate of change in public education spending between 1975 and 1999, Botswana's education spending increased at an average annual rate of 13.2 percent per year (World Bank 2004). As Table 14.1 also indicates, education spending has been increasing quite rapidly since 1970.

Early on, the government sought to provide "free" primary education to all children. Soon this was extended to cover students interested in secondary education. Later on, benefits were extended to students studying at the University of Botswana. Again, although there are undoubtedly gains from education, Botswana's commitment to engage in massive public spending to cover education expenses resulted in higher levels of government spending, new laws such as the National Policy on Education of 1977, and new bureaucracies such as the Teachers Union.[19]

The collective result of new spending on a number of different fronts was big government. In just over a decade, Botswana was beginning to make the transition from a small government to a big government. When we look at it now, four decades after Botswana gained independence, Botswana's government has gone from being fairly limited to a behemoth, comparable in size with that of many Western countries.[20] Increasing demands for governmental goods and services have brought about an expansion in government size. As one citizen put it, "Batswana are no longer asking 'What do we need to do to develop?' Instead, they are asking, 'What are you going to promise to give me if I vote for you?'"[21]

When we blend the various and seemingly isolated spending programs together, the reasons for why Botswana has turned into a large nation-state become clear. The government's decision to make promises to a number of different groups of people desiring government services has resulted in an increased tax burden for citizens and investors, a slow and steady erosion of civil liberties, a loss of individual responsibility, and the loss of a government committed to the promotion of sound economic policies.[22]

A recent study by Acemoglu, Johnson, and Robinson (2003) has tried to explain Botswana's remarkable growth while minimizing the impact government growth has had on Botswana's well-being. In fact, they claim that Botswana has managed to grow with big government because the government has, for the most part, been run efficiently. The facts of the matter are something much different: Botswana has enjoyed rapid economic growth in spite of big government. The economic growth is not because of big, efficient government but rather because of an earlier period when the country experimented with minimal government. In a fundamental sense, Botswana is still milking the benefits of its experiment with minimal government rather than benefiting from big government.

Botswana's postcolonial experience is not a story of efficient government but rather a story of "institutional sclerosis" (Olson 1982, 1996). In the period immediately after independence, Botswana's new government had a fairly blank slate. There was a minimal amount of governmental infrastructure, and interest groups were almost nonexistent. During this period, promoting good policy was not especially difficult. Khama and the BDP enjoyed high levels of support, and they did not have to worry about disappointing any well-organized groups. Policy could have gone in many different directions during this early period, but Botswana's leaders decided to pursue a fairly pro-market course.

Over time, though, the number of interest groups and the money flowing into interest groups increased rapidly. With more interest groups, the BDP's decisions became more complicated. Although concerns about growth-enhancing policies remained important to politicians, there were now new concerns about keeping different lobbying groups satisfied. With interest groups came an erosion of good policy. Even though Khama's rhetoric sounded fairly free market in the mid-1970s, the reality on the ground in Botswana was that Khama and the BDP were slowly selling out to interest groups and public demands for more government.

Interest group activity has steadily increased since the mid-1970s. With bureaucracy has come a crowding out of the private sector, but the public sector's crowding out of the private sector and the efficiency losses are not the only byproducts of Botswana's big government. With each new governmental program comes increased complexity in the overall system. The number of interest groups in conflict with each other multi-plies as the government's role expands. Discerning "real" interests from strategic interests becomes a more daunting task. And, ultimately, most attempts to serve the public good become futile as the government be-comes bogged down in bureaucracy. After this interest-group-dominated environment is in place, which clearly seems to be the case in Botswana, the task of pushing for reform becomes formidable. Moving the system at all becomes nearly impossible. Citizens are left with an incoherent hodge-podge of policies, few of which they would have desired *ex ante*.[23]

3. Botswana in a Comparative Perspective

Are things really as bad in Botswana as this story suggests? Careful readers could raise (at least) two criticisms of the story being told about Botswana's postcolonial government. First, maybe this analysis is being too harsh on Botswana. Although it has experienced rapid growth in the size and scope of government since the mid-1970s, perhaps it is still far better off than most other sub-Saharan African countries. In the subsec-tion that follows, we will look at how Botswana compares with its neigh-bors. Although Botswana's growth performance has certainly outper-formed that of other countries, its economic policies and government size are average to below average when compared with those of other African countries.

The second point that needs to be considered in this section relates to the studies the Fraser Institute has published regarding Botswana's economic policies. To a great extent, the story being told in this essay contradicts the story being told by the Fraser Institute. According to the thesis of this essay, Botswana's economic policies—especially its fiscal policies—have deteriorated since the early years. Yet the Fraser Institute's

Economic Freedom of the World Index reports that Botswana's fiscal policy has improved since 1975 (the first year the index started to track Botswana). According to the Fraser Institute's 2004 report (Gwartney and Lawson 2004, 60), Botswana has become more economically free in general, and its size-of-government score has also improved tremendously. If Botswana has actually been improving over time, then maybe this analysis is overstating Botswana's problems.

Although the Fraser Institute provides a good overall picture of Botswana's economy, its economic freedom scores are missing important microeconomic content on the size-of-government component. The EFW index has done a good job of tracking Botswana's excessive government spending since the mid-1970s. The EFW index lowered Botswana's "Government Consumption" rank from 4.5 (near average) in 1975 to 0.0 in 2002. At the same time, though, Botswana's scores on taxation have steadily improved since 1980. While nominal tax rates in Botswana have remained largely unchanged since 1980, the nominal tax rate is misrepresenting important changes that have occurred in Botswana's underlying fiscal structure.

From the mid-1970s to the present, Botswana's government has been supporting high levels of government spending by increasing the tax burden on the diamond industry. Although Debswana, a diamond mining company owned jointly by the De Beers Group and Botswana's government, does not publicly release information that relates to specific tax rates, it is clear that the tax burden for Debswana has been steadily increasing. Botswana's government has renegotiated contracts with De Beers a number of different times since diamonds were discovered. Each time, taxes on diamond profits have been increased. Estimates are highly speculative and vary greatly, but Debswana's contribution to overall government revenue has increased from 20 percent in the early 1980s to somewhere between 35 and 50 percent of government revenue today.[24]

Because the diamond industry accounts for nearly 40 percent of all economic activity in Botswana, heavy taxes on diamonds have allowed tax rates in other industries to remain flat. In effect, the government's choice to soak the diamond industry has allowed nominal tax rates in other sectors of the economy to remain fixed. In real terms, however, business conditions in Botswana have steadily worsened when we take into account the taxes on Debswana.

There is evidence that Botswana's mismanagement of the diamond industry is spinning the economy into a "natural resource curse." In his popular book, *The Future of Freedom*, Fareed Zakaria offers one of the clearest explanations of the "natural resource curse" when he writes,

> Why are unearned riches [like oil, diamonds, and gold] such a curse? Because they impede the development of modern political institutions, laws, and bureaucracies. Let us cynically assume that any government's chief goal is to give itself greater wealth and power. In a country with no resources, for the state to get rich, society has to get rich so that the government can then tax this wealth. In this sense East Asia was blessed in that it was dirt poor. Its regimes had to work hard to create effective government because that was the only way to enrich the country and thus the state. Governments with treasure in their soil have it easy; they are "trust-fund" states. They get fat on revenues from mineral or oil sales and don't have to tackle the far more difficult task of creating a framework of laws and institutions that generate wealth. (2003, 75)

Botswana's government has been getting fat on the revenues from diamonds. Diamonds have also allowed the government to support low taxes in other sectors of the economy. When the diamonds disappear—and there is evidence that diamond extractions are beginning to decline—Botswana's government will have no choice but to raise taxes in other sectors of the economy. When this occurs, the nominal tax rates that the EFW index pays attention to will return to their real levels.

Before concluding, one final question remains: Is this analysis being excessively pessimistic about Botswana's current economic conditions? Maybe we are asking too much of Botswana when we implicitly compare it with Western countries and the United States model. In order to get a clear grasp of just how Botswana is doing relative to other African countries, it makes sense to compare Botswana with other African countries. But with which ones should it be compared? Because we know Botswana is in far better shape than the Congo, Zimbabwe, and many other sub-Saharan African countries, it is unclear that all of sub-Saharan Africa should be regarded as Botswana's peer group.

Instead, it makes sense to compare Botswana with other African countries that have made it (so to speak). To a large extent, countries in the Southern African Customs Union (SACU) have, indeed, made it.

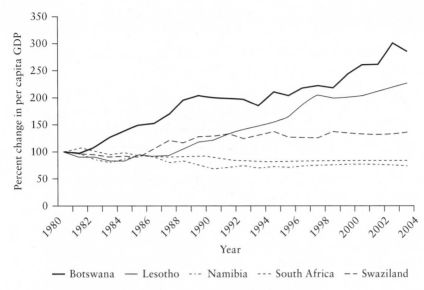

FIGURE **14.2**   GDP growth per capita for SACU countries, 1980–2003
SOURCE: World Bank (2004).

Along with four other countries, Botswana is a member of SACU.[25] The
SACU was formed in 1969, and member countries meet annually to discuss issues of free trade and to maintain common tariff standards among
member countries. Compared with other sub-Saharan African countries,
countries with SACU membership tend to be more stable politically, and
they are all beyond a minimum level of development. This makes SACU
countries an excellent peer group with which to compare Botswana because these countries are, in many ways, similar to Botswana. By looking
at SACU countries, we are looking at southern Africa's best countries, and
we are omitting extremely backward countries such as Zimbabwe.

As Figure 14.2 indicates, Botswana's rate of growth over the past
twenty-five years has been far in excess of that of other SACU countries.
In fact, Botswana has nearly tripled its real GDP per capita in the past
twenty-five years.

Tables 14.2 and 14.3 tell the story that the Fraser Institute also
tells us in its EFW index: relative to other SACU countries (and relative
to the rest of the world), Botswana has kept marginal taxes on corporate
profits and individual income quite low. In so doing, it has been able to

TABLE 14.2
Highest marginal tax rate on
corporate profits, 2002

Country	Rate
Botswana	15%
South Africa	30%
Swaziland	30%
Namibia	35%
Lesotho	N/A

SOURCE: World Bank (2004).

TABLE 14.3
Highest marginal tax rate on
individual income, 2002

Country	Rate
Botswana	25%
Swaziland	33%
Namibia	36%
South Africa	40%
Lesotho	N/A

SOURCE: World Bank (2004).

avoid the problems of corruption and black markets that have plagued South Africa and Namibia.

At the same time, though, Botswana's government spending has exploded in the past twenty-five years. Figure 14.3 shows how Botswana's government spending (as a percentage of GDP) compares with that of other SACU countries. Between 1980 and 2003, Botswana's government spending increased more rapidly than that of all other SACU countries. Only Namibia comes close to Botswana in its rate of government spending. Botswana averaged a 2.3 percent rate of government growth throughout this period, and Namibia was fractions of a percentage point less. In addition, when we look at the trend line from 1995 to 2003, Botswana's government has been growing while many other SACU countries have been cutting the size of their governments. While Botswana's overall GDP per capita has nearly tripled since 1980, its government size per capita has nearly doubled!

When we compare Botswana with other SACU countries, it becomes clear that Botswana's position relative to other SACU countries is somewhat mixed. On the one hand, Botswana's government has been

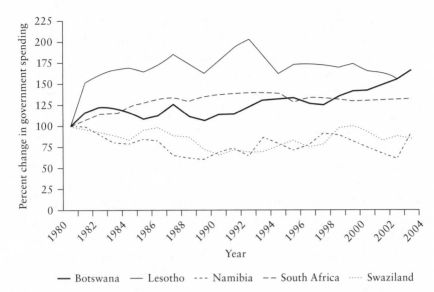

FIGURE **14.3**   Change in government spending in SACU countries, 1980–2003
SOURCE: World Bank (2004).

able to keep taxes lower and to avoid corruption problems; again, this is largely the result of heavy taxes on the diamond industry. On the other hand, Botswana has failed to constrain Leviathan, and there is evidence that it is being plagued by its own unique "natural resource curse." If Botswana is to remain a rapidly growing, entrepreneurial economy in the future, it will need to work hard to reclaim its postcolonial moment by trying to get the government out of the way. The next section deals with specific measures Botswana should take as it works to reclaim its postcolonial moment.

4. Reclaiming the Postcolonial Moment

Because Botswana had a taste of relatively free markets and limited government from 1965 until 1975, and given its increased reliance on big government since 1975, where does Botswana go from here, and what can be done to reclaim the postcolonial moment of limited government? Attempting to predict where any country is headed immediately forces us to consider the "if you're so smart . . ." question (see McCloskey 1990). Because most prognostications miss the mark, I will avoid speculation on where Botswana is going in the future, although I do find the doomsday forecasts of some (see, for example, Thurow 2002) far too gloomy.

There are many things that Botswana can do to reverse the growth of its government and to reclaim its postcolonial moment. The question that citizens of Botswana must answer is the following: Given our reasonable level of development, what is the role for government? Or, more to the point, can our current approach, which is based on big government, help us reach ever-higher levels of development? Seretse Khama's vision of a government limited in scale and scope was a reasonable one, but this vision was abandoned long ago. The new vision is a convoluted one that is difficult to summarize, but at its core, the new visionaries recognize the need for equality and economic growth. If high rates of economic growth remain a desired end for officials in Botswana today, there are some fairly simple rules Botswana must adopt to sustain rapid rates of economic growth.

A. The Role of Government

The government in Botswana has gone from being a proprietary state, concerned primarily with increasing growth, to a predatory state, concerned with maintaining power and redistributing income.[26] To achieve long-term economic growth, Batswana need to reduce their dependence on the government, but over time, the government's contribution to gross domestic product has been steadily increasing.

Government spending as a percentage of gross domestic product went from 19 percent of GDP in 1975 to 32 percent of GDP in 2003. Government spending in Botswana increased at an average annual rate of 10.7 percent per year between 1975 and 2003. Botswana's government growth looks especially high when we compare it with South Africa's; South Africa's government grew at an average annual rate of 2.8 percent over the same period of time. When compared with the governments of most other African countries, Botswana's government has been growing at a far more rapid rate, and, whether we compare Botswana's government with those of other African countries, middle-income countries, or highly developed countries, the government's growth in Botswana is higher.

Since its independence, Botswana has always been careful to avoid budget deficits. Even though a number of interview respondents thought that the government should be running deficits to cover costs associated with Botswana's HIV/AIDS crisis and to diversify the economy, legislators have resisted the temptation to increase spending beyond current revenue. In fact, during the late 1980s and early 1990s, Botswana was successful in building a "rainy day" fund to hedge against economic downturns, drought, or international instability.

There are a number of good reasons to avoid deficit spending. Over time, fiscal imbalances hamper long-term development (Easterly, forthcoming). In Botswana's case, fiscal imbalances would make the country ever more dependent on South Africa. Given South Africa's relative instability, Botswana has always tried to maintain a rainy day fund just in case "South Africa goes crazy and decides to close the borders." [27]

Although Botswana should be commended for carefully balancing its budget year in and year out, its overall level of spending is quite high. Today, nearly 40 percent of the economic activity in Botswana is somehow connected to the government. Increased government involvement creates efficiency losses, obvious distortionary effects in economic activity, and a greater dependence on further government interventions. In a fundamental sense, Botswana's government is deadweight on the Batswana. Given its relatively high level of spending, Botswana's government is crowding out the private sector.

B. The Private Sector

Secure property rights and a transparent legal code are crucial for the development of the private sector (Dixit 2004; Glaeser and Shleifer 2002; Rosenberg and Birdzell 1986; North 1981). Well-defined, well-protected property rights encourage people to obtain capital, bet on their ideas, and improve the resources in their possession. For countries to develop, then, reformers must take steps to secure property rights, constrain government officials, and enforce contracts. If the government can do the job of establishing the rules of the game, the market can take care of any remaining inefficiencies.

Although this secret to success seems fairly straightforward, Botswana's government has decided to abandon its role as referee by suiting up and trying to become a more active player in the private sector. It has gotten into the business of defining winners in some important sectors of the economy, subsidizing losers in other sectors, and intervening in labor disagreements. In addition, the number of new, special-needs bureaus has been growing rapidly in the last thirty years. Botswana has taken a path similar to that of most other developed countries by granting more and more power to meat commissions, agricultural boards, and water regulators. By trying to imitate other countries that have a regulatory authority for each important economic activity, Botswana has lost some of its competitive edge in the private sector.

In addition, the private agreements between Debswana and Botswana's government have been renegotiated a number of times. Although the renegotiations have resulted in longer leases for Debswana, Botswana's government has steadily increased its tax on diamond revenues.[28] Botswana's renegotiations with Debswana have given the nation of Botswana major shareholder status in the company and seats on the board. Because the renegotiations help Botswana keep more of the diamond revenue within the country's geographic borders, many view the renegotiations as a victory for Botswana (see, for example, Robinson and Parsons, forthcoming). However, there are at least two reasons to view the renegotiations as a negative for Botswana's long-term development.

The first reason is because Botswana may be in the early stages of the "natural resource curse."[29] The resource curse works something like the following. Countries with large resource stocks engage in massive spending. As resource stocks decline or as resource prices on products such as oil, gold, or diamonds fall, or as both occur, the government responds by levying harsher taxes on industry. This, in turn, contributes to a further decline in the country's economic fortunes.

As we discussed earlier, Botswana's government has been doing plenty of spending; since 1975, government spending has been increasing at a rate in excess of 10 percent per year. The only easy way to cover this spending is to squeeze the fairly immobile diamond industry for more money. Government's need to grab more revenue from the diamond industry by renegotiating the terms of trade seems indicative of bigger problems. But this spend-and-renegotiate approach cannot continue forever, especially because there are indications that available diamond stocks in Botswana will be rapidly declining in the next twenty years.

The second reason to be concerned with Debswana's mining renegotiations relates to the signal that renegotiations send to other industries. Continued renegotiations with Debswana have a negative spill-over effect on overall investment in other sectors of Botswana's economy. When the government chooses to renegotiate, it signals a willingness on the government's part to intervene whenever large revenue sources are present. According to a number of respondents, "the diamond industry is unique and Botswana leaves other industries alone." [30] Although Botswana's government might be leaving other industries alone for the time being, to date Botswana's grabbing hand has not been tested by any other large industries. Perhaps large industries have been staying clear of Botswana because they are concerned about how they will be treated by the government.

C. The Mixed Sector and Parastatal Organizations

Hopefully, a slice of the private sector in Botswana will remain unhampered by government intervention. One cannot be as optimistic about the government-regulated corporations and parastatal entities within Botswana's economy. As one respondent put it, "We have learned well from the United States. Government interest groups are Gaborone's [Botswana's capital] biggest growth industry. Just like you, we have our lobbyists and bureaucracies with far-ranging concerns." [31]

Although public choice economists have yet to provide an unambiguous explanation for the expansion of the regulatory state, after bureaucracy begins to grow, we can expect bureaucracies monitoring the original bureaucracies to multiply. There is no real rhyme or reason to the bureaucratic sector. It is not driven by profit and loss; nor is it directly involved in the formulation of policy. Instead, each parastatal corporation seems to be in search of maintaining or expanding its overall operating budget or doing both (Niskanen 1971).

Although Botswana's parastatal organizations have been relatively successful at avoiding corruption, there are reasons to be concerned about this mixed sector of the economy. For example, the mix between government and the private sector in Botswana's media has produced a number of perverse effects. Botswana's major media outlets are afraid to raise serious criticisms of other parastatal corporations or the government. Why are they afraid to do so? Because nearly 50 percent of their advertising revenue comes from the government. At any time, the government can decide to cut funding to a news outlet. If a media outlet is too critical in its news coverage, the government will often respond by cutting funding. Because many of the media outlets have fewer than ten thousand subscribers, they are unable to withstand the government's blacklisting and ultimately go out of business.[32]

The negative effect of parastatal organizations can also be seen when one looks at a number of different research branches connected to the government. Institutions such as the CEDA, the Botswana Institute for Development Policy Analysis (BIDPA), and the Botswana Development Corporation are all careful to toe the party line when discussing economic policy in Botswana. Criticisms of the government are generally limited to complaining about too much funding or not enough funding allocated to specific programs rather than asking whether the government should be involved in handling various activities. This story might sound a lot like our own experience in the United States, and therein lies Botswana's biggest problem: it should not aspire to be the United States of America or any other western European country. Its early success largely resulted from the fact that it *was not* like the United States of the twentieth century. If anything, it was like the United States during the Industrial Revolution. Its slowdown in development has occurred as it has steadily made changes to move from being like the United States of 1850 to being like the United States of 2007.

5. Conclusion

What are the lessons to be learned from Botswana's postcolonial development? Here the answer depends on what the reader wants to take away from Botswana's experience. One can learn a great deal about Botswana by studying the period when an extremely poor country successfully adopted free-market, laissez-faire policies. One can also try to make sense out of the transition period around 1975: What were the forces responsible for Botswana's transition to big government? One can look at the period from 1975 to 2003 and be awe-inspired by the power of markets: even though Botswana's government was expanding, the country was still one of the fastest-growing economies in the world. This tells us something about how resilient markets are even when the government becomes more activist. Finally, one can try to make sense of the big picture by asking what the future holds for Botswana; predicting Botswana's future is a difficult task, but there are a few things to keep an eye on in the years ahead.

First, the government's role in Botswana's economy has gotten out of control. When compared with Khama's vision, Botswana's government is way too big. Early on, the government in Botswana tried to set parameters for private behavior and to help build a minimal level of infrastructure. Its role in the early years was quite limited, and it did not offer its citizens public goods such as defense or education. Somewhere along the way, Botswana's government started to become all things to all people. Because the rest of the world had a national defense, Botswana decided to create one.[33] Education became something everyone "needed," and Botswana's government footed the bill for most education expenses. In a short period of time, Botswana's government went from being a nightwatchman state to a nanny state. Will the trend toward big government continue in the years to come, or will Botswana figure out a way to reduce its government's size and scope?

Second, the key determinant of growth in the private sector is profit. Early leaders in Botswana understood the importance of a market economy driven by profit and loss, but more recent generations have been inclined to subsidize industries that seem "promising" and to hand out government licenses to other industries. In so doing, they are distorting their market economy. Because the government has taken a helping-hand approach to the private sector, there will be more difficult decisions in the future when major industries start to deal with economic losses. Will the government follow its current course and continue to intervene, or will Botswana reach a crisis moment in which market interventions no longer beget further interventions?

Given the nature of government and the popularity of current public expenditures, Botswana will struggle to gain the momentum necessary to seriously reduce the size of government. A highly centralized, costly bureaucracy seems to be part of modern-day Botswana. The modern-day Leviathan was the product of a number of different factors ranging from cultural norms that preceded British colonialism to diamond discoveries in the mid-1970s to the formation of interest groups to the widespread belief that government must handle services such as education and defense. Whatever the reasons for the government's growth in Botswana, government in Botswana is not going to go away anytime soon.

Botswana's transition from a poor country to a middle-income country is deserving of praise. Within the development literature and popular media outlets, Botswana has been given plenty of credit for this accomplishment (see, for example, Acemoglu, Johnson, and Robinson 2003; Beaulier 2003). However, the past is no predictor of the future. Even though Botswana has had a remarkable run over the last forty years, it will struggle to solve its current problem of big government. Even if the Batswana understand that the solution to their problems is to return to the postcolonial institutions and government of 1965, this outcome is about as likely as the U.S. political system rolling back to the nineteenth-century period of classical liberalism.

Although Botswana's future remains uncertain and somewhat bleak, the case of Botswana in the early years could still serve as a useful reminder to trained economists: we need not get carried away when thinking about growth because the answers are right in our micro textbook. In the early years, free-market policies worked in Botswana. In the jargon of microeconomics, the choice to constrain government and to allow people to move freely in and out of the country led to a shifting of the production possibilities curve. Other countries looking to develop could profit from a study of Botswana's early years. As they will see, Botswana was able to pull itself up by its own bootstraps through sound economic policy, antiracist policies, and common sense. The depressing reality of modern-day Botswana is that Botswana's early development experience could also serve as a useful model for Botswana's current policymakers. If Botswana is to continue as "Africa's best-kept secret," it must not only tell others about its postcolonial experiment with good policy but also study its own history and return to good policies on the home front.

Notes

I thank Peter Boettke, Christopher Coyne, Gerald Gunderson, Jay Marchand, Skip Mounts, Benjamin Powell, and workshop participants at Campbell University, the Ludwig von Mises Institute, and San Jose State University for useful comments and suggestions on an earlier draft of this paper. Susan Anderson and Andres Marroquin helped gather a number of interviews used below and provided excellent assistance. John Holm, Hagen Maroney, Jack Parson, and Jay Salkin provided useful contact information. I thank the Mercatus Center's Global Prosperity Initiative (GPI) project for supporting my fieldwork in Botswana. The standard disclaimer applies.

1. The relationships among political institutions, policies, and growth have been the subject of a great deal of debate among economists. Most recently, Glaeser and colleagues (2004) find that good policies, especially when pursued by a dictator, lead to better political institutions and higher economic growth.

2. For more on ethnography, see Fetterman (1989) and Rose (1990).

3. For more on the role political institutions played in Botswana's development, see Beaulier and Subrick (2005).

4. The projects given first priority must pass both tests, but passing at least one test was a necessary condition for projects to be given consideration. A former Bank of Botswana deputy, Derek Hudson, provided information on the NDPs. During the interview, Hudson also told us that recent governments have not been strict in adhering to economic and social feasibility tests. According to Hudson, "things got bad" toward the end of President Masire's term as commissioner of economic feasibility studies: "Just before Masire retired as commissioner of economic feasibility studies, he wanted to build an ostrich farm. While driving to the airport with me, the commissioner says that this would never make a profit, let alone pass the social rate of return test, but he decided to build the farm anyway. Once a person disobeys the law of economic feasibility, you sort of create a rut where others attempt the same thing . . . never mind what the economists say." Interview with Derek Hudson on July 21, 2004, 12:30 p.m. to 2 p.m. at Fishmonger Restaurant at the Riverwalk Mall in Gaborone, Botswana.

5. Interview with Derek Hudson on July 21, 2004, 12:30 p.m. to 2 p.m. at Fishmonger Restaurant at the Riverwalk Mall in Gaborone, Botswana.

6. The idea of unanimous consent for additional government spending seems like it came straight out of Buchanan and Tullock (1962). Even though I was unable to find evidence indicating an intellectual connection between Khama's policies and Buchanan and Tullock, the fact that the government behaved as if it had read Buchanan and Tullock led to far better policy.

7. The question of why Botswana kept British colonial institutions in place in the postcolonial period while other new nations chose to scrap colonial institutions has been the subject of a great deal of debate among development economists and local citizens in Botswana. Beaulier (2003) argues that Khama's training in the United Kingdom and cosmopolitan attitude led to Botswana's postcolonial leaders being more willing to work with British institutions. Acemoglu, Johnson, and Robinson (2003) argue that Great Britain's "benign neglect" during the colonial period left Botswana with nothing to be angry about in the postcolonial pe-

riod. In a personal interview, an expatriate, who preferred to remain anonymous, offered an alternative explanation: on a per capita basis, Botswana had the most British expatriates during the postcolonial period. These individuals were quite influential in government decision making, and they were effective in locking in British legal and political institutions. This interview occurred from 12 P.M. to 2 P.M. on July 26, 2004, at Gaborone Sun & Casino in Gaborone, Botswana.

8. The move from the informal to the formal economy also explains some of Botswana's rapid economic growth in the early period. To some extent, Botswana's 10.74 percent growth between 1965 and 1975 is probably an exaggerated rate of growth because of the measurement problems associated with the move from an informal economy to a formal economy. But even if some of Botswana's growth is the result of existing businesses coming above ground, the amount of activity that became formal after 1965 is too small to explain Botswana's rapid growth. I thank Ian Campbell, a cultural historian of Botswana and expatriate, for discussing the structure of Botswana's postcolonial economy with us in a personal interview. Campbell was interviewed at his house on July 24, 2004, in Gaborone, Botswana.

9. This respondent preferred to remain anonymous. The interview was conducted from 12 P.M. to 2 P.M. on July 26, 2004, at Gaborone Sun & Casino in Gaborone, Botswana.

10. See http://www.botswana-tourism.gov.bw for more information on Botswana's tourism industry.

11. According to *World Development Indicators 2004*, Botswana's number of air departures per year increased from 1,600 in 1979 to 7,300 in 2002. Evidence on paved roads is more anecdotal, but according to Donald Stephenson of the Bank of Botswana, Botswana went from having "25 to 50 kilometers of paved roads at independence to a country that is essentially paved." According to *World Development Indicators 2004*, Botswana had ten thousand kilometers of paved roads in the year 2000. Interview with Stephenson took place at the Bank of Botswana on June 23, 2004, from 8:30 A.M. to 10 A.M. in Gaborone, Botswana.

12. The fraction of students completing primary and secondary school has been rising steadily since independence. At the same time, literacy rates have increased from approximately 50 percent in 1965 to nearly 90 percent in 2000.

13. According to Ribson Gabonowe of the Department of Mines, "Botswana's diamond mines have increased production from 4 million carats per year in the early 1970s to more than 30 million carats per year today." Interview with Gabonowe took place in the Department of Mines, Education Building, on June 16, 2004, from 10:30 A.M. to 12 P.M. in Gaborone, Botswana.

14. Support for Selebi-Phikwe has continued since Khama's death. While visiting Selebi-Phikwe, we had the opportunity to interview a number of people con-

nected to the mining industry. Despite the fact that Selebi-Phikwe is unprofitable and will one day be closed, most of the people we interviewed felt that the government should support the mine to make the costs of shutdown more bearable.

15. To date, the Bank of Botswana has been successful at maintaining sound money. Rates of inflation have been around 10 percent per year, which is well below Africa's average. The Bank of Botswana has also been effective in minimizing its inflation variability. Much of Botswana's monetary success comes from the fact that it replaced a fixed monetary regime with a regime that was based on a broad basket of currencies.

16. Since its creation, the BDF has been heavily criticized. The BDF's emergence was controversial in part because Khama's son, Ian, was appointed lieutenant colonel of the BDF. Ian Khama was quite aggressive and quite successful in extending the BDF's role to include an antipoaching branch, patrol boats to monitor the border with Zimbabwe, and air fighters.

17. E-mail response from an anonymous businessman and expatriate from Botswana. E-mail was received on October 6, 2004, at 6:43 A.M.

18. In fact, the biggest inconvenience we encountered during our time in Botswana was not a lack of technology, poor sanitation, or crime but rather the constant inspections and checkpoints we encountered whenever traveling around the country.

19. The National Policy on Education of 1977 (NPE) sought to improve the quality and quantity of education, guarantee nine years of schooling to all children, and push the curriculum in a direction that emphasized national values of democracy, development, self-reliance, and unity. For more on the National Policy on Education of 1977, see http://www2.unesco.org/wef/countryreports/botswana/rapport_1.html (accessed April 19, 2007).

20. Of course, in absolute size the governments of western Europe are much larger than Botswana's government.

21. Interview with an anonymous reporter at the President Hotel in Gaborone, Botswana, from 3 P.M. to 5 P.M. on July 20, 2004.

22. A number of local citizens in Botswana argue that the government is the only institution responsible for the loss of individual responsibility. According to Peter Freedman, an economic consultant for the Ministry of Mines, Energy, and Water Affairs, there is a concern that a new generation of "diamond babies" has a different set of values than does the older, hard-working generation of Batswana. In Freedman's own words: "After 25 years of relatively fast change in society, it is hard to see whether the traditional elements of honesty and integrity are still dominant, or whether modern ways of business and social organizations have actually changed the fundamental culture in a real way. The diamond babies have grown up with aspirations different from the earlier generations. They expect

more out of life. They are more willing to bend or break the rules in order to get more. They think that they are more entitled to things. With prosperity from the diamond industry comes this kind of undercurrent in the culture." Our interview with Peter Freedman occurred on June 25, 2004, from 11 A.M. to 1 P.M. in his office in Gaborone, Botswana.

23. For more on the role that bureaucracies and interest groups play in thwarting reform, see Wilson (1989) and Friedman and Friedman (1984).

24. Interview with the Honorable Baledzi Gaolathe, minister of finance and development planning, in his office in Gaborone, Botswana, on July 22, 2004 from 12 P.M. to 1:30 P.M.

25. Other member countries include Lesotho, Namibia, South Africa, and Swaziland.

26. See Beaulier and Subrick (2005) for a discussion of predatory versus proprietary states. For more formal models of predatory states, see Grossman (2000) and Grossman and Noh (1994).

27. Interview with Kenneth Matambo, president of Botswana Development Corporation, in his office in Gaborone, Botswana, on July 23, 2004, from 2 P.M. to 3 P.M.

28. Not all of the blame can be placed on a predatory state. As Clark Leith, professor at the University of Western Ontario and economic consultant for the Ministry of Finance and Development Planning in Botswana, pointed out in a personal interview, "part of the problem is the African view of land. Land is viewed as a communal resource, not alienable. But, as soon as you don't have a price allocation mechanism, who gets this valuable resource?" Thus the conflict over mineral rights is, in part, a result of different attitudes about ownership. Interview with Leith occurred on June 24, 2004, from 11 A.M. to 12:30 P.M. in his office in Gaborone, Botswana.

29. For more on the "natural resource curse," see Sachs and Warner (2001).

30. This view was expressed by a number of respondents, including Dr. Happy Fidzani, executive director of the Botswana Institute for Development Policy Analysis (BIDPA), in a personal interview on July 7, 2004, from 10 A.M. to 11:30 A.M. in a BIDPA office in Gaborone, Botswana.

31. Interview with the Honorable Baledzi Gaolathe, minister of finance and development planning, in his office in Gaborone, Botswana, on July 22, 2004, from 12 P.M. to 1:30 P.M.

32. Interview with an anonymous reporter at the President Hotel in Gaborone, Botswana, from 3 P.M. to 5 P.M. on July 20, 2004. Coyne and Leeson (2004) explain how the media affect economic development. According to their argument, free media create transparency and provide voters with good information. As such, the media serve as a check on politicians. If the media are not free, or the

government is partially involved—as is the case in Botswana—then the media do not serve as an effective constraint on big government.

33. There is a great deal of local frustration with Botswana's expanding military. According to Alec Campbell, a former British expatriate and cultural historian of Botswana, a lot of Botswana's defense spending is wasteful and inefficient. As Campbell put it, "Why do we need an air force? What country in this region would consider attacking us through the air?" In the development literature (Gupta, de Mello, and Sharan 2001), there is a clear relationship between defense spending and corruption: the more a country spends on defense, the more problems it has with internal corruption and secrecy. Campbell was interviewed by one of the authors at Campbell's house on July 24, 2004, in Gaborone, Botswana.

References

Acemoglu, D., S. Johnson, and J. Robinson. 2003. "An African Success Story: Botswana." In *In Search of Prosperity*, ed. D. Rodrik, 80–119. Princeton, NJ: Princeton University Press.

Ayittey, G. 1992. *Africa Betrayed*. New York: St. Martin's Press.

Beaulier, S. 2003. "Explaining Botswana's Success: The Critical Role of Post-Colonial Policy." *Cato Journal* 23 (2): 227–240.

Beaulier, S., and J. R. Subrick. 2005. "Political Foundations of Development: The Case of Botswana." Working paper. Macon, GA: Mercer University.

Buchanan, J., and G. Tullock. 1962. *The Calculus of Consent*. Ann Arbor: University of Michigan Press.

Carter, G., and E. P. Morgan. 1980. *From the Front Line: Speeches of Sir Seretse Khama*. London: Rex Collings.

Coyne, C., and P. Leeson. 2004. "Read All About It! Understanding the Role of Media in Economic Development." *Kyklos* 57:21–44.

Dixit, A. 2004. *Lawlessness and Economics*. Princeton, NJ: Princeton University Press.

Easterly, W. (Forthcoming). "National Policies and Economic Growth: A Reappraisal." In *Handbook of Economic Growth*, ed. P. Aghion and S. Durlauf. Amsterdam, Netherlands: North-Holland.

Easterly, W., and R. Levine. 1997. "Africa's Growth Tragedy: Policies and Ethnic Divisions." *Quarterly Journal of Economics,* 1203–1250.

Economic Survey Mission. 1960. *Basutoland, Bechuanaland and Swaziland*. London: H.M.S.O.

Fetterman, D. 1989. *Ethnography: Step by Step*. New York: Appleton, Century, Crofts.

Friedman, M., and R. Friedman. 1984. *Tyranny of the Status Quo*. San Diego, CA: Harcourt Brace.

Glaeser, E., and A. Shleifer. 2002. "Legal Origins." *Quarterly Journal of Economics* 117:1193–1229.

Glaeser, E., R. La Porta, F. Lopez-de-Silanes, and A. Shleifer. 2004. "Do Institutions Cause Growth?" *Journal of Economic Growth* 9 (3): 271–303.

Grossman, H. 2000. "The State: Agent or Proprietor?" *Economics of Governance* 1 (1): 3–11.

Grossman, H., and S. J. Noh. 1994. "Proprietary Public Finance and Economic Welfare." *Journal of Public Economics* 53:187–204.

Gupta, S., L. de Mello, and R. Sharan. 2001. "Corruption and Military Spending." *European Journal of Political Economy* 4:749–777.

Gwartney, J., and R. Lawson. 2004. *Economic Freedom of the World: Annual Report*. Vancouver, Canada: Fraser Institute.

McCloskey, D. 1990. *If You're So Smart: The Narrative of Economic Expertise*. Chicago: University of Chicago Press.

Niskanen, W. 1971. *Bureaucracy and Representative Government*. Chicago: Aldine Publishing.

North, D. 1981. *Structure and Change in Economic History*. New York: W. W. Norton.

Olson, M. 1982. *The Rise and Decline of Nations*. New Haven, CT: Yale University Press.

———. 1996. "Big Bills on the Sidewalk: Why Some Nations Are Rich, and Others Poor." *Journal of Economic Perspectives* 10 (2): 3–24.

Robinson, J., and N. Parsons. (Forthcoming). "State Formation and Governance in Botswana." *Journal of African Economies*.

Rodrik, D., ed. 2003. *In Search of Prosperity*. Princeton, NJ: Princeton University Press.

Rose, D. 1990. *Living the Ethnographic Life*. Newbury Park, CA: Sage.

Rosenberg, N., and L. E. Birdzell. 1986. *How the West Grew Rich*. New York: Basic Books.

Sachs, J., and A. Warner. 2001. "Natural Resources and Economic Development: The Curse of Natural Resources." *European Economic Review* 45: 827–838.

Thurow, R. 2002. "Botswana Watches Economic Success Destroyed by AIDS." *Wall Street Journal* (August 29).

Wilson, J. Q. 1989. *Bureaucracy*. New York: Basic Books.

World Bank. 2004. *World Development Indicators 2004*. Washington, DC: World Bank.

Zakaria, F. 2003. *The Future of Freedom*. New York: W. W. Norton.

Index

INDEPENDENT STUDIES IN POLITICAL ECONOMY

For further information and a catalog of publications, please contact:

THE INDEPENDENT INSTITUTE

100 Swan Way, Oakland, California 94621-1428, U.S.A.

510-632-1366 · Fax 510-568-6040 · info@independent.org · www.independent.org